CHINA'S NEW NAVY

CHINA'S NEW NAVY

*The **Evolution** of **PLAN** from the **People's Revolution** to a 21st-Century Cold War*

Xiaobing Li

Naval Institute Press
Annapolis, Maryland

Naval Institute Press
291 Wood Road
Annapolis, MD 21402

© 2023 by the U.S. Naval Institute
All rights reserved. No part of this book may be reproduced or utilized in any form or by any means, electronic or mechanical, including photocopying and recording, or by any information storage and retrieval system, without permission in writing from the publisher.

ISBN: 978-1-68247-775-5 (Hardcover)
ISBN: 978-1-68247-809-7 (eBook)

Library of Congress Cataloging-in-Publication Data is available.

♾ Print editions meet the requirements of ANSI/NISO z39.48-1992 (Permanence of Paper).
Printed in the United States of America.

31 30 29 28 27 26 25 24 23   9 8 7 6 5 4 3 2 1
First printing

For Tran, Kevin, Sharon, and Christina

CONTENTS

List of Maps viii

List of Abbreviations ix

Acknowledgments xiii

Note on Transliteration xv

Introduction. Operation and Transformation 1

Chapter 1. Light Navy for Coastal Defense 15

Chapter 2. "Limited Naval Wars" in the Taiwan Strait 50

Chapter 3. Naval Strategy and Combat Experience 85

Chapter 4. The Vietnam War and South China Sea 117

Chapter 5. Reform and New Strategy 140

Chapter 6. Sea Power in the Blue Water 166

Conclusion. Xi's New Navy 192

Notes 199

Selected Bibliography 245

Index 271

MAPS

Map 1. The People's Republic of China 17

Map 2. China and Taiwan 34

Map 3. Vietnam and the Ho Chi Minh Trail 120

Map 4. Chinese AAA Divisions in Vietnam 124

Map 5. Disputed Islands in the South China Sea 130

Map 6. China's Invasion of Vietnam 143

ABBREVIATIONS

AAA	antiaircraft artillery
AD-AFC	Air Defense–Air Force Command (NVA)
ADIZ	air defense identification zone
AMS	Academy of Military Science
ARVN	Army of Vietnam (South Vietnam)
BRI	Belt and Road Initiative
CCP	Chinese Communist Party
CCYL	Chinese Communist Youth League
CIA	Central Intelligence Agency (U.S.)
CMC	Central Military Commission (CCP)
CNOOC	China National Offshore Oil Corporation
CPVF	Chinese People's Volunteers Force (the Korean War)
CRLG	Cultural Revolution Leading Group (CCP Central Committee)
CSTIND	Commission of Science, Technology, and Industry for National Defense
CWIHP	Cold War International History Project (Wilson Center, U.S.)
DGS	Department of General Staff
DNA	Dalian Naval Academy
ECMR	East China Military Region
ECMRN	East China Military Region Navy
ECS	East China Sea
EEZ	exclusive economic zone
ESF	East Sea Fleet
FFC	Fujian Front Command

GMD	Guomindang (Chinese Nationalist Party, or Kuomintang, KMT)
GRDC	Guangzhou Riverine Defense Command
GNP	gross national product
HQ	headquarters
KGB	Security and Intelligence Service (Soviet Union)
LVT	landing vehicle, tracked
NDU	National Defense University
NKPA	North Korean People's Army
NLF	National Liberation Front (Viet Cong)
NPC	National People's Congress
NSF	North Sea Fleet
NSFL	Nanjing School for Foreign Languages
NVA	North Vietnamese Army
NVAN	North Vietnamese Army's Navy
PAP	People's Armed Police
PC	patrol craft
PLA	People's Liberation Army
PLAAF	PLA Air Force
PLAN	PLA Navy
PLANAF	PLA Navy Air Force
Politburo	Political Bureau (CCP Central Committee)
POW	prisoner of war
PRC	People's Republic of China
PT	patrol torpedo boat
QNB	Qingdao Naval Base
RMB	renminbi (Chinese currency)

ROC	Republic of China
SAF	Second Artillery Force (strategic force)
SAM	surface-to-air missile
SCMRN	South-Central Military Region Navy
SCS	South China Sea
SMAG	Soviet Military Advisory Group (China)
SSF	South Sea Fleet
SSN	nuclear attack submarine
UAV	unmanned aerial vehicle
UN	United Nations
USAF	U.S. Air Force
USN	U.S. Navy
USSR	Union of the Soviet Socialist Republics
VCP	Vietnamese Communist Party
Viet Minh	Viet Nam Doc Lap Dong Minh Hoi (Vietnamese Independence League, North Vietnam)
VNN	Vietnamese Navy (South Vietnam)
WOW	Way of War
ZC	Zhejiang Command
ZFC	Zhejiang Front Command

ACKNOWLEDGMENTS

Many people at the University of Central Oklahoma (UCO) have contributed to this book and deserve recognition. First, I would like to thank Interim Dean of College of Liberal Arts (CLA) David Macey, Assistant Dean of CLA Theresa Vaughan, and Chairperson of the Department of History and Geography Katrina Lacher. They have been very supportive of the project over the past years. As the Don Betz Endowed Chair in International Studies since 2020, I received funding from UCO Foundation for my research and trips to conferences. The UCO Research, Creative, and Scholarly Activities (RCSA) grants sponsored by the Office of High-Impact Practice, led by Director Michael Springer, made student research assistants available for the project during the past four years.

I wish to thank my Chinese colleagues and collaborators at the PLA Academy of Military Science (AMS), China Academy of Social Sciences, Military Archives of the PLA, National Defense University (NDU), Peking University, East China Normal University, Ji'nan University, China Society for Strategy and Management, China Foundation for International and Strategic Studies, Logistics College of the PLA, Nanjing Political Academy of the PLA, and provisional academies of social sciences and history museums in Heilongjiang, Jilin, and Liaoning. They made the many arrangements necessary for interviewing PLA officers and retired generals in 2017-19. I am grateful to Major General Chen Zhiya, Senior Colonel Ke Chunqiao, Li Danhui, Liu Zhiqing, Niu Jun, Shen Zhihua, Shao Xiao, Major General Wang Baocun, Senior Colonel Wang Zhongchun, Major General Xu Changyou, Yang Dongyu, Yang Kuisong, Colonel Yang Shaojun, Zhang Baijia, and Zhang Pengfei for their help and advice on my research in China.

I also thank the Sun Yat-sen Foundation, China Reunification Alliance, and Mainland Affairs Council, Republic of China (ROC). They provided financial assistance for my research trips to Taiwan in 2017-19 and arranged many interviews with military and political leaders such as Ma Ying-jeou. I am grateful to the staff of Academia Sinica at Taipei, National Palace Museum, National Military Archives, and Taiwan National University for their assistance and advice on my research in Taiwan. Yinuo Chang of the

National Cheng Chi University helped me with the primary and secondary sources in Taiwan.

Special thanks to Stanley J. Adamiak, who critically reviewed all the chapters. Chen Jian, Bruce A. Elleman, Sherman X. Lai, Steven I. Levine, Robert J. McMahon, Hai Nguyen, John Prados, David Shambaugh, Harold M. Tanner, David Ulbrich, James Willbanks, Peter Worthing, Yafeng Xia, Qiang Zhai, and Shuguang Zhang made important comments on earlier versions of some chapters as conference papers. Brad Watkins drew the maps. Travis Chambers copyedited the chapters. Several graduate and undergraduate students at UCO traveled with me to meet the veterans, transcribed the interviews, and read parts of the manuscript.

I also wish to thank the anonymous readers for the Naval Institute Press, who offered many valuable suggestions and criticism on both the proposal and manuscript. At the press, Padraic (Pat) Carlin, senior acquisitions editor, guided the review process of this project over the past two years. Any remaining errors of facts, language usage, and interpretation are my own.

During the research and writing period over the past years, my wife, Tran; our son Kevin and daughter-in-law Sharon; and our daughter Christina shared with me the burden of overseas traveling through China, Hong Kong, Taiwan, and Vietnam. Their understanding and love made the completion of this history project possible. I dedicate this book to them.

NOTE ON TRANSLITERATION

The *Hanyu pinyin* romanization system is applied to Chinese names of persons, places, and terms. The transliteration is also used for the titles of Chinese publications. The names of most Chinese people are written in the Chinese way, the surname first, such as Mao Zedong. For some popular names, traditional Wade-Giles spellings appear in parentheses after the first use of the *Hanyu pinyin*, such as Jiang Jieshi (Chiang Kai-shek), as do popular names of places like the Yangzi (Yangtze) River and Guangzhou (Canton). Exceptions are made for a few figures whose names are widely known in reverse order, like Sun Yat-sen (Sun Zhongshan), and a few places such as Tibet (Xizang).

INTRODUCTION

Operation and Transformation

Mr. Ma Ying-jeou hesitated for a couple of seconds after I asked him how to defeat a Chinese amphibious landing on Taiwan. Then the former president (2008–16) of the Republic of China (ROC) told me a landing would be the end of Taiwan's defense.[1] It seemed that any effective defense or a decisive victory should happen in the Taiwan Strait and be determined by naval battles. When tensions have risen in recent years between China and the United States in the South China Sea (SCS) and the Taiwan Strait, the American public has worried about possible naval conflict with China and asked important questions about the rapid development of the navy of the People's Liberation Army (PLA, China's armed forces). The PLA Navy (PLAN)'s aggressive behaviors toward the U.S., Taiwanese, and Japanese naval forces have certainly fomented distrustful, hostile, and even confrontational impressions. As a result, both Democratic and Republican administrations have held a tough-line policy against China and made commitments to the security of the Indo-Pacific region by selling high-tech naval weapons to Taiwan, promising U.S. protection to Japan and South Korea, and joining the Quadrilateral Security Dialogue with Australia, Japan, and India. If China goes to war with the United States, it must be at sea. A better understanding of the PLAN thus becomes a pivotal topic in public debates and strategic research in America.

The Chinese navy seems to have become one of the twenty-first-century naval powers overnight. Is PLAN strategy and behavior explicable? What are their intentions and capabilities? How do they operate in battles? How can we specifically characterize the Chinese navy? Although many Western military experts have studied China's shipbuilding and technological improvement, knowledge of Chinese naval operational capacity has almost been lost. There are few solid operational-level histories of the PLAN in English.

As a survey of Chinese naval operational history, this book focuses on the major battles and important engagements of more than 1,200 Chinese naval operations from 1949 to 2009. This work elucidates the origin of and changes within the PLAN by examining its evolution over the past sixty years. The book covers the war history of the PLAN, naval aviation, marine corps, and coastal defense troops, which are all under the PLAN's purview. Having gradually evolved from past Cold War experience, Chinese naval heritage and culture are clearly distinctive and differentiate the PLAN from other navies. Historically, the PLAN developed general patterns of strategic thinking and operational behavior forged from a half century of technology improvement, institutional reforms, sea battles, contested offshore landings, and far-sea operations. Some early experiences from its inception from 1949 to 2009 are relevant to contemporary Chinese leaders as they consider specific strategic and even operational challenges like those in the Taiwan Strait and SCS. Contemporary naval doctrine, organization, and training inherit, are derived from and draw on the experience and the maritime policy of the Cold War, such as "nuclear deterrence," "active defense," and "limited (or local) warfare." These strategic concepts are redefined and adapted to be meaningful in today's strategic, operational, and tactical context. This historical survey offers a new understanding of Chinese naval leadership, structure, development, and its role in Beijing's strategic thinking.

NAVAL TRADITION AND WESTERN MISPERCEPTIONS

China's naval war experience has become intertwined with its military history. Ancient Chinese military writers—especially in the preimperial age—produced impressive bodies of work about stratagems, generalship, military thought, and institutions from the Warring States period (475–221 BCE) to the Han dynasty (206 BCE–220 CE). Western scholars are familiar with and have explored Chinese warfare and military thought, including Sunzi (Sun-tzu)'s classic *The Art of War*, which has not only been studied in military institutes but has also been applied to diplomacy, geopolitics, and international relations due to its philosophical nature and strategic value as a work that can be "read in more ways than one."[2] The first recorded naval battle occurred in 549 BCE when the Chu state sent its "boat division" to attack the Wu state. Rear Admiral Wu Jiezhang describes the battle as the "beginning of riverine warfare."[3]

Rear Admiral Wu and his faculty at the PLA Naval Aviation Engineering University divide Chinese naval history into four phases. The first phase started in the Spring and Autumn period (770–476 BCE) and continued to the Han dynasty, when five out of seven warring states established their riverboat divisions attached to their armies as part of ground operations. Some military classics from this period detailed naval organization, combat boat designs, and river operational tactics. The second phase began during the Three Kingdoms (220–80) and lasted until the Tang dynasty (618–907). During this period, the unified imperial governments created state fleets with large numbers of troops and improved combat and transport boats and engaged in large-scale riverine battles. In the Battle of Chibi (Red Cliff), for example, overlord Cao Cao's 70,000 troops sailed east in the Yangzi (Yangtze) River to attack Sun Quan's fleet with 30,000 men. Sun lit up a dozen small boats loaded with plenty of firewood, flammable oil, and dry straw, then smashed the flaming vessels into Cao's fleet. With his fleet destroyed, Cao took the remnants of his army and retreated north of the Yangzi River.[4] The third phase of Chinese naval history took place from the Song (960–1275) to the Ming (1368–1644) dynasties. The Song had twenty-six shipyards and built three thousand naval boats. After establishing the Yuan dynasty (1279–1368), Mongol emperor Kublai Khan maintained a strong navy. During the fourth phase, however, Chinese naval technology stagnated and regressed from the Qing dynasty (1644–1911) to World War II.[5] According to Major General Xu Yan of PLA National Defense University (NDU), in the 1930s the ROC naval tonnage amounted to only 60,000, while Japan's totaled 1 million tons and the American and British each totaled 1.7 million tons.[6]

In the West, specialization in Chinese naval history study was a relatively new phenomenon. It had been understudied and overlooked in the past. Since the 1990s, Western military historians have begun to focus on modern Chinese military history in response to China's reform and modernization in the 1980s. China's rise as a new naval power in the 2010s, with demands of maritime interests, oceanic sovereignty, and overseas naval bases, attracted substantial academic attention among Western naval historians. As scholarship advanced, they argued that Chinese naval history should not be neglected, and they provided fresh interpretations and new conceptions of its significant development, which promoted military reforms, state-building, frontier defense, and territorial expansions of imperial China.

First, new research efforts challenged the conceptualization and generalization of Chinese Way of War (WOW) as Confucian pacifism that was defensive in nature. Whereas Geoffrey Parker links the Western WOW to technology, discipline, decisive victory, and training, John Keegan argues that China followed an "'Oriental' style of war-making characterized by caution, delay, the avoidance of battle, and the use of elaborate ruses and stratagems."[7] John King Fairbank points out that one of the Chinese WOWs was a tradition of defensive land warfare, principally using geography to either wear down or pacify enemies.[8] As a result, the imperial navies received minimal treatment in Chinese military history studies, and naval operations seemed insignificant in Chinese warfare. As more Chinese military writings became available, scholars such as William R. Thompson, Kenneth Swope, Hans Van de Ven, and Harold M. Tanner began to question previous views of the Chinese WOW, arguing that although there is a comprehensive and holistic set of Chinese principles that deals with war, those principles do not describe a separate, distinct, and mutually exclusive "way of war."[9] These scholars contend that the Chinese invented or adopted many of the supposedly Western ways of warfare. David A. Graff compares the military practices of the Sui (581–618) and Tang dynasties and the Byzantine Empire. His conclusion indicates striking similarities in their organizations, tactics, and cautious approach to warfare.[10]

Second, recent research indicated when and how imperial China built an effective naval force against foreign armies.[11] According to these findings, China has been interested in developing maritime capabilities since the Song dynasty. To protect commercial shipping against northern commercial raids and Japanese pirates, the Song prepared a new defense on water and financed the construction of warships. The Song navy numbered more than 50,000 seafarers, and its ships could hold up to 300 tons, with a capacity of 600 passengers.[12] "Previously, the Mongols had had little use for boats in their land campaigns,"[13] but the Song state established a fiscal structure with regard to naval building and mobilization. It instituted significant financial innovations, many of which can be attributed to the crucial connection between commercialized naval warfare and the monetized economy. The formation of financial systems in Chinese history was a state-centered scenario rather than an evolutionary process adapted to cumulative economic changes. After the Song fell in 1279, the Yuan court retained many of the taxes and fiscal structures of the Southern Song (1127–1279) in southern China and relied heavily on indirect taxation for revenue.

Third, the debate over gunpowder in China continued with regard to explosives and firearms in naval war against the Mongols.[14] In the Battle of Chenjia, Song admirals ordered sailors to throw fireballs and shoot explosive arrows to burn Jin naval boats and stop the attacks. Song general Rong Wen employed "shocking guns" in the Battle of Caishi to stop enemy troops. The Song navy also used the "burning box," which they filled with crude oil and floated into the enemy fleets. The Song's *Wujing zongyao* (*General Outline of Weapons*), published in 1044, introduced more than ten different gunpowder weapons for both army and navy, including firing weapons such as bamboo firing sticks.[15] Later in the Yuan dynasty, the Yuan military replaced bamboo barrels with bronze ones. It also described a fire-throwing pipe with "a tail fanning out like a pheasant's plumage at maximum display, immensely increasing the flammable area in comparison with the 'iron-beaked fire goose.'"[16] Ralph D. Sawyer points out that the navy's adoption of riverine incendiary combat was seldom mentioned until the Song, when the military texts detailed clashes on or in water: "Thereafter, the *Hundred Unorthodox Strategies* explicated the fundamental principles under the topic of 'Amphibious Warfare.'"[17] Peter A. Lorge agrees that the reason the Mongols took half a century to conquer the Southern Song was that the Song navy used incendiary gunpower weapons to prevent the Mongols from crossing the rivers.[18] However, as an expert on gunpowder technology in China, he emphasizes that the development of gunpowder did not transform the practice of warfare in China in the way it is commonly conceived of in the West.[19]

Fourth, recent research argues that previous works failed to acknowledge Chinese naval successes prior to the Opium War (1840–42), the beginning of a "century of humiliation." After the Yuan, the Ming emperors sponsored the most active phase of maritime activity. Peter Worthing emphasizes a naval supremacy at the height of the Ming, which built a strong navy to project their power and incorporated new tributary states into their empire by sending Admiral Zheng He on seven maritime expeditions in Southeast Asia, India, and Africa.[20] However, Paul Unschuld points out that when Ming emperor Hongxi (1378–1425) took the crown, naval activities suffered severe setbacks. The sixteenth-century decision disabled China's high-seas naval ability and technological knowledge and created a gap that allowed the Europeans to surpass China's capabilities.[21] Chinese naval modernization was no longer the result of Western expansion or a matter of Chinese "responding" to the West. New research indicates the origins of naval reforms toward modernization in indigenous movements prior to their military confrontations with British and French powers in the nineteenth century. Tonoi Andrade uses the "Great Military Divergence" of the nineteenth century and describes the British as being in the "Fire Weapon Era" during the Opium War, while the Chinese were in the "Mixed Era." Although the British engaged in multiple conflicts, the Qing army did not and thus lacked practice.[22] Bruce A. Elleman and others blame the internal conflicts within the Qing court for the failure in the war and in naval reforms.[23]

OPERATIONAL HISTORY: A LITERATURE REVIEW

Admiral Liu Huaqing, the PLAN commander (1982–88) known as "China's Sergei Gorshkov or Alfred T. Mahan," emphasized China's naval supremacy through ancient history, the imperial age, and the early modern period as an active force to project Chinese power status in East Asia and incorporated tributary states into the empire. China was an active participant, not merely a passive responder, in shaping international trade and global culture in the early modern age. By the nineteenth century, however, the Qing government proved unsuccessful at adapting to rapid changes in global political and economic trends that would keep their governance intact. According to the Chinese admiral, foreign naval powers attacked the Qing more than 470 times from 1800 to 1911, and the Qing navy failed to defend the country. Liu Huaqing blamed Chinese naval failures on the incompetent Manchu rulers, corrupt politicians, backward science and technology, and an outdated military system.[24] One major change in the way PLAN historians reconceptualized Chinese naval warfare is the development of a naval history independent of the West. In the 2010s–2020s, naval affairs have become one of the most discussed subjects in the military field. The Chinese naval publishers—PLAN Press (China's equivalent of the Naval Institute Press) and Ocean Wave Publishing House (海潮出版社 [*Haichao*]), under the command of the PLAN headquarters (HQ) and run by its Political Tasks Department—have published more than eight hundred books in recent years. A common starting point for these naval warfare studies centers on Chinese culture, tradition, and society.

In the West, a China-centric approach also developed from recent studies on Chinese naval history. Nicola Di Cosmo says the difference between Western and Chinese societies requires theories unique to military history, arguing that theories of Western context can be useful for comparative and theoretical models but that further exploration of the cultural evolution of Chinese warfare is required to advance "theoretical sophistication."[25] Recent approaches, incorporating the best methods and analyses from the entire historical discipline, broaden our understanding of naval warfare in China within the people, society, and culture that fought and that built them.

Combined scholarly efforts provide solid groundwork for this research on the PLAN history. Nevertheless, there is as yet no comprehensive operational history of the Chinese navy available in English. A comparable title to this work is Elleman's book, which collects fourteen cases of Chinese naval operations from the Tang dynasty to 2001. These cases characterize modern-day Chinese navy in a military culture and tradition.[26] Given that it covers a 1,380-year history of the modern Chinese navy, however, this concise and brief book cannot do more than skim the surface. There are four cases on the PLAN from 1954 to 2001, and each offers a short (up to six-page) summary of the event. As its back-cover blurb says, "This book will serve well as a useful overview for non-specialists and as a jumping-off point for readers who hope to explore specific aspects of China's naval history in greater detail."[27]

Toshi Yoshihara offers available Chinese-language sources and detailed historical accounts in his new book.[28] He criticizes the "conventional wisdom held that China's maritime thought was largely a Soviet derivative and that the founding naval officers—army officers selected for their loyalty to the Chinese Communist Party—contributed little to the nautical enterprise." He "became convinced that an understanding of China's prospects at sea in the twenty-first century requires an acquaintance with its maritime past."[29] Although the author offers the little-known story of Mao Zedong (Mao Tsetung)'s founding of the PLAN, the book only covers a very short period, about eighteen months, in 1949 and 1950.

In the second edition of their work, Yoshihara and James R. Holmes coauthored an overview of Chinese maritime strategy. The central theme of the book focuses on China's challenge of U.S. maritime strategy in the region and confrontation such has already been seen in maritime territorial disputes and other regional security issues. The book fills some major gaps in strategy research and indicates the destabilizing factors in the region largely from the rise of China. Its civil-military relations and political situation have produced uncertainties and instability. But the book does not set out to provide historical evidence to support the authors' important argument.[30] Another coauthored book, this one by Elleman and James C. Bussert, examines PLAN technology and its "increasingly modern combat system,"[31] providing "a warp of plainly technical threads of equipment characteristics and capabilities and ship construction programs."[32] The authors explain how the PLAN is making rapid advances in technology diffusion and why China is preparing to fight "informationization warfare." As its focus is the contemporary Chinese navy, only one of its twelve chapters (a sixteen-page chapter titled "China's Naval Technology Growth, 1949–1989") deals with the historical background. As Rear Admiral Eric A. McVadon describes in his foreword, this book is "an informative examination of equipment characteristics, acquisition processes, technology, and political military . . . factors,"[33] rather than an operational history of the PLAN.

The well-researched volume by Rear Admiral Michael A. McDevitt addresses important questions like "why China seeks to become a maritime power" and why Chinese leader Xi Jinping needs a "world-class" navy by midcentury.³⁴ While redefining "world-class navy," his analysis focuses on Chinese maritime security theory, strategic practice and implications, and civil-military relations between the party-state and the navy. Rear Admiral McDevitt puts the PLAN into the broader context of China's national goal to become one of the global economic powers. But he notes that his book "is not a history of PLA Navy; that book has already been well written, twice, by Dr. Bernard Cole."³⁵ Cole provides a comprehensive and insightful assessment of the continuity and changes in PLAN doctrine, organization, strategy, and technology. He connects Chinese economic development and global trade with PLAN development.³⁶ Cole argues that Beijing's hard-line position on its territorial demands results from China's dependency on oceanic resources.³⁷ Nevertheless, he summarizes the PLAN's history from 1949 to 1998 within ten pages. The analytical framework on the current Chinese naval development does not allow the author to offer operational details and campaign tactics of naval warfare in the past.

As a Chinese naval operation history, *China's New Navy* examines the major sea battles, landing campaigns, air engagements, island defense, foreign interventions, antipiracy missions, and oceanic voyages of the Chinese navy through the Cold War and beyond. Since the PLAN derived from the PLA Army, the book provides a broad view of China's naval development to tie PLAN modernization into the post-1949 history of the PLA and even the People's Republic of China (PRC). It explains how China actually employed its naval force to challenge U.S. East Asia–Pacific strategy in the past and how this kind of behavior remains evident today. It connects Chinese military culture and tradition to this reform and transformation and characterizes the PLAN not only by what they have but also by who they are and what they can do. Their goals of the naval modernization and their approach to naval warfare in practice are very important for a better understanding of today's Chinese navy.

CHINESE PERSPECTIVE AND AVAILABLE SOURCES

Based on Chinese documents, untouched materials, and personal interviews, this research work looks into the relatively neglected study of warfighting history of PLAN warships, submarines, air force, coastal defense troops, and naval special force. During the 1980s, Deng Xiaoping's reform and opening to the West provided some academic freedom to Chinese naval history studies. The archival offices, research divisions, and history committees of the Chinese Communist Party (CCP), PRC, and PLA published archival materials, official documents, military reports, and high command instructions.[38] Local archival materials are also vital for military historians who study Chinese naval warfare, not simply for filling in factual gaps but also to serve as the main source for discovering both new topics in the field. Memoirs, recollections, and interviews of veterans, officers, and prisoners of war (POWs) became important sources. No matter how politically indoctrinated they may be, the naval veterans are culturally bound to cherish the memory of the past. The immense detail recorded from their experience made a remarkable contribution to the study by adding another perspective. After the Cold War ended in 1991, some former Soviet documents were declassified at the Archives of the President, Party Central Committee, and General Staff of the Soviet Armed Forces, which revealed new perspectives on Russo-Chinese military relations and Soviet aid and advisory to the PLAN.[39] Some translated Russian documents were printed in the Wilson Center's Cold War International History Project *Bulletin*.[40]

After taking office as the PLA's commander in chief in 2012, Xi Jinping carried out Mao-like active defense strategy and repositioned China as the Indo-Pacific regional epicenter. But whereas Mao's active defense was to use neighboring countries like Korea and Vietnam to establish a "ground buffer zone" against the U.S. threat, Xi Jinping has adopted the defensive offense strategy by preparing naval war in the Taiwan Strait, East China Sea (ECS), and SCS. Since Xi launched the "Belt and Road Initiative" (BRI) in 2013, more naval studies, strategic research, and maritime policy analyses have become available in China. Some works focus on naval confrontations in China's strategy, which are designed to protect Beijing's so-called core interest.

This book explores Chinese official documents, strategic writings, military instructions, PLAN speeches, and high command communication of the top leaders like Mao, PLA Commander in Chief Zhu De, Vice President Liu Shaoqi, and Premier Zhou Enlai.[41] Their manuscripts and military works since the founding of the PRC in 1949 were collected and published by the CCP Central Archival and Manuscripts Press. The General Office of the PRC Ministry of Foreign Affairs also published large numbers of government documents in recent years.[42] The PLA collected and published military papers of the top Chinese military leaders like Marshals Zhu De, Peng Dehuai, Lin Biao, Liu Bocheng, Nie Rongzhen, Xu Xiangqian, Chen Yi, He Long, and Ye Jianying.[43] Their campaign plans, reform projects, conference records, writings on strategy, and telegrams are crucial for understanding the PLAN's development and modernization during the Cold War. Certainly, the writings and memoirs of the naval leaders like Xiao Jinguang, Su Zhenhua, Ye Fei, Liu Huaqing, and the others are essential for this research work.[44] The exploration of their strategic thoughts, operational system, and internal weaknesses shapes the PLAN's characteristics in the twenty-first century and differentiate the PLAN from other naval forces in the world.

Since 2008, my research trips have focused on the recollections and interviews of PLAN sailors and officers. I collected their memoirs and interviewed retired PLAN admirals and officers such as General Ye Fei, PLAN political commissar (1979–82); Major General Chai Chengwen; Senior Colonel Guan Zhichao; Major Hou Zhenlu; Captain Wang Xuedong; and others in Beijing, Shanghai, Guangzhou, Nanjing, Wuhan, Hangzhou, and Hainan.[45] The great details from their experience made a remarkable contribution to this study by adding alternate perspectives. Rear Admiral Xu Changyou, former political commissar of the East Sea Fleet (ESF)'s Air Force, helped me considerably to understand the PLAN's chain of command. I conducted more than two hundred veteran interviews, collecting direct testimony by Chinese naval officers and sailors themselves. The untold stories of the Chinese captains, boatswains, "faceless" sailors and gunners, and naval pilots provide original scenario and putting faces, or "flesh and bones," on a naval officer and his crew in a personal and intimate manner during the Cold War and beyond. They also indicate important lessons learned by the naval officers who faced the enemies during a period when the PLAN underwent a complex transformation after the Cold War. From 2010 to 2017, during four research trips to Taiwan, I also researched ROC government documents and interviewed Taiwanese leaders, generals, and naval officers.

The chapters follow the chronological development of PLAN operational experiences by discussing its strategy, tactics, and operation since the founding of the PRC in 1949. Through this operational history, the book establishes that PLAN battle performance was a fundamental factor for changes in war strategy and combat tactics. Its need to win in naval war was a driving force behind its modernization and its push for transformation. As the PLAN had more engagements, further and deeper reform became possible: the naval experience in conflicts produced changes in strategy and tactics. According to the chapters, on the one hand, the party controlled the PLAN in its political indoctrination and organization, but on the other hand, the admirals had their own ways to bypass conventional channels and ask for more. In this way, military reform was part of the persistent bargaining between the PLAN and the CCP. In most cases, the party and state decided to cater to the military demands for improvement, since they faced an immediate and direct foreign threat. In others, however, the Party Center rejected the demands for change by dismissing military leaders and purging the PLAN.

Chapter 1 begins with the birth of the PLAN in April 1949 and its early battles in 1950–53, when Mao Zedong fought the Chinese Civil War in the Taiwan Strait. The chapter also looks at how the Chinese navy received Russian aid during the Korean War and how the need to acquire new naval technology sparked debate among naval officers for the rest of the century. Chapter 2 examines naval battles and operations during the 1954–55 and 1958 Taiwan Strait Crises, including the amphibious landing campaign against the ROC-held offshore islands. Chapter 3 focuses on the PLAN's transformation from a coastal fleet to a naval force by examining its battles against the ROC navy and its air wars against Taiwanese fighters and U.S. spy aircraft through the 1960s. When Moscow broke with Beijing, the PLAN survived. Chapter 4 covers Chinese naval operations in the Vietnam War, including air defense, intelligence, sea transportation, southern infiltrations, minesweeping, and attacks on the South Vietnamese navy (or ARVN Navy) around the disputed islands in the SCS. Chapter 5 views Deng Xiaoping's military reforms from 1978 to 1989 as favorable and necessary for naval restructuring, which, however, was incomplete and limited in dealing with political and social problems that led to the 1989 Tiananmen incident. Chapter 6 explains how Jiang Zemin not only survived Tiananmen and the collapse of the Soviet Union but was also able to promote China's sea power, maritime interests, and oceanic sovereignty. After Jiang, Hu Jintao continued the favorable policy for naval modernization. From 1990 to 2012, the PLAN enjoyed double-digit growth in its annual budget and became one of the global sea powers. The PLAN sent ten formations to the Gulf of Aden and African coast to defend vessels against pirates in 2008-11. The conclusion discusses what Xi Jinping inherited from his predecessors in 2012 and how he draws his new maritime strategy from the past naval experience. The Chinese political leaders and naval leaders have adapted the PLAN to China's economic growth and changing international circumstances. When China played an increasingly important role on the international stage, the Chinese navy emerged as a great navy matching China's great power status.

CHAPTER 1

Light Navy for Coastal Defense

During the 1946-49 Civil War, the PLA did not have a naval force capable of engaging the Chinese Nationalist (Guomindang, GMD, or Kuomintang, KMT) navy. From 1949 to 1951, the major PLA landing campaigns against the ROC-held islands Dengbu, Jinmen (Quemoy or Kinmen), Hainan, and Zhoushan (Chou-shan) were predominantly army operations without naval support. New challenges and serious setbacks in offshore operations led the CCP leaders to restructure their military and adapt to a new naval warfare in the Taiwan (Formosa) Strait. In 1949, the PLA high command developed amphibious landing doctrine. Chinese generals shifted focus and conceptualization of amphibious operations, demanded naval and air development, and made important improvements to match their opponents, including new naval technology, airpower, landing training, and offshore logistics. On April 23, 1949, the PLA's Third Field Army establish the East China Military Region's Navy (ECMRN) to receive the former GMD seamen and vessels. April 23 is celebrated as the birthday of the PLAN.

On January 12, 1950, Mao Zedong, CCP chairman, appointed army general Xiao Jinguang (Hsiao Chin-guang) as the inaugural commander of the new "Chinese People's Navy." From the very beginning, Xiao shaped PLA naval doctrine by adopting army doctrine and tradition with some modifications in a naval environment. On April 14, his navy HQ became operational in Beijing as the PLA naval high command.[1] But the PLAN, established through "an arduous birth from the flame of war," as PLA Naval Command College's Gao Xiaoxing puts it, did not have a long-term development plan, an overall naval strategy, or effective combat tactics from 1949 to 1953.[2] Because of limited resources, Commander Xiao Jinguang believed that the

PLA should build a light navy with practical means like airplanes and torpedo boats for immediate and capable operations to support the army. Thereafter, his light navy began to develop its "air, sub, and speed" (空 *kong*, 潜 *qian*, 快 *kui*) capacities, including naval aviation, submarines, and torpedo squadrons to support the army's landing campaigns and coastal defense in 1950.[3]

The Korean War (1950–53) contributed to a jumpstart of Chinese military modernization when the Soviet Union rearmed more than sixty PLA infantry divisions and built fourteen Chinese air force divisions with 3,300 Russian-made warplanes. To win the ground war, however, Beijing concentrated its military buildup on the army and air force as 73 percent of Chinese infantry divisions (more than 3 million troops) and 52 percent of air force divisions fought against the U.S.-led United Nations (UN) force in Korea.[4] Mao Zedong convinced Xiao Jinguang to delay the PLAN development by tremendously reducing naval purchases from Moscow from 1950 to 1953. Chinese admirals agreed with Mao, since the navy had only one torpedo boat squadron and two coastal artillery companies in the Korean War. Because of Mao's decision, as PLA-NDU Xu Yan argues, the navy did not become an independent armed service during the 1950s and 1960s. "In fact, the navy merely served the army as its auxiliary force. . . . In retrospect, the PLA did not have an independent naval strategy during that period."[5]

This chapter examines these congenital deficiencies' negative impact on naval leadership, institutions, and operations from 1949 to 1953 and explains how the lessons learned from early unsuccessful operations informed the PLAN's construction, organization, and technological improvements. In retrospect, the Chinese navy's adaptation to a new naval war environment resulted from the assimilation of former ROC naval personnel and Russian technology. Fleet Admiral Xiao Jinguang's development strategy focused on a light navy to support army operations for coastal defense. Early naval engagements against the ROC navy in the Taiwan Strait show a learning curve for the PLAN. Major shortcomings manifested in lack of maritime experience, centralized coordination, modern warships, and seamen training. The findings indicate that the People's Navy, building on the army's historical legacy, carried on army organizational systems and combat tactics. When Russian naval assistance became available, the technology gap was increasingly apparent after the Korean War. The PLAN modernized the Chinese WOWs, slowly evolved through Chinese interactions with and observations of Russian advisers, and naturally outgrew its formative years.

NEW NAVY WITH ROC SAILORS AND PLA SOLDIERS

In 1949, the PLA high command prioritized amphibious warfare against the ROC-held Taiwan and other offshore islands in the last phase of the civil war. To ensure its successful landings, the PLA required effective air and naval supports. On January 8, 1949, the CCP Politburo passed a resolution, "Current Situation and the Party's Tasks in 1949," calling for its party and army to destroy Jiang Jieshi (Chiang Kai-shek)'s forces and liberate the country. In its instruction, the Party Center planned "to establish a navy capable of defending the coast and rivers" in 1949–50.[6] Its immediate intention to develop a naval force derived primarily from the CCP's plan to eliminate all

Map 1. The People's Republic of China

Prepared by Brad Watkins

enemy forces on the mainland and offshore islands. In his opening speech at the Chinese People's Political Consultative Conference First National Assembly on September 21, 1949, Mao Zedong called for building "a strong naval force" for New China.[7] (See map 1.)

In mid-October, Mao summoned Xiao Jinguang and discussed how to create the PLA's naval force. Mao told Xiao, "We need to learn from the Soviet Union to build our naval and air forces. We will depend on Russian assistance. You speak good Russian and know a lot about the Soviet military system. It seems a proper appointment for you to serve as the commander [of the PLAN]."[8] In December, the CCP Central Military Commission reorganized Xiao's 12th Army Group HQ into the PLA Navy Department.[9] On January 12, 1950, Mao appointed Xiao as the first commander of the new "Chinese People's Navy." In its initiation, the PLAN had three regional naval units: ECMRN, Guangzhou Riverine Defense Command (GRDC), and QNB Command.[10]

The newly established PLAN had no experience in offshore operations and sea warfare and no knowledge about naval technology and training. Naval Commander Xiao Jinguang felt tremendous "labor pain" when the PLA gave birth to its new navy. In 1950, there were no PLA commanders or soldiers capable of moving a ship. As such, former enemy seamen, or the ROC sailors, operated PLA ships and gunboats in the rivers and at sea. Moreover, Xiao Jinguang did not have any air support or coastal artillery protection for his warships, gunboats, and naval facilities against the frequent ROC air raids and attacks from the seas.[11] Perhaps most detrimental to the PLAN's inception was that all PLA naval officers, including Xiao himself, came from an infantry background without any basic naval knowledge or training. Xiao Jinguang became a CCP member in 1922 during his study of military science in the Soviet Union from 1921 to 1924. After he returned, Xiao served as a CCP representative in the GMD Sixth Division during the first CCP-GMD military and political coalition in the Northern Expeditionary War of 1926–27. Being fluent in Russian, he was sent to Russia again in 1927 and received a degree from the Leningrad Military and Political Academy in 1930.[12] Once back in China, Xiao joined the CCP's Red Army and became a chief of staff, political commissar, and commander of an army. Then he served as political commissar and superintendent of the CCP Central School for Military and Politics until 1937. During China's Resistance War against Japan (1937–45), Xiao was the Eighth Route Army's garrison force commander. After the civil war broke out in 1946, the CCP Shandong Regional Command had Xiao Jinguang as its deputy commander and chief of staff. In 1948, the PLA Fourth Field Army appointed him as the commander of its 12th Army Group. Thereafter, Xiao Jinguang served as the PLAN commander for twenty-six years from 1949 to 1966 and again from 1971 to 1980. He became vice defense minister in 1954 and ranked fleet admiral in 1955. (The PLA did not have rankings until 1955.)[13]

Thus, early Chinese naval development demonstrated, and was marked by, growing and learning pains thanks to the CCP's twenty-two-year military history (1927–49) without a navy. Xiao Jinguang's most imminent fear was former enemy officers and sailors operating his warships and gunboats. From 1949 to 1950, ninety-four ROC warships and gunboats (23 percent of the ROC tonnage) revolted or defected from the ROC navy to the PLA.[14] The Communist naval officers had to rely on former enemies, who received their training from British, American, and Japanese navies through World Wars I and II. PLA officers found it difficult to work with ex-ROC naval officers, often citing lack of trust, differing political ideologies, and bitter hatred exacerbated by the Chinese Civil War. From 1949 to 1951, Xiao Jinguang and his staff labored to convince PLA officers to work with defected and realigned ex-GMD seamen.[15]

On February 12, 1949, the GMD's *Huang'an* crew mutinied against the GMD navy. The *Huang'an* was a Japanese-made frigate with a displacement of 745 tons and a speed of 16.5 knots. It was commissioned to the Japanese navy in the summer of 1945, but Japan surrendered to the Allied forces on August 15 that same year. The ROC government received the Japanese frigate in July 1947 and renamed it *Huang'an* (Jie 22). By the end of the year, *Huang'an* was commissioned into the GMD navy's First Fleet and armed with new weapons and equipment. In January 1948, the CCP undercover agents serving on the frigate mobilized an anti-GMD rebellion among the sailors who complained about the civil war and blamed it on the ROC government. During the Chinese Lunar New Year, *Huang'an* captain and seven of twelve officers left the ship for holiday with their families on February 10–12. After commandeering the ship, the pro-CCP seamen sailed the *Huang'an*, with sixty-four sailors and five officers, from its base at Qingdao, Shandong, and to PLA-held Lianyungang, signaling the beginning of GMD warships and naval personnel's defections to the PLA.[16] *Huang'an* became one of the first PLA naval ships and was renamed the *Shenyang* in February 1950. It was remodeled and rearmed with Russian-made weapons and equipment in 1955. The frigate *Shenyang* was decommissioned from the Chinese navy in 1980.

On February 25, 1949, the GMD's *Chongking* (*Chongqing*) cruiser revolted with its captain and six hundred seamen. After World War II, Great Britain and the United States provided their warships and naval vessels to the ROC government, totaling 160,000 tons. On May 19, 1948, the British government sold its cruiser HMS *Aurora* to the ROC, and the British Royal Navy trained ROC officers and sailors in Britain for three months. When Captain Deng Zhaoxiang and his crew sailed the cruiser back to China in August, it was christened *Chongking* after the ROC's wartime capital. As the largest warship in the navy, with 5,220 tons standard load and three 152-mm guns, it became the ROC's flagship. In late 1948, however, some pro-CCP sailors began secretly organizing and planned a defection to the PLA. Although Captain Deng Zhaoxiang had been unaware of the plot, he joined his crew after they rebelled on February 25, 1949. The following morning, the cruiser left Shanghai and arrived at PLA-controlled Yantai, Shandong. On March 24, Mao and PLA commander in chief Zhu De congratulated the *Chongking* officers and sailors in their cosigned telegram, encouraging them "to serve as pioneers in the Chinese People's Navy."[17] The defection and surrender of ROC warships and naval personnel provided the foundation for and facilitated the creation of the PLA's naval force in 1949.

On April 23, 1949, the ROC Navy's Second Fleet revolted in Nanjing. The Second Fleet comprised sixty-two warships and naval vessels under the commander of Rear Admiral Lin Zun. CCP representatives negotiated with Fleet Commander Lin Zun from October 1948 to February 1949. Eventually Lin agreed to defect and leave Nanjing, his fleet base. However, when Lin called for a voting quorum of his commanders, eight of the attendees voted to stay at Nanjing, two vetoed defection, and six abstained. When the PLA captured the ROC's capital, Nanjing, on April 23, Lin Zun revolted. After Lin's declaration, the Second Fleet's 53 vessels and 1,500 personnel broke from the GMD navy and joined the PLA.[18] The nine ships left in the fleet returned to the GMD. Mao and Zhu telegraphed Lin Zun and his fleet on May 18, praising their defection as a "heroic action on the [Yangzi] River at Nanjing." Chinese leaders asked the former GMD admiral and officers to "learn the principles, thoughts, and systems of the People's Liberation Army, and make new efforts in the bright future of the Chinese People's Navy."[19]

On August 28, Mao Zedong met Rear Admiral Lin Zun and other former high-ranking GMD naval officers in Beijing. At the meeting, the CCP chairman told Lin, "You know science and technology. Our new [PLA] navy should learn from you. . . . You should also learn from the new navy. New and old [GMD] navies must unite, learn from each other, and work together to strive for building a strong, people's navy."[20] On September 23, Mao hosted a dinner for twenty-nine defected GMD generals and admirals, including Lin Zun. He and his fleet joined the PLA's ECMRN in May 1949, and Lin became the ECMRN deputy commander.[21] In 1951, he was appointed chairman of the Naval Faculty Committee of the PLA Academy of Military Science (AMS). Lin Zun was ranked PLAN rear admiral in 1955 and served as vice president of the PLA Naval War Academy in 1957.[22]

It was because of the GMD Second Fleet's defection in Nanjing on April 23 that the PLA's Third Field Army established its ECMRN on the same day to receive the former ROC fleet; April 23 is celebrated as the PLA Navy's birthday. Chen Yi (Ch'en Yi), Third Field Army commander, appointed Zhang Aiping as the ECMRN commander and political commissar.[23] Chen told Zhang, "The CMC [Central Military Commission] has just decided that the Northeast China Military Region Command will build an air force, while the East China Military Region Command will take charge of building a navy."[24] As an elementary school teacher, Zhang joined the CCP's Red Army in 1929. He was promoted to a regiment, brigade, and division commander and political commissar during the Resistance War against Japan. In 1946, he was deputy commander of the Central China Military Region. From December 1947 to January 1949, Zhang was sent to Vladivostok, Russia for treatment of his head injury.[25] After his return, Zhang Aiping accepted his new appointment as commander of the first PLA naval force. He was ranked general in 1955 and became deputy chief of the PLA General Staff in 1955–58 and 1977–80, China's vice premier in 1980–82, and defense minister in 1982–87.[26]

In the spring of 1949, Zhang Aiping, at thirty-nine years old, faced the same hurdles as Xiao Jinguang, lacking any knowledge, training, or experience in naval warfare. Compounding that, all 644 PLA officers transferred to his naval HQ were from an infantry division HQ. Nevertheless, after the PLA's decisive victory in early 1949, there was a wave of defections among GMD warships and naval personnel. Since the PLA was successful in recruiting former GMD army troops during the Chinese Civil War, Zhang turned his attention to former GMD seamen and sailors.[27]

After the PLA's Third Field Army took over Shanghai in May 1949, Zhang Aiping sent his officers and staff to the metropolitan area looking for former GMD captains, sailors, and naval technicians who left the GMD or surrendered to the PLA. ECMRN accepted the crew members and co-opted them into the new PLA naval force. Zhang also extended his recruitment to former GMD naval professionals. In June, after approval by the ECMR (East China Military Region) and Mao, he advertised recruitment in Shanghai's newspapers and publicly called on ex-GMD seamen, as *yuan haijun tongzhi* (comrades of the former navy, or ex-naval comrades), to overcome any barrier or hesitation regarding the GMD officers and sailors.[28] Zhang encouraged them to register and apply for the positions in the ECMRN. By August, more than one thousand ex-GMD naval personnel had registered and applied. Zhang screened and hired 788 of them. By September, more than four thousand former GMD naval professionals joined the ECMRN in Shanghai.[29] It became a reality in 1949 that the PLA infantry commanders held naval offices, but ex-GMD seamen operated the PLA ships. The PLAN depended on former GMD naval officers and sailors.

Refusal to follow Jiang Jieshi to Taiwan expanded beyond political factors and often involved personal reasons. Many GMD officers and seamen still had families, savings, and property on that mainland, not Taiwan. If they decided to remain on the mainland, GMD defectors did so both out of political considerations and, even more so, out of fear. When the PLA rapidly took over major Chinese cities in 1949, the CCP launched large-scale movements to identify supporters and opponents in the urban areas. Many former GMD officers were arrested, jailed, and executed. Their land, shops, business, houses, and properties were confiscated by the newly established CCP municipal governments. For those who had served in the GMD navy and wanted to avoid being labeled "counterrevolutionaries" or the enemy of the new regime, joining the Communist forces became a good way to survive the Communist revolution. Additionally, appealing to former GMD personnel was the PLA's protection of its officers and soldiers from class struggles and political accusations during the 1950s.[30] To serve in the PLAN, ex-GMD officers and sailors could continue their naval professions and use their skills with ships, while also escaping the brutal revolutionary movements.

In early 1949, the CMC decided to establish the naval academy, college, and training schools. The PLAN had to employ four thousand former GMD naval officers as the instructors and administrators to run PLA naval schools and train PLA officers, most of whom had no naval operational experience; many of them had never even seen the ocean before.[31] In May, the PLAN opened the Andong (or Dandong) Naval Academy in Liaoning, the first naval school in the PLAN's history. More than 550 former GMD naval officers and sailors who defected from the GMD navy cruiser *Chongking* arrived as the instructors and trainers. Then seventy-four more ex-GMD navy officers and sailors from GMD warship *Lingfu* joined the faculty and staff at the naval academy. The Andong Naval Academy trained and cultivated the PLA infantry officers and soldiers for naval warfare, marine navigation, and surface warship technology. The first superintendent was the *Chongking*'s captain, Deng Zhaoxiang, an honored graduate of Greenwich Royal Naval College. After GMD *Chongking*'s uprising, Captain Deng was appointed superintendent of the PLAN's Andong Naval Academy in March 1949 and Torpedo Training School at Qingdao in August 1950. He was ranked rear admiral in 1955 and joined the CCP in 1965. Rear Admiral Deng Zhaoxiang became deputy commander of the Qingdao Naval Base Command in 1957, deputy commander of the North Sea Fleet (NSF) in 1960, and deputy commander of the PLAN in 1981.[32] Vice Superintendent of the Andong Naval Academy Zhang Xuesi, who later became a rear admiral, was the brother of GMD General Zhang

Xueliang (Chang Hsueh-liang). The former GMD naval officers administrated the naval academy and developed the training curriculum. In August 1949, the PLAN opened the East China Naval Academy in Nanjing. In November, Zhang Xuesi participated in the establishment of the first Chinese Naval College in Dalian by following the Andong model. Thereafter, several more naval colleges and schools were established in Qingdao, Nanjing, and Guangzhou with the help of the former GMD naval officers.

Rear Admiral Yang Guoyu, PLAN deputy commander and chief of staff in 1978–85, points out that most ex-GMD naval officers and seamen successfully realigned with the PLAN and "made their important contribution" to the construction of the new Chinese navy.[33] To realign the former GMD naval personnel with the PLA's political doctrines, Zhang Aiping established the CCP system in the former GMD Second Fleet. Political commissars were appointed to each warship as the first leading commander, ahead of the captain, and several political instructors to the engine room, gunner group, and logistical crew. The ECMRN Command also carried out a series of reeducation programs with an emphasis on "consultation, inclusion, education, and thought reform."[34] The naval political commissars and political instructors organized the ex-naval officers to study communism, CCP theories, and PLA tradition. They also recruited some politically active ex-seamen to join the CCYL (Chinese Communist Youth League) and CCP. ECMRN Command also offered CCP membership to all former GMD captains, and four of them joined the party.

PLAN commander Xiao Jinguang, however, distrusted the former GMD naval officers. To take control of his warships, Xiao telegraphed the GRDC in April 1950, "Our first priority is to control the fleets. This effort definitely faced many challenges and difficulties since we currently depend on the skills of ex-GMD seamen. . . . We cannot rely on them during our major operations in the future. We have to appoint enough of our officers to run the fleet command."[35] Thereafter, the PLAN began a program of gradually retiring former GMD officers from administrative posts in the mid-1950s, when more PLA officers completed their naval education and training programs. During the Chinese Cultural Revolution (1966–67), many former GMD naval seamen were purged from the Chinese navy.

To train PLA infantry officers, the ECMR's navy opened the ECMRN Naval School at the former GMD navy HQ in Nanjing on August 15, 1949; Zhang Aiping served as its president. Many PLA officers who transferred to the navy were frustrated when they stepped on a warship for the first time. They were totally lost when faced with closely placed equipment, meters, thick electric wires, and pipelines. "They didn't dare touch or move anything. When burrowing down through hatch doors and climbing up stairs, they bumped their heads many times."[36] More than 1,500 transferred army officers enrolled for a two-month crash training by the former GMD naval officers. Soviet advisers arrived in 1950 and implemented their curriculum and instructions for seafaring technicians and helmsmen. Meanwhile, the naval school also provided political studies and training for the former GMD seamen on communist ideology and PLA tradition. On February 3, 1950, the Third Field Army transferred more than ten thousand soldiers and officers from its 35th Army to the ECMRN HQ under Zhang Aiping's command.[37]

During the early years, the PLAN had three sources of naval vessels. The main source of warships and gunboats were defected ships from the ROC navy. ECMRN was the PLAN's largest naval force since it had been established from the former GMD Second Fleet. By its first anniversary, ECMRN had 134 vessels, totaling 43,971 tons, including 51 warships and gunboats (16,382 tons), 52 landing craft (20,131 tons), and 31 assistant ships (7,458 tons).[38] Gao Xiaoxing of PLA Naval Command College states that the first-generation frigates "were the backbone of the PLAN's combat power in the early days."[39] The PLAN's largest warship in the early days was the frigate *Nanchang*, with its standard displacement of 1,200 tons and cruising speed of 14 knots. Its main weapons were 120-mm shipborne cannon. It was the former ROC *Changzhi*. In September 1949, its officers and sailors revolted against the ROC and sailed to the ECMRN harbor. However, the ROC air force followed the *Changzhi* and continued its aerial bombardment, trying to destroy the frigate. To protect the warship, the ECMRN Command decided to sink the frigate in the Yangzi River in late 1949 after removing the weapons and equipment. In February 1950, the *Changzhi* was salvaged and sent to the Shanghai shipyard for repair and refitting. It was renamed the *Nanchang* on April 23 and commissioned to the PLAN in July. The frigate *Nanchang* was retired in 1979.

The second source of PLAN vessels was confiscated ROC ships. Bussert and Elleman point out, "In 1949 the Chinese Communist Party (CCP) inherited a large number of navy ships—mainly of Japanese and American origin—from the retreating Nationalist forces."[40] By early 1950, the Chinese navy had captured and received 183 ROC warships and other vessels totaling 47,695 tons in shipyards and ports. Many of the ROC warships were from the Japanese navy: in 1946, after World War II, the Allied Powers dismantled the Japanese navy and redistributed its warships to the ROC, the Soviet Union, the United States, and Great Britain. The ROC received thirty-four Japanese frigates, which arrived in Shanghai and Qingdao in July–September 1947. The ROC navy repaired and reequipped them and called them into service with the code name *Jie* (received) *1–34*. During the Chinese Civil War, the PLAN took over the ROC frigates *Jie-5*, *Jie-6*, *Jie-12*, and *Jie-14* and renamed them *Wuchang*, *Ji'nan*, *Changsha*, and *Xi'an*. The defected ROC frigates *Huang'an* (*Jie-22*) and *Hui'an* (*Jie-4*) were renamed *Shenyang* and *Ruijin*.

The third source of PLAN naval vessels were a few Western warships. The PLAN frigate *Guangzhou* was the former British Castle-class corvette *Bowmanville*, taken over by the Chinese navy in Shanghai in 1950. The frigate *Luoyang* was the former Australian minesweeper *Bendigo* (880 tons), built in World War II and sold to a Hong Kong company after the war. The Chinese navy bought it in 1950 and remodeled it into a frigate. The PLAN also purchased other Western ships in Hong Kong and salvaged six from the Yangzi River, totaling forty-eight Western vessels (28,076 tons). The Chinese navy took over 169 small and medium-sized commercial vessels along the coast cities with a total of 71,501 tons. In 1949–50, the PLAN also repaired and refitted more than 130 vessels for army transportations, naval operations, and training purposes.

The PLAN named each warship after a geographical location in China. Frigates were named after large cities: for example, the *Nanchang* and *Guangzhou*. Gunboats, such as the *Yan'an* and *Ruijin*, were named for small cities. Landing craft took the names of famous geographic places, like the Yellow River (*Huanghe*) and Taihang Mountain (*Taihangshan*). Today the large and medium-sized Chinese naval surface ships bear both pennant numbers and ships' names. The small boats have only pennant numbers. Nevertheless, in 1949–50, only a dozen were warships, and many were medium or small ships and gunboats, mainly used for defense in the Yangzi River. As such, the PLAN was incapable of undertaking any major cross-strait operation against Taiwan in 1949. To eliminate Jiang's forces in Taiwan and conclude the civil war, Mao looked for Soviet naval assistance for the PLA's landing campaigns.

MAO'S PROBLEMS AND STALIN'S PROMISE

After founding the PRC on October 1, Mao Zedong still confronted over 1 million GMD soldiers in Taiwan and southwestern China.[41] At Taipei, the ROC's new capital, Jiang Jieshi deployed 200,000 troops to defend Taiwan and 280,000 men on other islands: 100,000 on Hainan, 120,000 on Zhoushan, and 60,000 on Jinmen.[42] Jiang also used Taiwan as a base and relied on the islands in the coastal regions for counterattacks, air bombings, and naval blockade against the mainland. Elleman argues, "Chiang shifted from a land-based offensive to a naval one, supporting a blockade strategy against the PRC."[43] The PLA faced the entirely new but immediate task of amphibious landing campaigns against the remnants of the ROC force, especially its navy. At that time, the ROC navy had 428 warships and naval vessels, totaling 100,000 tons. The newly established PLAN seemed like no match for the ROC navy in the Taiwan Strait, since it had only 200 medium and small warships, landing craft, and support vessels, totaling 43,000 tons.[44] Moreover, the PLAN could not even protect its warships from ROC air bombings.

In 1949–50, to defend Taiwan, the GMD air force took advantage of their command over the seas and air, searching for and bombing all possible naval targets, including warships, vessels, docks, ports, and shipyards, to destroy any naval potential for a large-scale landing campaign. After the GMD cruiser *Chongking* arrived at the PLA-occupied area on February 25, 1949, GMD airplanes followed it, bombed it from March 18 to 20, and finally sank it at Huludao harbor on March 20.[45] After its Second Fleet's uprising on April 23, 1949, GMD airplanes continuously bombed the fleet's major warships around the Nanjing-Shanghai area. The PLA's ECMRN had no air defense to answer the GMD's large-scale bombings. From April 26 to September 24, the air raids sank six out of nine warships and seriously damaged another in the former GMD Second Fleet. In February 1950, the heavy GMD air raids forced ECMRN to order its thirteen warships and gunboats to leave the East China coast and sail up the Yangzi River to Wuhan, Central China, to avoid further loss.[46]

Without direct naval support along the coast, in 1949 landing operations became an exceedingly difficult task for the PLA. The PLA's Third Field Army, totaling 1 million troops, learned harsh lessons when it commenced landing campaigns in the fall. On October 3, the 61st Division of its 21st Army landed five battalions on Dengbu Island, off the Zhejiang coast. The landing was successful when PLA troops annihilated six hundred GMD defenders and occupied the island that day. However, the GMD navy transported two reinforcement regiments the next day and counterattacked the PLA troops on October 4–5. After suffering 1,490 casualties, the PLA withdrew from Dengbu Island on October 6.[47] PLA Command quickly realized that amphibious assaults were nearly impossible without naval support.

Also in October 1949, the Third Field Army approved its 10th Army Group's landing on Jinmen (Quemoy or Kinmen), a group of small islands covering a total of sixty square miles. Jinmen Island is less than two miles away from Xiamen, Fujian and surrounded by the mainland on three sides. It had a population of 40,000 at the time. The 10th Army Group defeated the GMD defense and took over Xiamen on October 17. Thereafter, Ye Fei, commander of the 10th, ordered his 28th Army to collect boats and prepare a landing on Jinmen. With poor intelligence, the army command failed to address its ranks' battle readiness, transportation, and communication. The 28th Army launched ten thousand troops to attack Jinmen on October 24. After their landing, the three PLA regiments found themselves encircled by the GMD garrison in a small village. Most of the PLA's ground war tactics that had brought them great success on the mainland, like surprise attack to break enemy defense, mobilization and penetration deep into enemy rear, and separation and annihilation, proved unsuccessful in their amphibious applications. The next morning, GMD air strikes and naval bombardment destroyed the two hundred fishing boats that the 28th Army had collected from around Xiamen and used for the landing.[48] With no boats, the 10th Army Group's 150,000 men could not send reinforcements to Jinmen.

After three days of fighting on Jinmen, the PLA lost 9,086 landing troops, including more than 3,000 prisoners, while the GMD army lost only about 1,000 defenders.[49]

News that the Third Field Army's best army group had lost three regiments on Jinmen reached Beijing by October 28. Mao Zedong was shocked and telegraphed Lin Biao, Fourth Field Army commander, on October 31 to halt all amphibious landings on the SCS coast.[50] The PLA high command learned the hard lesson that naval and air forces were necessary for large-scale amphibious campaigns. Then Mao ordered Su Yu, deputy commander of the Third Field Army, in early November to postpone the attacks on the islands in the ECS.[51] Mao warned army commanders in November that the "cross-strait campaign is totally different from all experience our army had in the past. . . . [All commanders must] guard against arrogance, avoid underestimating the enemy, and be well prepared."[52] Following Mao's instructions, Su Yu called off all the offshore attacks on November 14. He warned his generals about the amphibious operation as "a new warfare" or "modern warfare, different from all the wars we have fought before."[53] It would be "extremely difficult to operate a large-scale cross-ocean amphibious landing operation without air and sea control."[54]

Nevertheless, the GMD army perceived the PLA's defeat on Jinmen differently. First, the PLA troops became arrogant and conceited after they took over Xiamen and hence underestimated the landing at Jinmen. Through GMD accounts, the PLA thought their immediate landing successful and did not have a plan for setbacks. Second, the PLA did not have accurate information on the GMD defense forces, which had received new reinforcements from the GMD 18th and 19th Armies. Third, the PLA focused on one landing point and landed there at the wrong time: the 28th Army reached its one landing site in the early morning. This gave the GMD a chance to concentrate its defense forces and firepower during the day. The PLA could have chosen two or more landing sites and landed at different times, including at night. Fourth, the landing troops did not have supporting naval firepower or antitank guns. And the final reason was lack of transportation: the PLA did not have boats for its second wave or any major reinforcement after they transported the first three regiments to Jinmen. During my interview,

General Jiang Weiguo (Chiang Wei-kuo) of the GMD told me that the Battle of Jinmen not only boosted the troops' morale but also convinced his father, Jiang Jieshi, that the ROC government could survive on these islands by building up a strong defense.[55]

The CCP's Party Center realized the huge gap between the ROC and PRC navies and believed a strong naval force was necessary for a successful landing campaign against Taiwan. Chinese leaders considered Soviet naval assistance as a quick solution for their problem.[56] Toward the end of the Chinese Civil War, the Party Center sent a delegation led by CCP vice chairman Liu Shaoqi to visit Moscow for Russian naval assistance and military aid in June–July 1949. Soviet leader Joseph Stalin advised Chinese leaders that "China should have its own navy, and we are ready to help you build naval fleets." Stalin's detailed suggestions included coastal defense, naval cooperation in the offshore areas, shipbuilding and repair, and warship weapons and ammunition.[57] To follow up with Stalin's proposal for a new Chinese naval force, the PLA high command sent a naval delegation to the Soviet Union in August–September. The Chinese delegation visited several Russian naval academies and negotiated three Soviet assistance agreements for Chinese naval academies, Russian naval advisers, and salvaging the sunken *Chongking* cruiser.[58] On September 13, 1949, ECMRN commander Zhang Aiping led another naval delegation to Moscow. They spent forty-three days in the Soviet Union and negotiated more agreements on Russian naval aid and advisory services. On October 25, the first group of eighty-four Soviet naval advisers arrived in Dalian, Liaoning to establish the first Chinese naval academy. On November 24, Rear Admiral Kuzmin and his high-ranking Russian naval advisory group arrived in Beijing. Later, Stalin appointed Kuzmin as the Soviet navy's chief adviser to the PLAN.[59]

In December, Lin Biao ordered his Fourth Field Army to prepare the Hainan landing campaign. The field army assigned its 15th Army Group for the task within three months. After receiving Lin's report, Mao drafted a lengthy telegram to Lin and provided detailed instructions for the Hainan landing campaign.[60] Mao warned Lin, "The cross-strait operation is totally different from all of our army's experience in the ground operations in the past. . . . [You] must concentrate and transport at least an entire army

(40,000–50,000 men) with supplies for at least three days before landing at the enemy beach.... You must study the lesson [of Jinmen]."[61] Mao's recommendations reflected a direct connection with the failure of Jinmen. He applied the Jinmen lessons to Lin's Fourth Field Army's landing campaign at Hainan (or Qiongya) and requested a centralized command, a larger landing force, and better preparation.

Mao's landing-campaign checklist was the first systematic consideration of PLA amphibious operation by the top Chinese leaders. It became the modern PLA's landing-campaign doctrine when Mao's generals and admirals, including Su Yu, Xiao Jinguang, Zhang Aiping, and Deng Hua, transformed his concepts into their offshore war strategies, landing plans, joint operations, and landing tactics. Practical and undogmatic, these army and naval officers could adjust to changing conditions and consistently reassess their own performance. Nor did the new landing doctrine take shape only in the crucible of combat or after suffering another Jinmen failure. The original doctrine included five major points. First, the Party Center should decide on an amphibious landing campaign. The war decision could serve a political purpose, since it came from the CCP leadership. Second, the PLA would establish a centralized chain of command for a large-scale landing campaign. Third, the landing forces must be superior to the defensive ROC garrison in terms of numbers and firepower. Fourth, the landing troops must receive proper training and exercises. Fifth, they should have naval support, cross-strait transportation, and adequate supplies. Soon the new doctrine provided guidelines for PLA landing campaign against the Taiwan-held Hainan Island.

Following Mao's amphibious doctrine, the 15th Army Group planned its Hainan landing campaign, which would deploy two infantry armies, 40th and 43rd Armies, three artillery regiments, and combat engineering troops, totaling 100,000 troops. While training their troops for landing, the 15th Command collected 2,130 fishing junks and employed more than 6,000 boat crews for cross-strait transportation. The PLA high command also instructed the guerrilla troops (about 20,000 men) on Hainan to support the landing campaign. On January 10, 1950, Mao instructed the CMC and the Party Center "to make an effort to solve the problem of the Hainan Island in the spring and summer seasons."[62] On February 1, the CCP Central China

Bureau held the Hainan campaign conference and decided the amphibious strategy would combine small-scale crossings with large-scale crossings to cope with the ROC naval and air superiority in the strait. The PLA needed immediate naval aid from the Soviet Union.

During Mao's first visit to Moscow from December 1949 to February 1950, he asked for Russian help to build a Chinese navy. Soviet leader Joseph Stalin agreed and further advised that "you send sailors, and we provide ships. After completing their training, these Chinese naval officers can sail these warships back to China."[63] After a long negotiation, Beijing and Moscow established military alliance by signing the Sino-Soviet Friendship and Mutual Assistant Treaty on February 14, 1950. Then Mao used the loan from the treaty to place a huge naval order to arm the new Chinese naval force with ships, aircraft, and equipment. Two days later, Stalin signed the $150 million agreement, about half of the total loan. On Mao's request, Stalin also agreed to send a couple hundred Soviet naval officers to serve in the Soviet Naval Advisory Group for the Chinese navy.[64] Mao was satisfied with the outcome of his visit and told Soviet ambassador Pavel Yudin after his return to Beijing, "You can help us build a navy. You can be our advisors. . . . You can train Chinese [officers] to fight against imperialism while you work as advisors."[65]

On Beijing's request for air defense of Chinese major cities, in February 1950 a Soviet air force division arrived in Shanghai. Division commander Lieutenant General Bakisky's mission was to protect major cities in East China like Shanghai, Nanjing, Hangzhou, and Xuzhou, which were suffering from prolonged exposure to Taiwan's air raids. From March 13 to May 11, the Russian pilots shot down five Taiwanese bombers and fighters and stopped ROC air raids and reconnaissance. The Russian air force division conducted regular patrols and set up antiaircraft artillery (AAA) defense on the ground, providing an effective air defense in East China.[66] In August, General Georgiy Belov of the Soviet air force arrived in Shenyang with another Soviet air force division. From October to December, the Soviet Union sent thirteen air force divisions to China, including nine MiG-9 and MiG-15 fighter divisions, one La-9 fighter division, two Yer-10 fighter divisions, and one Tu-2 bomber division. Each division had two or three regiments, including around 120 to

160 aircraft. These Russian air force divisions stationed in Northeast, North, East, and South China for air defense and patrol to protect major Chinese cities. During their missions, they also trained Chinese pilots, ground crew, and technicians. When the Soviet air force withdrew from China, they left all fighters, bombers, AAA guns, radars, and ground facilities (of fourteen air force divisions) to the Chinese.[67] With an effective Russian air defense around the Nanjing-Shanghai region, the PLAN warships and gunboats returned to the coastal area.

The PLA high command convened with Mao when he returned from Moscow on March 4, 1950. Mao appointed Acting Chief of the General Staff Nie Rongzhen and Deputy Commander of the Third Field Army Su Yu to plan an amphibious landing campaign against Taiwan. Mao recommended mobilizing additional infantry divisions and training airborne forces.[68] Su visited PLAN commander Xiao Jinguang on March 11 and detailed naval supports for Taiwan's liberation. The CMC approved the Su-Xiao plan in April. Meanwhile, the Third Field Army commenced amphibious training exercises. Half a million troops from the Third Field Army mobilized for landing attack, comprising the Seventh, Eighth, and Ninth Army Groups.[69] The Fourth Field Army also participated in the Taiwan campaign by deploying its 13th Army Group as landing reserve and its 19th Army Group as a mobile force along the coast. The Taiwan invasion forces consisted of nearly 800,000 men.[70] (See map 2.)

The Fourth Field Army's large-scale landing at Hainan in April and Third Field Army's successful campaigns over Zhoushan Island group in May bolstered morale and encouraged final preparation for Taiwan's invasion. Mao insisted that the party's priority was Taiwan and Tibet's liberation as the CCP's Seventh Congress held its Third Plenary Session on June 6-9 in Beijing. After Su Yu briefed the party leaders on PLA preparations for Taiwan's invasion, the Party Center decided to liberate Taiwan that summer.[71] However, Mao's priority was involuntarily altered, and the CCP was forced to shift their objectives when the Korean War broke out on June 25, 1950.[72]

Neither Russians nor the North Koreans informed Chinese leadership of the June 25 attack on South Korea.[73] Beijing also found that U.S. policy toward Taiwan shifted as Washington abruptly and unexpectedly switched

Map 2. China and Taiwan

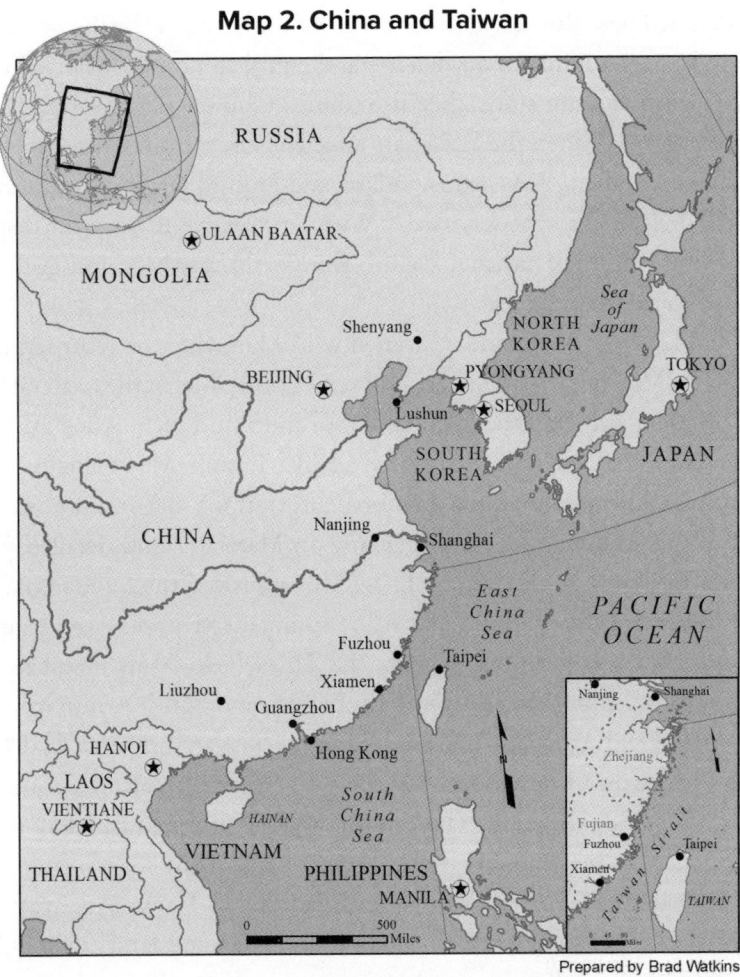

Prepared by Brad Watkins

from "hands off" to "hands on."[74] As a deterrent against potential Chinese Communist attacks on ROC-held Taiwan, President Truman deployed the U.S. Seventh Fleet to the Taiwan Strait two days after North Korea's invasion of the South. By the end of 1950, Truman's stance prevented the PLA's planned invasion and secured the ROC with the Seventh Fleet's patrols in the Taiwan Strait, which marked a major shift in the cross-strait scenario. Direct American involvement in the Taiwan Strait presented the PLA with a serious challenge.[75] Zhou instructed Xiao Jinguang to cancel major naval operations in the Taiwan Strait, since the PLAN had no match for the U.S. Seventh Fleet, even though the Chinese navy had received 7 gunboats, 19 airplanes, and 431 artillery guns from the Russians by that summer.[76] The CMC cabled Third Field Army Commander Chen Yi to postpone the amphibious assaults. Before June, the PLA's primary task was liberating Taiwan from Nationalist forces, but as Mao reflected in one of the speeches he gave after June, "The American armed forces have occupied Taiwan, invaded Korea, and reached the boundary of Northeast China. Now we must fight against the American forces in both Korea and Taiwan."[77] What had been a civil war quickly transformed into an international conflict, and Communist leaders faced a new challenge. Any decision on an amphibious strategy against Taiwan required consideration of U.S. military might after the outbreak of the Korean War in 1950.

LIGHT NAVY WITH RUSSIAN AID AND TRAINING

On August 10, 1950, Mao Zedong and Zhou Enlai, the CMC vice chairman and premier, chaired a PLA high command meeting about the development of naval and air forces. To carry out the CMC decisions, Commander Xiao Jinguang held the first PLAN high command conference in Beijing from August 11 to 30. As Toshi Yoshihara points out, "The Chinese navy's first planning conference in August 1950 had a lasting impact on the PLAN's doctrinal and force structure developments. Naval leaders insisted from the start that the PLA's fine traditions and its core values must be the foundation of Chinese sea power."[78]

Among the twenty-three attendees were Liu Daosheng, PLAN vice political commissar and director of the Political Tasks Department; Luo Shunchu, PLAN chief of staff, Zhang Aiping, ECMRN commander; and other top Chinese naval leaders. Liu Daosheng joined the CCP after he graduated from the Naval Academy of Leningrad in 1930. After his return, Liu became a company, battalion, and regimental political officer in the Red Army. He was the Eighth Route Army's regiment and division political commissar during the Resistant War against Japan in 1937–45. Liu Daosheng was promoted to deputy political commissar and director of the Political Tasks Department of the 12th Army Group under the command of Xiao Jinguang at the end of the

Chinese Civil War. When the 12th Army Group was reorganized into the PLAN HQ, Liu was appointed PLAN vice political commissar and director of the Political Tasks Department. Then, from 1953 to 1957, he was sent to Russia to study naval warfare at the Soviet Naval Academy. Liu was ranked vice admiral in 1955 and served as deputy commander of the PLAN from 1957 to 1967 and again from 1973 to 1982. During this time, he also served as superintendent of the PLA Naval Academy in 1957–62 and as PLAN Air Force commander in 1962–67.[79] Luo Shunchu had a similar military career, even though he worked in the Eighth Route Army's HQ as staff officer. In the civil war, Luo Shunchu became the commander and political commissar of the 40th Army. After the founding of the PRC, he was appointed PLAN deputy commander in 1952 and was ranked vice admiral in 1955.[80]

At the August 1950 naval conference, the Chinese naval leaders discussed naval development strategy and made a three-year plan (1950–53) for the Chinese navy. They all agreed that the navy's immediate tasks were assisting the army's landing campaigns to eliminate the GMD remnants, fight against GMD naval blockade and harassment, and defend the coast and guarantee China's security. To reach these objectives with limited time and resources, the twenty-three naval leaders believed it unrealistic and unnecessary to have large warships. Instead, they endeavored to build a light, small navy with some practical and effective means of immediate and capable operations, such as airplanes, submarines, and torpedo boats. This light navy would develop its "air, sub, and speed" (空 kong, 潜 qian, 快 kui) capacities of coast defense and landing assistance. The three priorities included the establishment of naval aviation, submarine forces, and torpedo fleets from 1950 to 1953.[81]

To achieve the three goals, the August conference passed the Three-Year Plan for the Navy's Development. According to the document, the PLAN would establish a new naval air force (air, 空 kong) with three divisions, including a torpedo bomber division, a fighter division, and a recon and transit division. Meanwhile, it should build a submarine brigade (sub, 潜 qian) and three torpedo boat squadrons (speed, 快 kui). The Three-Year Plan also included the construction of naval infrastructures like shipyards, supply depots, air force bases, coastal artillery force, and other facilities. According to Chinese naval leaders, the light naval force would serve PLAN strategic goals, including coastal defense, amphibious landings, and naval support to the Korean War at a realistic and low cost in a timely fashion. The Chinese naval leaders totally trusted the Soviet Union's technology, advice, and experience in building their new navy. Unfortunately, without input from Soviet naval advisers, Xiao Jinguang's Three-Year Plan lacked a long-term vision for a modern Chinese navy. Nevertheless, Commodore Wu Dianqing of the PLAN Political Tasks Department believes this plan "became the foundation of the PLAN's development for the next three decades"—that is, from the 1950s to the 1970s, not just the three years from 1950 to 1953.[82] Hence, the short-term, quick-fix plan handicapped the PLAN's future development for more than twenty years.

After approving the PLAN's Three-Year Plan, Mao Zedong cabled Stalin on October 8, 1950, asking for more Soviet naval aid and advisers. His lengthy purchase focused on China's three priorities, including 7 destroyers and frigates, 36 torpedo bombers, 124 pursuit airplanes, 10 coast transit airplanes, 500 vehicles, 194 heavy coastal guns, and 6,550 naval mines and depth charges. The Chinese requests also included 408 additional naval advisers.[83] Mao cabled Stalin again on October 28 and informed him that Beijing would send a naval delegation to Moscow to finalize the arms purchase. The Chinese delegation included Xiao Jinguang, Luo Shunchu, and Soviet chief advisers in the PLAN. Xiao Jinguang's six years of higher education and military training in the Soviet Union established his close contacts and affiliation with Russian admirals and made him successful in Sino-Soviet naval negotiations and agreement regarding Soviet aid for PLAN essentials.[84] The Chinese delegation made a formal proposal to the Soviet government on December 18 that included the purchase of naval aircraft, submarines, advisory assistance, and technical training.[85]

According to the Sino-Soviet agreement, the first group of Russian naval advisers and experts arrived in China. They helped the PLAN found the first Chinese naval school in Dalian, Liaoning in February 1950. It later became the PLA Naval Academy. Because Dalian was a coastal resort city, the PLAN could not find a site for its new naval campus there. The Russian advisers removed their artillery regiment from the city and made the land available for the new naval academy. Soviet naval advisers, totaling ninety-two in 1950, decided on the campus layout, designed the shipyard, planned training programs, outlined entire curricula, and provided hundreds of naval texts and tens of thousands of Russian books.[86] The Russian advisers and instructors also helped build another naval academy in Nanjing in April. According to Xia Guang, the inaugural president of the Nanjing Naval Academy, Russian advisers worked in the academy at all the administrative positions from 1950. The Russian advisers made all executive decisions, hired instructors, supervised academic affairs, and managed facilities, labs, classrooms, and equipment. It was not until 1954 that Chinese administrators, instructors, and technicians began administrating the academy, upholding the curricula, and maintaining the campus.[87]

General Vasilievich Zahalov, deputy chief of the Soviet General Staff and head of the Soviet Military Advisory Group (SMAG) in China, assigned 711 Soviet advisers to the PLAN HQ and naval bases in 1950-51.[88] The Russian military advisers were under the Soviet Red Army high command. Major General Kecherjn wrote in his report to the Soviet General Staff on June 16, 1951 that "the Chinese comrades are very friendly to our military advisers. They always listen carefully to all of our advice, suggestions, and considerations."[89] In 1951-53, after General Zahalov left China, General Mikhail Kalasovski became SMAG chief.[90]

PLAN commander Xiao Jinguang worked closely with top Russian naval advisers in Beijing to establish his naval aviation (air, 空 kong), submarine force (sub, 潜 qian), and torpedo boat fleet (speed, 快 kui) as the priority in Chinese naval development. With Russian aid and advisory help, Xiao and PLAN leaders decided on Qingdao, a seaport city in Shandong, as the central location for PLAN's "air, sub, speedboat" development strategy. In April 1950, the Fourth Field Army established the Qingdao Naval Base Tasks Commission, with Zhao Yiping as commander. In September, the Second Field Army joined the force at Qingdao, transferring its 11th Army's HQ to the naval base and establishing the Qingdao Naval Base (QNB), with Yi Yaocai as the base commander. At that time, the QNB had only two patrol gunboat squadrons. On October 21, the PLAN established its first coast artillery battalion, equipped with Russian-made 130-mm coastal guns, at the QNB.

By 1952, the artillery troops had 99 coastal guns at Qingdao. On December 26, 1950, the first naval antiaircraft artillery regiment was established in the QNB and equipped with Russian-made 37-mm guns for air defense.[91]

In December 1950, the second group of 621 Soviet naval advisers arrived. The PLAN faced a serious shortage of Russian translators. In January 1951, the Soviet navy sent twenty-four Russian translators to the PLAN for one year. Soon the Russians decided to extend the translators' contracts for an additional year, until 1953.

With readily available Soviet advisers and experts in naval aviation (air, 空 kong), the PLAN opened its aviation academy in Qingdao on November 1, 1950.[92] The First PLA Naval Aviation Academy established a dual Chinese-Russian administrative system, with two officers for each position. Zhao Huichun, chief of the Operation Division, ECMRN, was appointed as Chinese superintendent of the PLAN Aviation Academy, while Colonel Imyanov was the Russian superintendent. Yang Li, chief of the PLAN Training Department, served as the Chinese assistant superintendent, while Lieutenant Colonel Gemolov served as the Russian assistant superintendent. Jian Ming, deputy chief of staff of the Hebei Provincial Command, served as Chinese provost, while Lieutenant Colonel Makelenko served as the Russian provost at Qingdao.[93] There were seventy-six Russian academic instructors, aviation experts, and air force pilot trainers at China's first naval aviation academy that winter. The Russian air force officers were dedicated and hardworking instructors with strict and critical attitudes toward their Chinese students. They were usually serious and tough in class but were social and easy to approach outside the classroom. They occasionally complained about how Stalin had banned their families from joining them in China and how the school mess hall never had enough Russian-made vodka. More than 240 Chinese pilot students and 570 ground crew students enrolled in different majors and fields in the first year.[94]

From August 6 to 30, 1951, PLA commander in chief Zhu De visited the QNB and the PLAN First Aviation Academy with Luo Ruiqing, Xiao Hua, and General Kalasovski, adviser general of the Soviet Red Army in China (1951–53). Xiao Jinguang and Liu Daosheng met Zhu at Qingdao. At their meeting on August 30, the PLA and PLAN's top leaders decided to establish the Chinese navy's air force as one of the three priorities, "naval aviation (air, 空 kong) development," in the Three-Year Plan. Zhu De wrote a letter to Mao Zedong on the same day and suggested that the "PLAN aviation should consist of 20 percent of China's air force."[95] On January 20, 1952, after Mao and CMC's approval, Xiao Jinguang summoned Zhao Huichun to PLAN HQ in Beijing and assigned him to work with Russian advisers on PLAN Air Force's establishment. After many revisions, the PLAN Command submitted the final plan to the CMC in April.

In May 1952, the PLA high command approved the PLAN Air Force's (PLANAF) establishment. The CMC appointed Zhao Huichun as PLANAF chief of staff on June 1, Li Keru as the director of the Political Tasks Department in July, and Zeng Kelin as the deputy commander in September. On September 16, the PLAN established its first air force division in Shanghai. The PLAN First Air Force Division included a torpedo bomber regiment, a fighter regiment, and a support regiment. On February 10, 1953, the high command appointed Dun Xingyun as the PLANAF commander. The PLANAF established two more air force divisions on February 21. The PLAN Second Air Force Division was a jet fighter division based at Ningbo, Zhejiang, and the Third Air Force Division was a torpedo bomber division based at Jiaoxian, Shandong.[96] By 1953, the PLAN had accomplished its first goal of "naval aviation (air, 空 kong) development" in its Three-Year Plan.

To establish its submarine (sub, 潜 qiang) force as the second goal in the plan, the Chinese government purchased two Russian-made small Type C submarines (built in 1943) in the fall of 1950. The Chinese navy asked the Soviet navy on December 18 to use the two submarines to train the PLAN crews for two years (1951–53) in Russia.[97] After the Soviets agreed, the first group of 275 Chinese submariners traveled to the Russian Pacific Fleet on April 20, 1951. In Russian uniforms and following Soviet regulations, the Chinese worked and lived with their Russian counterparts, learning submarine technologies and operations. Their training, which began on May 14, 1951, was extended to 1954.[98] After three years' training in Russia, on June 19, 1954, the Chinese submariners sailed the two submarines back home. The PLAN established its first submarine division at the QNB on July 22. China bought two more Type Cs in 1954 and six more Russian submarines in 1955.[99]

To fulfill the third priority listed in the Three-Year Plan, "speed" (快 *kui*) for its boat fleet, the PLAN purchased new Russian-made torpedo boats in the fall of 1950. They were *T-123* speedboats with a standard displacement of only 22.86 tons and a navigational speed of 52 knots. Each patrol torpedo (PT) boat had two torpedo tubes and two 12.7-mm dual-barreled antiaircraft machine guns. With its small body, this kind of PT boat was a high-speed and flexible attacking vessel.[100] However, there were no accommodations or sleeping bunks on the narrow torpedo boats, and the men had to stand at post all the time. It was also impossible to cook on the PT boats, so daily meals were a major issue. Although the boats were small, they were fast with torpedo firepower, much more effective than the worn-out ROC warships and fishing boats the Chinese navy had. By importing the torpedo boats, the PLAN was able to establish operational fleets with attacking capacity to sink the ROC warships. Meanwhile, the Russian advisers and experts helped the PLAN establish its speedboat (torpedo boat) school at the QNB in August 1950. The Russian navy also provided six torpedo boats for training. From 1951 to 1953, the school trained more than nine hundred officers and crew members.[101] In October 1952, the PLAN established four torpedo squadrons with forty-two torpedo boats. During this period, the Soviet navy also provided two hundred vessels and helped the Chinese form nine gunboat squadrons.

As a navy of learning, the PLAN assimilated Russian naval technology and imitated small Russian ships and weapon systems. In 1952, the Chinese navy negotiated with the Soviet navy for the purchase of a complete set of semifinished warship instruments and technical materials. The Russian naval experts and naval engineers came to China with the shipbuilding packages and helped China establish a new naval industry. They created navigation research and development, shipbuilding and repair, shipyard and dock construction, and weapon system upgrading. Bussert and Elleman add, "In 1953 the USSR assisted China in establishing the first new military shipyard in Bohai at Huludao, which would construct the most modern submarines."[102] At this point, 621 Soviet advisers assisted the PLAN at their shipyards.[103] To meet increasing needs for naval leadership and guiding services, the CMC transferred the 10th Army's HQ from the Second Field Army to the navy in 1952. After 1953, the Chinese naval industry began to assemble these parts and manufacture its own gunboats, including torpedo boats, minesweepers, and submarine chasers, in six of its main shipyards. For example, the Wuhu Shipyard built fifty-one torpedo boats from 1955 to 1959. Even with Russian technology and assistance, imitation was difficult because of overall low industrial capacity and backward technology in China.

By 1953, the PLAN had achieved the three goals (air, sub, and speed) in its Three-Year Plan. The light-navy development strategy adhered perfectly to the high command's priority in 1950–53, when the Chinese army and air force desperately needed more financial resources and Russian aid in the Korean War. Mao Zedong visited PLAN HQ on December 12, 1952 and tried convincing his admirals to reduce, if not cancel, their naval purchases from the Soviet Union. Mao told Xiao, Liu Daosheng, Wang Hongkun, and Luo, "Currently [the War of] Resisting the US and Aiding Korea demanded airplanes. We have to concentrate our foreign currency on helping the Air Force.... Our foreign currency is not enough [for both air and naval forces]. How about purchasing airplanes first for the Air Force? Is it OK to postpone your planned purchase of warships to a later time?" The naval leaders accepted Mao's request and agreed to reduce their budget and cancel their orders from the Soviet Union.[104] Many senior naval officers attributed the PLAN's slow start, a decade-long budget restraint, and poor performance in the 1950s to the Korean War.

LANDING SUPPORTS AND COMBAT TACTICS

According to the PLAN's war strategy in 1949–53, its two naval forces were tasked with supporting the regional army's offshore operations against the ROC forces in the Taiwan Strait. The South-Central Military Region's Navy (SCMRN) and ECMRN were under the direct regional army's command for their operations, battle preparations, and combat trainings. There was no centralized PLAN chain of command for the local landing campaigns. During their early years, the two naval forces lacked maritime experience, battle coordination, firepower, air defense, modern warships, and trained seamen. The findings indicate that SCMRN and ECMRN, fighting along the landing troops, carried on infantry combat tactics. They waged "guerrilla warfare on the seas," launching surprise attacks to neutralize GMD firepower, operating at night to avoid air strikes, and using hand grenades to engage in close combat against much larger enemy ships. On the seas, the Chinese navy had no choice but to rely on the infantry tactics they knew. Gao Xiaoxing of PLA Naval Command College summarizes the early naval tactics as "concentrating fire, fast breakthrough, and going ahead full blast. . . . This was the typical PLA ground military tactics when storming heavily fortified positions."[105] Early operational difficulties and naval battle losses indicate the sequelae of an overnight transition from PLA Army to PLAN.

After taking Guangzhou, the largest city in South China, in October 1949, the Fourth Field Army established the Office of Naval Takeover to receive and manage former GMD warships and naval personnel. On December 15, the field army command combined the naval office with the received warships to establish the GRDC, appointing the deputy commander of the 13th Army Group Hong Xuezhi as the new river force commander.[106] Since it had only five small warships and a dozen gunboats in the Pearl River (Zhujiang), the GRDC did not participate in the Fourth Field Army's large-scale landing campaign against the ROC-held Hainan Island in March–April 1950. Jiang Jieshi concentrated 100,000 ROC defense troops, including fifty warships and gunboats, on Hainan, the second-largest Chinese island next to Taiwan.

On March 5–10, the 15th Army Group began its small-scale, battalion-sized night landings across the Qiongzhou Strait. The vanguard landing troops quickly overran the defense garrison and reached local guerrillas. Then, between March 26 and 31, the 15th Army Group's 40th and 43rd Armies sent two regiments with artillery units to cross the strait and successfully landed at Hainan. These vanguard troops established their bases and prepared the sites for the 15th Army Group's large-scale landing. At 7:30 p.m. on April 16, the first landing wave of 50,000 troops on 350 boats sailed to Hainan. The ROC air patrol reported the PLA assault as soon as it left the shore. Through the night, six ROC warships attacked the PLA landing force but failed to stop the crossing, while one ROC warship was sunk and two damaged in the engagements.[107] By six o'clock the next morning, the first wave landed at Hainan. By April 22, the ROC defense collapsed and the PLA took over Haikou, the capital city of Hainan. On April 23, the second landing wave of 50,000 PLA troops left the mainland and landed at Hainan. By May 1, the PLA had won the Battle of Hainan.[108]

In May–August 1950, the GRDC participated in the PLA's landing campaign at the Wanshan Island Group, including forty-eight islands about twenty miles off the mainland. Guangzhou was the largest commercial port in South China. Moreover, Hong Kong, bordering on Guangzhou, was a transfer hub for trade between the newly founded PRC and the West. However, the city was in a predicament as the ROC forces blocked the port and the outlets of the Pearl River shipping on the Wanshan Islands. With more than three thousand troops stationed there, the Wanshan Islands became a choke point for Guangzhou's navigation channels and foreign maritime trade. To take over the Wanshan Islands, GRDC naval command and the 131st Infantry Division established a joint front command, including the landing force commanders and GRDC chief staff and deputy political commissar. Vice Admiral Yang Guoyu points out, "The Battle of Wanshan was the first time in the PLA history when the navy and army coordinated."[109]

In May 1950, the joint front command planned an amphibious landing on the Wanshan Islands for May 26. GRDC commander Hong Xuezhi sent twenty-four warships, gunboats, and landing vessels from Guangzhou to the Wanshan area to participate in the landing campaign.[110] The joint landing command divided the Guangzhou vessels into three groups by using 80 percent of its naval gunboats to transport and protect the landing troops while deploying only 20 percent of its naval force to attack the enemy navy. The first naval group had only one warship and two gunboats to attack the estimated two to four ROC warships at the anchor site in the Lajiwei (Trash Tail Island) harbor of the Wanshan. The second group included eleven warships and gunboats to cover the flanks of the landing troops. The third group comprised one warship and eight landing vessels to deposit two landing battalions on Lajiwei Island.[111]

As a surprise attack, GRDC Chief Staff Li Huaizhang sent off the first naval group on the night of May 25 to attack enemy warships at the main anchor site at Lajiwei harbor and clear the way for landing troops. Lack of sea communication and reliance on infantry walkie-talkies between the warship and gunboats resulted in the PLA ships losing contact and heading in different directions during the twenty-mile sail. Due to the shortage of technical personnel, there was only one mechanical sailor for two ships and one navigator for three ships. By the late night, only the gunboat *Jiefang* (*Liberation*; 28 tons, navigational speed 10 knots) and the warship *Guishan* (*Laurel Mountain*; 358 tons) had reached the bay of Lajiwei. As the largest ship in the fleet, the *Guishan* was the GRDC flagship, with two 40-mm cannon. *Jiefang* arrived at Lajiwei first, around 4 a.m., and Assistant Captain Lin Wenhu found the entire ROC Third Fleet—more than twenty warships and gunboats—stationed there.[112]

As the only PLA gunboat present, Assistant Captain Lin Wenhu launched the dangerous, single-boat attack in the dark and ordered his crew to get closer to enemy warships. Although *Jiefang* had only one small cannon and two machine guns, all its sailors opened fire with small arms, including machine guns, rocket launchers, and recoilless rifles, as if they were infantry. *Jiefang* maneuvered between the ROC ships and fired from about 100–300 yards. It also fired in unison at the ROC fleet flagship *Taihe*, a 1,500-ton frigate. Surprised and confused, the ROC warships could not use their big guns to return fire at such close range. *Jiefang* moved deep among the ROC ships and engaged in switch-hitting, which made things even more chaotic.[113]

Forty minutes later, the *Guishan* warship arrived and joined *Jiefang*'s suicidal attack in the harbor. During the hour-long battle, *Jiefang* and *Guishan* sank one ROC gunboat and seriously damaged several others. Nevertheless, by the early morning, *Jiefang* lost thirteen out of nineteen sailors, and Assistant Captain Lin Wenhu was killed during the attack.[114] *Guishan* also lost all crew, including its captain. After being badly hit, the warship ran ashore. Although the sailors fought like tigers, the attack was of little impact or significance. The ROC Third Fleet remained in its station in the Wanshan Islands. The Chinese navy failed at the operational level, since they lost all offensive ships, including their flagship, during the attack. But despite the navy's operational failure, the campaign was successful, since its main objective was the army's landing. Assistant Captain Lin Wenhu became the first naval propaganda hero. SCMRN established the Lin Wenhu Martyrs Monument near its HQ in Guangzhou. The Guangdong provincial government renamed Lajiwei "Gui-shan Island," after the warship *Guishan*.

The next morning, other SCMRN gunboats engaged ROC warships east of Lajiwei harbor, sinking one enemy ship and catching another. During the naval battle, small PLAN gunboats again drew close to the large ROC ships as PLAN sailors jumped over enemy gunboats and engaged in hand-to-hand combat like infantry soldiers. The PLAN's combat history started with small gunboats to attack large ROC warships by using guerrilla strategy and infantry combat tactics. With naval support, the PLA began its landings on the Qingzhou (Green Islet) and Sanjiao (Triangle) Islands of Wanshan under cover provided by naval gunboats. In late May, the PLA attacked more islands and islets in the archipelago.[115]

In June, the ROC reinforced the Third Fleet with several frigates and minesweeping ships at the Wanshan Islands to stop the PLA landing campaign. SCMRN discovered the ROC's new anchoring area at Sanmen Island, which was not occupied by ROC troops. In the late night of June 26, the PLA shipped eighteen heavy artillery pieces to Sanmen, and SCMRN sent three gunboats to the island. At about five the next morning, the PLA's 100-mm cannon from the islands and guns from the three boats commenced heavy shelling on the ROC warships at Sanmen. After a few hours of shelling, the PLA had sunk one enemy gunboat and damaged one cruiser and two minesweeping ships.[116] In July, the ROC navy withdraw all its ships from the Wanshan area. By August 3, the PLA landed at Wanshan's last island and completed the landing campaign. During the naval battles from May to August, the PLA sank four and damaged twelve ROC warships and gunboats and captured eleven enemy vessels.[117] Yoshihara states that "the pitched battles at sea and the contested landings on offshore islands had a lasting influence upon the Chinese military's institutions, outlook, strategy, doctrine, and force structure."[118]

In October 1950, GRDC Commander Hong Xuezhi joined the 13th Army Group and went to the Korean War. On December 3, the Fourth Field Army Command transferred some infantry officers and soldiers from its Second and 173rd Divisions to the Riverine Defense Command and reorganized it into SCMRN, with Fang Qiang as the commander and political commissar. In October 1952, more officers and soldiers were transferred to SCMRN from the 44th Army of the Fourth Field Army.[119]

To break through the ROC's coastal blockade, the ECMRN participated in PLA landing campaigns against ROC-supported pirates on the islands around the Yangzi River outlet, off the Zhejiang coast. In June–July 1950, the PLA planned a landing campaign against the ROC/pirate-held islands. ECMRN organized a landing fleet with several gunboats (25 tons each, with one double-barrel 13-mm machine gun) and landing craft to support the landing campaigns. Although some former ROC sailors questioned the small river gunboats' capacity to engage in the ECS, the PLA captains led the landing operations. On June 16, the fleet landed troops on Tanzhushan Island, eliminating the garrison and capturing forty-six pirates.[120] On July 8, the fleet attacked Chenshan Island, and PLA landing troops destroyed the garrison and captured three hundred enemy troops. On December 15, the fleet ordered twenty-three gunboats and landing craft to attack the ROC navy and landed the PLA troops at Nancongshan and Shantoushan Islands, sinking five enemy boats and destroying the garrisons of six hundred on the two islands.[121] These naval battles and landing campaigns enabled the PLA to break the ROC's blockade and open the coastal waters for commercial shipping and fishing.

In September 1950, ECMRN began its second minesweeping operation along the waterways and sea-lanes near Shanghai. The ROC Navy laid a large number of underwater mines in and around the Yangzi's outlet to block Shanghai's harbors and the Yangzi's shipping. During that time, many merchant ships struck the mines and sank, including foreign ships.[122] ECMRN organized the minesweeping brigade in April with only ten small landing craft (28 tons), since the fleet had no designated minesweeping ship. On June 19, the minesweeping brigade entered the area, but it had little success. Three commercial cargo ships struck mines and sank on June 20–21. The brigade suspended its operation and the first minesweeping effort ended on July 2.[123] The Chinese government partially shut down the sea-lanes in and out of Shanghai on August 28. In August, the Russian water-minesweeping experts arrived in Shanghai. They helped the ECMRN reequip four heavy landing craft (420 tons) with Russian supplied MT-3 minesweeping equipment. On September 21, the second minesweeping operation began with eight ships around the Yangzi River outlet. Within a week, they swept four water mines in the area, destroying three and disarming one for research. By the end of October, the minesweeping operation was successful and had cleared most of the underwater mines. The Shanghai government reopened the sea-lanes from the Yangzi to the ECS.[124]

The ECMRN faced new challenge during the Korean War. Jiang Jieshi increased ROC attacks from the offshore islands against PLA coastal defenses by taking advantage of the PLA's intervention in Korea. On the evening of July 9, 1950, ECMRN gunboats *3* and *103* anchored near Langjishan Island to guard the harbor. The next morning, gunboat *3*'s captain, Shao Jianming, spotted an ROC gunboat approaching the island. After asking *103* to return to the harbor and report the situation, Captain Shao ordered his small gunboat (25 tons) to attack the larger enemy ship. The ROC warship retreated, lured *3* from the island, and then opened fire at sea. The ROC warship's superior firepower scored two hits on *3*'s control room, killing Captain Shao Jianming and his deputy. As *103* arrived at the battle, *3* suffered four more hits and sank with its twenty-two crew members.[125] The Chinese navy's loss revealed its severe lack of training and its reliance on outdated equipment and weapons.

In September 1951, Jiang Jieshi sent General Hu Zongnan to the Dachen Islands to command ROC army and navy operations against the Chinese eastern coast. The Dachen consisted of a dozen small islands within hit-and-run range of both the ROC and the PLA. Hu strategically erected strong defenses on the coastal islands and aggressively harassed, sabotaged, and counterattacked from the offshore islands like Dachen, Mazu, and Jinmen. In 1950 to 1953, ROC troops raided more than two thousand fishing boats along the Zhejiang coast and captured ten thousand fishermen.[126]

Jiang Jieshi escalated tension during the Korean War with the hope that the ROC could return to the mainland with U.S. military support. On June 15, 1953, General Hu Zongnan launched the ROC's largest attack from Jinmen, on the PLA-occupied Dongshan Island off the Fujian coast. He organized a landing force of more than 11,000 troops with a fleet comprising one destroyer and nine warships. The next morning, Hu landed ROC troops on the island and overwhelmed the PLA garrison, about one thousand troops, with strong air and naval firepower.[127] The PLA garrison defended the island

and waited for reinforcements. The ECMRN sent four gunboats to protect the reinforcements for Dongshan Island. The PLAN gunboats managed to avoid ROC warships' firepower and reached the island the next day. The gunboats provided the PLA reinforcements with combat support and defeated the ROC landing troops. On June 17, the Battle of Dongshan ended with a PLA defensive victory. The ROC lost 3,400 troops, 2 tanks, 2 airplanes, and 3 landing craft. The PLA suffered 1,250 casualties.[128] In 1953, the ECMRN engaged the ROC navy in fifty-two battles off the eastern coast.[129]

In July 1953, Chinese leaders suspected that President Dwight Eisenhower wanted to "unleash Jiang" after the Korean War, since he had ordered the U.S. Seventh Fleet no longer to prevent Jiang's attack on the mainland.[130] The PLAN, however, as a light naval force, was neither battle tested nor ready for a major naval showdown in the Taiwan Strait. Lacking the necessary naval power, Mao decided to deal with Washington diplomatically after the Korean War, if possible. However, the Chinese navy would continue its operations against the ROC-occupied islands in limited naval war.[131]

In retrospect, the PLAN was merely the "army at sea" fighting with infantry weapons and tactics on the gunboats during their first four years. Xu Yan concludes that at that time the Chinese navy "was an auxiliary force to the army. Its operations were to serve the needs of the army in the military region. For example, the North Sea Fleet (NSF) was under the command of the Ji'nan Military Region, East Sea Fleet (ESF) under the Nanjing Military Region, and South Sea Fleet (SSF) under the Guangzhou Military Region."[132] Thus, the regionalized fleets became involved in the Chinese army's sectional or factional politics and established their own regional networks. PLAN commander Xiao Jinguang had faced this extraordinary challenge, or "the issue of cohesion," in the PLAN since the early 1950s.[133] Sherman Xiaogang Lai describes the navy's inherent deficiency as "mountaintop-ism," which "would plague the PLAN for decades."[134]

CHAPTER 2

"Limited Naval Wars" in the Taiwan Strait

The PLA focused on new amphibious campaigns against the Taiwan-held offshore islands along the mainland coast after the Korean War ended in 1953. Chinese naval leaders saw an invasion of the Taiwanese islands as an opportunity to get back the funds they lost to the army and air force in 1950–53. However, Mao Zedong realized China's military limits in the Korean War and modified its civil war strategy in 1954–59. Moreover, after Stalin died in 1953, the CCP adopted a moderate foreign policy to relax international tensions. Mao cooperated with the new post-Stalin Soviet leaders who were striving for détente with the United States. Therefore, Chinese leaders did not want any major international crisis or a war with the United States in the Taiwan Strait, especially following recent settlements that ended two conflicts close to China: namely, the Korean Armistice in 1953 and the Indochina settlement in 1954. On December 22, 1953, while rejecting Marshal Chen Yi's plan to deploy five armies to attack Jinmen Island, Mao Zedong instructed the ECMR commander to keep offshore operations defensive and on a small scale, with no direct engagement with U.S. armed forces in Chinese waters.[1]

Because of the Korean War in which the Chinese army and air force received the lion's share of the military budget, Chinese naval development was delayed in 1950–53. After Mao's foreign policy shift, it was postponed again. To avoid any confusion and high expectations on the part of naval officers, Mao told the navy at an enlarged CCP Politburo meeting on December 4, 1953, "We should make a plan to gradually develop a strong navy step by step in a relatively long period time according to [our] industrial growth and financial availability."[2] Thus, the PLAN's short-term plan, or the "1950 Three-Year Plan," focused merely on "air [空 *kong*, naval aviation], sub [潜 *qian*, submarines], and speed [快 *kuai*, speedboats]" and became a long-term plan during the 1950s. This meant that the Chinese navy would remain a light navy with no large ships. In 1955, ECMR navy was renamed the PLAN's ESF; the SCMRN navy, the SSF; and the QNB, the NSF. Naval development remained slow and limited through the 1960s, since the navy's modernization was secondary to that of the army and air force. Sherman Xiaogang Lai adds another reason to the PLAN's problems: "The decline of the PLAN's combat efficiency in the late 1950s was closely linked to Mao's catastrophic Great Leap Forward Movement campaign in 1958 and the resulting famine that cost over 30 million lives."[3]

However, Mao never lost a chance to test America's intentions and commitments in East and Southeast Asia. Beginning in 1954, the PLA engaged in "limited wars" (or, in Chinese, "local wars") in the Taiwan Strait. By limiting the scope of each operation in regard to scale and time, the PLAN avoided direct confrontation with the U.S. Navy. By conducting limited landing campaigns and offshore bombardments, China maintained its important international position in East Asia after Korea. On December 2, Washington signed the Mutual Defense Treaty with Taipei to commit U.S. armed forces to the security and safety of Taiwan. In his official response on December 8, Premier Zhou Enlai issued a strong statement denouncing it as a "treaty of aggression" and reaffirmed the PRC's determination to "liberate Taiwan." Zhou declared that the "Chinese people must defeat the traitorous Jiang Jieshi clique," but he did not mention any possible military confrontation against the United States in the Taiwan Strait.[4] Since the U.S.-Taiwan defense treaty was ambiguous about these offshore islands between China and Taiwan, Mao intended to probe and test American resolve by attacking the Taiwan-held offshore islands in 1954–55 and again in 1958, causing two Taiwan Strait Crises.[5]

This chapter examines the mixed results of Mao's détente foreign policy and "local war" strategy for the Chinese navy from 1954 to 1959. The PLAN made do with a decentralized chain of command, small ships, weak firepower, and inadequate adaptation of Russian naval experience, which led to the navy's poor performance in the First Taiwan Strait Crisis. Soviet aid and advisory services remained available, and as a result, the PLAN maintained its slow, steady development following the Soviet model with new but limited capacities. With an exceptionally low annual operational budget, about 100 million RMB (about $40 million at that time) throughout the 1950s, the Chinese navy managed to integrate Russian naval technology with its own experience and lessons learned from naval battles. The PLAN established a capable torpedo boat fleet, developed speedboat combat tactics, and transformed itself from an inshore defensive force to a light naval force capable of offshore attacks by the end of its first decade.[6]

MORE RUSSIAN AID AND "ENLIGHTENED" MENTORS

From 1954 to 1959, Defense Minister Peng Dehuai continued the Chinese military modernization begun during the Korean War. Following the Soviet model, Marshal Peng improved military technologies, reorganized defense industries, and spent about $2 billion on arms purchases from Russia.[7] However, he followed Mao's strategy and prioritized the army and air force's developments during his military reform movement. In March 1956, Peng Dehuai made it clear at an enlarged CMC meeting that "the navy should follow the original plan [the Three-Year Plan] to focus on continuous development of submarines and torpedo boats."[8] The Chinese navy continued to follow Fleet Admiral Xiao Jinguang's Three-Year Plan (1950–53) for six more years, until 1959, with the same goal of building a light navy while making new efforts in submarine construction, torpedo boat combat operations, and naval aviation. Moscow sent more naval advisers and shared Soviet technology and Russian naval experience with the PLAN in 1954–59.

On June 4, 1953, Beijing reached an important naval assistance agreement with Moscow, known as the 6-4 Agreement, for delivery of 137 naval vessels to the PLAN in 1954–56, including four destroyers. In October 1954, the first two destroyers (*Rekordny* and *Reshitelny*) arrived at Qingdao.[9] With a displacement of 1,600 tons, these old Russian-made warships, which entered service in 1937 and 1941, had been refitted and repaired before being sold to China. The PLAN named them *Anshan* (DD 101) and *Changchun* (DD 102). The second pair of destroyers, named *Jilin* (DD 103) and *Fushun* (DD 104), arrived in June 1955. They certainly improved Chinese naval surface striking power in the mid-1950s. However, these destroyers continued as the PLAN's only major warships for the next twenty years, garnering reverence from Chinese seamen as the "four kings" until the early 1970s.[10]

In the 6-4 Agreement, the Chinese government requested more Russian advisers to help with the PLAN's building and training. There were about 3,400 Russian naval advisers in the PLAN by 1958. As they imparted rudimentary naval knowledge to PLAN officers, Russian advisers developed unique ways of working with their PLAN counterparts. The Russians worked with the Chinese on a one-on-one basis: there were equal numbers of Russian advisers and Chinese officers at the PLAN Command, fleet headquarters, and naval bases. In most cases, Chinese officers listened to Russian recommendations, accepted their comments and suggestions, and implemented Russian advice in the orders and instructions. Russian advisers were also paired with each departmental head for operation, intelligence, logistics, political tasks, and human resources at PLAN HQ. In November 1954, Russian advisers and Chinese officers organized a PLAN landing exercise at the Shandong Peninsula. In January 1955, they executed naval battles and a joint amphibious landing campaign at the Yijiangshan Island, defeating the Taiwanese garrison and taking over the island.[11] In 1957, the first Chinese-Russian joint naval exercise was conducted in the Yellow Sea.

At the SSF, more than fifty Russian naval advisers paired with the Chinese officers at the fleet HQ from 1950 to 1955. The fleet commanders included Commodore Buphalov; advising fleet commander Vice Admiral Fang Qiang; Lieutenant Commodore Savenski, working with the fleet's chief of staff, Zhou Wenjie; and another senior Russian adviser with the Chinese political commissar. The Russian fleet commanders advised the Chinese during fleet maneuvers and exercises, established coastal defense and communications, and taught ship maintenance and repair.[12] The same Russian advisers continued working with their Chinese partners for three to five years. They dealt with many problems immediately and answered most questions from their Chinese partners.[13]

When the Russian-made destroyers arrived at the PLAN's Qingdao base, the Soviet navy sent the entire chain of command as advisers, instructors, and technicians to show the Chinese how to operate the destroyers. Russian captains worked side by side with Chinese captains on the bridge for ship combat readiness, coastal patrol, and ship-to-ship communications. Russian chief petty officers, boatswains, weapon control officers, engineers, and electricians taught their Chinese counterparts how to operate and maintain the engines, communication systems, electricity, radar, and shipboard weapons.[14] During the first period, the Soviet officers and crew operated the destroyers, while the Chinese followed Russian operational manuals and guidelines. Afterward, there was a cooperative period when the Russians allowed the Chinese to take over part of the operation, maintenance, and repairs. After six months, when the Chinese crew took over the destroyers and began operating them independently, all Russian personnel below chief petty officer returned to the Soviet Union. But higher-ranking Russian advisers, like captains, deputy captains, and navigation officers, stayed at Qingdao for another year.[15]

According to the 6-4 Agreement of 1953, the Chinese navy also purchased 14 submarines, 22 torpedo boats, 148 naval airplanes, and 452 torpedoes to fulfill the three priorities of "air [naval air force, 空 kong], sub [submarines, 潜 qian], and speed [torpedo boats, 快 kuai]" in PLAN commander Xiao Jinguang's Three-Year Plan.[16] In June–July 1954, the PLAN received four Russian-made World War II submarines (Models 51-53 and 57). With 1,070 tons submerged weight and seventy-two-hour maximum submerged time, the S-class submarine had six torpedo tubes and six reloads apiece. James C. Bussert and Bruce A. Elleman point out, "China's first semi-indigenous submarine was a direct adaptation of a Late-1950s Russian design." From 1950, the Chinese began to assimilate the Russian models and produce their own submarines.[17]

The post-Stalin purchases saw the PLAN importing semifinished vessels and blueprints to assemble in China, thus giving birth to the PRC's domestic warship-building industry. In the 6-4 Agreement, 95 out of 137 vessels were partially constructed ships or shipbuilding materials, including engines, equipment, and weapon systems.[18] The Soviets delivered forty-nine unfinished ships to the PLAN in 1954-56, including four frigates, seven submarines, fourteen minesweepers, and twenty-four torpedo boats. According to the agreement, the Soviets also provided designs, blueprints, and building materials for forty-six ships, including sixteen submarines and thirty torpedo boats.[19] The naval 6–4 Agreement also included Soviet assistance on naval shipbuilding, repair, and equipment supply.

In the 6–4 Agreement of 1953, the Chinese government requested more Russian advisers to help with the PLAN's shipbuilding.[20] The Soviet navy sent more than 450 advisers to China for that purpose. The Russian advisers established a solid foundation for the Chinese naval industry. Cole adds, "The Soviets helped the Chinese establish a large shore-based infrastructure, including shipyards, naval colleges, and extensive coastal fortifications."[21] The Chinese navy depended on Soviet advisers and experts to assimilate Russian naval technology and experience. By November 1954, there were 288 Russian shipbuilding advisers in the PLAN, including 4 admirals, 30 designing officers, 136 shipbuilding advisers, 44 assembly experts, 16 manufacturing advisers, and 58 testing and inspecting advisers. They supervised shipyard construction; designed testing institutes, technology labs, and weaponry development centers; and established training centers. The Russian advisers not only helped the Chinese build new warships but also trained a new generation of naval experts, designers, engineers, and technicians for the PLAN.[22]

In September 1954, Soviet new leader Nikita Khrushchev visited Beijing and agreed to provide $260 million in new military aid for China's ongoing military reform. In the Soviet-China agreement, Khrushchev also included the withdrawal of Russian armed forces from Port Arthur (Lushun Naval Base) in Liaoning, one of the most important Soviet naval bases in the Pacific, and transfer the Dalian Ship Building Corporation from the Soviet Union to China.[23] Bussert and Elleman argue, "With Dalian's return in 1955, China's shipbuilding capabilities grew quickly."[24] Starting in 1954, the PLAN designed its own 75-ton small gunboat. After successful tests, the model *55-Jia* gunboats were built at Dalian and Guangzhou shipyards.[25] By 1955, the PLAN manufactured its own torpedoes under Russian supervision. In 1956, the Chinese imitated the first Russian 03-model of W-class submarine. The last substantial naval purchase before the Sino-Soviet split, the so-called 2–4 Agreement, was finalized on February 4, 1959. The agreement provided the PLAN with conventional submarine launched ballistic missiles, ship-to-ship missiles, submarines armed with missiles, and missile-launching ships. The Soviet Union shipped the vessels and weapon systems to China with designs, blueprints, equipment, sample missiles, and shipbuilding materials, including the R-class submarine.[26] From 1961 to 1979, China manufactured thirty-three R-class submarines.[27]

In May 1955, the Port Arthur Naval Base was returned to the PLAN, after sixty years of foreign military occupations (by Imperial Russia from 1895 to 1904, Imperial Japan from 1905 to 1945, and the Soviet Union from 1945 to 1955), when 12,000 Russian ground, air, and naval troops withdrew.[28] The PLAN received most of the Russian aircraft, vessels, vehicles, and equipment, including 64 torpedo bombers, 14 training airplanes, 39 torpedo boats, 12 frigates, 18 support ships, 412 torpedoes and naval mines, 122 AAA guns, 66 heavy coast artillery pieces (180-mm and 130-mm), 3.25 million artillery shells, 2,642 tons of explosives and bombs, 35 radar sets, 1,684 vehicles, and 22,000 tons of gasoline. The Soviet navy also returned shipyards, coast defense works, hospitals, warehouses, research labs, and additional naval equipment in Dalian, Liaoning to the Chinese navy. The army received 357 Russian tanks and 1,113 heavy artillery pieces. The PLA Air Force also received 328 Russian airplanes and assumed 9 airfields in Liaoning province. To manage the naval base and maintain the equipment, the NSF HQ hired back more than 140 Russians as advisers to train Chinese naval officers at the Lushun base until 1959.[29] By 1958, there were a total of 3,390 Russian naval advisers in the PLAN.[30] The Russian navy strongly influenced Chinese naval development through its advisory assistance in the 1950s.

Meanwhile, the Chinese naval schools established educational partnership with Russian naval academies, technological institutes, and training programs. The Russian advisers in the PLAN schools helped with recruitment and admissions of Chinese naval officers to study in their "sister schools" in the Soviet Union. For example, the PLA Nanjing School for Foreign Languages (NSFL, later Nanjing Institute for Foreign Languages) had exchange programs with the Moscow Institute of International Relations. The Russian advisers at the NSFL worked with Marshal Liu Bocheng, NSFL superintendent, and made regular recommendations to the Russian school board to send their selected Chinese students to study at Moscow and receive intelligence training from the KGB. The Chinese naval intelligence students learned electronic signals, radar technology, and data analysis at the Russian institute. All NSFL officer trainees participated in major PLAN exercises like the Liaodong Peninsula coastal defense exercise and Russo-Chinese joint naval exercise.[31]

By 1959, more than six hundred Chinese naval officers had studied military technology, aviation, and maritime science in Soviet naval college and institutes, including high-ranking officers like Liu Daosheng, PLAN vice political commissar and director of the Political Tasks Department; Fang Qiang, commander and political commissar of the SCMRN in 1950–53; Zhang Xuesi, vice superintendent and vice political commissar of the Dalian Naval Academy (DNA) in 1950–55; and Liu Huaqing, DNA vice superintendent and vice political commissar in 1950–54. Fang Qiang, Zhang Xuesi, and Liu Huaqing were classmates who studied at the Voroshilov Naval Command Academy (currently Kuznestsov Naval Academy) in St. Petersburg from 1954 to 1957, 1956 to 1958, and 1954 to 1958, respectively. During his study in Russia, Fang Qiang was ranked vice admiral in 1955. After his graduation, Fang became PLAN deputy political commissar in 1959–65 and vice commander in 1979–82.[32] Zhang Xuesi was ranked rear admiral in 1955 and became PLAN chief of staff in 1960–66.[33] Liu Huaqing was ranked rear admiral in 1955 and served as NSF deputy commander in the 1960s and PLAN deputy chief of staff in 1970–75. Liu Huaqing became PLAN commander in 1982–88 and CMC vice chairman in 1989–97. He was ranked admiral in 1988. Liu Huaqing became the CCP Politburo's Standing Committee member in 1992 as one of China's top seven leaders from 1992 to 1997.[34]

Toward the end of the 1950s, the PLAN boasted twenty-three naval brigades with 860 vessels, including 4 destroyers, 28 frigates, 16 submarines, 200 small warships and gunboats, and more than 200 torpedo boats. There were six air force divisions and two independent regiments under the PLAN Air Force command. The PLANAF had more than five hundred fighters, bombers, reconnaissance, and cargo planes.[35] The PLAN also commanded nineteen artillery regiments and eight antiaircraft artillery regiments along the coast areas. These artillery regiments had nearly seven hundred heavy (130-mm) coastal cannon and AAA guns with Russian-made fire-control radar.³⁶ The PLAN totaled 188,000 men, including 114,000 transferred infantry soldiers (80.6 percent of the total), 6,000 transferred air force personnel (3.2 percent), 30,000 new recruits who were high school graduates (16 percent), and 4,000 former ROC sailors (2.1 percent). Most former ROC sailors worked on the warships among the 22,000 sailors. On October 24, 1955, the ECMRN was renamed the PLAN ESF, and the SCMRN became its SSF. Mao was satisfied with the navy's early development. The president said at the PRC Central Government's Thirty-Third Plenary that "Taiwan will be unified when our naval and air forces get stronger."³⁷

JOINT OPERATIONS AND PT BOATS IN THE 1954 TAIWAN STRAIT CRISIS

The PLA's limited engagement in the Taiwan Strait assumed different forms to serve China's security concerns and strategic needs. Before each naval or amphibious attack, the PLA first established limited goals with a practical objective and military strategies, which would not cause any major international crisis. During the landing campaigns, the local command tried to reduce international tensions by limiting battle areas in the air and at sea so the PLAN and air force would not risk war with U.S. armed forces in the Taiwan Strait. The PLA joint amphibious landing operations developed and evolved more from their successful warfighting experiences than from technological modernization.

In early 1954, Chief of Zhejiang Command (ZC) Zhang Aiping proposed to the ECMR Command his landing campaign against twelve Taiwan-held islands off the Zhejiang coast. The ECMR forwarded the landing proposal to the CMC. At that time, however, Beijing was organizing its delegation for the Geneva international conference in April and preparing for Indochinese and Korean settlements with the United States. In its reply, the CMC emphasized the "local war" concept: in other words, the ZC would restrict its attacks on the small islands and identify the weakest point of Taiwanese island defenses.³⁸ Following CMC orders, General Zhang submitted to the PLA General Staff a "piecemeal" attacking plan and suggested attacking one island at a time, beginning with the Dongjis and Dachens, the northernmost small islands in the ECS, more than two hundred miles from Taiwan.

"Limited Naval Wars" in the Taiwan Strait   **59**

Zhang's proposal completely avoided the U.S. Seventh Fleet, located about one hundred miles away in the SCS. After his success, Zhang Aiping would attack larger islands in the south.[39] The PLA high command approved his plan with the request that he protect the ECS's fishing season in the spring, since the Dachen area was the largest fishing ground in Zhejiang.[40]

Zhang's landing plan commenced with an amphibious assault involving land, air, and naval forces and was the PLA's first implementation of joint operations. In January 1954, Zhang Aiping chaired a joint commanders' meeting including Lieutenant General Nie Fengzhi, ECMR Air Force commander; Rear Admiral Ma Guansan, ECMR Navy's chief of staff; and Major General Huang Chaotian, deputy commander of the 20th Army. As a Korean War veteran, Nie Fengzhi supported Zhang's cautious step-by-step, or island-by-island, plan for the landings at the Dongji and Dachen Islands. After joining the CCP's army in 1929, Nie became a commander of the Red Army company, battalion, and regiment. In 1937–45, he was a regiment and brigade commander. In 1948–49, Nie served as the Third Field Army's 27th Army commander. In 1950, he became Chinese People's Volunteers Force–North Korean People's Army (CPVF-NKPA) Joint Air Force commander in the Korean War. In 1953–55, after his return, he served as air force commander of Zhejiang Front Command (ZFC) and ECMR.[41] Nie Fengzhi was ranked air force lieutenant general in 1955. In March 1954, Zhang Aiping established his new joint command, the ZFC. It was a tripartite HQ that included commanders from the air force, navy, and army. With Zhang as the ZFC commander, Nie, Ma, and Huang served as deputy commanders of each service's subheadquarters. Although Zhang Aiping combined three services in his amphibious campaign, the PLA joint operations would not become a specific policy until much later.

To prepare the amphibious operations, the Chinese navy continued its effort in establishing a capable marine force. The earliest unit of the PLAN marine unit was created by the Riverine Defense Command of the PLA Guangdong Military Region in December 1949. However, the marine battalion did not develop landing operation capability during the early years. To attack the ROC-held islands in the ECS, the ECMR Navy formed the First Marine Regiment in Shanghai in April 1953. It was equipped with landing combat weapons, light artillery pieces, and amphibious vehicles and tanks for fierce assault firepower, high maneuverability, and solid protecting power. In December 1954, it became the First Marine Division, including two marine regiments and one tank regiment, as the formal PLAN Marine Corps.[42]

In the spring of 1954, the ZFC joint command decided on major campaign issues at the strategic level. First, the PLAN and PLANAF should stop, or at least reduce, the Taiwanese naval transportation and air patrols around the Dachens. Second, through PLA air and sea control, ZFC should isolate and weaken the Taiwanese garrisons on these islands. Third, meanwhile, the PLA ground troops should receive landing training. Zhang Aiping emphasized close cooperation among the services and sent landing troop commanders to the navy and air force for joint operation training. However, Zhongtian Han argues that the PLA successfully implemented the joint operation at the strategic level, but that they failed at the operational level in 1954. His findings show that the army, navy, and air force exhibited uneven performances in the joint landing campaign, since one of the four Chinese frigates was sunk by Taiwanese air raids.[43]

To control the water and airspace around the offshore islands, Zhang Aiping initiated the campaign to fight for sea and air control to isolate ROC garrisons on the Dongji and Dachen Islands. It was the Chinese navy's first large-scale offensive operation since its founding in 1949. ECMR Navy sent four frigates, six medium escort ships, twelve torpedo boats, twenty-four gunboats, and six rocket-artillery boats, with a total of 3,700 sailors under the command of Rear Admiral Ma Guansan. Ma joined the Eighth Route Army and the CCP in 1938 and became an infantry commander at battalion and regimental levels in the Anti-Japanese War. Ma served as a division and army chief of staff and commander in the Chinese Civil War. Without any naval knowledge or experience, he was appointed as the ECMRN chief of staff in 1949 and later as the PLAN deputy chief of staff. Ma Guansan was ranked rear admiral in 1955.[44] In March 1954, Rear Admiral Ma anchored his fleet at Sanmen Bay between the Dongjis and Dachens, and then sent warships to patrol the area, looking for opportunities to attack Taiwan's ships, weakening their naval defense, and controlling the surrounding waters. To conceal the landing campaign, the Chinese fleet operated as if they were escorting Chinese fishermen and protecting Zhejiang's fishing ground.

From March 18 to May 17, the Chinese navy attacked the Taiwanese navy in twelve engagements around the Dachens but failed to sink any Taiwanese warship.[45] In the early morning of March 18, ECMRN sent the frigates *Xingguo* and *Yan'an* with several patrol boats to the waters near Dachen. When the Chinese squadron met a Taiwanese frigate and a minesweeper, they opened fire. Both sides engaged in distant fighting due to bad weather and low visibility. After Dachen reinforced two more Taiwanese warships to the area, the Chinese squadron disengaged. In the afternoon, four Taiwanese F-47 bombers raided Chinese squadron and hit two patrol boats. The PLANAF responded immediately by scrambling two fighters to the area and shooting down two Taiwanese bombers. Vice Admiral Hu Yanlin considers it the "first successful naval-air joint battle in the PLA history."[46] On April 27, ECMRN set an ambush at 5:30 p.m. by deploying the *Xingguo* and *Ruijin* near Dachen and the frigates *Guangzhou* and *Kaifeng* north of the island. Around 7:50 p.m., one Taiwanese warship embarked from Dachen and opened fire on *Xingguo* and *Ruijin*. A Taiwanese destroyer, a frigate, and other patrol boats followed and joined the attacks on *Xingguo* and *Ruijin*. The two Chinese frigates feigned retreat and lured the Taiwanese ships to the north, where four Chinese warships opened fire on the Taiwanese ships. After sixteen minutes of firing, the Taiwanese ships disengaged and returned to Dachen. Since Chinese naval guns were small and inaccurate, only one Taiwanese frigate was damaged.[47] Although Ma Guansan's fleet failed to sink any GMD warship, his active naval operations around the Dachens reduced Taiwanese naval patrols and other activities.

The situation in the area grew favorable for the PLA's planned joint landing campaign. Nevertheless, at the command meetings, Lieutenant General Nie Fengzhi, ZFC Air Force commander, disagreed with the Russian advisers' strategic bombing plan on Dongji. Nie recalled that the Russian plan, borrowed from their World War II concentrated bombing strategy, did not work on scattered targets on the small island. Russian advisers irritated Nie Fengzhi after circumventing his command and asking the PLAN air force wing commanders to carry out the bombing plan. Nie personally called all the wing commanders and ordered them to follow the ZFC decision.⁴⁸ The offshore bombings and air support marked the beginning of Chinese PLAN officers' willingness to say no to their Russian advisers.

Facing an imminent PLA attack, Jiang Jieshi personally visited Taiwanese garrisons on the Dachens on May 6–7.⁴⁹ General Jiang Weiguo (Chiang Wei-kuo, ROC army) recalled in my interview that to strengthen his troops' morale and quell rumors of an evacuation from the islands, his father promised possible U.S. support to the ROC offshore island defense. After Jiang Jieshi's visit, the Dachens' garrison received reinforcement and more supplies.⁵⁰ On May 17, Taiwan's Ministry of Foreign Affairs informed Taiwanese ambassador Gu Weijun (Ku Wei-chien) at Washington that the PLAN controlled the waters and air north of the Dachen Islands.⁵¹

In May, Zhang Aiping and his ZFC readied their joint amphibious attack on the Dongjis, a group of three small islands north of the Dachens, including Toumen, Tianshan, and Jiangershan. At 6:30 p.m. on May 15, the air-navy-army command launched the joint operation. First, Rear Admiral Ma Guansan ordered four frigates and one torpedo squadron to enter the area and protect the landing troops' flanks against possible Taiwanese naval attack. Then the naval commander sent twelve gunboats to provide cover fire for the landing vessels. At 7 p.m., the joint command sent two landing ships and sixteen transit boats to carry the 180th Regiment to the Dongjis. Meanwhile, the joint command prepared air support from the PLAN Second Air Force Division's Sixth Regiment and First Division's Fourth Regiment. The troops of the 180th Regiment of the 60th Division first landed at Toumen, without meeting much resistance. Then they attacked Tianshan Island. When they reached Jiangershan, a Taiwanese garrison organized defensive fire with machine guns and small mortars. The 180th Regiment broke through the defense and captured sixty prisoners.

By 5:30 p.m. on May 15, two Taiwanese P-51 planes had flown into the Dongji area. To protect the landing campaign, the Second Air Force Division ordered Deputy Battalion Commander Song Guoqing and Captain Chang Huachen to scramble immediately and intercept the enemy planes before they entered the Dongji area. After Song Guoqing reached Dongji, he lowered his

"Limited Naval Wars" in the Taiwan Strait   **63**

MiG-15bis fighter from 3,600 to 2,400 feet and saw two Taiwanese planes coming toward him about 900 feet. He opened fire and shot down one of the Taiwanese planes. With air and naval supports, the PLA troops occupied the Dongji Islands without any major enemy interruption.[52]

It took the Taiwanese navy almost eight hours to respond to the PLA's landing at the Dongjis. In the early morning of May 16, the Taiwanese navy sent five warships to the Dongjis. From 2:30 a.m. to 10:50 a.m., Taiwanese troops from the Dachens launched four counterattacks with naval support.[53] To stop Taiwanese counterattacks, the joint command sent four frigates to attack the Taiwanese warships and eventually drove them away from the Dongjis. About 5:30 p.m., four Taiwanese F-47 bombers raided the landing area, but they immediately returned to Taiwan after the PLAN Second Air Force Division scrambled fighters to Dongji. From May 16 to 20, the Taiwanese air force used bombers and fighters to carry out seventy-eight sorties against the Dongjis. But the 20th Army's 60th Division successfully defended the islands. In the Dongji landing battle, the PLA's joint operations evolved due to army and air force commanders' abilities to adjust to changing conditions, while the naval commanders continued to learn their lessons.

On May 18, when two PLAN frigates, *Ruijin* and *Xingguo*, returned to Dongji after their refuels at the mainland, Taiwanese planes assaulted the Chinese warships. Due to bad weather over the PLANAF base, the naval air force could not send any air protection. Meanwhile, *Ruijin*'s captain miscalculated the situation: he neither "serpentined" his ship nor organized effective air defense fire. Around 6:45 p.m., four F-47s bombed the *Ruijin* at a low altitude. After the first F-47 missed, one bomb from the second plane hit the ship's port side, then two more bombs from the third plane hit its starboard side. By 6:52 p.m., the *Ruijin* began sinking. Although the captain survived, he lost his political commissar and fifty-six crew members.[54] After receiving the battle report, Mao Zedong instructed the PLAN on May 22 to "avoid any negative impact from the loss of one warship."[55] During the Dongji landing campaign from May 11 to 20, both the army and the air force achieved their battle objectives by, respectively, occupying five of the Dongji's islands and shooting down eight Taiwanese planes. However, the navy lost one frigate without destroying any Taiwanese warships or gunboats in battle.

On June 1, ECMR deputy commander Su Yu reported to Beijing that eight U.S. cruisers and destroyers had sailed to just north of the Dachen Islands accompanied by American planes that morning. The ECMR Command ordered all its air, naval, and landing forces in the area not to fire on Americans and, if possible, to avoid any conflict. Mao Zedong wrote to Su the next day, "Correct reaction. Do not open fire first on Americans. Only hold defensive position and try your best to avoid any conflict."[56] Beijing was increasingly concerned about what the future might hold for Taiwan. Events indicated that the U.S. Seventh Fleet would not withdraw from the strait and that China might face a permanent separation from Taiwan. Mao feared that if the status quo continued, the world would soon get used to considering the division across the Taiwan Strait as another accepted situation, similar to the 38th Parallel in Korea or the 17th Parallel in Vietnam. On July 23, Mao telegraphed Zhou Enlai, "We must stress the issue of Taiwan's liberation." Otherwise, "we would make a big political mistake."[57] At a CCP Politburo meeting in August, after discussion of the Taiwan liberation propaganda campaign, it was decided that a stronger signal would be sent via military action. Diplomatic means seemed limited, but a bombardment of Taiwan-held Jinmen Islands, coupled with the propaganda campaign, would strongly demonstrate Beijing's determination to handle Taiwan as its own domestic affair.[58] The CMC ordered Fujian Military Region commander Ye Fei on August 25 to conduct "a punishing bombardment on the GMD forces on the Jinmen Islands."[59]

At 1:50 p.m. on September 3, when a Taiwanese convoy of cargo ships arrived at Jinmen, Ye Fei ordered 150 heavy artillery guns to shell Jinmen. It is known as the 9-3 Bombardment. In two hours of shelling, the PLA sank one GMD gunboat and two transit ships and damaged seven others. By the end of the day, the Jinmen Islands had been hit with seven thousand rounds, and two American advisers were killed.[60] On September 9, after learning of John Foster Dulles's visit to Taiwan, Ye requested another shelling, and Mao approved it on September 14.[61] Ye Fei organized four artillery groups composed of more than 130 guns and commenced shelling on September 22.

Since Zhang Aiping had been successful at the Dongji Islands and had avoided any American intervention, the CMC ordered him in July 1954 to attack the Dachen Island group.[62] On October 31, Zhang Aiping was promoted to PLA deputy general chief of staff. Nevertheless, Zhang learned from his joint operation in the battle of the Dongjis and realized the complication of air, naval, and ground troops' communication and coordination in the landing. Joint operations did not simply involve engaging the enemy in the air, on the sea, and on the beachhead but instead required systems with better communication and cooperation.

In the fall of 1954, Zhang's naval force under Rear Admiral Ma Guansan was eager to improve their performance by employing new tactics against the Taiwanese navy at Dachen. Ma Guansan accepted that PLA gunboats were inferior to Taiwanese warships in terms of tonnage, speed, and firepower. The Taiwanese navy had more than twenty warships and gunboats in the Dachen area. Their largest was a leviathan: the destroyer *Taiping* (DE 22), with displaced 1,430 tons, 220 crewmen, and 18 cannons of 76 mm and 40 mm. Commissioned into the U.S. Navy as USS *Decker* (DE 47) in 1943, it was transferred to the ROC navy in World War II. *Taiping* was the Taiwanese navy's strongest warship, and no Chinese warship could match its firepower. The main force of Ma's fleet were four frigates like *Ruijin* and *Xingguo*. Both were rebuilt World War II U.S. cargo ships, 600 tons of displacement, with two 76-mm cannon, two 37-mms, and four 25-mms. (The *Ruijin* was sunk on May 18.) Thereafter, Ma and his staff decided to use their torpedo boats against larger Taiwanese warships.[63]

Rear Admiral Ma Guansan ordered twelve PT boats from the PLAN's 31st Torpedo Squadron to Dachen to attack the largest Taiwanese warships. They were Russian-made *T-123* (or *P-4*) torpedo boats with 22 tons of displacement, a speed of 52 knots, two 12.7-mm dual-barreled antiaircraft machine guns, and two torpedo tubes. The small surface combatant was an effective weapon against large warships because of its speed, agility, and torpedoes. However, each PT boat had only two 450-mm torpedoes, and they were inshore craft with a limited fuel load for short distances. Moreover, the Chinese PT boats did not have radar system with very limited operational radius. Ma Guansan had to use small islands around the Dachens to conceal his deployment of the torpedo boats for surprise attacks.[64]

In late October, according to ECMR intelligence, the Taiwanese navy was redeploying its warships, which would sail, bypassing Gao Island, in the next few days. On October 31, Rear Admiral Ma Guansan sent six PT boats from the 31st Torpedo Squadron to Gao Island for an ambush. He ordered escort ships to tow the PT boats to the standby site at night because of their limited fuel load. The ROC radar station immediately discovered the PLA naval movement toward Gao. Ironically, the Taiwanese naval officers ignored the radar signal, since it showed that the Chinese fleet (of escort ships) made a round trip and returned to their coastal homebase two hours later, in the early morning. They did not know that six torpedo boats were hidden at Gao Island on November 1. Two days later, one Taiwanese warship appeared in the predetermined attack area. Although the PT boats were ready to attack, the winds and waves were above sea state 4 level, which could not guarantee the accuracy of torpedoes. Tie Jianghai, 31st Squadron deputy commander, decided to wait again for another chance. It was already early winter, and the men had to stand at post on deck for many days in the rain, because there were no sleeping bunks or places to take shelter on the small boats. The sailors were soaked and trembled with cold. Moreover, it was impossible to cook on the boats. Tie Jianghai had to send his men a good distance in a fishing boat to cook and then brought meals back to the speedboats.[65]

Around midnight on November 14, Ma Guansan informed Tie Jianghai that a Taiwanese warship had left Dachen and sailed toward Gao Island. At 1:05 a.m., the 31st reported the ship's direction and speed instantly, and drafters located it on a sea chart. At 1:21 a.m., Tie Jianghai ordered *PT-155, 156, 157,* and *158* at full speed to follow the coastal radar direction to search for the target. When they were about six or seven miles away, the PT boat captains identified the Taiwanese destroyer *Taiping* by its bridge and the anchor. They immediately assumed battle formation.[66]

Taiping captain Tang Tingrang received a patrol order very late that evening. He ordered his crew of 198 officers and sailors to get ready and sail northeast into the dark about 12:10 a.m. Deputy Captain Zhou Guanying recalled that *Taiping*'s planar radar had some problems at that time and failed to provide clear signals when the PLA torpedo boats rushed toward *Taiping* at high speed.[67]

When the PT boats were about four miles from the *Taiping*, Tie Jianghai ordered *PT-155* and *156* to launch the attack first, followed by *157* and *158*. At 1:35 a.m., *156* fired two torpedoes from ten cable lengths, then *155* and *157* fired. At 1:37 a.m., *PT-158* fired two torpedoes from five cable lengths. One of them hit the destroyer *Taiping*, causing onboard explosions, and it capsized. At 7:24 a.m., the *Taiping* sank into the sea; 29 Taiwanese officers and sailor died, 37 were wounded, and 145 were rescued.[68] It was the PLAN's first big victory using torpedo boats in naval battle. *PT-158* is still displayed at the China People's Revolution Military Museum in Beijing today. The naval officers continued their "guerrilla tactics," including surprise attacks, night operations, and close combat. Nevertheless, accurate information, appropriate positions for ambush, and sufficient torpedo training all contributed to the 31st Torpedo Squadron's successful attack. The *Taiping* was the largest vessel the PLAN had sunk to that point.

AMPHIBIOUS LANDING OF YIJIANGSHAN, 1955

At a joint command meeting in the fall of 1954, Zhang Aiping, Nie Fengzhi, Ma Guansan, and Huang Chaotian decided to launch the next landing campaign at ROC-held Yijiangshan in January 1955. The Yijiangshan Islands consist of two islets, along a narrow trench, that creates a barrier seven miles north of the Dachen Archipelago. The islands are bounded by steep cliffs that stand erect over the sea. The landing area was less than a thousand meters long. The ROC garrison at Yijiangshan numbered about a thousand men. They had built permanent and semipermanent defense works.[69] The island was vital to the Dachen campaign. Mao Zedong approved the ZFC plan in late October 1954, placing Zhang and the ZFC under the CMC's direct command in November. With Cold War politics in mind, Mao Zedong did not intend to jeopardize China's improved international position after the two settlements signed at the Geneva Conference in the summer. Mao continued a wait-and-see policy toward ongoing negotiations between Taipei and Washington for a mutual defense treaty.[70] He instructed Zhang Aiping to continue his landing preparation and training while maintaining control of the air and waters around Dachen and further weakening ROC defenses before the landing.[71] To carry out Mao's instructions, ZFC finished its torpedo boat base construction, landing troops exercises, and coastal artillery placements by December. Zhang also reported to CMC that the U.S. Seventh Fleet "left for the typhoon season" in November and that the PLA would not have "any conflict with the American forces" in the ECS.[72]

The PLANAF sent more planes to ZFC. After reinforcement, Lieutenant General Nie Fengzhi had five bomber and fighter divisions, totaling 184 planes. He began his assault on November 1, 1954. For four days, the PLA Air Force (PLAAF) raided the Dachens and Yijiangshan, carrying out one hundred sorties and dropping more than one thousand bombs.[73] The PLAN Air Force avoided any conflict with the U.S. Air Force (USAF) during the battles. Nie Fengzhi talked personally about this policy with every participating PLANAF pilot. Nie's message was that there should be no exchange of fire with U.S. airplanes without his permission. "To avoid any pilot accidentally engaging American airplanes, the headquarters has explicitly commanded that only I shall determine whether to fire on U.S. airplanes." He recalled, "Throughout the whole campaign we had an excellent result with no involvement with foreign air forces."[74] Then his air force launched five heavy bombings between December 21 and January 10, 1955, with 28 bomber and 116 fighter sorties.[75]

On January 10, bad weather reached the Dachen area. The massive waves and high winds forced all Taiwanese vessels to anchor in the Dachen harbor. The PLANAF saw a good attack opportunity and launched another bombing raid. At 10:30 a.m., the PLAAF and PLANAF joined forces and launched 130 sorties to bomb the anchor site of the Taiwanese ships. Three regiments from the 20th Bomber Division raided the targets in three waves. They sank ROC *Zhongquan*, a tank-landing ship (3,000 tons with 130 crew), and damaged four others.[76]

After his successful sinking of *Taiping*, Rear Admiral Ma Guansan planned another PT boat ambush operation. In late November, he deployed six PT boats from the First Torpedo Squadron to standby positions at Baiyanshan Island, a good place for surrounding the strategic passage around the Dachen Islands. What the PT boat officers and sailors did not know was that they would have to wait there for more than forty days. On January 10, after the PLANAF heavy bombing, the surviving ships fled the harbor and scattered around the area in the open sea. Several Taiwanese ships reached Baiyanshan Island, where the Chinese PT boats were ready for their ambush.

At dusk on January 10, the First Squadron commander ordered four torpedo boats to sail out from Baiyanshan and attack the Taiwanese warships. Due to the harsh conditions at sea, two of them fell behind. *PT-102* dashed out at thirty knots and got about thirty cable lengths away from an ROC warship. When Captain Zhang Yimin gave the order to fire, however, he discovered that one torpedo shot out unusually slowly, and the other couldn't be launched at all. He missed the target. Meanwhile, the two torpedoes from *PT-101* strayed off target due to strong winds and big waves. After a short chase, the First Squadron had to order its boats back to Baiyanshan Island, since the strong winds and large waves could capsize the small boats. Two hours later, the First's radar captured a trace of another ROC warship, and its commander ordered *PT-102, 105,* and *106* out to attack. Since *PT-102* had launched its left torpedo, it had only one torpedo in the right tube. A one-ton torpedo exerted great impact on the balance of a speedboat of only twenty-two tons. Worse were the strong north winds (5–6 on the Beaufort scale) and large waves, which caused the boat to heel over fiercely. Five crewmen leaned to port to keep the boat from capsizing. Then Captain Zhang Yimin could not find any trace of *PT-105* and *106*. About fifteen minutes later, he saw the target: the Taiwanese *Lingjiang*. Zhang dashed his boat at thirty-five knots to get as close as one thousand feet from the warship and gave the order to fire. The torpedo hit the *Lingjiang* within ten seconds, and this former U.S. gunboat soon sank. After January 10, the PLAN controlled the air and water around the Dachen Islands.

Chinese officers and their Russian advisers could not agree on the landing's timing. Commodore Antonov, Soviet adviser to ECMRN, insisted that the PLAN should sail at night and land the troops at dawn, in a navy-centered campaign, and utilize a master combat schedule based on Soviet World War II experience and the Red Army's combat handbooks. He also cited the Allied landings at Normandy, on Sicily, and Okinawa to make his point that nighttime sailing and daybreak landing was the only way to win a battle for the Yijiangshan Islands, because PLAN ships under sail could then escape harassment by Taiwan's planes and larger warships. Chinese naval officers disagreed with the Russian adviser in a heated face-to-face argument. Vice Admiral Tao Yong, ECMRN commander, argued that it would be harder to sail at night than in daylight because of the huge differences among the Chinese ships and the lack of experience in coordinated operations. With air and naval control of the area, Tao Yong felt the PLAN could land successfully in the daytime. As a senior PLA commander, Tao had served as a squad, platoon, company, battalion, and regiment commander in the Red Army. In World War II, he became a regiment and divisional commander and political commissar. In 1946–49, Tao Yong was appointed the 23rd Army commander, and then deputy commander of the PLA and CPVF's Ninth Army Group in the Korean War. As the ECMRN commander, he was ranked vice admiral in 1955. Tao Yong became the navy's deputy commander in 1956–63.[77]

There was a standoff. Vice Admiral Tao Yong would not yield. He argued that it would be especially advantageous to sail at noon and land in the afternoon, when the tide was in.[78] Antonov packed his books and stormed out the door in the heat of the moment. Zhang said to his joint chiefs, "You dare to squeeze out the Soviet advisers. Well, we may be better off without them. We can now do things in our own way."[79] The ZFC commanders decided that if weather permitted, they would land at noon on the eighteenth.

On January 18, the PLANAF sent fifty-four bombers and eighteen fighters to commence a joint attack by hitting key Taiwanese positions and defense works at both Yijiangshan and the Dachens. At 8 a.m., one Du-2 bomber regiment raided Dachen defense command, artillery size, and other targets. Around 2 p.m., another bomber regiment attacked beach defense works and Taiwanese positions on Yijiangshan. The bombers dropped 127 tons of ordnance for over six hours. Starting at 12:20 p.m., naval coastal artillery bombed Yijiangshan for two hours. Four artillery battalions and twelve artillery companies barraged the island with 40,000 shells. During the cannonade, four escort ships and two gunboats fired from the surrounding waters at the island's defense positions between 1:18 p.m. and 2:15 p.m. The prelanding naval bombardment destroyed almost all the defense works, artillery positions, and communications on Yijiangshan. The heavy repeated shelling also neutralized the Dachens' supportive fire.[80]

Around 12:15 p.m., more than 140 landing craft transported Huang Chaotian's ten-thousand-man invasion force to Yijiangshan. The first wave included three thousand troops from the 178th and 180th Regiments, 60th Division, under the command of Lin Weixian and Huang Chaotian. The First Battalion, 178th Regiment (1/178), rushed the eastern beach from their twenty-eight landing craft, while the Second Battalion, 180th Regiment (2/180), attacked the southern beach. Coordinating with the naval bombardment and amphibious landings, Nie Fengzhi's MiG-15s initiated low-altitude strikes on defense beachheads at 2:25 p.m. Between 2:29 p.m. and 3 p.m., the first amphibious wave landed at Yijiangshan. In the east, the Sixth Company, 1/178 Battalion, suffered more than thirty casualties before landing as Taiwanese 60-mm rockets hit two of their transports. Its First and Fifth Companies rushed the beach, took over defensive positions, and charged Height 203, the island's highest point. The First Company lost forty men in the attack. From the south, the 2/180 Battalion landed around 2:37 p.m. and sent its Fifth and Seventh Companies to attack the heights. Its Fifth Company broke through the defenses and took over the height around 3:03 p.m. With support from the second amphibious wave, the 178th Regiment occupied Heights 180 and 190. By 5:30 p.m., the entire island fell under PLA control.[81]

By two o'clock the next morning, the PLA had wiped out all remaining defensive pockets. Taiwan lost its garrison of 1,086 men, with 567 killed and 519 captured. The PLA had 2,092 casualties. The army suffered heavy casualties, including 893 dead and 1,037 wounded, nearly 50 percent of its first wave lost during the landing. As the PLA's first joint amphibious landing campaign, the Yijiangshan landing was still an army-centric operation. Air and naval supports were only a contributing factor rather than a determining factor during the landing. The air force had no loss, but eight bombers and fighters were damaged.[82] The naval force had 23 killed, 139 wounded, one landing craft lost, and twenty-one ships damaged.[83] Naval firepower and technology did not become the determining issue until much later. The naval force was very young, and most of its officers came from the army, which enjoyed a reputation as an important part in combat.

After the victory of the Yijiangshan landing, General Zhang Aiping ordered two hundred bombers to bomb Dachen on the same day, the largest air raid in PLA military history.[84] Taiwanese leaders questioned the Dachens' defense after Yijiangshan's loss. The U.S. government convinced Jiang Jieshi to retreat from Dachen and other islands in the ECS. With American assistance, Taiwan withdrew 25,000 troops and evacuate 18,000 civilians from the Dachens on February 8 and 12.[85] After the United States informed the ROC that it would not defend Nanjishan Island, the GMD evacuated again on February 22, 1955. By February 26, all twelve ECS islands along the Zhejiang coast were occupied by the PLA.[86]

After Taiwan lost Yijiangshan to China on January 19, the Eisenhower administration tried to stop the PLA's ongoing "piecemeal" landing campaign.[87] Eisenhower requested congressional support for the offshore islands' defense in the Taiwan Strait. The U.S. Congress acted immediately and passed the Formosa Resolution on January 29, authorizing the president to employ U.S. armed forces in the protection of Taiwan and surrounding areas. Meanwhile, the United States warned of nuclear options as it attempted to stay the tide of Chinese communism. On March 6, Eisenhower and Secretary of State John Foster Dulles reaffirmed their commitment to the offshore islands' safety and mentioned the possible use of nuclear weapons.[88] On March 16, the president directly answered the question: "Yes, of course they could be used." Eisenhower later explained that "in any combat where these things can be used on strictly military targets and for strictly military purposes, I see no reason why they shouldn't be used just exactly as you could use a bullet or anything else."[89] Just one year after signing the Korean Armistice, the United States and China faced another showdown. Nevertheless, on April 26, Beijing backed down as Premier Zhou Enlai suggested truce negotiations.[90] At that time, the 1954–55 crisis in the Taiwan Strait was over, and the Sino-American ambassadorial talks began at Geneva on August 1, 1955.

THE SECOND TAIWAN STRAIT CRISIS, 1958

In mid-July 1958, Mao Zedong counted on a Middle East crisis to divert American attention and limit their involvement in the Taiwan Strait.[91] The crisis seemed a good opportunity for Mao to test America's commitment to the ROC-held islands by renewing PLA offshore attacks. On July 17, he made the decision to bomb Jinmen Islands to blockade Taiwan's supply to its garrison "to support the Arabs' anti-imperialist struggles."[92] The next evening, at the CMC's planning meeting, Mao talked to CMC vice chairmen and army, air force, and navy chiefs. He believed that shelling Taiwanese troops on Jinmen would not provide any chance for an American intervention and that a successful blockade might take two to three months.[93]

The Jinmen Island group had a population of 50,000 at that time. Jiang Jieshi deployed six infantry divisions and two tank battalions, totaling 88,500 troops and armed with 308 artillery pieces and 146 AAA guns. The Jinmen garrison required at least four hundred tons of supplies per day and totally depended on Taiwan, about 140 miles away, making transportation and logistics critically vulnerable for the garrison.[94] According to Mao, the PLA only needed to cut off or restrict Jinmen's supply lines to undermine its garrison's effectiveness and force a Taiwanese withdrawal from the islands, similar to the 1955 Dachen evacuation after the PLA blocked Taiwan's supplies. It seemed to Mao that PLA ground artillery bombardment should meet the blockade objective.[95]

At the CMC meeting on July 18, Marshal Peng Dehuai supported Mao's plan, and the chiefs agreed with Mao and Peng that an effective blockade could produce a decisive result against the island's defense and lead to Taiwan's withdrawal from Jinmen. The bombardment of Jinmen would begin on July 25.[96] In addition to the bombardment, the chiefs also suggested PLAN patrols and air bombings against Jinmen. The chiefs decided to deploy air force units in Fujian and eastern Guangdong by July 27. The joint blockade would be able to isolate the Jinmen garrison. However, Peng warned the chiefs of a possible Taiwanese counterattack on China to create tension in the Taiwan Strait, necessitating a U.S. response. At the meeting, Peng Dehuai established the joint Fujian Front Command (FFC), including the army, navy, and air force. General Ye Fei was appointed as FFC commander, Lieutenant General Nie Fengzhi as FFC air force commander, and Peng Deqing as FFC naval commander and political commissar. The PLAN's assignment was to support the army's bombardment by deploying naval coastal artillery companies to Fujian, patrolling the Jinmen area to attack enemy transit ships, and sending naval air force divisions to Fujian. After the meeting, Beijing did not inform Moscow about the bombardment or about the air force deployment to Fujian.[97]

After returning to Fujian on July 19, the FFC commander, General Ye Fei, prepared the bombardment against Jinmen. As former commander of the Tenth Army Group, Ye had failed the Jinmen landing and lost nine thousand men in 1949. To conduct an effective blockade, Ye chaired a FFC planning meeting at Xiamen on July 20. According to his generals and admiral, as long as the United States did not intervene, coastal batteries, assisted with naval attacks and air raids, could shut down the Jinmen harbors and airfields.[98] The FFC decided to concentrate thirty-two artillery battalions and six naval coastal artillery companies with Soviet-made 152-mm and 122-mm howitzers, and American-made 105-mm howitzers. The navy would shell the ships in Jinmen harbors. Meanwhile, the PLA high command transferred three more artillery divisions to Fujian.[99]

In response to the initial PLAAF buildup across the strait, Jiang Jieshi announced in late July that the GMD troops on Taiwan, Penghu (Pescadores), Jinmen, and Mazu were all "on emergency alert."[100] After July 17, the Taiwanese high command conducted antilanding and artillery exercises, increased naval patrols in the straits, and sent more reconnaissance planes to China's coastal areas along the strait. Jiang understood artillery operations, since he had studied military in Japan from 1906 to 1908 and served in the Nineteenth Artillery Regiment of the Japanese Imperial Army in 1909–10. Jiang Jieshi equipped the Jinmen garrison with ninety-six American-made 155-mm howitzers, twenty 155-mm cannon, and 192 pieces of 105-mm howitzers, totaling 308 guns. On the other side, Ye Fei and his FFC had 223 pieces of 105-mm howitzers, seventy-three 100-mm and bigger cannon, and nineteen 130-mm and four 100-mm coastal guns, totaling 319 guns. Jinmen's artillery pieces were superior in quality to the PLA's. Moreover, since July, the U.S. Seventh Fleet had deployed two aircraft carriers, two heavy cruisers, and eight destroyers in the area about sixty to one hundred nautical miles northeast of Taiwan. The PLA high command also received intelligence that there were two or three American submarines approaching China's southeastern coast and following the deployment of PLAN vessels from the ECS to the Taiwan Strait.[101]

Hence, Mao Zedong worried about a possible U.S. intervention in the Taiwan Strait if such a large bombardment took place. The risk of war with the United States kept the chairman awake through July 25–27. Mao wrote to

Defense Minister Peng Dehuai and suggested that it might be "more appropriate to withhold the attack on Jinmen for several days." The chairman hoped for "the best scenario": if Jiang Jieshi's army was lured into attacking the mainland, the Jinmen bombardment would appear retaliatory. Mao asked Peng to "telegraph this letter to Ye Fei and ask him to think about it very carefully. Let me know his opinion."[102] After receiving a copy of Mao's July 27 letter, Ye held an emergency meeting of the FFC at Xiamen. Ye shared Mao's points with Nie Fengzhi and Peng Deqing. All the field generals agreed that postponing the bombardment of Jinmen would allow them to make better preparations.[103] Khrushchev visited Beijing from July 31 to August 3. Mao kept the impending PLA operations against Jinmen to himself during the Russian leader's visit.[104]

From August 17 to 30, Mao Zedong chaired the CCP Politburo Standing Committee meeting at Beidaihe, Hebei.[105] In the morning on August 20, Marshal Peng Dehuai briefed Mao with Department of General Staff (DGS) intelligence that Jiang Jieshi was chairing a strategic meeting debating whether Jinmen should be defended or evacuated and that Jiang and his defense minister were going to visit Jinmen soon. (In fact, Jiang visited Jinmen on August 19–20, and ROC defense minister Yu Dawei visited Jinmen on the evening of August 22.) Mao saw an opportunity to push Jiang's withdrawal by commencing the PLA's bombardment. Mao asked Peng about the bombardment preparations.[106] Peng confirmed the artillery troops' readiness and detailed shelling plan.[107] But Mao summoned FFC commander Ye Fei to Beidaihe on August 21 for more operational details.

During Ye Fei's briefing, Mao questioned Ye about any potential casualties among American military advisers, with so many artillery pieces (almost ten thousand) deployed along the front. Ye immediately answered, "Yes, [we] will hit them [Americans] for sure." Mao then asked Ye whether American casualties were avoidable, but Ye explained that it would be nearly impossible. Marshal Lin Biao suggested that Mao instruct Wang Bingnan, China's representative at the U.S.-China ambassadorial talks in Warsaw, to inform the Americans of the shelling. Mao did not accept Lin's suggestion.[108] Mao decided to begin the bombardment of Jinmen on August 23. He adopted a step-by-step shelling strategy: "Take one step first, and look carefully before taking another step." The chairman predicted the Taiwanese garrison's withdrawal if the PLA successfully cut it off.[109] At 9 a.m. on August 22, the PLA high command ordered the FFC "to launch a large-scale bombardment against the Jinmen Islands on the 23rd. Your shelling should concentrate on the commanding HQ, artillery sites, radar stations, and naval vessels in the Liaoluo Bay harbor. The bombardment will continue for three days, but the next step depends on international response and Taiwan's reactions."[110]

At 5:30 p.m. on August 23, General Ye Fei issued final orders from Beidaihe to fire on the Jinmen Islands. It became known as the 8-23 Artillery Battle.[111] The first barrage, delivered by seventy-two artillery pieces from six artillery battalions, fired some six thousand shells in just fifteen minutes on the Jinmen Defense HQ. Meanwhile, sixty guns from five battalions fired five thousand shells on the ROC Ninth Division HQ, and thirty-six guns from three battalions fired more than three thousand shells on the ROC 58th Division HQ. Among the others, seventy-two artillery pieces from six battalions fired some six thousand shells on the 25th and 27th Regimental HQ. Twenty-four coastal guns from six naval artillery companies fired one thousand shells on harbor facilities and Taiwanese ships in the Liaoluo Bay. After a five-minute break, the second barrage began at 5:50 p.m. against Jinmen artillery positions where the ROC returned fire. Within thirty minutes, the PLA fired more than 30,000 rounds and killed some six hundred ROC officers and soldiers, including three deputy commanders of the Jinmen Garrison HQ: Lieutenant General Ji Xingwen, Major General Zhao Jiarang, and Major General Zhang Jie. Moreover, Taiwan's defense minister, Yu Dawei, was wounded as he visited Jinmen. Jinmen launched retaliatory bombardment at 5:18 p.m. on August 24, firing 3,500 shells on the PLA's artillery positions. After Ye Fei's order, the Chinese guns returned fire with 9,808 shells in forty-five minutes and silenced Jinmen's artillery troops.[112]

By August 25, the PLA's bombardment had significantly reduced the Jinmen supply from Taiwan. On August 28, Taiwan changed its shipping schedule from daytime to nighttime and shifted its loading location from the large harbors to small harbors to avoid bombardment.[113] For a total blockade, Ye Fei tried to isolate Jinmen Island from its surrounding islands with two more artillery divisions as reinforcements that arrived in Fujian before the end of the month. Moreover, Ye Fei also requested searchlight units and began nighttime shelling on August 30 to stop Taiwanese night shipments.[114] The PLA continued its overwhelming barrage and silenced ROC counterbattery fire. But according to Chief General Hao Bocun (Hau Pei-tsun, ROC army, served as the garrison commander on Jinmen), recounting the incident years later, the bombardment did not destroy many ROC artillery pieces.[115] By September 3, Jinmen received meager supplies through limited, ineffective airlifts and night shipping. The PLA readied to make another move, Ye Fei recalled.[116] That evening, however, Mao ordered a sudden halt to the bombardment from September 4 to 6 to gauge the American response.[117]

The Eisenhower administration responded immediately to the escalated PLA attacks in the Taiwan Strait. The Pentagon directed the U.S. Taiwan Patrol Force to help "protect the shipping lanes supplying Jinmen." Vice Admiral Roland N. Smoot, commander of the U.S. Taiwan Defense Command (1958–62), worked with the Taiwanese navy on a U.S.-escorted ROC supply convoy, code-named Operation Lighting, to supply Jinmen.[118] On the morning of September 7, American warships joined that Taiwanese convoy, totaling thirteen ships. Among six American warships was USS *Helena* (CA 75), a *Baltimore*-class heavy cruiser with a displacement of 13,600 tons and a top speed of 33 knots. Around 9 a.m., Ye Fei recognized the American warship immediately as it embarked from Taiwan and reported the new development to Mao Zedong in Beijing. Mao ordered a salvo on the combined fleet, targeting Taiwanese ships only, including two destroyers, three gunboats, and two transit ships. Moreover, Ye could not open fire until the fleet reached the harbor, so he interpreted Mao's order as "Do not fire." Ye Fei followed Mao's commands without question or hesitation and did not fire a single shell, since the American ships were so close to the Taiwanese vessels.[119] Protected by the American ships, at 11:25 a.m. Taiwan's supply reached Jinmen unmolested.[120] Frustrated and angry about their failed blockade, Ye and the FFC asked for another heavy shelling on Jinmen on September 8. The CMC approved their request at midnight the next morning.

However, that morning, another American-Taiwanese convoy made way for Jinmen in the same escort pattern used the day before. USS *Helena* led five American destroyers to escort seven Taiwanese ships. At 10 a.m., when the combined fleet was reaching Jinmen, the American warships stopped about three miles from the island. Then the transit ships continued toward Liaoluowan Bay. Around 11 a.m., the DGS ordered Ye Fei to carry out the bombardment as planned after the Taiwanese ships reached Liaoluowan harbor. Ye immediately phoned Lieutenant General Wang Shangrong, chief of the DGS's Operation Division, and asked what he should do if the Americans fired at him. Wang Shangrong told Ye "not to return fire" on the Americans without a specific order. At 12:43 p.m., Mao Zedong ordered Ye Fei to open fire. Ye directed the shelling on the transit ships in the harbor. The PLAN 149th and 150th Coastal Artillery Companies sank one of the ships with their 130-mm guns. Meanwhile, on September 8, thirty-six artillery battalions fired 21,700 shells on Jinmen.[121] When the heavy shelling began, the American ships rapidly turned around and sailed away from Jinmen about six to twelve miles without firing a single shot.[122] Elleman points out that U.S. ships were told "to remain at least three miles from shore. U.S. Navy ships were particularly warned not to shoot at the mainland."[123]

On September 11, the U.S.-Taiwanese joint convoy tried again with four American warships and eleven Taiwanese ships, including four transit ships and seven warships. When the joint fleet approached Jinmen at about 3 p.m., Ye Fei ordered fire with forty artillery battalions by following the same method used on September 8. Having learned from the previous lessons, the ROC ships did not attempt to reach the harbor or allow the American escort to get out of range. All the ships turned around. The U.S.-Taiwanese combined fleet unsuccessfully retried two days later but were again repulsed by fierce PLA fire.[124]

In mid-September, Taiwan used a different landing vessel—an LVT (landing vehicle, tracked), a much smaller (6-ton load) and flexible amphibious vehicle that could land and unload on the beach.[125] On September 14, Taiwan sent seventeen fully loaded LVTs from large ships, and fifteen reached the island's beach. On September 15, after receiving reports on the LVTs, the PLA high command ordered the FFC to zero in on the LVTs with its guns and stop them before they could reach the beach.[126] However, "with USN assistance, Nationalist supply ships began to reach Jinmen in sufficiently large numbers that by mid-September they had broken what was being called a

PRC artillery blockade of the island. By September 19 a total of nine convoys had reached Jinmen; the final four were able to land an average of 151 tons of supplies."[127] By October 5, Taiwan's transportation to Jinmen gradually resumed by using LVTs, which sent in 170 tons of supplies per day. The Jinmen garrison received about 40 percent of their needs, a huge increase from the 5 percent since late August.[128]

SPEEDBOATS VERSUS WARSHIPS DURING THE JINMEN BLOCKADE

While the blockade by the PLA Army's bombardment faced increasing difficulties, the PLAAF and PLAN also faced more problems in the Second Taiwan Strait Crisis in 1958. After the PLAAF's extensive preparations, on July 27 forty-eight MiG-17 fighters arrived at the two air bases located at Liancheng in Fujian and Shantou in Guangdong.[129] Lieutenant General Nie Fengzhi was appointed commander of the FFC air force that summer. Over the next year, the PLAAF would deploy twenty-three fighter regiments totaling 520 aircraft, mostly MiG-17s, on the front. After the PLA deployed its air force in the two southern provinces at the end of July, its fighters challenged the ROC air force over the Taiwan Strait.

At first, the PLAAF's MiG-17s performed at higher altitudes than American-made F-84 Sabers deployed by Taiwan. On July 29, the PLAAF 18th Division responded to several F-84Gs that approached Shantou, Guangdong. At 11:11 a.m., Division Commander Lin Hu sent four MiG-17s under Regimental Commander Zhao De'an to stop the GMD fighters. Zhao found four F-84Gs around 11:45 a.m. and organized his attack in a swirling dogfight. Within three minutes, two F-84Gs were downed and one damaged. Zhao and his MiG-17s returned without casualties.[130] Although PLA pilots improved their combat skills and gained control of the airspace over the Taiwan Strait, they only chose battles with favorable conditions.[131]

On August 13, 1958, for example, eight F-86 fighters escorted two RF-84 reconnaissance planes that came over the Fuzhou airport. Around 12 p.m., four MiG-17 fighters from the Fourth Air Division attacked the Taiwanese planes, damaging two of them and forcing them back.[132] The next day, a MiG-17 formation cruised over Pingtan Island and encountered eleven F-86s. During the dogfights, they shot down two Taiwanese fighters and lost one of their own. On August 25, eight Chinese-made Jian-5 fighters from the Ninth Air Division encountered GMD fighters while patrolling the Fujian coast. PLA pilots shot down two F-86s during fourteen minutes of combat. One PLA fighter was downed by AAA friendly fire from the ground. Although PLAAF pilots preferred fighting over land rather than water for their familiarity and safety, they often faced fire from their own antiaircraft ground crews.[133] Between July 29 and August 22, the PLA fighters downed four GMD fighters and damaged five, while the PLA lost one fighter.[134] Thereafter, the PLA controlled the airspace along the Fujian coast.

The PLAN's performance during the Second Taiwan Strait Crisis was mixed, like it had been in 1954-55. After Marshal Peng Dehuai established the FFC, Rear Admiral Peng Deqing served as the naval chief in the joint command. Having served as a company commander in the Red Army, Peng Deqing became a company, battalion, regiment, and brigade commander or political commissar for the New Fourth Army during World War II. He was promoted to a brigade and division political commissar, chief staff, and commander in 1946-48; in 1949, he became deputy commander of the 22nd and 23rd Armies and then commander of the PLA's 27th Army. In the Korean War, Peng was commander of the 27th Army, CPVF Ninth Army Group, and participated in the Battle of the Chosin Reservoir. After returned to China, he became deputy commander of the ECMRN. The PLA ranked him rear admiral in 1955.[135] Before the 8-23 Artillery Battle, Rear Admiral Peng Deqing was conducting a naval exercise with an Indian cruiser near Wusongkou, Shanghai in late July. As the ESF deputy commander, Peng deployed the frigate *Chengdu*, twelve torpedo boats, nine torpedo bombers, and twelve fighters in the exercise.

After the CMC meeting, on July 19 PLAN commander Xiao Jinguang ordered his fleets to deploy naval ships to Fujian to participate in the blockade of Jinmen. The SSF would send two torpedo boat brigades, one submarine hunter brigade, and one speed gunboat squadron to Fujian, while the ESF would send one torpedo boat brigade and one submarine hunter brigade to the front by August 5. Rear Admiral Peng Deqing was summoned to Beijing by Xiao Jinguang for detailed instructions on preparing naval operations in the Taiwan Strait. According to Peng's notes, Xiao's guidelines were to "attack Jinmen, not Mazu; attack the Jiangs, not Americans; attack near water, not high sea; block only, no landing; and joint operations to support the army."[136] On July 20, after returning to Shanghai, Peng passed Xiao's instructions on to the ESF commanders. Then Peng led the ESF PT boat Sixth Brigade to travel by train to Fujian. On July 24, after arriving in Fujian, Rear Admiral Peng Deqing established FFC naval HQ. He deployed fourteen coastal artillery companies to Fujian, including fifty 130-mm guns and other artillery pieces, for bombardment. Meanwhile, he organized a blockade fleet in Xiamen, including thirty-one frigates, six submarine hunters, forty-seven torpedo boats, and eight landing craft. Peng also ordered the PLANAF to send two air force regiments, including fifty-three fighters and transit planes, to Fujian.[137]

During the August 23 shelling, Rear Admiral Peng Deqing and his PT boats were waiting for battle opportunity. At 6:10 p.m. on August 24, three large Taiwanese landing craft, *Zhonghai* (LST 201), *Meisong* (LSM 353), and *Taisheng* (LST 237), fled Jinmen during the shelling and headed for Taiwan. At 6:30 p.m., Peng sent six PT boats (22 tons each) under the command of Zhang Yimin after the enemy transit ships. Zhang Yimin, the captain who sank the Taiwanese ship *Dongting* in 1955, was now a battalion officer. He trained his sailors with the "three rules" of not releasing torpedoes: first, do not fire a torpedo unless you are within three cable lengths (500 meters) of the target; second, do not fire a torpedo beyond 45–100 degrees between you and the enemy ship; and third, do not fire a torpedo when your boat is unstable.[138] The PT boats were directed by two coastal naval radar stations.

Around 6:40 p.m., the PT boats saw two of Taiwan's landing ships, *Taisheng* and *Zhonghai*, with two submarine hunters and two gunboats thirteen nautical miles northwest of Jinmen. Each landing craft had a standard displacement of 4,080 tons; they were almost 100 meters in length, with 130 crew members and eight 40-mm and twelve 20-mm guns each. Both were among the largest Taiwanese ships. On *PT-184*, Zhang Yimin ordered the speedboats to split into two groups and attack the enemy at close range. At 6:50 p.m., when these PT boats got within fifteen cable lengths, the two

Taiwanese warships opened fire. The PT boats' speed helped them avoid shells from the eight 40-mm guns and twelve 20-mm guns on each ship. They quickly got within four cable lengths of the warships, and Zhang ordered the PT boats to launch torpedoes. Twenty seconds later, two of five torpedoes hit *Taisheng*. Soon, after two explosions, it sank. *Zhonghai* captain Zheng Benji tried to avoid the incoming torpedoes, but he failed. One out of eight torpedoes hit *Zhonghai* and badly damaged the ship.[139]

Nevertheless, Zhang Yimin lost one of his torpedo boats, *PT-175*, in the August 24 battle. It was hit by enemy shells after it fired one of its two torpedoes. Zhang asked the captain of *175*, Xu Fengming, about the damages. Xu said he had lost one of his two engines, but the boat was still operational. He asked Zhang and other PT boats to leave immediately as planned. Soon after the PLA PT squadron left, *175* sank. Captain Xu abandoned the boat and led his crew to swim back to the mainland. Only five out of twelve crew members were saved by Chinese fishermen two days later, and three were captured by the Taiwanese navy. Captain Xu Fengming and the other three swam to Jinmen but were killed in a beach engagement with the garrison.[140] *PT-175* was not the only speedboat the PLAN lost in the 1958 crisis.

Rear Admiral Peng Deqing lost two more PT boats in the battle on September 1. He received intelligence from Beijing that an ROC convoy had left Taiwan at 2:20 p.m. and would arrive at Jinmen around ten o'clock that evening. Grand General Su Yu, PLA chief of staff, ordered an attack, emphasizing that there should be "no accidental nor mistaken fire on American ships."[141] At 4:30 p.m., the naval radar stations reported to Peng Deqing that a large landing craft loaded with supplies, *Meijian*, was on its way to Jinmen, escorted by three submarine hunters. Peng deployed six PT boats from the First PT Squadron, and three speedboats (75 tons each) and four gunboats (50 tons each) from the 31st Gunboat Squadron to intercept the Taiwanese convoy and destroy the *Meijian*. At 10:03 p.m., the radar station informed the Chinese fleet that the enemy ships were about twenty-seven nautical miles from Jinmen and traveling at a speed of eleven knots. At 11 p.m., the PT boats under the command of Zhang Yimin rushed to their targets at full speed. However, the radar stations lost *Meijian* and mistook a sub hunter, *Weiyuan*, as the landing craft.

At 11:40 p.m., Commander Zhang Yimin saw *Weiyuan* and ordered his boats *PT-103*, *177*, *178*, and *180* to attack at thirty cable lengths. *Weiyuan* opened fires with two 76-mm cannons, one 40-mm cannon, and five 20-mm guns. Due to the high winds and large waves, the torpedo boats failed to hit the enemy sub hunter with any of their eight torpedoes. Meanwhile, *PT-174* fired at another sub hunter, *Tuojiang*, but it missed too. Zhang ordered his boats to evacuate from the battle site at 11:53 p.m. Then *174* and *180* collided into each other at high speed when they made their U-turns. Soon both boats sank. Nevertheless, all twenty-five crew members were rescued by the Chinese gunboats around three thirty the next morning. Zhang blamed his failure on the bad weather and misinformation by the radar stations, which made the battle situation very difficult for his PT boats.[142]

After the PT boats left, at 11:35 p.m., the three Chinese speedboats, *556*, *557*, and *558*, met the three Taiwanese submarine hunters. The Chinese-made small speedboat, with a displacement of 75 tons and two 37-mm guns, had been newly designed and commissioned about a month before. At 11:50 p.m., the submarine hunter *Tuojiang*, about 450 tons with one 76-mm and six 20-mm guns, opened fire on the Chinese gunboats from three miles. The gunboats did not slow down and continued to rush to the enemy warship at full speed. The three gunboats returned fire at about seven hundred meters. The captain of *556*, Hua Keyi, ordered his guns to fire at the *Tuojiang* 76-mm cannon, and soon it fell silent. *Tuojiang* then turned around and ran toward *556*. Speedboat *556* did not run away from the *Tuojiang*, and instead Hua Keyi followed *Tuojiang* and got closer and closer while keeping fire on its right side. Soon *557* and *558* joined the fire. After losing its guns, *Tuojiang* disengaged and turned around. Around 12:08 a.m. on September 2, the Chinese gunboats pulled out of the battle site. The submarine hunter *Tuojiang* sank before it could reach Taiwan. It was the first time in Chinese naval history that small gunboats had sunk a larger enemy warship.[143]

On September 19, Taiwanese naval patrol gunboats met two Chinese blockading gunboats. The PLAN lost one gunboat during the battle.[144] Thereafter, the PLAN focused on its supportive role in assisting the army's artillery battles rather than establishing a naval blockade. On October 20, Fleet Admiral Xiao Jinguang, PLAN commander; Rear Admiral Zhang Xuesi, PLAN chief of staff; Vice Admiral Tao Yong, ESF commander; and Vice Admiral Kang Zhiqiang, ESF political commissar, visited the FFC naval base, torpedo squadron, coastal artillery companies, and radar troops. Although the PLAN did sink one escorting ship, they failed to destroy any transit ship to enforce the blockade due to a navigation error by the FFC naval command.[145]

After forty days of shelling, the PLA's blockade of Jinmen failed. Jiang Jieshi showed no signs of withdrawing his garrison from the island. Mao Zedong had to accept that China would not fight the United States over the offshore islands. The CMC issued instructions, drafted by Mao, rationalizing the slowdown of the bombardment on October 5. Pressed to find an excuse, Mao wrote to his marshals and generals, "Our batteries should not fire a single shell on October 6 and 7, even if there are American planes and escort ships. If the enemy bombs us, our forces should still not return fire. We will cease our activities, lie low, and wait and see for two days. Then we will know what to do."[146] The Second Taiwan Strait Crisis was over.

From August 23 to October 6, the PLA shelled the Jinmen Islands with 474,900 rounds and claimed to have sunk twenty-one Taiwanese warships and transport ships, damaged another seventeen, shot down eighteen Taiwanese airplanes, and inflicted more than a thousand casualties.[147] Jinmen's garrison returned fire with more than 120,000 shells during the same time. The PLAN reported that it had sunk five enemy ships, destroyed eighteen LTVs, and damaged fifteen ships. Mao was satisfied with the 1958 shelling of Jinmen and made it a model of "diplomacy through the military" in the Taiwan Strait. It happened again in 1962 and became a principal means for Beijing to send signals to Washington for many years to come. China left Jinmen linked to Taiwan to avoid giving the United States a pretext for instigating a "two Chinas plot."[148] Mao called it the "noose strategy." It meant that Beijing would leave the islands in Jiang Jieshi's hands as a burden on America.[149] Thereafter, Mao's policy toward the Taiwan Strait changed from one of military confrontation to one of political considerations based on the nature of the Cold War and, ultimately, international politics over the civil war.[150] The regular PLA shelling continued until January 1, 1979, when the PRC and the United States normalized diplomatic relations.

CHAPTER 3

Naval Strategy and Combat Experience

From 1959 to 1965, China's "local war" strategy faced new challenges from neighboring Russia. During the great polemic debate over international communism in 1960, the ideological foundation of the China-Soviet alliance collapsed. One major contributing factor was China's newly acquired position as the dominant center of international communism in East Asia.[1] Mao Zedong criticized Nikita Khrushchev as a "new revisionist" who "betrayed international communist movements" with "socialist imperialist" aggressive policy.[2] Khrushchev labeled Mao "an ultra-leftist, an ultra-dogmatist and a left revisionist." On a broader scale, the new confrontation between Beijing and Moscow changed the dynamics of the global Cold War.[3] The Sino-Soviet split undermined the characteristics of the Cold War as a confrontation between the contentious ideologies of communism and capitalism.[4] Soon, political conflicts between the two communist parties extended to their diplomatic relations, defense coordination, and military operations. What once existed as the cornerstone of international communism in the 1950s was dealt a final blow by strategic differences on military developments within the Sino-Soviet military alliance. Having lost Soviet nuclear protection, Mao Zedong expedited the PLA's efforts to develop a strategic force in the early 1960s. The communist Cold War not only triggered the development of nuclear and missile programs but also determined their eventual targets.

The Sino-Soviet split and Mao's failed Great Leap Forward in 1958 divided PLA officers between the so-called rightists, on the one hand, and the leftists loyal to Mao, on the other. The political earthquake began in 1959 when a gap emerged between Mao and Defense Minister Peng Dehuai.

The latter was dismissed from all his positions and was under house arrest for many years. Marshal Lin Biao took over the administration of the CMC and Defense Ministry in September 1959. Lin's command emphasized "leftish" politics for the PLA and promoted Mao's personality cult. In 1962, Lin appointed Lieutenant General Li Zuopeng, his longtime lieutenant, as the navy's first deputy commander in an attempt to take over naval leadership from Fleet Admiral Xiao Jinguang.

During China's nationwide famine, Jiang Jieshi called for a "return to the mainland" in 1962 and launched new, small-scale attacks along China's coast during the Sino-Soviet split. By 1964, the Taiwanese navy had launched twenty-four operations against China's commercial shipping, offshore fishing, and island defenses and had captured 370 Chinese fishing boats. In early 1964, Mao Zedong instructed Xiao Jinguang and the navy to fight back against "Jiang Jieshi's harassments and sabotages along the southeastern coast."[5] In 1965, the Chinese navy engaged in three major naval battles. The PLAN claimed that all of them were victories over the Taiwanese navy. In the same region, the PLANAF also fared better against the Taiwanese air force. Although Taiwan had recently received American F-84 fighters, the ROC air force had yet to deploy them. Moreover, Taiwanese pilots were no match for the Chinese pilots, fresh from the Korean War, nor was the F-84 a match for the PLANAF's Soviet-made MiG-15 jet fighters.

In retrospect, the Chinese navy centralized its chain of command, land–sea communications, battle coordination, and offensive tactics. The PLAN's new combat tactics seemed effective while their small patrol craft (PC) and torpedo boats (PT) were engaged against the large Taiwanese warships; they were different from the army's tactics. The PLAN's primary strength in 1958-65 could maintain its initiative in the Taiwan Strait, its ability to develop its combat tactics both in the air and at sea, its flexibility in obstruction methods, its advantageous use of offshore areas, and its assimilation of Russian naval technology. Nevertheless, the PLAN lacked major warships in the Taiwan Strait and experienced low morale, factionalism and regionalism, and disconcertment among top naval leaders after the CCP Lushan conference.

DE-RUSSIANIZATION AND REJECTION OF THE "JOINT FLEET"

The Soviet Union played an active role in Chinese military modernization in the 1950s and not only developed communist military cooperation but also created a new Chinese air force and a PLA navy capable of fighting against technologically advanced Western forces and the GMD air force over the Taiwan Strait. Technology consumed a larger and larger portion of the defense budget throughout the 1950s. By 1959, the PLA had purchased $2 billion in Soviet arms.[6] The last huge naval purchase before the Sino-Soviet split, the so-called 2–4 Agreement, was finalized on February 4, 1959 and provided the PLAN with ballistic submarine-to-surface missiles and ship-to-ship missiles, submarines armed with missiles, and missile-launching ships. They were shipped to China with their designs, blueprints, equipment, sample missiles, and shipbuilding materials. This agreement was then considered a "high-tech" deal for the PLAN.[7]

In April–June 1958, Fleet Admiral Xiao Jinguang, PLAN commander, proposed to Defense Minister Peng Dehuai that the navy could use more Russian assistance to update its technologies, including nuclear submarines and guided missiles. Xiao worried about future Soviet naval aid, since relations between the CCP and the Russian Communist Party had become increasingly tense after the Communist Party of the Soviet Union Twentieth National Congress, when Khrushchev criticized Joseph Stalin as a dictator in his report.[8] In 1957–58, Mao Zedong mobilized the CCP and started a massive propaganda campaign criticizing post-Stalin Soviet leaders as "revisionists" and "social imperialists." Xiao Jinguang realized the urgency of the need to update Soviet naval technologies. Peng Dehuai agreed, and in March 1959, Xiao and PLAN Command submitted the PLAN Ten-Year Development Agenda to the CMC and Mao, recommending a transformation of the PLAN to a modern navy with medium and large surface warships and nuclear submarines for near-sea defense.[9] Peng and PLA leaders supported Xiao's agenda, which argued for the importance of continuing Soviet naval aid, advisory, and technology assistance.

By 1958, there were 3,390 Russian naval advisers in the PLAN.[10] The Russian navy had a strong influence on the Chinese navy's development through advisory assistance in the 1950s. However, disagreements between

Russian advisers and Chinese naval officers arose at all levels. In his report to Moscow, Major General Kecherjn complained on June 16, 1951, "Whenever they felt like [we forced something on them], they would immediately say that 'our opinion is different from your opinion on these issues.'" He also complained about the Russian advisers: "Our advisers did not express their supposed determination and persistence when they helped Chinese comrades to overcome the wrong ideas and practices on their troop deployments and operation tactics. Whenever the Chinese declined their advice (by saying please wait for the next time or no hurry), [our advisers] often stepped back and gave up."[11]

First, the PLAN opposed Russian attempts to copy their naval system in China. Russian advisers tried to centralize the naval command structure by limiting the appointment and promotion authority of regimental and divisional commanders. The PLAN derived this system from the army, where the regimental commander promoted the first and second lieutenants, and division command appointed captains. Russian advisers demanded that the Chinese use the Soviet system, where only the division command promoted the first and second lieutenants, and the army command appointed captains. Reports of the disagreement reached Mao's office on October 27, 1950. Mao suggested that Zhou Enlai talk to the Russian advisers in Beijing and solve the problem. Mao complained about this later to Pavel Yudin, the Soviet ambassador in Beijing, telling him, "We wish to learn from the Soviet Union, but primarily we ought to take our own experiences into consideration, giving them priority."[12]

Vice Admiral Zhang Xusan recalled that although the Russian advisers intended to make the PLAN as good as the Soviet navy, they often ignored the geographic settings, demographical characters, cultural tradition, and military experience unique to the Chinese. Zhang studied naval technology in the Soviet Union in 1952–54. During his training, Zhang endeavored to modify the Soviet system to better fit China's situation. After his return, Zhang became the first captain of the destroyer *Changchun*. He had to work with Commodore Chibeholov and more than thirty Russian advisers who sailed the destroyer from Russia to China and were to stay with the ship for six months to one year. According to Zhang, the Russian advisers were very friendly and tried their best to help the Chinese in any way they could. But disagreements and arguments persisted as the Russian advisers wanted to enforce Russian standards, regulations, and systems on the Chinese and were not interested in developing a new Chinese naval institution. Their recommendations were inflexible and sometimes unrealistic for the PLAN.[13] Zhang was promoted to vice admiral in 1988 and Chinese navy's deputy commander in 1990–92.

A conceptual gap regarding civil-military relations also existed between the Russians and Chinese. The Russians tried to separate the populace from national defense, but the PLA welcomed local involvement in the "people's war" against any foreign threat. In February 1952, when the CMC designated Dingling Island for coast defense, Russian advisers requested the evacuation of all residents from the island. Except for relocating inhabitants with a criminal history or those with no valid identification, Chinese officers refused to accept the Russians' advice. Eventually, the Russian advisers dropped their demands.[14]

Russian advisers did not conduct research on local Chinese islands, coastal areas, and defense positions. Many had only brought their handbooks and training manuals to China. Some of their ideas, plans, and decisions did not apply to China's situation. At coastal artillery positions, Russian advisers deployed the heavy guns only forty meters apart, making it easier for a shell depot nearby. But the PLAN, unlike the Soviet Red Army, had insufficient AAA, and the Russian plan presented dangers during possible air raids.[15] When the PLANAF designed its air base at Ningbo, Zhejiang, a Soviet adviser proposed that the runway slope be built beyond the normal standard. Chinese naval air engineers worried the slope might cause accidents, so the PLAN refused the Soviet's runway design.[16]

Last, the Chinese disdained the Soviet's control of advanced technology. In October 1957, Fleet Admiral Xiao Jinguang asked the Soviet high command in Moscow to help the Chinese navy build nuclear submarines with missile-launching capacity. The Soviet navy's chief responded that the Soviet Union would sell these submarines to the PLAN so that the Chinese did not need to develop and build their own nuclear submarines.[17] After his return to Beijing, Xiao commented to Marshal Peng that the PLAN still built outdated Russian ships from 1950, when the Soviets were producing 1956–57 models. Peng passed the navy's complaints on to Zhou Enlai in early 1958. On June 28, Zhou wrote to Khrushchev that the Soviet designs and blueprints of the new warships and submarines should be available to the Chinese navy. On the same day, Zhou approved the PLAN's proposals on China's own nuclear submarines' research and development.[18] Major General Kecherjn of Russia reported to the Soviet high command that the "[Chinese] told us very carefully that 'they are not happy' since they did not receive modern technology and equipment."[19] Meanwhile, some Chinese officers believed that the American and British naval technology was more advanced than the Russian, so they called for learning naval technology from the United States and United Kingdom and learning politics and organization from the Soviet Union.[20] From January 1956, the Soviet Union began to reduce the number of the Russian military advisers in China. By May 31, the Russian advisers at the PLA high command were reduced from 592 to 422. The Russian advisers at the PLAN HQ were reduced from 145 to 93.[21]

On July 21, 1958, Moscow announced its intention to establish a Russo-Chinese joint fleet. Mao Zedong was so upset about the Russian proposal that he summoned Soviet ambassador Pavel Yudin to his office the next day. Mao complained to Yudin, "You made me so angry yesterday that I didn't sleep a wink last night. . . . Why now again the idea of a naval 'cooperative'? How would you explain your proposal of a naval 'cooperative' to the whole world and to the Chinese people?" The Chinese leader told the Soviet ambassador, "You don't trust the Chinese, only the Russians. The Russians are superior, while the Chinese are inferior, clumsy, hence the question of joint operation. Speaking of that, how about putting everything under joint operation: the army, navy and air force, industry, agriculture and education? Should we hand over to you our coastline of over 10,000 kilometers, while we ourselves engage solely in organizing guerrilla forces? You have had some success with atomic energy, so you want to control others, to enjoy the right of lease."[22] Surprised by Mao's anger and accusations, Yudin immediately called Moscow and reported to Khrushchev. Khrushchev was also shocked and decided to talk to Mao directly.[23] However, Khrushchev failed to convince

Mao that the Soviets did not intend to control the Chinese navy through the Russo-Chinese joint fleet when he visited Beijing from July 31 to August 3.[24] Khrushchev did not give up and fought back by telling Mao, "You said that you spent a night without sleep. I also had a sleepless night when I received this information." The Soviet leader told Mao, "We [the Soviets] build our Navy and can use it. This is a formidable weapon. . . . The [joint] fleet cannot be owned by two countries. The fleet needs to be commanded. When two are in command it is impossible to fight a war."[25] Mao shot back, "Your adviser (an admiral) advised us four times to send a cable asking for assistance in building the fleet. . . . We understood it as follows: if we want to obtain [Soviet] assistance, then we must build a joint fleet aimed primarily against the US. . . . I said then that we could give you the entire Chinese coast, but we disagree with a joint fleet."[26]

Then Khrushchev suggested a joint Soviet-China long-wave radio/radar system. Before Khrushchev's visit to Beijing on July 31, Soviet defense minister Malinovsky had telegraphed Peng Dehuai about the purpose of a joint long-wave radar observation station on the Chinese coast. It was aimed at improving Moscow's communication with its nuclear submarine fleet in the Pacific and providing China with a more effective nuclear protection. Malinovsky also suggested splitting the total cost of 110 million rubles: Moscow would pay 70 million and Beijing 40 million.[27] When Yudin informed him of this idea, Mao got upset. He told the Soviet ambassador, "A 'cooperative' involves a question of ownership, and it will be 50 percent by each side according to the proposal. . . . This request is similar to that for naval 'cooperative,' which we will be unable to explain to our people or the outside world; it is politically harmful."[28]

At their first conversation on July 31, Khrushchev tried to further clarify the radio/radar station to Mao, explaining that "when needed, one could command Soviet submarines in the Pacific. . . . We need it, and you will need it, too, when you will have a submarine fleet." Mao again questioned the ownership, saying, "This station may be built. It will be the property of China, built with investments of the Chinese government, and we could use it jointly." Khrushchev countered, "I would suggest that credit is needed, assistance from our side." Mao got angry again and ended the discussion: "If you insist on assistance, then we will not build the station at all." The Soviet leader, saddened by this comment, asked Mao, "Now, do you really consider us red imperialists?"[29]

Disappointed and frustrated, Khrushchev wanted to withdraw the Soviet military advisers from China. He asked Mao, "Why do you need military advisers? You won wars, acquired such an experience. Of what use are they to you? Our advisers have been brought up under different conditions." Mao still needed Russian military advisers and answered, "We need specialists in technology. . . . I am talking about individual cases, not about the recall of all of them." He emphasized that "99.9 percent and perhaps even more of them who stayed here for the last seven to eight years are good advisers and only some individuals do not take up their duties such as they should have done." Mao even apologized to Khrushchev about the misunderstanding: "We are not posing the question about the advisers. Perhaps we posed incorrectly the question about the shortcomings in the work of advisers?"

But the Chinese leader did want to limit the power and influence of the Russian military advisers, so he instead suggested, "Perhaps we should change all the advisers into specialists? . . . Let them work, but in a slightly different way." Khrushchev had nothing else to say and agreed with Mao: "That's right. Leave them with the right to advise. Let them work."[30] At that moment on August 1, Khrushchev regarded the PLA's problems with the Russian advisers as some isolated mistakes made by a few Soviet military advisers and some misunderstanding of their duties and responsibilities in China. "Yes, there was a contradiction, but not a conflict," the Soviet leader concluded.[31] He did not think it as a control or trust issue at all. The Chinese, however, saw it differently.

The next day, Premier Zhou Enlai drafted a document on Soviet military advisory assistance that was signed by both governments on August 2, 1958. The new agreement changed all the military advisers into "specialists" who would continue their assistance to the PLA.[32] The Soviet military advisers' administrative and executive roles were also reduced. These naval specialists in the PLAN could no longer attend the fleet command briefings and planning meetings, take part in decision-making, or visit the troops or inspect ships without an invitation or permission from the PLAN.[33] In August,

Beijing had prepared a large-scale bombing and shelling campaign against the Taiwan-held islands without informing Moscow and Khrushchev during his visit. During the Second Taiwan Strait Crisis in October, Khrushchev wrote twice to Mao, offering Russian C-75 bombers with surface-to-air missiles (SAMs) and Soviet advisers. In his replies, Mao only accepted Russian bombers and SAMs; he did not want any more Soviet advisers. Russian aid and new technology never came.[34]

In 1959, the PLAN began to install listening devices on the telephones in the Russian advisers' offices and hotel rooms. The monitors recorded the naval advisers' phone conversations both with the Chinese and with Russians in the Soviet Union. Many Russian advisers also complained that their mail and family letters had been opened and checked.[35] More and more naval advisers felt uncomfortable working with the Chinese naval officers. Khrushchev did not expect at all that within less than two years, by August 13, 1960, all 12,000 Soviet "specialists" would have to leave China.[36]

COMMANDERS' CHANGE: FROM PENG TO LIN, FROM XIAO TO LI

The Sino-Soviet split caused confusion and division in the party and army. The political earthquake began in the PLA in 1959 when a rift between Mao Zedong and Peng Dehuai created political criticism against Mao's domestic policy.[37] Defense Minister Peng wrote a long letter to Mao that explored the problems during the Great Leap Forward. At the CCP Politburo and Central Committee meetings at Mt. Lushan from July 2 to August 16, Mao mobilized the conference attendees and initiated a major assault on Peng, accusing him of being the leader of a "right opportunist clique," a "military club," and of conducting "unprincipled factional activity" in the party and army.[38] Ellis Joffe describes it as "the most serious leadership struggle since the establishment of the Communist regime."[39] Fang Zhu points out that Mao feared that Peng would use "his military power to defy Mao's authority in the party leadership." In other words, Peng's criticism was perceived "as a sign of military disloyalty to Mao's personal authority." However, Zhu believes that Peng "never intended to threaten the party center or Mao Zedong. There was no sign of his plotting any military action against anyone."⁴⁰ After the Mt. Lushan conference, Peng Dehuai was dismissed from all his positions in the army and party and placed under house arrest.⁴¹ From September to February 1960, Mao launched a top-down purge to dismiss or jail 1,848 PLA generals and high-ranking officers believed to be Peng's followers or "rightists."⁴²

The extended political struggle and large-scale purge caused fear among the naval rank and file about their career, positions, and even their lives. Furthermore, Marshal Lin Biao emphasized the leftist policy after he took over the CMC and Defense Ministry in September 1959, which caused confusion between professionalism and the radical leftist line. The former seemed wrong and dangerous, while the latter was safe. Naval technology development, combat training, and educational programs slowed, when they did not completely stop, after the purge against Marshal Peng and the pro-Soviet naval officers.⁴³ Soon some serious accidents took place in 1959–60, including a submarine collision in the ESF.

The ESF *Submarine 418* accident took place on December 1, 1959, killing thirty-nine out of forty submariners. *Sub 418* was one of the two M-class, Russian-made small submarines (about 200 tons) received from the Soviet navy in June 1954. It served in World War II as Soviet navy *M-279*. From November 24 to December 1, 1959, the ESF conducted an offensive exercise for the "liberation of Taiwan" near Zhoushan Islands off the Zhejiang coast. ESF deployed the 18th Frigate Brigade and 22nd Submarine Squadron for the exercise, including the three frigates *Kunming*, *Chengdu*, and *Hengyang* and the two submarines *Sub 416* and *418*. During the exercise, however, the 18th Brigade commander and political commissar attended a commanders meeting to criticize Peng Dehuai and Huang Kecheng at the naval base and did not command this exercise. So did the captains and political commissars of the frigates *Chengdu* and *Hengyang* and the political commissar of *Sub 418*. The exercise was commanded by *Kunming*'s captain.

On November 28–29, *Sub 418* conducted antiship and sub-to-sub attack exercises. Because the submarine had aging equipment and an out-of-date weapon system and had been in disrepair for a long time, Captain Zhang Minglong, a graduate of the Leningrad Naval Academy, had a hard time operating it. During the attack drills, the torpedoes fired from *Sub 418* failed to hit any target. The sub also lost one of the training torpedoes, worth about 150,000 yuan RMB. At the end of the exercise, about 1:40 p.m. on December 1, *Kunming*'s captain ordered *Hengyang* frigate to secure an area for *418*'s float-up. Due to the lack of joint operations with the submarines, he mistakenly ordered the frigate to stop its engine while waiting for the submarine. *Sub 418* came at full speed fifty meters underwater, and its sonar man did not hear any sound, since *Hengyang* had shut down its engine. According to the regulations, surface ships should leave their engines running to allow submarines to detect those sounds and thereby ensure that it was safe to ascend. The frigate had no idea where *418* was, since the submarine did not have the radio capacity to send or receive any signal underwater. The exercise command ordered the frigate to throw three hand grenades into the water to signal the *418* to emerge. It was the only way for a surface ship to communicate with the submarine, given the lack of electronic communication.

After *Sub 418* received the signal from the three grenades, Captain Zhang Minglong ordered to "prepare to float" at thirty meters underwater. He had no idea that the frigate *Hengyang* was right above him, since the submarine did not have a radar system that could detect surface ships. Zhang also failed to make sure that all the watertight compartments were fully closed: it was standard procedure to shut down all the doors before a float-up, but in this case only two out of five watertight hatches were closed. *Sub 418* rose toward the frigate. Soon the sharp bow of *Hengyang* halved the floating *418* boat bridge and opened up the submarine at the middle, which had a diameter of 1.6 meters. Within three minutes, water filled three cabins and killed twenty-four officers and submariners, including Captain Zhang. The submarine sank to the bottom of the sea. Chief Engineer Wang Faquan and other sixteen men were still alive in the other two cabins, five in the first cabin and ten in the last (sixth) cabin, with their hatches closed. The *Hengyang*'s captain did not know about the accident until an hour later, when his sailors reported the fuel spills in the water from the submarine.

The bad news of *Sub 418*'s sinking shocked the PLA high command and the Chinese navy, which had only eight submarines at that time. Naval commander Xiao Jinguang ordered an emergency rescue mission, including the ESF, the PLAAF, and the Shanghai Municipal Party Committee. Tao

Yong, the ESF commander, led a couple dozen ships to the accident water to look for the sunken submarines on December 1. The Chinese navy, however, had only learned Russian standard procedures, which ignored rescue operation, counteraccident methods, and wrecked-ship rescues. The rescue team could not mark the exact wreck position for two days and failed to establish contact with the remaining submariners underwater during their rescue. At that time, the Chinese measurement technology was backward, and the sub's position was not determined until three days later.

At 5 a.m. on December 2, the ten submariners in the last cabin had little oxygen left and decided to leave the boat. Diving medicine has confirmed that if a person rises quickly from the bottom of the sea to the surface, the sudden change in pressure causes great damage to human organs, and the mortality rate is high. Unfortunately, the Chinese submariners did not have such training, and their broken depth gauge inaccurately indicated that they were only eight meters below the surface rather than forty. When Wang Faquan opened the torpedo tube and everyone climbed out, the huge water pressure quickly floated everyone to the surface, and most were sacrificed due to the different pressures the rapid rise caused inside and outside the body. Among the ten men who escaped, the only survivor was Chief Marine Sergeant Wang Faquan, who carried some food and tools with him and thus rose more slowly than the others. The five men in the first cabins died while they waited for rescue: they ran out of oxygen on December 2.

More trouble came to the PLAN when Second Lieutenant Liu Chengsi, a new pilot of the PLAN Sixth Air Force Division's Sixteenth Regiment, flew his MiG-15 jet fighter to Taiwan. Liu graduated from the Air Force Academy in July 1961 and joined the PLANAF later that year. According to the PLAN's investigation, Liu defected over a mere watch. At that time, watches were a luxury item; only a few people in the country had them. The PLAN actually issued a watch to each pilot, but Liu's superior, a battalion commander, lost his own watch and decided to keep Liu's watch for himself. Liu Chengsi was so disappointed about not receiving his watch that, in protest, he bought a desk clock and hung it around his neck whenever he flew his MiG-15. Because this was a safety violation, the battalion stopped his regular flight training. This punishment pushed Liu to his decision to fly to

Taiwan. In the early 1960s, Taiwan increased its political propaganda efforts and psychological warfare on the PLA by offering huge gold prizes for the Chinese pilots who flew to Taiwan. (A MiG-15 pilot would be awarded fifty kilos of gold and a MiG-19 pilot two hundred kilos.) Moreover, the PLAN investigation report concluded that Liu Chengsi listened to Taiwan's radio broadcast on a regular basis and that he wanted the money and a different lifestyle. To reach his goal, Liu feigned deep regret about his wrongdoing and promised, in his confessions and self-criticism reports, that it would not happen again. His battalion commanders accepted his apologies and resumed his flying schedule.

On March 3, 1962, Liu Chengsi took off from the PLAN Luqiao Air Force Base for a regular training flight. When his MiG-15 fighter (No. 1765) reached Taizhou, he turned off the radio, lowered his altitude, and changed direction, heading toward Taiwan. Thereafter the Chinese radar lost the fighter. The PLAN did not know Liu Chengsi had landed at the ROC Taoyuan Air Force Base in Taiwan until the Taiwanese radio broadcasted this breaking news. Liu became the first PLA pilot to defect. The Taiwanese government held a big welcome ceremony and awarded him fifty kilos of gold. Then Liu served in the Taiwanese air force as deputy director of a radio station and achieved the rank of air force colonel. When he married in 1964, the wedding ceremony was officiated by the Taiwanese air force commander.

After the PLAN investigation of Liu's defection, the PLANAF experienced top-down discipline. The commanders of the ESF Air Force, Sixth Division, 16th Regiment, and its battalion were dismissed from their positions, and some faced punishment and court martial. However, Defense Minister Lin Biao was not satisfied with the navy's investigation and sent his own investigation team, headed by Lieutenant General Li Zuopeng, chief of the DGS's Department of Training and one of Lin's longtime subordinates in the Fourth Field Army. Li had followed Lin since 1933, when he served as a Red Army officer. In World War II, Li Zuopeng was a planning officer in the 115th Division under the command of Lin Biao. From 1946 to 1949, Li became a division and army commander and then the chief of staff of the 15th Army Group in Lin Biao's Fourth Field Army. Li Zuopeng was ranked lieutenant general in 1955.

In April 1962, Li Zuopeng and his team completed the investigation and submitted their report to Lin Biao and the CMC, accusing the navy's leaders of failing "to raise high the flag of Mao Zedong's Thought."[44] The report describes the "rampant existence of a phenomenon of discord" through the CCP hierarchy in the navy. Li noticed that the factional struggles were so bad in many naval units that the CCP networks did not work as they were supposed to. Among the consequences of the neglect of the party's control was erosion of discipline. Captains of some warships held drinking parties on board while they were on duty. Some prominent officers were pursuing "corruptive ways of life." A reflection of the problems in the navy's leadership was a series of scandals ranging from sailors' suicides and revenge homicides to murders of civilian officials and attempts by officers to organize mass defections to Taiwan.[45]

After receiving Li Zuopeng's report, Marshal Lin Biao appointed Li as standing deputy commander of the Chinese navy; later, from June 1967 to 1972, he became the navy's political commissar. As one of the top military leaders, Li Zuopeng was appointed the PLA deputy chief of staff in October 1968.[46] After taking over the naval command, Li Zuopeng launched a political campaign in the navy to "help" Xiao Jinguang deal with some of the problems, since Xiao's health was declining. The PLA official biography of Fleet Admiral Xiao Jinguang points out that the naval commander lost his commanding authority over the PLAN to Li Zuopeng after the latter became naval deputy commander.[47] With Defense Minister Lin Biao's support, Li Zuopeng chaired a series of high-ranking naval commander conferences to identify the major issues, point out who was responsible, and undermine Xiao's leadership while establishing his own authority in the PLAN. The most important meeting was the extended conference of the PLAN Party Committee from December 5, 1962 to January 17, 1963. The entire naval senior officer corps above the divisional level attended the conference in Beijing and blamed the naval problems on Xiao Jinguang as the principal target of criticism. Because of the unbearable harsh criticism and great political pressure, Xiao had to excuse himself and be admitted to a hospital. Li Zuopeng criticized Xiao's "authoritarian leadership style of the household head" (*Jiazhang zuofeng*). Along with Xiao, Li also criticized Su Zhenhua, the navy's political commissar, for his "failure to adhere to principles" and his "insufficient attention to his duty in the PLAN's political tasks."[48]

After the December–January 1963 naval conference, Mao Zedong approved the navy's new leadership structure, comprising "three lines," suggested by the DGS. In this new leading group, Li Zuopeng and Zhang Xiuchun, director of the PLAN's Department of Political Tasks, were in the "First Line" and in charge of the navy's daily administration. Xiao Jinguang was in the "Third Line," without much of a leadership role in the navy. Sherman Xiaoguang Lai points out, "Xiao was not happy with this arrangement and wrote to Mao, but Mao ignored him. From this moment until his official retirement in 1980, Xiao was the PLAN's commander in name only."[49] From 1963 to 1966, 158 senior naval officers above division level were dismissed or jailed. Commodore Cui Xianghua and Chen Dapeng of China's NDU state in their work, "After Lin Biao sent Li Zuopeng to the navy, Li began to develop his own personal network and divided the naval officer corps."[50]

PLANAF AND AIR WAR

From 1952 to 1957, the Chinese air force followed the Soviet model for major institutional developments: building a centralized command system, multiple levels of administration, and various air defense forces, it acquired 4,400 aircraft and thus became the world's third largest air force. In 1952–54, the PLAAF transferred three divisions to the naval aviation to form the PLANAF.[51] In the late 1950s, however, the PLAAF and PLANAF departed from the Soviet air force's influence and control. Chinese officers agreed that since China's air force had grown, it should operate independently, with or without Russian advisement or assistance.

Then the Chinese air force and navy aviation began to emphasize having its own strength and depending less on the Soviet Union. By the late 1950s, the Chinese comanufactured Soviet-model aircraft in China. The Chinese also learned to reengineer, modify, and produce their own domestic variations beginning in the late 1950s.[52] In 1956, the PLAAF tested the Jian-5 fighter (J-5, a Chinese version of the Russian MiG-17 fighter), PT-5 (training aircraft), and Yun-5 (Y-5, transport aircraft).[53] Thereafter, the

Chinese air force received and equipped itself with Chinese-made aircraft. In 1959, China manufactured the Jian-6 (J-6), a modified MiG-19 fighter.[54] However, the Sino-Soviet split slowed down, though it did not completely stop, the modernization of Chinese aviation, since the Chinese lost their only source for technological improvement and development. Major General Xu Yan of China's NDU explains that China's aviation technology experienced "a period of lingering, groping, and winding," without major development, through the 1960s.[55] Chinese aviation slowly introduced domestically made aircraft for service. In the late 1960s, China manufactured the PT-6, Jian-7 (J-7), the Hong-5 (H-5, light bomber), and engines for the Wopen-5 (WP-5, turbojet).

When Jiang Jieshi called for the "return to the mainland" and launched military activities along the Chinese coast, the PLAAF and PLANAF were able to engage the GMD air force and achieve victories in the air wars. The PLAAF deputy commander, Lieutenant General Lin Hu, divided China's early air warfare between 1954 and 1965 into three phases: first, a transition from the Korean War to the Taiwan Strait in 1954–57; second, a territorial air defense along the southeastern coast in 1958–61; and third, an antiaerial reconnaissance war from 1962 to 1965 to stop U.S. and GMD spy planes over the mainland, especially over China's nuclear testing grounds in the northwestern regions.

During the first phase, from 1954 to 1957, the navy's aviation outperformed PLAAF divisions. After its founding in September 1952, the PLAN air divisions were stationed in China during the Korean War. The PLANAF boasted three fighter divisions by war's end and routinely engaged the GMD in the Taiwan Strait.[56] The PLANAF fared better against the Taiwanese air force in the same area. Although Taiwan had recently received American F-84 fighters, its air force had yet to deploy them. Moreover, Taiwanese pilots were no match for the PLANAF's Soviet-made MiG-15 jet fighters, manned by pilots with fresh experience from the Korean War. For example, the Sixth Regiment of the PLAN Second Air Force Division was a seasoned PLAN fighter regiment transferred to the PLAN in 1954 after the regiment returned from the Korean War.[57] In six air engagements, the PLANAF shot down eight Taiwanese fighters and bombers, while it lost only two.

On March 18, 1954, four Taiwanese F-47 planes raided Chinese naval vessels in the Sanmen Bay. The PLANAF scrambled two MiG-15 fighters from its Second Division. The MiG-15s possessed higher speed and more firepower than the F-47 fighters and shot down two during the engagement. On May 11, two MiG-15 fighters from naval aviation shot down another Taiwanese F-47 in the same area.[58] On the nineteenth, when four F-47 planes raided the Chinese naval base, four MiG-15s sortied off and contested them. During the battle, the naval pilots shot down three Taiwanese fighters. From April 1955 to April 1956, the newly established PLAN Fourth Division launched 404 sorties, shooting down five Taiwanese planes and damaging four in 124 engagements.[59]

In fighting the American-equipped and -trained Taiwanese, Chinese naval pilots became familiarized with American aviation technology and GMD air war tactics. By 1956, the PLANAF had six fighter-bomber divisions. Nevertheless, naval aviation faced a significant learning curve during this period. In 1953, a year after its founding, the PLANAF had forty-five training accidents, losing thirteen planes and ten pilots. In the first half of 1955, the navy had forty-two aviation accidents, losing nine planes and eight pilots. By 1957, the PLANAF had learned a hard lesson, improved its training, and reduced the number of accidents to thirty and the losses to three planes and four pilots.

The second phase of China's air war manifested in a "territorial air defense" from 1958 to 1961. During this period, the Chinese air force was newly equipped with Russian technology and gained coastal air defense capabilities. In the 1958 Taiwan Strait Crisis, the air war intensified as the PLAAF reinforced the Fujian front with seventeen MiG regiments comprising 520 fighters.

However, in September, the momentum in the air war shifted in favor of Taiwan after the United States secretly armed the F-86s with newly designed Sidewinder (AIM-9A) air-to-air missiles. The Sidewinder's first casualty occurred on September 24 after a Taiwanese fighter destroyed one MiG-17 from the 16th Air Division. That morning, the division command received a radar report that twelve F-86s had taken off from the Taoyuan airport. Divisional command launched sixteen MiG fighters to intercept the enemy planes. When the Chinese fighters met the F-86s, they engaged in a dogfight. One of the Chinese pilots, Wang Zizhong, was left behind by his comrades. A Taiwanese fighter fired a Sidewinder missile on Wang and shot down his MiG. On October 10, a Sidewinder claimed another MiG-17 after eight PLAAF planes attacked six F-86s.[60] Thereafter, the PLAAF avoided engagements with the Sidewinder-equipped fighters and awaited technological solutions from the Soviets, who were working on copying a captured missile by a PLAAF pilot. During the 1958 Taiwan Strait Crisis, a Taiwanese pilot fired an AIM-9B and hit a MiG-17, but it failed to explode. The MiG pilot, with undetonated ordnance lodged in his frame, carefully returned to base. Russian missile engineers quickly followed the design and developed their own air-to-air missile, the Vympel K-13, which entered service in 1960. After the shelling of Jinmen started, Khrushchev wrote twice to Mao in October, offering Russian C-75 bombers with SAMs and Soviet advisers. In his replies, Mao only accepted Russian bombers and SAMs; he declined the offer of Soviet advisers. Neither Russian aid nor new technology ever arrived.[61]

The third phase of Chinese air warfare was an antiaerial reconnaissance war from 1962 to 1965. The PLAAF focused its defense efforts on stopping Taiwan/U.S. strategic and tactical reconnaissance aircraft over the mainland by improving radar systems and individual combat training. After the Korean War, the USAF strengthened its collaboration with Jiang Jieshi in Taiwan by providing new planes, advisers, and intelligence personnel. The U.S. Fourth Air Force directed and instigated the GMD's frequent incursions into the Chinese mainland, going deep inland to conduct strategic reconnaissance. The Taiwanese air force was equipped with advanced American-made P2V, RB-57A, RB-57D, RF-101A, and U-2 spy planes.[62] Air combats became the primary implementation of war as Taiwan's reconnaissance planes continuously penetrated mainland China's airspace and heightened cross-strait tensions. The PLAAF trained its MiG pilots in night missions, low- and ultralow-altitude operations, and close combat.

The Taiwanese air force equipped a squadron (the 34th Squadron) with P2V spy planes. It was also known as the Black Bat Squadron, since their fuselage and aircraft body were painted black for low-altitude night reconnaissance. During the early 1960s, the MiG-17 was the PLAAF's primary implement for night air defense. However, the Taiwanese P2V proved difficult for the high-speed, high-altitude MiG-17 to track and eliminate. In 1961 alone, the P2V flew over the mainland more than ten times. Although the PLAAF sortied their MiGs several hundred times, they failed to intercept and destroy any P2Vs. The PLAAF continued researching P2V flying patterns and upgraded its MiG-17's radar and communication. Charged with stopping GMD reconnaissance, Chinese MiG pilots observed their opponents closely while using precise tactics. After more than a year of difficult training and observation, they were finally ready to take down a "Black Bat." Late at night on June 19, 1963, a Taiwanese P2V plane entered China conducting photographic reconnaissance and reached Nanchang airport, about three hundred miles inland. PLAAF pilot Wang Wanli received orders and took off at 12:18 a.m. on June 20th. When he approached the P2V, the spy plane activated its signal-jamming system and took maneuvering measures. Wang opened fire but missed as the P2V's signal suddenly disappeared from his radar. However, with ground radar guidance, Wang reacquired his target and reduced his speed to minimum, nearly stalling. Wang quickly closed within three hundred feet, nearly colliding with his foe, and pressed the fire button for about two seconds. The P2V went up in flames, plunged down through the sky, and crashed into the ground.

On June 11, 1964, NSF Air Force received the urgent information that a Taiwanese P2V was flying along the Shandong coast in the evening. The PLAN Fourth Air Force Division scrambled two J-6 fighters around 11:50 p.m. to intercept the spy plane at Laiyang, Shandong. Soon the PLANAF pilots Chen Genfa and Shi Zhenshan discovered the P2V and opened fire. The GMD plane crashed at fifteen miles north of Laiyang, killing all thirteen crew members on board.[63] Five days later, Zhou Enlai, Nie Rongzhen, and Luo Ruiqing met Chen, Shi, and PLANAF officers in Beijing, congratulating them on their successful attack.[64] From that point on, the "Black Bat's" stealth operations into the mainland stopped.

Beginning in 1961, Taiwan sent RF-101A supersonic spy planes to China's southeastern coastal areas for high-speed low- and ultralow-altitude reconnaissance missions. Within a year, the RF-101A flew over China more than nine times, and Chinese fighter pilots failed to intercept them due to late radar confirmation and delayed takeoffs. It proved difficult for the subsonic MiG-17 to pursue the supersonic RF-101A. Not until June 1964 did the PLANAF deploy the J-6, a domestic supersonic fighter, which turned the tide of battle along the southeastern coast. Mao Zedong instructed Zhou Enlai, CMC vice chairman, to send the J-6 fighter air force regiments to the front and stop Taiwan's RF-101A spying activities over the mainland. After Zhou and the PLA DGS passed Mao's order on to the navy, PLAN commander Xiao Jinguang and PLANAF commander Liu Daosheng decided to transfer the Tenth Regiment of the PLAN Fourth Air Force Division from Qingdao to the Luqiao Air Force Base in Zhejiang. On December 2, 1964, Division Commander Zhou Kelin led the Tenth PLANAF Regiment under Deputy Commander Wang Honglin to Zhejiang.

Next day, the Luqiao Air Force Base sent an alarm that one RF-101A had taken off from Taipei. Wang Honglin and Gao Shaoying scrambled two J-6 fighters immediately but failed to find the spy plane due to the delayed radar signals. At 2:18 p.m. on December 18, two RF-101A aircraft flew into the mainland. Wu Changwu, commander of the Luqian Air Force Base, ordered two J-5 fighters to take off as a decoy as two supersonic J-6s took off at 2:42 p.m. and flew to an altitude of 12,000 feet, hid, and waited. Soon, one RF-101A approached at an altitude of 900 feet, but Chinese ground guiding radar lost it because of an operator error. J-6 pilot Wang Hongxi quickly decided to use a speculative guidance method and steered his fighter toward the enemy's possible route. Radar recaptured the target at 3:03 p.m. and discovered the RF-101A ascending rapidly along the presumed route. Wang Hongxi quickly tailed the spy plane, aligned itself, and commenced firing on the target at 3:16 p.m. The RF-101A was shot down, and the Taiwanese pilot, Major Xie Xiangpeng, was captured after parachuting.[65]

On the following day, December 19, Zhou Enlai and Luo Ruiqing met Zhou Kelin, Wang Hongxi, and other eight naval aviation officers in Beijing. On December 31, Mao Zedong met them at the Great Hall of the People. Mao asked Wang Hongxi about the characters in his name. Wang described the two characters as meaning "big happiness." Mao Zedong beamed and said, "You have a good name. [Your] shooting down the [spy] plane makes us happy!"[66] Three months later, the PLANAF shot down another RF-101A along the southeastern coast.[67]

To collect information on China's nuclear weapon testing and long-range missile development, the United States started to send unmanned aerial vehicles (UAVs) into Chinese airspace for reconnaissance in 1964, more than twenty times that year. The PLANAF faced new challenges, since the new MiG-19 fighters divisions had received a static ceiling of 52,800 feet and thus could barely reach the U.S. AQM-34A "Ryan Firebee" UAV, which had a powerful turbojet engine for high-altitude reconnaissance, up to 55,800 feet. The PLAN Fourth Air Force Division established a tasking team at Hainan with its best pilots to prepare the air battle against UAVs. On March 24, 1965, a UAV was discovered over Haikou, capital city of Hainan, flying at 52,000 feet. The Fourth Division's Tenth Regiment quickly departed at 1:27 p.m. to meet the enemy. Pilot Wang Xiangyi, in his MiG-19 fighter, ascended to 50,000 feet and found the unmanned plane. He accelerated and continued to ascend to 52,000 feet, firing three times at 411 meters. He eventually shot the plane down. It was the PLANAF's first record of a fighter dispatching an enemy plane in the stratosphere. However, it was not a "perfect air battle." First, PLANAF commander Liu Daosheng had instructed his pilots to down U.S. spy planes in China's territories. However, the UAV Wang shot down fell into international waters. It did not fit the CCP propaganda machine, since the United States could charge that China was violating aviation conventions to attack U.S. aircraft in the international airspace. Second, Wang Xiangyi ran out of fuel on his way back. He was lucky, as there was a nearby airport for his MiG-19 to land. Otherwise, it could have been a disaster. Nevertheless, Wang's success convinced PLANAF pilots that they could shoot down U.S. unmanned, high-altitude spy planes.

At 2:03 p.m. on March 31, the Fourth Command's radar signaled a UAV flying at 52,000 feet over Hainan Island. Its Tenth Regiment scrambled Wang Xiangyi and Shu Jicheng to intercept the U.S. spy plane. Shu Jicheng discovered the enemy plane, chased it as close as 110 meters, and opened fire. He downed the UAV, which crashed at Sanya, Hainan. On April 3, China's Ministry of Defense granted Shu Jicheng the status of "air combat hero." Then Mao, Zhou, Zhu De, and other Chinese leaders met Shu and officers from the PLANAF Tenth Regiment in Beijing.

On August 21, a U.S. transit plane carrying two UAVs flew north along the Vietnamese coast. At 12:51 p.m., it released one UAV over Da Nang; at 1:11 p.m., the other was released over the Gulf of Tonkin. Soon, the first UAV made a turn and flew toward Hainan. The Tenth Regiment sent Shu Jicheng to find the enemy plane, but he was not able to find the UAV. Shu pulled his MiG-19 up to 52,000 feet and discovered the spy plane. After his attack, the UAV was in flames. On December 29, the Defense Ministry celebrated the PLANAF's air war victory and named the Tenth Regiment the Naval Air Great Eagle Regiment.

Three months later, the PLAAF shot down another UAV. Over the next few years, Chinese pilots used a variety of aircraft and tactics to shoot down or damage more U.S.-made UAVs. Between 1954 and 1969, the PLAAF built an effective air defense, shooting down 81 enemy planes and damaging 177. Among the planes shot down were 32 USAF warplanes, including 20 unmanned high-altitude reconnaissance aircraft.[68]

However, the Chinese lost their only source for technological improvement and development of an air-to-air missile after the 1960 Sino-Soviet split. On July 5, 1969, they produced the Jian-8 (J-8), the first entirely Chinese-made high-altitude, high-speed fighter. Lu Xiaoping, a professor at PLAAF Command College, believes it "show[ed] that China was capable of domestic development of a new type of fighters, and that the PLA Air Force equipment had entered a new era."[69] By the mid-1970s, most PLAAF and PLANAF combat planes were made in China. Meanwhile, air defense troops were equipped with domestically produced SAMs.

COMBAT EXPERIENCE IN 1965

When the Taiwanese navy increased its harassment and sabotage activities against China's offshore islands and coastal areas in 1962, the PLA high command decided to stop Taiwan's aggressive naval operations by looking for opportunities to fight back. On May 31, Chief of the PLA General Staff Luo Ruiqing came to Shanghai and chaired a planning conference at the ESF HQ. Then Admiral Zhang Xuesi, chief of staff of the navy, visited the ESF and discussed the operational details with the naval officers who would be dealing with Taiwan's small-scale operations. From 1962 to 1966, the PLAN sank thirty-five Taiwanese boats and captured twenty-six to stop Taiwan's harassment and sabotages.[70] In 1965, the Chinese navy engaged two large-scale naval battles, the Battles of August Sixth and East Chongwu. The PLAN claimed all the victories over the Taiwanese navy through centralized chain of command, land-sea communication, battle coordination, and attacking tactics. The new PLAN tactics of using small boats to attack large warships, or the torpedo attack covered by frigate gun powers, seemed to work well in the naval engagements.

After China experienced nationwide famine and economic difficulties in 1960–62, the Taiwanese Defense Ministry took the opportunity to make a new antimainland offensive plan in 1963; its official name was Guoguang jihua (National Light Plan). In 1964, the Taiwanese navy command established an operation division called Guoming zuoyeshi (Brightness Operational Office) to coordinate naval operations with the Guoguang jihua, including naval war planning, attack preparation, and landing training.[71] On July 14, 1965, Jiang Jieshi visited the navy HQ and instructed his admirals "to reach the mainland's coastline and probe the PLA's responses."[72] Following Jiang's order, the ROC navy planned a joint operation on July 30, Haixiao yihao zuozhan (Operation Tsunami No. 1), in which the army would land a special force unit at the PLA-held Dongshan Island off the Fujian coast, destroying the radar station and capturing PLA prisoners there.

After the plan was approved by the Defense Ministry, the ROC navy assigned Rear Admiral Hu Jiaheng, commander of the Taiwanese navy's Second Fleet, to command two Taiwanese submarine hunters, *Jianmen* (PCE 45) and *Zhangjiang* (PC 118), to carry out the attack plan on August 6. *Jianmen* was a large U.S. submarine hunter (MSF 387) that had been transferred to the Taiwanese navy in April 1965. As Taiwanese 045, it had a standard displacement of 595 tons, a speed of 18 nautical miles per hour, one 76.2-mm gun, four 40-mm guns, and four 20-mm guns under Commodore Wang Yunshan. *Zhangjiang*, a smaller U.S. sub chaser (PC 1232), transferred to Taiwan in 1954 as Taiwanese 118, displacing 298 tons and with one 76.2-mm gun and one 40-mm gun, and five 20-mm guns under Lieutenant Commander Li Zhuan. Rear Admiral Hu Jiaheng led his fleet and special force unit, departing from the Zuoying harbor around 5 a.m. on August 5.[73] After setting sail, the two warships shut down their onboard communication to avoid PLA radar detection.

The PLAN received intelligence in Beijing that two Taiwanese warships, *Jianmen* and *Zhangjiang*, had left Zuoying Naval Base for China's southern coast. The PLAN HQ informed the SSF Command in Guangzhou at 5:45 p.m. Around the same time, two PLAN front radar stations also spotted the Taiwanese warships about eighty-four nautical miles from Zuoying and thirty nautical miles from the Chinese coast. At his HQ in Guangzhou, SSF commander Wu Ruilin immediately decided to take the battle opportunity. Having joined the Red Army in 1932, Wu Ruilin became a commander and political commissar of battalion, regiment, and division in the War of Resistance of Japan. In 1948–53, he was commander of the PLA and CPVF 42nd Army. After his return from the Korean War, Wu was commander of the Hainan Military Region in 1954 and was ranked lieutenant general in 1955. Wu became SSF commander in 1959 and PLAN deputy commander in 1968.[74]

At 7 p.m. on August 5, 1965, Lieutenant General Wu Ruilin made a plan by using both PC and PT boats to attack the two large enemy warships. His PC boats included a newly commissioned *Shanghai*-class PC of seventy-five tons. It had two cannons (one 75-mm, one 37-mm), two 25-mm double-barrel guns, and a top speed of twenty-seven knots. His battle tactics were to employ the PC boats to provide gunfire to silence the enemy guns and cover the PTs as they engaged in high-speed charging and torpedo launchings to sink the Taiwanese ships.

While reporting his attack plan to PLAN HQ and Guangzhou Military Region Command, Wu Ruilin established a "task squadron," including five PC boats from the 41st PC Brigade at the Shantou Marine Security District and twelve PT boats from the 11th Torpedo Brigade at the Haimen naval base. To guarantee a successful interception of the Taiwanese warships, Wu divided his task squadron into an attack group and a reinforcement.[75] The attack group included four PC boats under the command of Kong Zhaonian and Wang Jin. Cui Yudong, commander of the 11th Torpedo Brigade, on *PT-131*, led the attacking torpedo boats. The reinforcement group included one PC and six PT boats to follow the attack group and stand by. Political

Commissar Liu Weihuan and Deputy Commander Zhang Shouying from the 11th Brigade led the standby group at *PT-119*. Lieutenant General Wu Ruilin asked the Jingangshan and Zhoutian Radar Stations to make sure these were not American warships and report the enemy ships' movements every ten minutes.[76] Jingangshan Station, under the ESF Command, is located at the top of a hill across the water from Jinmen Island. Wu also called Kong Zhaonian from Guangzhou and instructed him to concentrate his firepower and try to destroy one enemy ship at the time.[77]

It was the first time that Kong Zhaonian, deputy commander of the Shantou Marine Security District, would be engaging with large Taiwanese warships, even though he had commanded many naval battles against small Taiwanese and pirate gunboats along Guangdong's coast. Kong joined the anti-Japanese guerrilla troop in 1940 and the CCP in 1942. He served as squad and platoon leader in 1942-45. He became a PLA captain, battalion commander, and regiment chief staff in 1946-49. After transferring from the army to the navy in 1951, Kong Zhaonian served as frigate chief staff and squadron commander near Guangzhou. He studied naval warfare at PLAN Naval War College from 1958 to 1961. After his graduation, Kong became the PLAN 73rd Submarine Hunter Squadron commander in 1961 and deputy commander of the PLAN Shantou Marine Security District in 1964.[78]

At 9:24 p.m., Kong Zhaonian led the first group of four PC boats departing from Shantou for the interception site east of Xiongdi Island, about eighteen miles southeast from the Dongshan Islands. Kong set up his command on *PC-598*. At 11:43 p.m., the first group of six PT boats left Haimen to meet the PC group at the interception site. Since the Chinese PC and PT boats had only lower-power radar, they depended on land-based high-power radar at the Jingangshan Radar Station to provide enemy positions and battle directions to intercept Taiwanese warships *Jianmen* and *Zhangjiang*.[79] Following Operation Tsunami No. 1, at 11 p.m. Rear Admiral Hu Jiaheng of Taiwan landed the special force unit at Dongshan Island. Hu did not have any major concerns, since the PLAN did not have any large warships like frigates or destroyers along the Fujian and Guangdong coast.[80]

After confirming the enemy ships' movement, the PLA General Staff approved the SSF plan at 11:10 p.m. with Zhou Enlai's instructions. Admiral

Zhang Xuesi, PLAN chief of staff, and General Tao Hanzhang, chief of staff of the Guangzhou Military Region, called Wu Ruilin and passed on Zhou's detailed instructions: to make sure they were Taiwanese ships (not American warships); to let the enemy ships in (the closer, the better); to attack within thirty nautical miles of the shore; to concentrate firepower; to attack in the night, disengaging before dawn; and not to mistakenly fire on our own or any foreign ships.[81] However, the SSF HQ miscalculated the direction and speed of the two enemy warships. When Kong Zhaonian and the first group of the Chinese squadron reached the interception site at twelve thirty-one the next morning, *Jianmen* and *Zhangjiang* had already passed the point and were about fourteen nautical miles away. The planned interception immediately turned into a chase. About 1:42 a.m. on August 6, Kong Zhaonian and his squadron spotted the two enemy warships east of the Xiongdi (Brothers) Islands.[82]

At 1:40 a.m., at his flagship bridge, Rear Admiral Hu Jiaheng received his radar report that the PLAN PC formation was approaching *Jianmen*. At 1:58 a.m., he ordered his 76.2-mm guns to fire on the Chinese gunboats from six nautical miles with illuminating projectiles at them for fire corrections. Then all the guns on the submarine hunters, including 40-mm and 20-mm guns, fired on the Chinese at four nautical miles. It was still beyond Chinese PC firing range, since each Chinese PC boat had only two 37-mm double-barrel and two 25-mm double-barrel guns. Kong Zhaonian ordered his group to make close contact with *Jianmen* and *Zhangjiang* at high speed without firing. Then *Jianmen* turned to the east and fled at high speed from the Chinese PCs.[83]

After *Jianmen* disappeared in the dark, Kong ordered his four gunboats to advance to about three cable lengths from *Zhangjiang* and then open fire from five hundred to one hundred meters at 2:41 a.m. Kong instructed his gunners to concentrate their fire on *Zhangjiang*'s guns, bridge, and crew members on deck. *Zhangjiang* captain Li Zhuan made a sharp right turn and let the Chinese PCs pass. He did not expect the Chinese gunboats to come back for their second attack, killing many of his crew members and causing a fire on the deck. During the third attack around 2:54 a.m., however, *PC-601* was hit by several shells, losing its captain and many crew members. *PC-611* was also badly damaged after being struck by seventeen shells and lost three out of the four engines. Engineer Mai Xiande was wounded severely on the head, but he was determined to operate in the forward and aft engine room from which *PC-611* continued to fire on *Zhangjiang*.[84] The guns fitted on the PCs were of small caliber, but their firing rate was very high.

Meanwhile, Kong Zhaonian ordered a torpedo attack. However, the six torpedo boats in the first group missed their attack opportunities due to the lack of communication and radar guidance: they went the wrong direction. When they found a "target" in the distance, five PT boats fired ten torpedoes on it. Nothing happened. When the PT commander led his speedboats to approach the target, they discovered that it was a large rock. Their efforts were in vain. Five out of six PT boats returned to the base, since they had run out of torpedoes.[85]

After his PT boats failed, Kong ordered his PCs' fourth attack, instructing to fire armor-piercing shells below the waterline of *Zhangjiang*. After an hour's fierce fighting, Captain Li Zhuan changed his tactics from avoiding the Chinese fire to facing the PC boats. *Zhangjiang* turned around and headed toward the PCs to break the Chinese attack formation. It worked for a while: the PC boats ran different directions and fired on their own. Kong, however, regrouped his PCs and carried on with his fifth attack. Eventually the Taiwanese submarine hunter caught fire after the repeated attacks, and its ammunition exploded during the sixth PC attack. After a ninety-minute fight, *Zhangjiang* sank around 3:33 a.m. at twenty-five nautical miles southeast of Dongshan Island. Captain Li Zhuan and most of his crew were lost in the sea.[86]

When *Zhangjiang* sank, *Jianmen* lingered about five miles from the battle site. Rear Admiral Hu Jiaheng waited for the Taiwanese air support he had requested. *Jianmen* captain Wang Yunshan was not sure about his ship's safety and suggested that they immediately return to Taiwan. But Hu refused, instead wanting Taiwanese bombers to retaliate by attacking the Chinese squadron at dawn and turning the battle situation around for a Taiwanese victory.[87] (The Taiwanese air force did not have much experience with night bombing at sea.)

While *Jianmen* waited, Kong Zhaonian received Wu Ruilin's order to continue the attack on *Jianmen*.[88] The PLA Jingangshan Radar Station provided

Kong with *Jianmen*'s position, about six miles from Kong's. He ordered three PC boats and five PT boats to get into a new attack formation and pursue *Jianmen* before the Taiwanese air force could reach his attacking point. At 4:40 a.m., *Jianmen* captain Wang Yunshan discovered the PC boats about three miles away and ordered his artillery to fire on the fast-approaching gunboats. Kong ordered his PCs not to fire while keeping up a high-speed charge. At 5:10 a.m., when the PCs had closed in to about seven cable lengths, Kong's men opened fire on *Jianmen*. During the second Chinese attack on *Jianmen*'s deck, Rear Admiral Hu Jiaheng was killed at the bridge. Meanwhile, the torpedo boats led by *PT-119* reached their firing position about two cable lengths from *Jianmen*. About 5:19 a.m., Deputy Commander Zhang Shouying on *PT-119* ordered five speedboats to fire. Three of the ten torpedoes hit the target. Three minutes later, *Jianmen* began to sink at thirty-eight nautical miles southeast of Dongshan. In the battle, Rear Admiral Hu Jiaheng of Taiwan was killed with 170 sailors and soldiers. Captain Wang Yunshan and thirty-three sailors were captured. When Kong Zhaonian and his men picked up surviving Taiwanese sailors, four Taiwanese bombers came to the area, which was a salvage spot. Soon eight PLAN fighters appeared, and the Taiwanese planes turned around. The August 6 naval battle was a victory for the PLAN, which had sunk two Taiwanese warships with only four PLAN officers and sailors killed, twenty-eight wounded, and two PC and two PT boats damaged.[89]

On August 9, the PLAN sent in the battle report to the high command cosigned by Li Zuopeng, PLAN deputy commander; Wu Ruilin, SSF commander; and Fang Zhengping, SSF political commissar. Their report described the August 6 battle as "the largest victory of naval engagements in recent years. . . . The engaged [PLAN] units took full advantage of human factors by their brave and tenacious fight, full use of our traditional tactics of close and night combats, and concentration of our force against isolated enemy. This battle victory has proved not only that small boats can attack large warships, but also that they can sink enemy warships."[90] On August 15, Mao Zedong read and approved their report.

Two days later, Mao, Zhou, Liu, and Deng met Kong Zhaonian and officer and sailor representatives from the August 6 naval battle in Beijing.

Then Premier Zhou and Marshal He Long attended the battle presentation. Zhou Enlai concluded with a traditional PLA perspective, pointing out that "the main reasons for the naval victory of using small boats to sink large warships were close combat, night attack, and concentration of firepower. The naval war should fight [like a ground war] in close combat, night attack, and concentration of forces, separating the enemy, attacking the weak and small ship first, and then isolating and destroying the bigger and stronger ship."[91] China's Defense Ministry granted the title of "Battle Hero" to engineer Mai Xiande. It was the first time in PLA history that a technician was honored as a battle hero, an indication that the PLAN had shifted its emphasis to machine and technology in battle rather than individual men. The navy titled the *PC-611* the "Heroic Ship at Sea" and the *TP-119* the "Heroic Speedboat." Gao Xiaoxing concluded, "Among all these [naval battles], the August Sixth Sea Battle was the largest battle, and it was also the biggest PLAN victory."[92]

The Taiwanese military leaders blamed their naval failure on their underestimation of the PLAN's combat effectiveness, lack of cooperation between the navy and air force, poor training in fighting against small speedboats, poor communication and information, and outdated equipment (e.g., slow gunfire and poor personnel protection on deck). President Jiang Jieshi believed that his navy ignored the enemy, so their warships were not prepared for a night attack. Moreover, Jiang also blamed his air force for being unable to provide effective air protection before the warships were destroyed. Disappointed by the lost naval battle, Jiang Jieshi removed Admiral Liu Guangkai from his post as commander of the Taiwanese navy on August 11. Although the American naval advisers tried to convince Jiang to give Liu a second chance, Jiang Jieshi stuck with his decision.[93] After his dismissal, Admiral Liu Guangkai pointed out the problems in naval planning, arguing that Operation Tsunami No. 1 was designed for such a battle disaster.[94] Before August 6, his admirals believed that the PLAN could attack only their small gunboats at sea and that the Chinese would avoid their large warships, since the PLAN did not have warships. In fact, the PLAN squadron was close to the coast and had accurate information and land-based radar support and guidance. Major General Xu Zuyuan, then deputy chief of the Operation Department, ROC Defense Ministry, emphasized that the PLAN had better information and communication than the Taiwanese navy did.⁹⁵ When *Jianmen* and *Zhangjiang* were out of Taiwan's radar range, they were on their own with respect to the PLAN movements and coastal situation. The Taiwanese warships did not know the Chinese were coming until it was too late. Moreover, the Taiwanese navy failed to share the information about its operation with the air force. After Hu Jiaheng called in, it took more than two hours for Taiwanese bombers to get ready and take off to support the two warships. It was too late.⁹⁶

The PLAN also assessed its naval battle performance on August 6. The Chinese admirals realized that the new *Shanghai*-class PC boats had made a big difference in combat because they had better speed and stronger firepower than the 1955 *Guangzhou*-class PC craft. The Chinese navy began to emphasize the importance of technology development and for the first time to honor a naval engineer as the "Combat Hero." The PLAN continued to employ their successful tactics of using small speedboats to attack large warships. It worked again in the next naval engagement, the Battle of East Chongwu (also known as the Battle of Wuqiu [Wuchiu] in Taiwan), on November 13–14, 1965.

On November 13, the PLAN high command received information that two Taiwanese warships, *Yongtai* and *Yongchang*, had departed Magong Island for the Chongwu coast at 1:20 p.m. The PLA front radar station also reported the Taiwanese ships' location and speed when they got within range. Zhou Enlai and Marshal He Long met at the PLA General Staff Operational Room and decided to attack the Taiwanese ships. Zhou reiterated to the DGS that the key principles were concentrating force and firepower on one ship first; attacking at close range at night; avoiding mistakenly firing on our own; and disengaging before dawn.⁹⁷ The DGS passed Zhou's instructions on to the PLAN HQ and Fuzhou Military Region Command. The PLAN issued the order to Zhou Renjie, ESF deputy commander, who was charged with the operation that afternoon.

After receiving the order, ESF Command planned to intercept the Taiwanese warships at eight nautical miles south of Wuqiu Island around 11 p.m. They would use the same tactics that had given them victory in the previous battle. While the command submitted its attack plan to DGS in Beijing, ESF in Shanghai, and Fuzhou Military Region Command, Zhou Renjie dispatched a squadron with six PC boats and six PT boats under the command of Wei Hengwu, deputy commander of Haitan Marine Security District, to the interception area. Meanwhile, the navy's Fujian Command deployed four PCs to fifteen nautical miles east of Chongwu to guard the task squadron and serve as a rescue team, while sending three PCs to the waters around Dongyin, where the Taiwanese navy had several warships in the harbor.[98] Soon the Fuzhou Military Region Command received approval of its attack plan from the high command, along with Premier Zhou Enlai's instructions.

At the assembly area, Commander Wei Hengwu held a captain meeting, passing on the high command's instruction, organizing three attack formations, and giving assignments to each captain. He ordered *PC-573*, *574*, *576*, and *579*—the first attack group, under his command—to fire on the first Taiwanese warship to slow it down. Meanwhile, *PC-588* and *589*—the second group, under the command of Ma Gan—would attack the second enemy ship. After the GMD ships stopped or slowed down, the third attack group, the six torpedo boats commanded by Zhang Yimin, would launch their attack to sink the Taiwanese warships. Taiwan's *Yongtai* and *Yongchang* were two submarine hunters with displacement of six hundred tons and strong firepower.[99]

At 10:16 p.m., Wei Hengwu's squadron embarked to locate their Taiwanese targets. Wei commanded from a larger, newly remodeled *PC-588*, known as the Tiger Boat, that displaced 125 tons. Around 11:14 p.m., his radar discovered the two enemy warships about 10.5 nautical miles away, with a speed of twelve knots. Wei ordered his gunboats to speed up toward the enemy ships, which did not know the approaching PLAN boats. About thirteen minutes later, Wei's formation met the Taiwanese warships. He ordered his PC boats to run through between the two ships and separate them. At 11:33 p.m., when *PC-588* reached the first ship, *Yongchang*, about five cable lengths from its right, Wei Hengwu opened fire. Four PCs concentrated their guns on *Yongchang*'s deck and rapidly fired two thousand shells within several minutes.[100] Then Wei ordered the torpedo attack. Zhang Yimin led the first group of PT boats into the attack on *Yongchang*. However, *PT-131* missed the target after it fired all two torpedoes at 11:52 p.m. *PT-152* missed *Yongchang* again at 12:02 a.m. due to the long distance of twelve nautical miles. Meanwhile, *Yongtai* fired on Chinese PC boats from behind with its bigger guns, hitting Wei's flagship *PC-588* in two minutes and killing three officers. Wei was badly wounded.[101]

After his first torpedo attack failed to hit *Yongchang*, Zhang Yimin split the second PT group into two formations for frontal and flanking attacks. Around 12:30 a.m., *PT-145* reached within four cable lengths of *Yongchang* and fired two torpedoes within three hundred meters. One of them hit *Yongchang* and it began to sink. At 1:06 a.m., *Yongchang* (PG-61) sank about fifteen nautical miles south of Wuqiu. Soon after the battle, two U.S. destroyers from the Seventh Fleet (or Task Force 72), USS *O'Brien* (DD 725) and USS *Leonard F. Mason* (DD 852), arrived and rescued the captain and fifteen officers and sailors from the water.[102] On November 26, Zhou Enlai and Luo Ruiqing met the representatives from the task squadron in Shanghai and congratulated their victory in the naval battle of East Chongwu.[103]

Successful combat experience indicated the improvement of naval chain of command, land-sea communication, battle coordination, and offensive tactics. The tactics for small patrol boats and speedboats to attack large enemy warships included surprise ambushes and close PC fire to cover torpedo attacks. From 1958 to 1965, the Chinese navy could maintain its initiative in the Taiwan Strait, develop its combat tactics both in the air and at sea, and take advantage of offshore areas for battle opportunities. Naval Command College's Gao Xiaoxing and other PLAN historians argue, "Further, the three naval defeats came as severe blows to the KMT Navy in Taiwan, altering the military balance across the Taiwan Strait. With the defeats, the dominance of the KMT Navy over the Taiwan Strait was a thing of the past."[104] Taiwanese strategist Zhong Jian agrees with the Chinese naval historians and concludes, "After three consecutive months when our navy lost three warships to the Communist navy's ambushes, President Jiang's dream of recovering the mainland and rebuilding the nation completely diminished."[105]

CHAPTER 4

The **Vietnam War** and **South China Sea**

The Chinese navy experienced ups and downs from 1966 to 1976 during the Great Proletarian Cultural Revolution, a nationwide political struggle with massive purges. To fight his political rivals, Mao Zedong launched the Cultural Revolution on May 16, 1966, by issuing a Party Center circular to purge the "bourgeois representatives who wormed their way into the party, government, and army."[1] Targeting Chinese president Liu Shaoqi and CCP secretary general Deng Xiaoping, Mao used student organizations like the Red Guards to "bomb the bourgeois headquarters." The Politburo formed the Central Committee's Cultural Revolution Leading Group (CRLG), including Defense Minister Lin Biao and Jiang Qing, Mao's wife, and handed over the party's authority to the CRLG from 1966 to 1976. In June, all K–12 schools, universities, and colleges dismissed their classes and encouraged tens of millions of students to join the Red Guards and participated in the new revolution. In the summer, the Red Guards took over their schools, patrolled neighborhood streets, and controlled local business, transportation, and media by attacking officials, administrators, and local party leaders. Their radical actions quickly became a frenzy, with a wild spree of home searches, detainment of residents, property confiscation, tortures, and even murder.

Marshal Lin Biao was elected the CCP vice chairman at a plenary session of the party's Eighth National Congress on August 12, 1966, second only to Mao. Later that month, Lin Biao called the PLA to participate in the Cultural Revolution through "three months of turmoil." In October, the PLA high command dismissed all classes in the military academies, naval colleges, and aviation institutes to allow the cadets to join the Red Guards in the revolution. Soon the Red Guards seized school administrators, attacked PLA HQ and departments in Beijing, and kidnapped generals, admirals, and their families. By 1967, it was reported that 80,000 generals and officers had been detained and tortured. About 1,169 of them died of physical abuse, starvation, or by execution. PLAN political commissar Li Zuopeng, one of Lin Biao's loyalists, called for a revolution in the navy, criticizing Fleet Admiral Xiao Jinguang and labeling Xiao's leadership the "Rightist Headquarters." Li orchestrated a "struggle between the two headquarters" in the navy, the "Leftist Headquarters" and "Rightist Headquarters." In 1966–68, 258 senior naval officers above divisional command levels were dismissed, purged, or jailed. Twenty-three of them died by torture, and two died in jail. Eleven died by suicide, including Vice Admiral Tao Yong, deputy commander of the PLAN and commander of the ESF, and Rear Admiral Zhang Xuesi, the PLAN's chief of staff.

In 1970, a new political conflict emerged between Mao and Lin due to their different worldviews, defense strategies, and personalities. Their contradictions erupted at the Ninth Party Central Committee's Second Plenum in August 1970. Zhu states, "By disagreeing with Mao during the plenum, for whatever reason, Lin had provided Mao with hard evidence of his political ambition. The relationship between the two men had deteriorated to the point of open confrontation."[2] Threatened by Lin's ambition and control of the military, Mao decided to remove Lin from his leadership role. Lin and his family felt Mao's directing the spearhead of his political power against them. The power struggle peaked after Lin's son attempted to assassinate Mao. On September 13, 1971, Lin and his family fled the country. Their plane crashed in Mongolia, however, killing everyone on board.[3] After Lin Biao's death, there was another top-down purge through the PLA, and thousands of officers were arrested, sentenced, or executed.[4] In that month, Li Zuopeng was jailed as one of Lin's lieutenants after having controlled the PLAN for ten years (1962–71). Admiral Su Zhenghua, former PLAN political commissar, was released from custody by Mao's order in March 1972 and returned to the navy's leadership from 1972 to 1979. Su was dismissed from all his positions in June 1967 and sent to a labor camp in the mountains of Hunan, where he worked as a farm field hand for nearly five years.[5]

Although the Chinese naval leadership was traumatized during the Cultural Revolution, the PLAN also experienced some significant developments and expanded its operations from coastal areas to the near sea in Southeast Asia in 1966–73 and the SCS in 1974–75. Among the major reasons were, first, its active involvement in the Vietnam War, fighting against the U.S. Navy (USN) and the ARVN's navy (VNN) from 1965 to 1973.[6] Chinese admirals quickly realized the disparity between Russian-made ships and weapons and American naval technology. They demanded new warships and better naval technology. Second, from 1967 to 1971, the PLA moved to the center of domestic politics through nationwide military administration. The navy was able to militarize China's shipbuilding industry, maritime research and development, and oceangoing voyages and establish a centralized naval research, development, and manufacturing system. Third, in 1974 the Chinese and Vietnamese navies clashed at the Paracel Islands (Xisha in Chinese and Quan Dao Hoang Sa in Vietnamese). The PLAN's first foreign naval war required its new capabilities in navigation technology, long-distance communication and logistics, and advanced weapon systems. The PLAN's victory placed China in a powerful position to deploy its warships and submarines into the deep water of the SCS.

PLAN SUPPORT TO THE SOUTH

As tensions between North and South Vietnam intensified, the Vietnamese Communist Party (VCP) passed a resolution at its Fifteenth Plenum, in January 1959 in Hanoi, to mount an "armed" struggle against Ngo Dinh Diem's South Vietnamese government in Saigon.[7] Relying on the Viet Minh model's former success, the VCP formed the National Liberation Front (NLF, Viet Cong) in the South in December 1960. Ho Chi Minh visited Mao Zedong in Beijing in the summer of 1962 and explained about Hanoi's NLF-based "South-first" strategy. Ho Chi Minh requested that China provide food, weapons, and ammunition to the NLF from China to South Vietnam through the Ho Chi Minh Trail.[8] Soon after the plan's inauguration, complaints of supplies not reaching the NLF surfaced. Grand General Luo Ruiqing, chief of the PLA General Staff, led an investigation team to Vietnam in March 1963 to find the causes of Chinese logistical setbacks. The DGS discovered that

55–68 percent of Chinese supplies were either destroyed, lost, or redirected in transit along the Ho Chi Minh Trail.[9] Upon his return, Luo reported to Mao Zedong and President Liu Shaoqi that if Beijing was going to follow through with deliveries to the NLF in South Vietnam, then the situation required a new, reliable transportation system through the Gulf of Tonkin.[10] (See map 3.)

Map 3. Vietnam and the Ho Chi Minh Trail

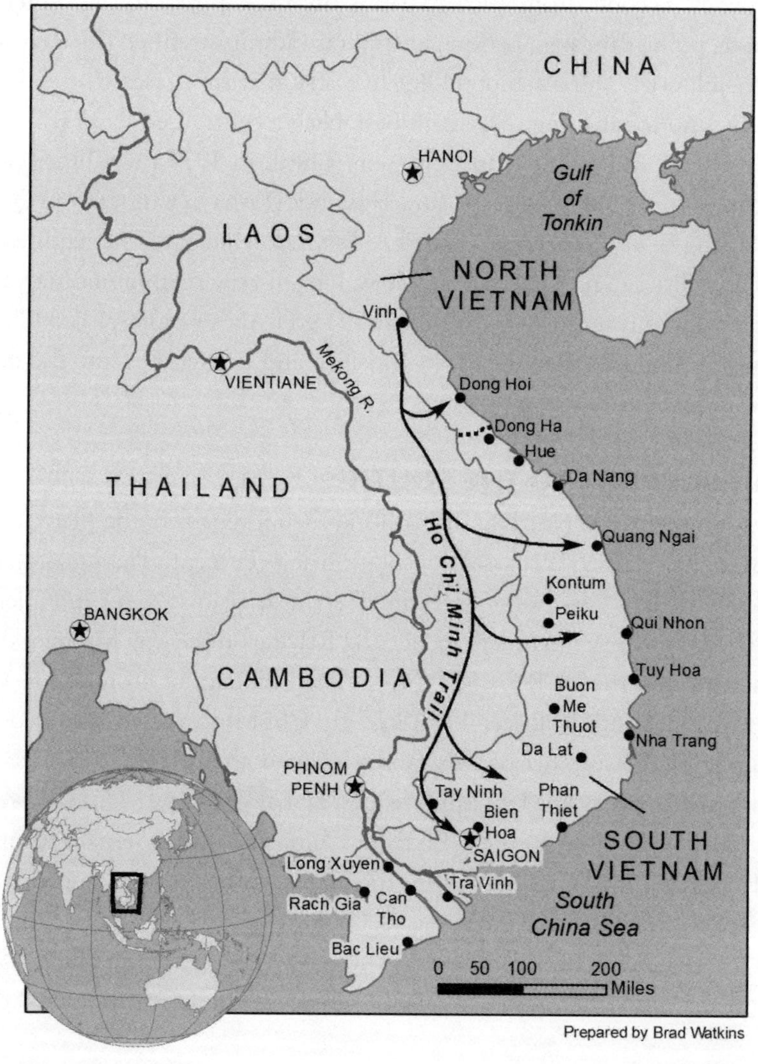

Prepared by Brad Watkins

To establish North Vietnam–PLA cooperation, Defense Minister Vo Nguyen Giap and General Van Tian Dung, chief of staff of the North Vietnamese Army (NVA), visited the PLA high command in Beijing on April 21–22, 1965. Luo Ruiqing and General Yang Chengwu met North Vietnamese military leaders and agreed on PLA-NVA joint operations. The PLA high command would send seventeen divisions from the PLA Army, Navy, Air Force, and Combat Engineering Corps to Vietnam. The Chinese forces would be under the dual command of PLA and NVA General Staffs.[11] To provide direct naval support and coordinate seaborne infiltrations into the South, the PLAN, NLF, and NVA Navy (NVAN) established a joint naval command at the Hainan Island in the Gulf of Tonkin. The tripod naval command would facilitate the water-route transport of supplies to South Vietnam, organize air defense to protect transportation lines, supply depots, and warehouses in the North, collect information on U.S. naval and air forces, and train Vietnamese naval officers and sailors.

First, the PLAN, NLF, and NVAN officers worked together at Hainan to transport Chinese supplies to the South. To make arrangements for Chinese naval deliveries, agents were sent into the South.[12] Along the southern coast, they guided PLAN vessels to unload cargo onto small fishing boats out at sea, which then delivered to the NLF. Shipping military supplies via water routes constituted 75 percent of Chinese aid prior to 1966.[13] Starting in 1966, seaborne transportation to South Vietnam was hindered, if not entirely shut down, by the USN and VNN warships, which searched and seized Chinese cargo ships and merchant vessels to blockade the southern coast. The PLAN employed naval guerrilla infiltration tactics to circumvent the USN-VNN blockade. Although the VNN regularly patrolled the eastern coast, the PLAN utilized smaller boats for tossing inflatable, waterproof supply bags into the water, which then floated to NLF guerrillas awaiting delivery on the shore.[14] The Hainan Command facilitated the movement of 214 artillery pieces, 416 AAA guns, 1,149 tons of ammunition, 881 vehicles, and 57,535 Chinese troops to Vietnam from 1965 to 1967. Hainan also repaired 163 NVAN vessels and ensured that 256 NVAN ships received 1,350 tons of supplies.[15] But the PLAN's delivery methods, although ingenious, were insufficient in supplying the NLF.

A new oceanic route connecting supply lines from China to South Vietnam gained Mao's approval and was dubbed the Ho Chi Minh Trail at Sea. First, PLAN transit ships sailed to Cambodia from Hainan Island. After trucks were loaded with Chinese supplies at the Sihanouk harbor, they drove north through Cambodia to reach Svay Rieng and Chiphu, two border towns close to NLF bases in southwest Vietnam, where NLF troops received shipments. A new port, Sihanoukville, was constructed for the sea trail after heavy expenditures from Beijing. New truck transportation, warehouses, and distribution depots were built by the PLA in southern Cambodia. In 1967, annual shipments reached 12,000 tons as the Ho Chi Minh Trail at Sea became operational.[16] The NLF received Chinese supplies much more quickly and with fewer losses. While more than half of the supplies entering from the Ho Chi Minh Trail's north end were destroyed, General Creighton Abrams of the U.S. Army estimated at the time that "virtually all supplies entering through Sihanoukville reached destination until Cambodia incursion of May 1970."[17]

Even after the American incursion into Cambodia, sea transportation continued. For example, the NLF received 15,000 tons of rice that June by sea from Shanghai.[18] From 1966 to 1973, support to the NVA and NLF doubled as transportation advanced through both land and sea trails. Chinese annual military supplies and provisions increased from 462 tanks and vehicles in 1968 to 8,978 in 1972; heavy artillery pieces from 3,362 in 1966 to 7,087 in 1968 and up to 9,912 in 1973; artillery shells from 1.06 million in 1966 to 2.08 million in 1968 and 2.2 million in 1973; and automatic rifles from 141,531 in 1966 to 219,899 in 1968 and to 233,600 in 1973.[19] The American military was unprepared to engage the NLF on both conventional and unconventional levels, which was enabled by China's successful supply of military aid to the South. A resourceful foe in China countered the advantages that the American armed forces thought they possessed.

Second, the PLAN sent its AAA troops to participate in the air defense in North Vietnam. After the Johnson administration started Operation Rolling Thunder on March 2, 1965, the PLA high command reached a quick decision on April 8 to send hundreds of thousands of Chinese AAA troops to North Vietnam to secure transportation lines and provide air defense for

Hanoi and key points. Another American miscalculation with Rolling Thunder was that "destruction of industrial and communications system would force North Vietnam to abandon the Southern insurgency."[20] In fact, North Vietnam successfully pressed China and the Soviet Union for increased and direct involvements by using Rolling Thunder to serve their war objective of defeating the South. Soon Beijing mobilized all PLA AAA troops from the army, navy, and air force to be ready for the Vietnam War. The PLA's DGS and the NVA Air Defense–Air Force (AD-AF) established a command for joint air defense in North Vietnam. The Chinese generals cooperated with the NVA officers to collaboratively design battle objectives, plan operations, mobilize local support, share intelligence, and assess combat performance.[21] On August 1, 1965, the first Chinese air defense troops, the 61st AAA Division, left Yunan and entered Vietnam along the La Cai–Hanoi lines in the northwest. By December, there were about 160,000 PLA soldiers in Vietnam, including 21,000 AAA troops. The navy selected three regiments and six battalions from its AAA troops in the NSF, ESF, and SSF. The first naval AAA unit entered Vietnam in October 1966. By the fall of 1967, the air defense troops in North Vietnam, including Vietnamese, Chinese, and Russians, totaled 72,500 men. The Chinese had 32,000 men, over 44 percent of the total.[22] (See map 4.)

On October 19 and 26, 1966, the first naval AAA units, First and Third Battalions, entered Vietnam and joined the 29th Regiment of the 31st Division. The division had old Russian-made weapons used in the Korean War. Their major cannon were 100-mm and 75-mm guns, which launched shells up to 20,000 to 30,000 feet. Some newly Chinese-made small guns, including 57-mm and 37-mm antiaircraft machine guns, provided a fire zone from 8,000 to 15,000 feet. The two naval AAA battalions were assigned by AD-AF to protect the railroads in the east zone. The division command deployed the First Battalion at a bridge and the Third at the Kep train station. The naval commanders concentrated their AAA firepower on one of the enemy airplanes for an "ensured shot down."[23] To reach the battle objective, the naval officers also emphasized "close combat" and "aiming the second plane" tactics. They employed effective combat tactics and reached their battle objectives, even though their weapons were not new.

Map 4. Chinese AAA Divisions in Vietnam

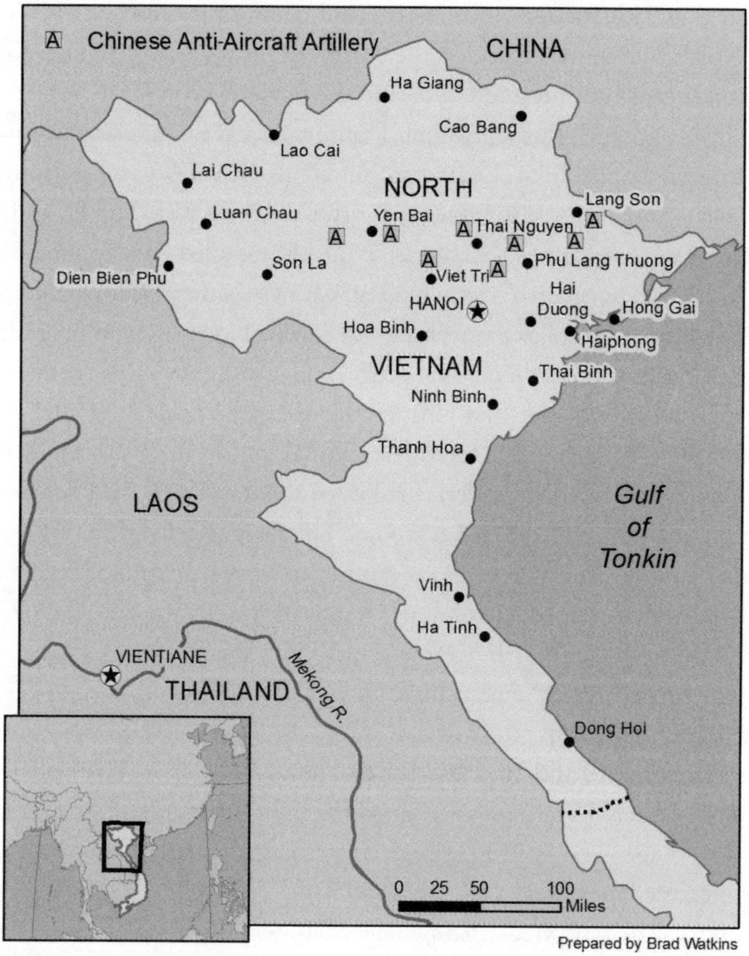

Prepared by Brad Watkins

About 3 p.m. on November 3, Third Battalion commander Qiao Xingyi was informed of eight F-105 Thunderchief fighter-bombers coming in his direction. Then his first outpost called and confirmed eight F-105s, at middle speed, at 18,000 feet, and from southeast to northwest. Soon the second outpost reported, "Eight 105s in two groups are coming!" Qiao Xingyi ordered one company to fire on the first F-105 and concentrated the rest of his guns on the second. When the second plane reached 2,500 meters, he ordered the two companies to fire. His tactics worked: the Third Battalion shot down one F-105 and damaged another. This was the first time the naval AAA troops shot down an American plane in Vietnam. At 11:20 p.m. on April 20, 1967, the Third Battalion shot down an A-6 fighter-bomber at night with the help of a naval searchlight company—the first time the naval air defense force shot down an American plane at night.[24] Spencer Tucker states, "Despite [Russian] SAMs and MiG interceptors, guns remained the most deadly threat to attacking aircraft. Of 3,000 U.S. aircraft lost during the Vietnam War, some 85 percent were downed by guns. Missiles accounted for only 8 percent, less than 2 percent of some 9,000 SAMs fired at U.S. aircraft reached their targets."[25]

However, the technology gap between the American and Chinese forces in Vietnam was huge. Major General Xu Changyou, the ESF deputy political commissar, pointed out, "When the Americans developed the post–World War II jet fighters in 1950, we used Russian-made World War II radar and antiaircraft artillery pieces. There was a five-year gap between the Chinese AAA technology and the UNF [United Nations Force] navigation in the Korean War. Then, when the Americans had the most advantaged aircraft in the world by the mid-1960s, we still used the same air defense weapons. There was a twenty-year technology gap between the Chinese AAA force and the US Air Force in the Vietnam War."[26] The major general believed that the PLAN's technological stagnation resulted from the Sino-Soviet split and the Cultural Revolution.[27]

The technology gap caused the naval casualties in the air defense. The PLA high command began to rotate their AAA divisions in December 1965 because the Chinese troops were suffering from casualties, sickness, exhaustions, and low morale in Vietnam. Each division served six to eight months as one tour in country. On June 7, 1967, the naval Sixth Battalion replaced the Third Battalion at Kep. Its First Company completed the setup of the AAA positions near the train station on August 3. Around four the next afternoon, nearly twenty F-105Fs and F-105Gs flew over Kep, splitting into two groups and attacking the train station from the southeast and northeast. Colonel Jerry N. Hoblit recalled that in a typical bombing mission, his F-105F, equipped with newly available Shrike antiradiation missiles, would accompany two or three F-105D fighters to provide protection against enemy ground fire.[28] The second group of F-105Gs hit the First Company's positions, killing eight Chinese soldiers and wounding twenty-three others.[29] To avoid casualties, naval AAA units made frequent changes of their artillery positions. For example, in September–October 1967, the Eighth Regiment of the PLAN changed the sites of its HQ four times and its company positions thirteen times within two months to avoid enemy retaliation.

Third, the Hainan Command conducted naval intelligence by collecting the signals of the U.S. armed forces and sending agents to South Vietnam and the SCS. Hainan's electronic observation stations intercepted U.S. armed forces radio transmissions as far away as Clark Air Force Base in the Philippines. Through their partnership, Vietnamese field agents procured human information collected in the South, and the Chinese attempted to determine American war objectives by cracking U.S. codes. The Chinese navy's involvement in the Vietnam War opened a new window of opportunity to learn from the USN, the most advanced naval force in the world.

The PLAN began collecting information on U.S. naval and aviation technology after quickly recognizing the disparity between Soviet-manufactured equipment and American military technology. Field agents in the South and near USN bases in Thailand relayed information back to Hanoi, where PLAN intelligence worked at the embassy.[30] Major U.S. naval bases at Da Nang and Hue were targeted by more than thirty NVA-assisted PLAN agents gathering information on U.S. and ARVN naval technology from May 9 to November 28, 1968. American water mines, including models MK-42, MK-50, and MK-52, were the priority of five NVA-accompanied PLAN mine experts in 1969. The PLAN's development of the model-311 and -312 mine dredgers, in response to their knowledge about American water mines, proved effective in the PLAN's minesweeping operations against Nixon's mine blockade in 1972–73.[31]

Fourth, the PLAN conducted a minesweeping operation along the coast of North Vietnam in 1972–73. In a public speech on May 8, 1972, President Richard Nixon announced that the United States would mine the major harbors along North Vietnam's coast. Hours later, U.S. warships and planes began the mine-laying operation. "Navy A-6 and A-7 bombers dropped 2,000-pound mines at the entrance to Hai Phong harbor, beginning the isolation of the DRV [Democratic Republic of Vietnam] from seaborne resupply."[32] In less than ten days, all the major seaports, including Haiphong, were totally blocked by mines, and the sea routes in and out of North Vietnam were paralyzed. The Vietnamese ambassador made an urgent request to Premier Zhou Enlai during their emergency meeting in Beijing on May 9, saying that North Vietnam needed China's immediate help in minesweeping. That evening, Zhou summoned naval officers and discussed a PLAN minesweeping plan. On May 10, the Central Committee's Politburo had a special meeting and approved the navy's plan to help the Vietnamese clear the mines. Nevertheless, the Politburo instructed the navy to investigate and do research on American water mines before its minesweeping operation.[33] Mao Zedong approved the plan on May 20, and the PLAN sent a mine countermeasures team to Vietnam under the command of Zhang Shouying.

The PLAN's research team entered Vietnam on May 27 with three model-312 and one model-311 mine dredgers plus two escort warships and four supply vessels.[34] On May 28, at the NVA naval base at Haiphong, the North Vietnamese navy's commander and political commissar met with the Chinese mine research team and the Chinese military attaché from Hanoi. The next day, the Vietnamese naval deputy chief of staff and other officers presented two captured U.S. MK-52 and MK-42 water mines and a map of minefields along the coast. By the end of the month, the Chinese team decided to begin the minesweeping while continuing their research. On June 4, Commander Zhang Shouying and Political Commissar Guo Baolan made a trip to Hanoi and reported their plan to the Chinese embassy.[35] Beijing asked the team leaders to brief the high command in person after the CMC received the embassy's report on June 6. That same day, Zhang and his group left Hanoi for Beijing. He briefed the PLAN Command two days later.[36]

When Zhang Shouying returned to Haiphong on June 28, he brought back more ships and troops. By July, the Chinese minesweeping troops had twelve model-312 minesweepers, four technology-support vessels, seven logistics vessels, and three escort gunboats, with 1,380 sailors and soldiers.[37] The team command designed a minesweeping operation that involved using depth charges to clean the mines and then guiding commercial ships out of Haiphong harbor. When the Chinese naval officers reported their plan to the Vietnamese, the NVAN Command expressed their disapproval of the depth-charge method, even though they were happy to see more Chinese ships arriving. The research team had to find another way to clean the mines in Vietnam.[38] From late July, Zhang recalled, the Chinese minesweeping fleet worked closely with the Vietnamese navy.[39]

Then the Vietnamese proposed the priority targets, and they made a joint plan with the Chinese about where and how to clean the mines. On August 2, the Vietnamese navy command held a minesweeping joint operation conference and decided that the Chinese minesweeping fleet should start its operation according to the Vietnamese shipping priority. Around 7 p.m. on August 12, the Chinese minesweeping operation began with MS-05 (model-312) sailing to the Haiphong minefield. The next evening, Vietnamese *HQ-412* sailed to the same minefield for a sweeping operation. *HQ-412*, one of the Chinese-made landing vessels transferred to the NVAN, was remodeled into a minesweeping boat. After it successfully detonated one MK-52, *HQ-412* hit another mine and sank with all its crew.[40] The Chinese and Vietnamese discovered the reason for *HQ-412*'s failure and learned a lesson. On August 14, Chinese MS-02, 04, and 05 continued their minesweeping operations and successfully cleaned and denoted five MK-52 mines.[41] Meanwhile, Fleet Commander Zhang Zhouying transferred three of their model-311 mine dredgers to the Vietnamese navy and trained Vietnamese naval officers and sailors to operate them. The joint minesweeping improved the operation by doubling the number of mines discovered and destroyed.[42] It took another month for the port of Haiphong to reopen in October 1972.

SU'S RETURN AND THE BATTLE IN THE SOUTH CHINA SEA

In the summer of 1966, Mao Zedong used the Red Guard youth to publicly attack, or "bomb" (*paoda*), the CCP and PRC hierarchy officials, including PRC president Liu Shaoqi and party secretary general Deng Xiaoping. On September 22–23, Marshal Lin Biao visited the navy's HQ to support Li Zuopeng and his followers in the PLAN. Li orchestrated a "struggle between the two headquarters" in the navy, the "Leftist Headquarters" and "Rightist

Headquarters." Many naval officers, labeled as rightists by Li Zuopeng and his followers, faced dismissal, torture, and prison in 1967. Eleven of them died by suicide, including Vice Admiral Tao Yong and Rear Admiral Zhang Xuesi.[43]

In 1965, Vice Admiral Tao Yong walked out from a PLAN Party Committee conference chaired by Li Zuopeng, who was using the conference to develop his personal power. In May 1966, Tao refused to attend another top naval officer conference for the same reason. On January 21, 1967, the vice admiral went to his office in Shanghai and met two reporters with Liao Zhengguo, commander of the Shanghai Municipal Security District. After lunch, Tao Yong asked his aide to get his barber for a haircut. When his aide and barber came back about ten minutes later, the naval deputy commander had disappeared. Around 2:30 p.m., they found Tao Yong's body in a small well in the backyard garden.[44] Soon Li Zuopeng labeled Tao Yong a traitor who had committed suicide against the CCP and PLA. Many naval officers in the ESF were purged or jailed as Tao's followers after his death. However, his wife, Zhu Lan, believed her husband had been murdered and thus did not kill herself. She wrote many letters to the PLAN HQ and PLA high command, pleading for an investigation of Vice Admiral Tao's death. She got no reply. In August 1967, Zhu was arrested and charged with being a "Japanese spy." She was tortured until she died in jail in October. In November 1971, after Lin Biao's death, Mao instructed the PLA to investigate the death of Tao Yong. Eventually, after Mao's death in September 1976, the CMC decided to rehabilitate Vice Admiral Tao Yong.[45]

In July 1967, Lin Biao's wife, Ye Qun, called Li Zuopeng and said, "Zhang Xuesi opposed Lin Biao in the Northeast [during the civil war]. Zhang had connections with the GMD."[46] Thereafter, Li began an investigation and sent in a report accusing Zhang as one of the rightists in the navy. With Lin Biao's approval, at 4 a.m. on September 11 Zhang Xuesi was arrested and his home was raided. Beginning in October, Zhang was brought to public criticism meetings in the naval HQ thirteen times and endured physical abuse and harassment. He was tortured continuously because he refused to accept accusations that he was a traitor and a GMD spy. Zhang Xueshi became very sick in February 1970 due to long-term torture and the lack of food and water in jail. The admiral died on May 29, only fifty-four years old.[47]

Map 5. Disputed Islands in the South China Sea

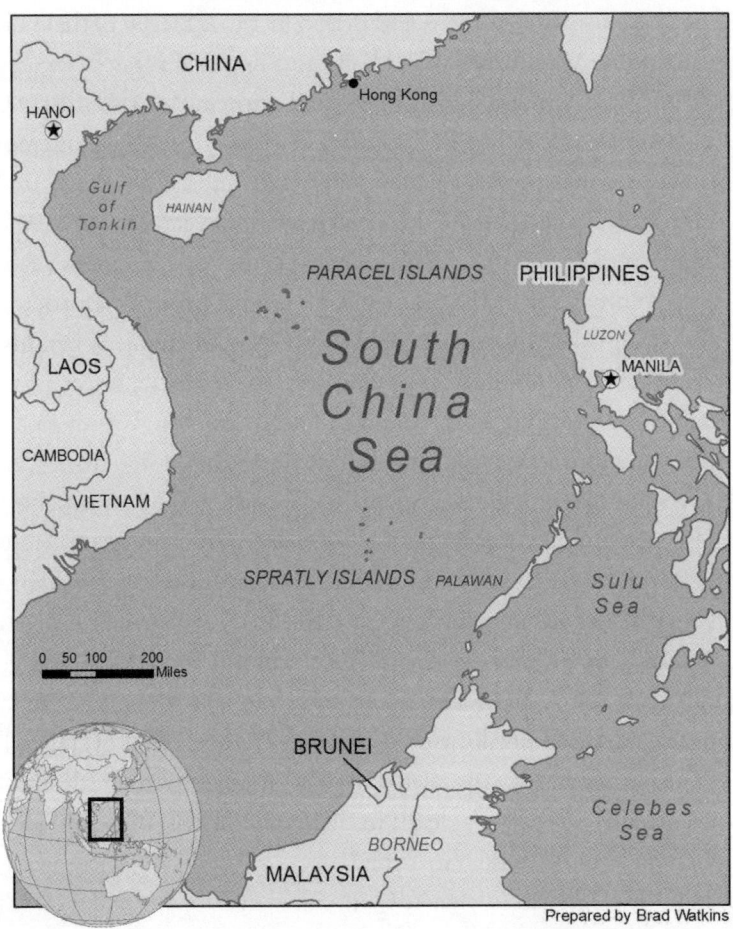

In September 1971, after Lin Biao's death that month, Li Zuopeng was jailed as one of Lin's lieutenants. Admiral Su Zhenhua reassumed his position as the PLAN political commissar in 1973, and on May 22, 1974, the CMC appointed him the navy's first deputy commander. On September 21, Admiral Su conducted a large-scale naval parade for Marshal Ye Jianying, China's defense minister, including Chinese-made, conventionally powered submarines, nuclear submarines, guided-missile destroyers, missile frigates, and naval fighter-bombers. On May 2–3, 1975, Mao Zedong chaired his last

Politburo meeting in Beijing. He held Su Zhenhua's hands at the end of the meeting and asked him "to build a good navy, which should deter the enemy."[48] Admiral Su organized planning committees, coordinated with the State Council, and drafted the Ten-Year Plan on Naval Development and Shipbuilding that summer. However, Su was caught in a new power struggle between Zhou-Ye and Jiang Qing, who continued to dominate the media and preach class struggle. Su's new plan did not take off during the Cultural Revolution, which lasted until Mao's death in September 1976.[49] Nevertheless, in October 1976, Admiral Su Zhenhua became the mayor of Shanghai and preoccupied by the municipal administration of China's largest city after the end of the Gang of Four. He also successfully commanded the PLAN's battle over the disputed Paracel Islands in the SCS against the South Vietnamese Navy.[50] (See map 5.)

The Paracel (Xisha) Islands are composed of Xuande, Yongle, and thirty other islands that occupy an ocean surface of 15,000 square kilometers and are located 330 kilometers southeast of China's Hainan Island. Many of the islands are mere islets: sandbanks and reefs. The major island is Yongxing (1.6 square kilometers). The South Vietnamese government occupied some of the Paracel Islands in the 1960s. After American troops pulled out of Vietnam in March 1973, the PLA high command saw an opportunity to seize some of the disputed islands. Admiral Su Zhenhau instructed the SSF to "safeguard national independence and state sovereignty and prepare a resolute fight against the provocations by the Saigon authority." The admiral also ordered the SSF "not to shoot first under any circumstances. But if the intruders attack, Chinese ships must fight back relentlessly."[51] After receiving the order, Rear Admiral Zhang Yuanpei, commander of the SSF, worried about increasing tension over the Paracels since he did not have any warship for a naval battle.

Admiral Hu Yanlin considered the SSF the weakest link among the three fleets. At that time it had only seven frigates that could sail to the Paracel Islands, and five of them were under direct command of the DGS and PLAN HQ and thus not available for South Sea Fleet operation. The rest of the frigates were either overhauled or out of order. The remaining escort and patrol boats (PCs) were small (about 300 tons), with limited voyage capability, and could not be used for naval operations at sea.⁵² At the SSF's Yulin Naval Base, Rear Admiral Zhang Yuanpei had six Type 6604 submarine chasers and three minesweepers, which had just returned from Vietnam. Rear Admiral Zhang appointed Wei Mingsen, deputy commander of the base, to command the Xisha naval battle.⁵³ Wei Mingsen had joined the Eighth Route Army in 1937 and the CCP in 1938. He became an intelligence officer in the PLA. After the founding of the PRC, he studied and taught at the PLA Advanced Infantry Academy. Wei became chief of the PLAN Department of Transportation in 1961 and deputy commander of SSF Yulin Naval Base in 1970.⁵⁴

After receiving the order on January 15, Wei Mingsen chose two submarine chasers, 271 and 274, about 332 tons each, in the best condition and fitted them with the best equipment and weapons available. However, due to the sub chasers' age and low level of automation, all crew members were required to be on deck when they fired their weapons. This made the men vulnerable to artillery shells coming from enemy warships. These sub hunters had been used only for routine patrols, not as combat warships for the front line. Nevertheless, it was what the South Sea Fleet had. Wei Mingsen led these two submarine hunters as a battle fleet and departed with some landing infantrymen from the Yulin Naval Base on January 16. About eight hours later, they reached the waters near the Paracel Islands.⁵⁵

On the morning of January 17, the two Chinese submarine chasers weighed anchor between Jinqin and Chenhang (Crescent) Islands. The next afternoon, the VNN sent the destroyer *Tran Khanh Du* (HQ 4) and the frigate *Nhat Tao* (HQ 10) (about 720 tons) to the waters of Yongle Island as reinforcements. This Vietnamese destroyer was a USN *Savage*-class convoy destroyer with a displacement of 1,750 tons. Wei Mingsen realized that his two submarine chasers, totaling 664 tons, faced four Vietnamese warships, a total tonnage of over 6,600, in the conflicted area. The Vietnamese had more than thirty cannons of various calibers installed on these warships. The Chinese formation faced a most unfavorable battle situation. Wei called for reinforcements.⁵⁶

Rear Admiral Zhang Yuanpei, SSF commander, responded to Wei's request by sending two more submarine chasers, 281 and 282, as reinforcements, joined by two Chinese minesweepers, 396 and 389, that were in the area. These minesweepers, about 628 tons each, were transporting supplies to the Paracel Islands. One of them, *389*, had been in repair for a year and had just returned to service three days before. On January 18, *396* and *389* reached the Chinese anchor site and joined the two submarine chasers.

At 5:47 a.m. on January 19, VNN destroyers *Tran Khanh Du* and *Tran Binh Trong* (HQ 5) moved toward the Palm Island from south of Antelope Reef. Then the destroyer *Ly Thuong Kiet* (HQ 16) and the frigate *Nhat Tao* appeared to the north of Palm Island, approaching the SSF's anchoring area. Zhang Yuanpei immediately ordered *396* and *389* to intercept the Vietnamese destroyer *Ly Thuong Kiet* and frigate *Nhat Tao*. He also ordered *271* and *274* to move to the southeast of Palm Island and monitor the activities of the Vietnamese destroyers *Tran Khanh Du* and *Tran Binh Trong*. Around 7 a.m., Wei Mingsen reported to Zhang that *Tran Khanh Du* and *Tran Binh Trong* had used rubber boats to land forty Vietnamese soldiers on Palm Island, where there were already more than one hundred Chinese troops.[57] The soldiers began to fire on each other. Without a beach stronghold and outnumbered, the Vietnamese landing troops retreated to the warships. Then the Vietnamese destroyer *Ly Thuong Kiet* sailed at full speed with its muzzle tilted high toward the Chinese ships and rammed the PLAN formation. During the ramming, the supports of the bridge, the railings on the port side, and the minesweeping apparatus on *389* were severely damaged by *Ly Thuong Kiet*.[58]

At 10:22 a.m. on January 19, the VNN destroyer *Tran Binh Trong* shelled the Chinese *274*. Wei Mingsen ordered the Chinese ships to return fire. To give full play to the smaller boats' maneuvering advantage, the Chinese formation fought at close quarters. Wei ordered *271* and *274* to attack *Tran Khanh Du* and *Tran Binh Trong*, while *396* and *389* were to attack *Ly Thuong Kiet* and *Nhat Tao*. The Vietnamese tried to keep their distance from the Chinese formation so that they could take advantage of their bigger cannon. But the Chinese ships continued to pursue tightly and at full speed. Very soon, the two sides had gotten into position for line-to-line combat.[59]

The captain of *274*, Li Fuxiang, fired on *Tran Khanh Du* from one thousand to three hundred meters. In the first round, the Chinese submarine chaser destroyed *Tran Khanh Du*'s navigation radar antenna. The PLAN warships simultaneously fired small-caliber guns with a high firing rate.

According to the memoir of a charge-man on 274, he loaded 180 rounds nonstop, loading the gun continually although his hands were severely chafed and bleeding.[60] He was later awarded the first-class merit distinction. 271 found the *Tran Khanh Du*'s firing range dead zone and concentrated its fire on the bridge, cutting off its communication. Irreparably damaged by the Chinese submarine chasers, *Tran Khanh Du* fled to the open seas trailing smoke.[61] Meanwhile, 396 and 389 attacked *Ly Thuong Kiet*. The 389 captain, Xiao Dewan, concentrated his guns on the *Ly Thuong Kiet*'s bridge. The Vietnamese destroyer was hit by shells, and its deck caught fire several times. It quickly fled the area too. 389, however, was also severely damaged and caught fire. Captain Xiao directed his minesweeper to land on the shore of a nearby reef.[62]

Then the Chinese warships concentrated their fire on *Nhat Tao*. Around 11:49 a.m., 281 and 282 moved to *Nhat Tao*'s starboard and sprayed it with bullets and shells. Soon the Vietnamese frigate caught fire. The 281 pursued the damaged *Nhat Tao*, which attempted to move to Antelope Reef but failed. As the two ships closed within a dozen yards, the 281 sailors rushed from their cabins and sprayed the Vietnamese soldiers with machine guns and grenades. The frigate exploded and sank at 2:52 p.m. south of Antelope Reef. After a ninety-minute fight, the remaining Vietnamese warships fled the Paracel Islands.[63]

When the VNN vessels left, the Vietnamese garrisons at Pattle, Robert, and Money Islands did not retreat. After the sea battle, Ye Jianying, Deng Xiaoping, and Su Zhenhua reported to Mao Zedong and suggested that China finalize control of the islands. Mao agreed. At 9 a.m. on January 20, 1974, the Chinese navy launched landing operations against the Vietnamese troops defending the islands. Under Chinese gunfire from both warships and landing troops, ARVN soldiers on Robert Island surrendered. Those on Pattle and Money Islands continued a stubborn defense from several positions. Later that day, after Chinese troops took the beachhead, most of the Vietnamese soldiers surrendered and laid down their weapons. During the battle, more than one hundred ARVN officers and soldiers were killed or wounded and forty-nine captured, including one American; sixty-seven Chinese sailors were wounded and eighteen killed.[64] The SCS battle was the first time the Chinese navy had conducted operations away from the coastal line. It was also the first time the PLAN had fought a foreign navy since its establishment in 1949. Despite outmoded warships and weak firepower, PLAN officers and sailors fought successfully by using shrewd naval tactics and sank one Vietnamese frigate and damaged three destroyers, while the 389 was merely damaged. The PLAN's successful operations provided China with a powerful position for deepwater deployment in the SCS.

NEW CAPABILITIES TOWARD THE BLUE WATERS

Before the 1960s, Chinese shipbuilding was based on existing Russian designs and reverse-engineered Soviet components and equipment. From the mid-1960s, China began to design and build its own medium-sized and more advanced guided-missile destroyers, frigates, and submarine chasers. The PLAN also developed antiship missiles, torpedoes, and shore-to-ship missiles. The first-generation frigates were the backbone of the PLAN's combat power in the early days. They performed brilliantly in operations to attack near-shore islands and safeguard coastal areas and territorial seas in the 1950s. In June 1957, the Type 01 frigate, built using Soviet technology, came into PLAN service. Its standard displacement was 1,249 tons, and the cruising speed was 14.5 knots. Its main weapons were 100-mm guns, 37-mm guns, and several antisubmarine weapons. In 1959, China designed and manufactured its first frigate, Type 062. In September 1966, the first Chinese-made Type 065 frigates were delivered to the navy. The standard displacement was 1,263 tons and the standard cruising speed 16 knots. In December 1975, Chinese-made Type 053H missile frigates went into service. These vessels' standard displacement is 1,469 tons, and their main weapons are 100-mm guns, 37-mm guns, ship-to-ship missiles, and depth-charge launching projectors.

Gao Xiaoxing and the others from the Naval Command University have identified three important transitions in the Chinese naval development in the late 1960s. First, the PLAN shifted its focus from buying and copying foreign warships to making its own; second, it moved from making small ships to building medium-sized warships and submarines; and third, missiles replaced guns as the weapon system for surface warships.[65] From 1967 to 1971, China constructed eight Type 051 *Luda* destroyer keels, a copy of the Soviet *Kotlin*. But as James C. Bussert and Bruce A. Elleman point out, "Most significant was the replacement of the torpedo tubes with two twin CSS-N-1 Styx SSM [surface-to-surface] missile launchers, including an FC radar." The new *Luda* destroyers had six surface-to-surface missile launchers and twenty guns from 130 mm to 25 mm. The PLAN received seventeen *Luda*-class destroyers as "primary open-ocean surface combatants" before 1993.[66] In the late 1970s, China manufactured improved Type 051G missile destroyers, improved Type 0-053K and Type 053H frigates, and new Type H2 missile frigates. The navy also received Type 037 and Type 037I submarine chasers, Type 027 large torpedo boats, Type 520T missile boats, and Type 082 minesweeping ships.[67]

In the 1960s, the Chinese also researched and developed their own medium-sized, conventionally powered submarines, attack submarines, and strategic nuclear-powered submarines. Before the Sino-Soviet split, the Soviet Union agreed to a compensated transfer to China of the right to build the new *Romeo*-class conventional torpedo submarine (which China called the Type 033) and *Golf*-class conventionally powered ballistic missile (Type 031 in China). In the early 1960s, the Type 033 submarine was manufactured at the Jiangnan Shipyard in Shanghai using Russian technology. The first Type 033 was delivered to the PLAN in 1965. Its submerged displacement is 1,881 tons, its submerged speed 13 knots. The main weapons are torpedoes, and it carries mines. In April 1974, the first Type 035 *Ming*-class diesel submarine launched in Wuhan. Its submerged displacement is 2,325 tons, its submerged speed 18 knots. In 1975, the second Type 035 was delivered to the navy. This marked a new era of China's own, self-designed and -manufactured conventionally powered submarines. Submarines 341 and 342 were the improved *Romeos*.[68]

China's first nuclear bomb test on October 16, 1964 promoted its missile program and nuclear-powered submarine research and development. Beijing's limited nuclear deterrence strategy was to be able to attack enemy vulnerable targets when making reprisals. The basic strategic thinking was to use limited numbers of nuclear weapons to achieve an asymmetrical balance with formidable enemies that have many nuclear warheads. Thus, China's few nuclear bombs should convince enemies not to use such weapons against China.

To pursue its limited nuclear deterrence strategy, China must make sure it is capable of inflicting a second strike. For this purpose, the ideal and reliable means was to employ nuclear-powered, missile-bearing submarines to provide a longtime concealed nuclear retaliation underwater. When the Soviet Union refused to help China develop a nuclear-powered submarine after the Sino-Soviet split, Chinese leaders grew determined to make their own. Mao Zedong famously said, "Even if it takes us 10,000 years, we must manufacture our own nuclear-powered submarines!"[69] The construction of the nuclear submarines was successfully carried out through a highly centralized civil-military cooperation. Cole points out that "Beijing invested heavily in developing nuclear-armed missiles and the nuclear-powered submarines" and considered them the "national projects."[70] On March 13, 1965, the Second and Sixth Industrial Ministries proposed establishing the Joint Institute of Nuclear Submarine to design and manufacture the nuclear submarines. Premier Zhou Enlai held a civil-military hearing in Beijing on March 20, including national research institutes, universities, the PLAN, and the State Council. After founding the joint institute, Zhou chaired twenty-two nuclear submarine working conferences from 1965 to 1970, evaluating the progress, discussing the issues, coordinating collective efforts, and solving administrative and material problems. In November 1966, the Joint Institute of Nuclear Submarine finished its first design.[71]

On December 7–10, Marshal Nie Rongzhen chaired an assessment conference, including the navy, all industrial ministries, and research institutes, to evaluate the design, provide improvement suggestions, and discuss how to deal with the chaotic situations during the first year of the Cultural Revolution. Vice Premier and CMC vice chairman Nie Rongzhen militarized the nuclear research institutes in order to save the researchers and protect the programs. Generally speaking, the nuclear program and defense facilities attracted professionals and scientists because these national projects provided social privileges and political protection. After the founding of the PRC, the most serious campaign against intellectuals and academics occurred in

1966, when Mao launched the Cultural Revolution. In 1967, Marshal Nie sent the PLA troops to all the research institutes and nuclear testing facilities and transferred most civilian employees at the nuclear and missile research institutes into military service. It was apparently important for these returning students from the United States and the West, both for themselves—for their personal safety and job security—and for their country, as they became part of the PLA.

Construction of the nuclear submarine began on November 23, 1968. This vessel, the first *Han*-class (Type 91) attack submarine, was completed in April 1969 at Bohai Shipyard in Huludao. From July 23 to August 28, 1970, the nuclear reactor was tested and reached its designed levels. During the torpedo nuclear submarine's manufacturing, the PLAN also started the research and design of its missile nuclear submarines from 1967 to 1972. On December 26, 1970, China's first nuclear-powered submarine launched as *401* during the middle of the Cultural Revolution. In August 1974, it was commissioned into the PLAN's battle array as the *Long March 1*. After it completed the construction, the first missile nuclear submarine launched in late 1976.[72] The second *Han*-class nuclear submarine began its construction in 1975 and became operational in 1980 as *402*.

By the late 1970s, the Chinese navy was also developing and manufacturing service vessels, including salvage-and-rescue ships, rescue tugboats, comprehensive depot ships, mine layers, minesweepers, and other service ships for engineering, reconnoitering, transport, maintenance, medical care, and other tasks. The ocean survey vessels displaced more than 11,000 tons. The PLAN also developed new weapons and equipment for the marine corps and navy coastal defense units. Thus, the navy was equipped with a modern framework to carry out maritime combat operations, base defense operations, and sea-based self-defense nuclear counterattack, with near-shore combat as a focus and operational and tactical maneuvers as a complement. Guo Xiaoxing from the Naval Command University states that by that time, "the overall technological level of the PLAN's equipment and vessels rose to international levels."[73]

On the last day of 1976, Chinese submarine *252* surfaced in the Pacific Ocean. Captain Xu Zhiming and his young officers and sailors rushed topside and shouted to the vast sea, "Pacific, here we are!" The PLAN had worked for nearly thirty years toward sailing on the open ocean, as it had been the dream of two generations of Chinese seamen. From the 1950s to 1970s, the PLAN lacked the technological capabilities to do so; patrols could be conducted only near shorelines and within the first island chain. By the late 1970s, the Chinese navy could move from the yellow waters of the near shore to the deep-blue waters of the ocean. Captain Xu and his *252* cruised the Pacific underwater for thirty days and nights, voyaging over 3,200 nautical miles. They were able to maintain communication with the PLAN through its ultra-long-wave radio station, which became operational on October 24, 1965. On January 9, 1977, submarine *252*'s sonar reported an aircraft carrier formation sailing south in the Pacific. Xu Zhiming ordered his submarine to follow the carrier formation. On January 24, 252 returned to its base in Qingdao. By opening new routes for the Chinese navy, the *252*'s voyage was a landmark for the PLAN's sailing history. It indicated China's new capabilities in shipbuilding, navigation technology, and long-distance communication and logistics. These oceangoing voyages convinced Chinese naval officers that they were no longer a "small navy," confined to the near sea; they became a modern navy, capable of reaching the oceans' deep waters.

CHAPTER 5

Reform and New Strategy

The PLA experienced a new reform movement and temperamental changes from the 1970s to the 1990s. During China's economic and military reforms, the Chinese military evolved from an army on foot to a mechanized, modern force, and civil-military relations culminated in qualitative change. As the PLA's "least important service," the navy struggled to find its new place in post-Mao China. The PLAN had four different chiefs through this period: Generals Su Zhenhua (1972–79) and Ye Fei (1979–82) and Admirals Liu Huaqing (1982–88) and Zhang Lianzhong (1988–96). Without basic naval skills or education and restricted to their experience in the army, the first two commanders—Su Zhenhua and Ye Fei—could provide nothing beyond coastal defense. After Liu Huaqing became PLAN commander in 1982, the Chinese navy had a new beginning.

Admiral Liu Huaqing, known as China's Sergei Gorshkov or Alfred T. Mahan, had a long vision for the PLAN to become a "blue-water navy." Long before assuming the naval command, Liu Huaqing proposed to Deng Xiaoping a naval development plan that included designing and manufacturing 40,000-ton aircraft carriers, 4,000-ton destroyers, and 2,000-ton frigates.[1] From his observations, Liu argued that the world's successful navies operated farther and farther from their coasts and that international trade was increasingly important to China's economy. Liu predicted that it was only a matter of time before the Chinese navy would have to engage in operations to protect China's sea lines of communications. Liu's vision for the PLAN's new strategy and its future development impressed Deng Xiaoping. On September 4, 1975, the day after receiving Liu's report, Deng forwarded it to Su Zhenhua, then the naval administrator and its political commissar, instructing him, "Take this report into your consideration. Some points deserve our attention."[2] After Deng Xiaoping commenced economic reform in 1978, rapid economic growth and overseas trade made the coastal regions, sea-lanes, and maritime development more important to national security interests and the country's economic activities. The Party Center supported Liu's plans and shifted its focus to the navy's modernization.

The 1970s became the turning point in Chinese naval development and modernization, when the navy received more than 20 percent of the annual defense budget. However, it took seven years—until 1982, when Liu Huaqing became its commander—for the PLAN to develop a new strategy as a blue-water navy. In the 1980s, Admiral Liu emphasized China's sea power, maritime interests, and oceangoing development by constructing a modern Chinese navy. After his promotion to CMC deputy secretary general and then vice chairman, Liu continued his efforts to build a strong navy. In 1992, Admiral Liu Huaqing was elected as a member of the CCP Politburo's Standing Committee and became one of China's seven top leaders. He administrated the PLA's daily operations, managed China's defense budget, and continued promoting naval development as the CMC vice chairman alongside Jiang Zemin.

DENG'S REFORM AND YE'S POLICY

After Mao Zedong died on September 9, 1976, an internal power struggle ensued between the Gang of Four, including Mao's wife, Jiang Qing, and the PLA marshals. During the showdown on October 6, Mao's successor, Hua Guofeng, along with Ye Jianying, arrested the Gang of Four and Mao's cousin Mao Yuanxin in a bloodless coup.[3] After serving five years in prison, navy chief Su Zhenhua remained cautious upon his return to the navy in 1973. He followed Hua Guofeng closely and earned Hua's trust by successfully disarming radical militias in Shanghai, their home base, through negotiations. Hua Guofeng appointed Su as the First Secretary for Shanghai's CCP Municipal Committee, the official administering China's largest city, while he continued serving as the PLAN's political commissar.[4] (Fleet Admiral Xiao Jinguang was in the hospital.) Admiral Su remained preoccupied by his municipal post and did not attempt any significant changes to the PLAN from 1977 to 1979. Under Hua Guofeng's patronage, Su Zhenhua refused to rehabilitate the Cultural Revolution's victims in the PLAN.

After the demise of the Gang of Four in October 1976, Deng Xiaoping returned to Beijing. He ended the Cultural Revolution, started new reform policies, and represented a new generation of Chinese leadership.[5] He opened China to the outside world for international support for the Four Modernizations, including the modernization of defense.[6] After China established diplomatic relations with the United States on January 1, 1979, Deng became the first Chinese Communist leader to visit Washington. The Sino-U.S. normalization led to the rapid creation of an institutional and legal framework for expanded economic cooperation.[7] Deng's drive to improve relations with the United States paid off. In July 1979, the U.S. government granted most favored nation trading status to China and gradually loosened trade restrictions, shifting the PRC to the category of "friendly, non-allied" country in May 1983.[8]

Deng Xiaoping had worked as extensively in the military as Mao Zedong before and after the founding of the PRC. Popular and trusted, Deng was one of the PLA's most influential and senior commanders in the PLA. He removed Hua Guofeng as the chair of the CMC and made himself the chief of the PLA General Staff. In February 1979, Deng decided to punish Vietnam as a warning to some neighboring countries and sent 220,000 PLA troops to invade Vietnam. He was disappointed by the PLA's poor discipline, low morale, and combat ineffectiveness and the high casualties in the Sino-Vietnam border war (see map 6). From February 17 to March 6, the PLA suffered 26,000 casualties, about 1,350 per day.[9] Gerald Segal points out that "in contrast to Korea, Chinese troops performed poorly. In Korea, they adequately defended North Korea, but in 1979 they failed to punish Vietnam. China's Cambodian allies were relegated to a sideshow along the Thai frontier, and China was unable to help them break out."[10] During the brief war, 37,300 Vietnamese troops were killed, and 2,300 were captured. Hanoi believed that the Vietnamese army had taught the Chinese army a lesson in that China lost militarily and beat a hasty retreat: "After we defeated them, we gave them the red carpet to leave Vietnam."[11] Henry J. Kenny points out,

"Most Western writers agree that Vietnam had indeed outperformed the PLA on the battlefield."[12] The Sino-Vietnamese border conflict continued to the mid-1980s.

The 1979 Vietnam incursion explored that the PLA had some serious problems and were not ready for such a "local war." Deng Xiaoping planned a new military reform in the wake of the 1979 Sino-Vietnamese border war and established a Military System Reform Leading Group in February 1982.[13] The CMC held a landmark conference from May 23 to June 6, 1985 that became the starting point of Deng's 1980s military reform. His new strategy included two central principles: first, the PLA should not expect a "total war" or a "nuclear war" in the future; second, the next "local war" or "limited war" needed a professional army with modern technology. This was another strategic transition from Mao's "people's war" doctrine to a new "people's war under modern conditions" doctrine.[14] The PLA reform followed Deng's new doctrine and emphasized the development of new military technology. Deng Xiaoping downsized the PLA forces by 1 million over the next two years. Theoretically, the money saved from the

Map 6. China's Invasion of Vietnam

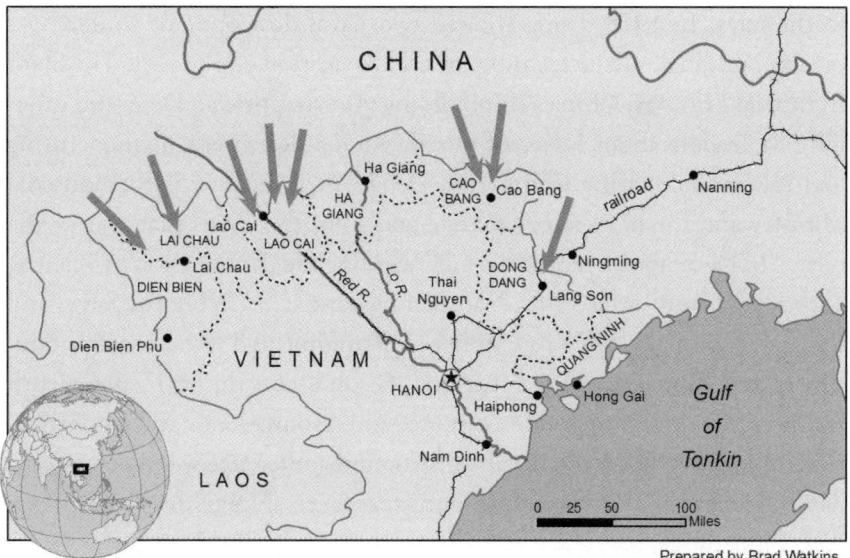

Prepared by Brad Watkins

troop reduction would be available for upgrading defense technology.[15] However, the PLA did not get what it wanted in terms of bigger budget. According to Deng, the PLA had to wait for national economic growth as a prerequisite for its technology improvement. Deng emphasized that "only when we have a good economic foundation will it be possible for us to modernize the army's equipment. So we must wait patiently for a few years."[16] He believed that defense building must be subordinated to serve national economic development and that the two causes should be promoted in a coordinated manner.

However, Deng Xiaoping's emphasis on international trade "shifted China's economic center of gravity to the coast."[17] Chinese trade with other nations has steadily expanded and affected some 60–70 percent of China's annual revenues. With more opening to the global market, Deng Xiaoping focused on the PLAN's development. He provided some guiding thoughts for Chinese maritime strategy beyond the PLAN's traditional role as a coastal defense force. Deng believed Chinese maritime interests should develop the country's maritime economy, protect China's maritime sovereignty over territorial waters, and sustain the ocean environment. He projected China as a maritime power to fulfill these important missions. In the 1970s, more than 20 percent of the national defense budget went to the navy. In 1978, Deng chaired two naval development conferences on shipbuilding, missile technology, and navigation equipment. The Sixth Industrial Ministry, China's shipbuilding ministry, briefed Deng and other military leaders about issues of missile-guided destroyer's manufacturing and nuclear submarine technology. Deng instructed the Sixth Industrial Ministry and the navy to collaborate and solve the issues that year or the next.[18] In December, a national team including the Commission of Science, Technology, and Industry for National Defense (CSTIND); the navy; and the State Council formed to improve shipbuilding and naval construction. The State Council mobilized the First, Second, Fourth, Fifth, and Eighth Industry Ministries to provide assistance and resources for naval modernization. In January 1979, the naval construction conference was held at Qingdao and included 240 naval units, ministry offices, shipbuilding enterprises, and companies.[19]

In March 1978, one of the PLAN's largest surface warships exploded in its home port of Zhanjiang, an SSF base. *Guangzhou* was a Chinese-designed guided-missile destroyer, commissioned as *160* in June 1974, with a displacement of 3,200 tons. The destroyer *160* was manned by 280 seamen, including 45 officers. According to the PLAN's investigation, control officer Lai Sanyang had a domestic dispute with his girlfriend, who killed herself. The ship's command disciplined him with an immediate discharge from naval service and return to his home village. Commissioned Warrant Officer Lai Sanyang, an expert in depth charges and water mines, remained disgruntled and decided to take revenge. Around 9 p.m. on March 9, Lai acquired a key to the destroyer's ammunition cabinet and detonated one depth charge with a high-voltage (380V) electric lighter. Soon the explosion caused a chain reaction and detonated the ship's remaining ordnance. At 9:40 p.m., the huge explosion blew the destroyer in half, killing 134 officers and sailors and wounding 28 on board and on shore.[20] It became the most serious naval incident in PLAN history. The destroyer *160*'s captain and political commissar were arrested at home and faced court martial the following morning. The South Sea Fleet's base commander and deputy commander were also disciplined regarding the explosion. Deng Xiaoping criticized Admiral Su Zhenhua as being "insensitive" toward such a serious naval incident.[21]

On February 7, 1979, PLAN political commissar Su Zhenhua had a heart attack and died in Shanghai. Deng Xiaoping appointed General Ye Fei as the navy's new chief on February 12. Born in the Philippines, Ye Fei grew up in Fujian and joined the CCP in 1932. He then became a Red Army political instructor and commander. In World War II, Ye was a regiment, brigade, and division commander and political commissar. He commanded the PLA Tenth Army Group in 1947–50. Ye was appointed as commander of the Fujian Military Region in 1953 and attained the rank of general in 1955. He became governor of Fujian from 1956 to 1966. During the Cultural Revolution, Ye was purged and dismissed from all his position. After his "rehabilitation," Ye served as China's transportation minister from 1975 to 1979. Deng appointed General Ye as the PLAN political commissar in 1979 and as PLAN commander in 1980 after Xiao Jinguang retired.[22]

At the time, Ye Fei prioritized rehabilitating the victims of the Cultural Revolution (1966–76). As the PLAN political commissar, Ye dealt with the issue because it affected tens of thousands of naval officers' careers. He separated them into two groups. The first group of PLAN officers had lost their positions, jobs, and pensions as victims of the Cultural Revolution. The second group, however, had earned their current positions at the expense of the victims, either directly or indirectly, throughout the previous two decades' relentless political struggles. With no naval experience in his career, General Ye faced a daunting task.[23] However, he knew a significant number of them and some shared experience with the naval officers during his military career. He knew a significant number of ESF's senior officers well and had shared experiences with them in the Third Field Army from 1949 to 1951. Ye also coordinated with the navy during the Taiwan Strait Crises when he commanded the Jinmen bombardment and blockade operations in Fujian. During his tenure as the minister of transportation, Ye Fei worked closely with the navy on issues of shipping, coastal security, and offshore rescue missions. He impressed Deng Xiaoping when he demonstrated the ability to revive a paralyzed ministry during his service as the minister of transportation.[24]

After assuming his navy command, General Ye Fei confirmed that factional disputes and struggles plagued the PLAN. He believed that it would take at least three years to reorganize the navy, put it in order, and establish good morale. On April 3, 1979, Ye reported his findings and suggestions to Deng Xiaoping. China's new leader was unsurprised by Ye's findings. Deng reiterated that the PLAN's main problems were "demoralization, factional fights, and lack of teamwork."[25] Solving these problems became Ye's top priority. Deng asked him to consider three other issues concerning the PLAN's new strategy. The first was the direction of its future development. Specifically, the issue was what kind of navy the PLAN would become. Deng stated that China did not seek hegemony and must instead adopt a defensive naval strategy and that the PLAN would not sail to oceans far from China's coasts. Nevertheless, the PLAN must be combat capable, reliable, and small but efficient. The second issue sought to improve the PLAN's culture, stressing professionalism and upright behavior. The third was excluding officers who had gained their station through the Cultural Revolution's political machinations.[26]

Ye Fei worked hard for the next three and a half years (1979–82), trying to make Deng's demands a reality. As the PLAN's morale and factional influence were intricately linked to the Cultural Revolution, Ye's first step was rehabilitation and de-Maoization that Admiral Su Zhenhua had failed to do since 1977. Because Su was responsible for much of the victimization and demoralization, Deng supported Ye in his investigation of Su beginning in 1981, as part of Ye's reconciliation efforts.[27] The top-down investigation took more than eight months and permeated the entire naval force. The investigation report, which was delivered to the entire PLAN, diplomatically criticized Su Zhenhua and identified his deficiencies. During his reorganization and reform, Ye selected new naval officers with college degrees to serve in the PLAN. During the 1980s, twelve naval schools enrolled thousands of cadets in the PLA Naval Command University, Naval University of Engineering, Naval Aeronautical Engineering Institute, Dalian Naval Shipbuilding College, Navy Submarine Academy, Navy Amphibious Warfare Institute, Naval Aviation College, and Navy Officer Academy. Thereafter, the navy's higher education institutes cultivated many talented professionals at various levels in the two major categories of naval command and engineering technology. They also served the navy's strategic studies and scientific and technological research and development.[28]

From July 20 to 31, 1979, the PLAN's new Party Committee convened at the NSF at the Qingdao Naval Base. To support new leadership, Deng Xiaoping met the naval leaders at the meeting in Qingdao on July 29. During his speech to the officers, Deng emphasized the importance of historical problems being solved by the new leaders. "It will be very difficult to do so by the next generation," Deng said.[29] On the same day, Deng came to the NSF air force field, reviewed the Chinese-made seaplanes, and met with the pilots. Vice Admiral Rao Shousheng informed Deng about the new seaplane's functions and features, while a squadron demonstrated a series of flight maneuvers, formations, and ultra-low-altitude attacks.[30]

Ye Fei invited Deng to also visit the Yantai Naval Base. During their conversation on the train to Yantai, Deng Xiaoping requested that Ye visit the Paracel Islands himself, because China "must guard the islands firmly."[31] On August 2, Deng boarded the first Chinese-made missile destroyer *105* at

Yantai and met all the officers and sailors. He toured the new warship with Captain Liu Zigeng as it sailed to the bay. Deng asked about the warship's functions, weapon systems, and crew morale. Deng proclaimed to Captain Liu and his officers that China wanted to be a rich country, which required entering the world and sailing its oceans. He continued that the Chinese navy should build up oceanic defense rather than near-sea defense. During his six-hour sailing tour, Deng also visited weapon controls, communications, engine rooms, and other parts of the new warship and inscribed a calligraphy for the navy: "Build a strong navy able to fight a modern war!"[32]

Deng Xiaoping's support and Ye's reorganization and rehabilitation improved the PLAN's capabilities. In June 1978, the PLAN made a progress report on the guided-missile destroyer's development and manufacturing. Deng instructed the navy to "concentrate [its] resources and overcome the key problems of building the missile destroyer. We must solve the problems. If not this year, [we must] solve [them] next year."[33] By the early 1980s, the navy developed and manufactured new combat warships, submarines, and large support vessels for oceangoing operations. The PLAN was equipped with new types of guided-missile destroyers, fighter-bombers, antisubmarine helicopters, and other high-performance equipment and weapons. The number of missile-carrying warships increased from twenty to two hundred by the end of the 1980s. From 1972 to 1982, the PLAN's submarine force grew from thirty-five to one hundred conventional submarines. Meanwhile, the navy developed nuclear attack submarines (SSN) and nuclear-powered ballistic missile submarines. In April 1980, the submarine 256 expanded its range and sailed into the Pacific. Afterward, more submarines sailed to the Pacific and reached the second island chain.

With new warships and new technology, the PLAN expanded its operations from the near shore (brown water) to the near sea (green water). The SSF dispatched 794 vessels and 262 aircraft between July 1980 and the end of 1982 for patrol, surveillance, and other tasks and was able to ensure the security of fisheries, the Paracel Islands, and the drilling platforms in the Gulf of Tonkin. On November 8, 1980, the PLANAF sent two H-6 bombers to patrol the Spratly Islands in the SCS for the first time. Then the PLANAF began its regular patrols in the area.[34] Those oceangoing voyages convinced Chinese naval officers that the PLAN, as a modern navy, was now capable of reaching deep waters (or blue waters, the far sea). For the joint operations and amphibious campaigns, the navy also developed a modern equipment framework to carry out maritime combat operations, including a sea-based nuclear counterattack, with near-shore combat as a focus and operational and tactical maneuvers as a complement. In October 1982, the PLAN launched its first ballistic missile, Julang-1, from a Type 31 conventional submarine. In 1988, the navy launched another ballistic missile from its Type 91 nuclear submarine.

On May 18, 1980, China successful tested an intercontinental ballistic missile, from its own territory to an ocean area about 4,350 miles northwest of the Fiji Islands in the South Pacific. The long-range carrier rocket crossed through the Southern and Northern Hemispheres and splashed down as hoped. Throughout testing, a PLAN convoy safeguarded the rocket's flight and landing for thirty-five days, covering 8,733 nautical miles. The PLA high command and the navy established a task force to retrieve the long-range carrier missile's data bin. From April to July 1980, the Task Force Formation crossed the equator and sailed to the South Pacific for the carrier rocket's testing.[35] The fleet had eighteen ships, including six destroyers (*106*, *107*, *108*, *131*, *132*, and *162*), two auxiliary vessels (*X-615* and *X-950*), two ocean salvage-and-rescue vessels (*J-302* and *J-506*), two marine survey ships (*Xiangyanghong-5* and *Xiangyanghong-10*), four ocean tug ships (*T-154*, *T-710*, *T-830*, and *Deyue*), and two main scientific survey ships (*Yuanwang-1* and *Yuanwang-2*). The Task Force Formation had a nineteen-member formation command. Rear Admiral Liu Daosheng, the first deputy commander of the navy, served as the task force commander, while Rear Admiral Yang Guoyu, PLAN deputy commander, served as the formation's deputy commander. The formation's command flagship was *Xiangyanghong-5*, which included a marine survey command, naval battle command, and logistics and rescue command. Commodore Gao Xizeng, ECS deputy commander, and Nie Jukui, commander of the SSF Yulin Naval Base, served as deputy commanders for the naval battle command. Rear Admiral Zhang Xusan, PLAN chief of staff, served as the battle command's chief of staff.[36]

On the morning of April 27, 1980, the PLAN held a ceremony at Wusongkou, Shanghai for the Task Force Formation's departure. Vice Premiers Wang Zhen and Geng Biao flew from Beijing to attend the ceremony. General Zhang Aiping, the defense minister, spoke to the formation officers, sailors, and scientists. In the afternoon, the two vice premiers, defense minister, and General Ye Fei visited the fleet at the Wusongkou harbor. The Task Force Formation embarked from Wusongkou on April 28-30.[37] The formation crossed the first island chain on May 1 and entered the Pacific, following an operational route designed by Tang Jiahua, chief of nautical voyages at PLAN HQ. Their nautical route avoided reefs, typhoons, and sovereign waters. On May 4, after his meteorologist officers reported a possible typhoon headed their way, Liu Daosheng diverted their route and avoided the bad weather conditions. On May 8, the fleet crossed the equator. Around 12 p.m. on May 9, a U.S. P-3C plane followed the Chinese fleet at a low altitude for a long period.[38] The Test Fleet Formation reached the designated area on May 12 and awaited the carrier rocket in the South Pacific. Admiral Liu Daosheng could hear the launching HQ's commands and countdown from the flagship's bridge on May 18. They also observed the rocket's flight into space and its return to earth. Soon the rocket and data bin splashed into the water. Liu ordered four helicopters to secure the area and retrieve the data bin. On June 1-2, the Test Fleet Formation returned to Shanghai, where Defense Minister Zhang Aiping awaited the fleet. On June 2, Marshal Ye Jianying met all the formation's officers and scientists at the celebration meeting.[39]

In 1980, General Ye Fei reestablished the navy's marine corps. After learning from the Battle of the Paracel Islands of 1974, rebuilding the marine corps became his priority. In the PLA's efforts to recapture disputed islands from the Vietnamese forces, the army sent its infantry from Hainan to aid in the navy's SCS landing mission from December 1973 to January 1974. The army officers and soldiers, however, lacked experience in amphibious landings and could hardly bear the motion of the sea's rolling waves. Their ability to fight Vietnamese soldiers on the islands was inhibited by seasickness.

On May 5, 1980, the SSF established the First Marine Brigade at Hainan Island. The marine brigade totaled more than five thousand troops, including three marine battalions, a tank battalion, an artillery battalion, an amphibious armored vehicle battalion, and a reconnaissance and communication battalion among other technical units like air defense, combat engineering, helicopters, diving, transportation, and antichemical companies.[40] Soon the ESF and NSF also established their own marine brigades. The marine brigades were equipped with *T-59* tanks, newly manufactured *T-63* tanks, *S-77* amphibious armored vehicles, and 122-mm self-propelled guns. The marine battalions also have *Hongqi-8* antitank missiles and *Hongying-5* and *Qianwei-1* antiaircraft missiles. The Marine Corps became an important ship-to-shore attack and coastal defense force of the Navy Joint Maneuver Formation. In the 1980s, the Marine Corps joined naval operations such as the defense of the Spratly Islands, the Sharp Sword Operation, earthquake relief, and ocean escorts. At the age of sixty-eight and in declining health, Ye Fei completed Deng's assignment and retired from the PLAN commander's post in 1982.[41]

LIU'S NAVAL STRATEGY

The appointment of Liu Huaqing as the navy's commander in August 1982 marked a new era in PLAN history, since he was the first naval officer to lead the Chinese navy and was very close to Deng Xiaoping and then Jiang Zemin. After joining the Red Army in 1931, Liu became a Red Army staff member in the division and army's Political Tasks Departments. He headed the 129th Division's Propaganda Office in World War II. He became a PLA brigade, division, and army deputy political commissar in 1946–49. During his study at the Naval Academy in the Soviet Union from 1954 to 1958, Liu was ranked rear admiral in 1955. He served as commander of the NSF Lushun Naval Base and deputy commander of the NSF after his return from Russia. He became vice minister of the Sixth Industrial Ministry in 1965 and deputy chief of the CSTIND in October 1966. He was promoted to deputy chief of the PLA General Staff in January 1981.

As CSTIND deputy chief, Liu Huaqing worked with Marshal Nie Rongzhen and pushed several major naval projects through research and development in the 1970s, including strategic nuclear submarines, guided-missile frigates, guided-missile destroyers, diesel-powered conventional submarines, antiship missiles, attack submarines, and submarine chasers. In 1982, Liu

Huaqing became PLAN commander. The Chinese navy was now sizable, with nearly all types of warships, and had become a regional naval power. Its underwater fleet had SSBNs, SSNs, and nuclear-powered submarines.[42] Its surface warship fleet included destroyers, frigates, corvettes, minesweepers, mine layers, missile boats, torpedo boasts, landing ships, and auxiliary vessels. Its aviation fleet was equipped with medium and light bombers, fighters, attackers, ship-based helicopters, and reconnaissance/surveillance planes, assisted by a radar network that covered all of China's coasts. Its offshore defense force had replaced coastal cannon with antiship missiles.

As a result, China's shipbuilding industry, navigation technology research and imports, and naval training and education systems backed its impressive naval development in the 1980s. Liu Huaqing transformed the PLAN from brown-water operations to a green-water development through reconstruction, qualitative improvement, higher educational standards for personnel, and new Western technology. Richard A. Bitzinger and other scholars point out that "prior to the 1989 Western arms embargo, China had secured valuable access to key foreign technologies to help kick-start indigenous naval S&T [science and technology]. . . . European naval technologies enabled China to institute its new-con warship programs, best manifested in the *Luhu*, *Jiangwei*, *Houjian*, and *Song* series, which served as test beds for subsequent designs."[43]

When Liu Huaqing became the navy commander, Li Yaowen was his political commissar. Li joined the CCP in 1937 and became an infantry company political instructor and then regiment and brigade political commissar in World War II. He was a PLA division and army political commissar in the civil war. Li Yaowen participated in the Battle of Chosin Reservoir in Korea as the CPVF 26th Army's political commissar. After his return, Li became the director of the Ji'nan Military Region's Political Tasks Department. In 1955, he was made a major general. Li was promoted to the Ji'nan Military Region's political commissar in 1965. Premier Zhou Enlai approved Li Yaowen's appointment as vice minister of the PRC's Ministry of Foreign Affairs in 1970. He was then appointed as China's ambassador to Tanzania in 1972, the first Chinese ambassador to Madagascar in 1975, and ambassador to the Soviet Union in 1976. He worked with Liu Huaqing after he became the CSTIND political commissar in 1977. After Ye Fei's retirement, Li Yaowen was appointed as the political commissar of the navy in October 1980. He attained the rank of admiral in September 1988.[44]

By the time Liu Huaqing took over the navy in August 1982, with Li Yaowen as his political commissar, the PLAN had grown from nothing into a maritime force of considerable size, supported by China's indigenous industry and education systems. When Mao Zedong was determined to make China a continental power in East Asia in the 1950s–70s, the PLAN, the PLA's least prioritized service, was intended to play only an auxiliary role in a total land war against coastal invasions. When Deng resolved to bring China into the global community in the 1980s–90s, the PLAN had to find its new place in post-Mao China and thus found new reasons to update its technology, which required an overhaul. This was a daunting task. The PLA therefore developed a new strategy when Liu Huaqing assumed command.[45]

After taking office, Admiral Liu continued Ye Fei's reorganization and rehabilitation of the naval force by addressing personnel problems from the Cultural Revolution, reducing factional and regional differences, and training the officer corps with modern naval war concepts. He organized the design and drafting of the *Naval Officers Training Manual*, the *Captains Training Outlines*, and the *Training Handbook for the Officers above the Divisional Level in the Navy*.[46] The new guidelines and regulations further defined the duties and responsibilities of the naval officers and improved the chain of command. He also removed some of the aging admirals and rebalanced the ratio of officers to seamen.

Liu Huaqing called for China's sea power, oceanic interests, and global strategy to be supported by a strong navy. In 1984, he persuaded admirals to draft the Seventh Five-Year Plan for the PLAN and "The Navy in 2000." Liu made a three-step development plan for China's blue-water navy by breaking through three "island chains" in 1988. The PLAN would establish its presence in the first island chain, running south from Japan past Taiwan to the Philippines, by 2010. The goal for the Chinese navy's establishment in the second chain from Sakhalin to the islands of the Southwest Pacific Ocean was targeted for 2025. The third island chain would reach from the Aleutian Islands in the north to Antarctica in the south by 2050. As David Shambaugh points out, Liu's plan and "the operational task would be to establish a 'sea' or 'area denial' capacity in a progressively phased fashion."[47]

According to Liu Huaqing, China endeavored to build a modern, blue-water naval force by 2000 with aircraft carriers and new high-tech warships. Shambaugh considers it a "principal shift" in China's security and PLA's defense "from continental to maritime and national to regional definitions."[48] Liu Huaqing's strategy envisioned the Chinese navy with capabilities in the Pacific and Indian Oceans, aircraft carriers and airplanes, and high-tech weapon systems. His new strategy pushed the research, development, and manufacturing of new warships, medium- and long-range missiles, and attacking weapon systems for naval modernization in the 1980s.

In 1981, China's nuclear submarine *Long March–1* set out on a nearly month-long voyage. In 1983, it went even further. On October 12, 1982, the PLAN successfully launched its underwater ballistic missile from a submarine, after its first test failed five days before. Rear Admiral Yang Guoyu congratulated the submarine crew after their return to Qingdao Naval Base.[49] In August 1983, China's first missile-bearing nuclear submarine entered service. In 1986, the navy had two *Xia*-class SSBNs armed with twelve CSS-N-3 missiles, and three *Han*-class SSNs armed with six SY-2 cruise missiles. In September 1988, the successful underwater launch of a ballistic missile by a nuclear submarine showed that the PLAN could provide underwater strategic deterrence and limited nuclear counterattack.

Thus, by the 1980s, the PLAN's overall technological level had become competitive with that of other global navies. The tactics and technological performance of the Chinese-made naval equipment had improved a great deal. The main surface combat warships were much better in terms of being fitted with missiles, integration between command and control, and implementation of stereoscopic combat zones. Starting in 1985, the PLAN fleet formations sailed to continents on goodwill visits and began participating in joint military exercises with warships from many countries. In 1987, the naval logistical ship *Fengcang* began supplying fuel and food to Chinese missile destroyers and missile frigates in the Pacific, which solved the last of the Chinese navy's three problems for ocean voyages, including long-distance communication, ocean sailing guidance, and ocean voyage logistics.[50]

In 1984, after approval from the State Council and CMC, the PLAN actively participated in the preparation of an Antarctic expedition to establish China's Great Wall Research Station at the South Pole. Admiral Hu Yanlin justifies the Chinese plan thus: "With the rapid economic development and population growth, [our] land resources [have been] consumed tremendously. It is an inevitable trend [for China] to demand new resources and new living space from the oceans. Therefore, to explore oceanic resources and to maintain [our] sea power are critical to the existence and development of Chinese people."[51] On November 22, the Antarctic expedition formation left Shanghai, comprising the PLAN *J-121* rescue ship with 308 naval sailors. Around 2 a.m. on December 26, the fleet arrived at the South Pole. On February 14, 1985, the fleet command reported to Beijing that China's Great Wall South Pole Research Station had been completed.[52] In 1986, China bought an Australian aircraft carrier, the *Melbourne*, for study and then scrap, even though the high command was not ready yet to build China's own carrier. By 1987, the PLAN had become the third largest navy in the world, with 350,000 sails and 1,000 ships, including 350 oceangoing warships.

As one of the military top leaders, Admiral Liu Huaqing was promoted to deputy secretary general of the CMC in 1987. Although he left the PLAN commander's post in 1988, Liu continued his efforts in naval development and modernization. That year, when he oversaw the PLA's development of military science and technology, Liu made new plans for naval technology improvement, including naval aviation technology. Since the late 1980s, the PLAN has been equipped with new guided-missile destroyers, fighter-bombers, antisubmarine helicopters, and high-performance equipment and weapons. In September 1988, the successful underwater launch of a ballistic missile by a nuclear submarine showed that the PLAN could provide underwater strategic deterrence and limited nuclear counterattacks. The PLANAF began testing the *JH-7* "Flying Leopard" (the *FBC-1* is the export version) in 1988. The *JH-7* filled the vacancy of a long-range (1,600 kilometers) strike aircraft for the navy. While the PLAAF adopted the Russian-made Su-27 fighters, the PLANAF adopted the *JH-7* as its main strike aircraft in the 1990s. Meanwhile, Admiral Liu Huaqing made three trips to the Paracel Islands in the SCS to inspect construction of the Yongxing airstrip and harbor.

Admiral Zhang Lianzhong became the navy's commander in 1988 after Liu became the CMC vice chairman. Admiral Zhang, who joined the CCP and the PLA in 1946, served the PLA as a platoon and company commander in the 31st Army and studied modern military technology at the PLA Advanced Infantry School in 1956–58 and the navy's Submarine Academy in 1960–64. After his graduation, Zhang served as a submarine control officer, second-in-command officer, and captain. Then he studied at the PLA Academy of Military Science. Beginning in 1980, Zhang Lianzhong became NSF deputy chief staff, commander of the Lushun Naval Base, and PLAN deputy commander. In January 1988, Zhang Lianzhong was appointed as the commander of the Chinese navy. Compared with his predecessors, he had the longest career in the navy. Commander Zhang Liangzhong was promoted to vice admiral in September 1988 and then admiral in May 1993. After taking the naval commander's position, Zhang prepared more naval battles against the Vietnamese in the SCS after the Battle of the Paracel Islands.

When the Sino-Vietnamese border war broke out in February 1979, the PLAN reinforced the SSF and ordered it to conduct marine and seaway surveys in the SCS. SSF Command assigned Wu Buyun as chief of the survey squadron. Wu Buyun led his squadron and sailed throughout the SCS, surveying more than two thousand islands and reefs, mapping navigation conditions, and drawing marine charts. In April 1986, PLA intelligence reported that Vietnamese agents had sent a ship and attempted to capture Wu and his team as they mapped a seaway in the Gulf of Tonkin. The PLAN requested Wu's return to Yulin Naval Base in Hainan immediately. However, Wu remained on the mission and completed his tasks while escaping Vietnamese agents.[53]

In 1987, China announced plans to establish No. 74 Marine Observatory at the Spratly Islands in the SCS. The Spratly Islands (Nansha in Chinese) are the largest group in the SCS; they lie over 550 nautical miles from China's Hainan Island, cover a water area of 61,775 square miles, and include approximately one hundred small islands (see map 5). Although most of these islands are rocky, small, and uninhabited, the competing claims reflect the interest in oil and gas reserves beneath them. Among the countries occupying some of the islands, the PRC controls seven islands, Vietnam twenty-nine, the Philippines nine, Malaysia nine, and the ROC only one, Taiping Island (also known as Itu Aba Island).[54] The Taiwanese established a permanent presence in the Spratly Islands in 1956. In December 2007, the Taiping Island airport was completed.[55] On February 2, 2008, Taiwanese president Chen Shui-bian visited the island accompanied by a large naval force. On January 28, 2016, ROC president Ma Ying-jeou led an official Taiwanese government delegation to the largest island (about 110 acres) in the Spratly Island group, the ROC-controlled Taiping Island. Ma Ying-jeou continues to claim ROC's sovereignty over the island. During an interview in 2017, President Ma gave me one of his three books on the legal status of the disputed islands from an international maritime legal perspective.[56]

In the spring of 1987, the border conflict between China and Vietnam intensified. In April, Admiral Zhang Lianzhong, the new PLAN commander, ordered the SSF to escort Chinese survey ships, while they were looking for the possible construction sites for the marine observatory at the Spratly Islands.[57] On May 8, SSF Command sent a large formation to escort marine research and logistical ships to the islands. After their research, the survey team chose the Yongshu Reef as the site for No. 74 Marine Observatory. The bottom of the Yongshu Reef was about sixteen miles long and four miles wide. During high tide, only a small portion of the reef was visible above sea level. Nevertheless, Admiral Hu Yanlin describes the Yongshu as the front line for China's southern frontier.[58]

Commander Zhang Lianzhong learned from the Battle of the Paracel Islands and sent troops to occupy the Spratly Islands before construction on the marine observatory commenced. In early January 1988, Commodore Chen Weiwen, chief of staff of the SSF Yulin Naval Base, led a battle formation toward the islands and occupied them three days later. Chen deployed two frigates, *553* and *556*, to patrol the islands and the Yongshu, where the construction site would soon be, while he ordered *502* and *503* frigates to secure the reefs around the islands by building several high outposts. During the nineteen days of preconstruction patrol, Chen Weiwen received several intel reports that the Vietnamese navy was preparing some operations against them.[59]

On January 31, 1988, two Vietnamese warships approached the Yongshu Reef. Chen Weiwen ordered frigates to intercept the Vietnamese ships and prevent their reaching the reef. After several attempts, the Vietnamese failed to land and retreated. After receiving Chen's engagement report, the State Council and CMC ordered construction of the No. 74 Marine Observatory as soon as possible. The SSF sent more warships to protect the engineering, research survey, construction, and logistical ships around the Spratly Islands. The first task was to open a two-hundred-meter path through the reefs for the construction ships. As soon as construction began, skirmishes between the Chinese and Vietnamese navies broke out over the reefs.

On February 17, Chinese missile destroyer *162* and frigate *508* escorted transit ship *147* to the Huayang Reef for surveying. In the early evening, *147* met one Vietnamese minesweeper and one transit ship, which also sailed toward the Huayang Reef. The Chinese survey team and construction workers on board *147* were all armed with guns and grenades. They maneuvered their ship and tried blocking the Vietnamese landing at the reef. The Chinese warships also aimed at the Vietnamese ships, while maintaining a policy of "no shooting first." During the standoff, the Vietnamese sent dinghies with armed personnel and their national flag. Lin Shuming, captain of the Chinese construction team on *147*, also rushed toward the reef with six armed workers and the Chinese flag. A race ensued, and the Chinese boat was the first to reach the reef, where they hoisted the flag up on a steel brazing as the sign of sovereignty. The Vietnamese stopped about a hundred yards out, since they faced a machine gun and several automatic weapons. After Chinese reinforcements arrived at the reef, the Vietnamese returned to their ships. Within three days, the Chinese construction workers had built a shelter at the Huayang Reef to protect their flag.[60]

At 4 p.m. on March 13, the Chinese frigate *502*'s radar reported to Commodore Chen Weiwen that a Vietnamese formation had reached the Chigua Reef, which was five thousand meters long and four hundred meters wide and not far from the Yongshu Reef. The Vietnamese formation included two armed transit ships, *604* and *605*, and a landing ship, *505*. Commodore Chen sent a group of sailors on a motorized sampan to occupy the reef at

9 p.m. The next morning, the Vietnamese armed transit ship 604 landed troops and armed workers at the Chigua Reef. Then Chen sent ten more sailors as reinforcement for the Chinese occupiers. Soon two Chinese frigates, *531* and *556*, arrived to support *502*. The Chinese sent more sailors to the reef.

By 7 a.m. on March 14, 1988, there were forty-three Vietnamese soldiers and fifty-eight Chinese sailors on the Chigua Reef. Both sides shouted and moved carefully toward each other. *502*'s political commissar, Li Chuqun, and the Chinese shouted in Vietnamese, asking the Vietnamese to leave the reef, while the Vietnamese asked the Chinese to return to their ships in Chinese. When both sides met in the middle of the reef, a Chinese sailor grasped the Vietnamese flag. The Vietnamese flag holder jumped out and tried to recover the flag. Eventually someone opened fire, and the first round from the Vietnamese wounded Deputy Weaponry Captain Yang Zhiliang in his left arm. Accounts conflict on who fired the first shot.[61]

The Vietnamese armed transit ship *604* opened fire on the Chinese on Chigua Reef. Chen Weiwen ordered frigate *502* to attack *604*, frigate *531* to concentrate fire on the Vietnamese landing ship *505*, and frigate *556* to fire on another armed transit ship, *605*. Soon the Vietnamese *604* was hit and caught fire, and it sank around 9 a.m. on March 14. Then frigate *502* joined *531* and fired on the landing ship *505*. After suffering heavy damage, the Vietnamese ships left the remnants on the reef and fled the Spratly Islands. The Vietnamese soldiers surrendered to the Chinese on Chigua Reef.[62]

After the Battle of the Spratly Islands, Commodore Chen Weiwen and his staff were given awards by the PLAN, and Yang Zhiliang became the battle's hero. During his hospitalization in Beijing, Yang Shangkun, China's vice president; Chi Haotian, PLA chief of General Staff; and Admiral Li Yaowen, the navy's political commissar, visited Yang Zhiliang. On August 1, the No. 74 Marine Observatory Station became operational. It was built on an artificial island and included a seaport, airstrip, naval facilities, radar and warning system, island defense, and living quarters.[63] A year later, Yang Zhiliang got married, and Admiral Liu Huaqing and Political Commissar Li Yaowen attended his wedding ceremony.

COMMERCIALIZATION AND TIANANMEN

The PLA generals described Deng Xiaoping's economic reform as a "double-edged sword." "It [globalization] plays a positive role in promoting world economic development. However, one must not underestimate its negative impact as it may pose more challenges to under-developed countries."[64] First, Deng reduced the defense budget in the mid-1980s military reform to generate desperately needed resources for national economic reconstruction. The PLA's annual military budgets thus suffered a gradual reduction. In 1975, China's annual defense budget was 17.4 percent of the national governmental expenses. By 1985, the annual defense budget had been reduced to 10.4 percent of the national budget. By 1995, it had shrunk to 8 percent of the annual national budget. In 1990, the PLA annual budget was 1.64 percent of China's gross national product (GNP). Then the annual military budget declined to 1.63 percent of the GNP in 1991, 1.57 percent in 1992, 1.36 percent in 1993, and 1.26 percent in 1994.[65] By contrast, in 1990 the U.S. defense budget was 6.4 percent of its GNP, and the Soviet Union's defense budget was 10 percent. In 1985, the PLA's annual budget was only $5.6 billion for its 4.3 million troops, about $1,300 per year, or $3.56 per day, for each officer or soldier. The budget cuts failed to provide even one meal a day for individual troops and created a serious financial crisis in the military. Each naval officer received only one pair of leather shoes every four years. The East Sea Fleet requested construction of a naval base on Chongming Island, a strategic point at the mouth of the Yangzi River, but the high command rejected it due to defense budget cuts.

Second, with industrialization and shifting to a market economy, PLAN recruitment declined, and the morale among seamen was low. A naval officer earned only about half the salary of an average urban worker.[66] Zhoushan Naval Base lacked financial resources and could not solve its issues with potable water, leading to serious conflicts over fresh water with the island's local fishermen. PLAN admirals still cite the Party Center and government's *qianzhai* (owing money) to the military; CCP leaders and the Deng administration owed the PLA a big debt in the 1980s. The high command only provided 60 percent of the military budget, and PLA units were forced to make up the 40 percent difference by their own financial means.

To address the shrinking defense budget, on May 4, 1985, the CCP allowed, and even encouraged, PLA units to engage in commercial manufacturing, business activities, and foreign trade.[67] The Party Center's document instructed the PLA DGS to establish the Baoli (Poly) Corporation for domestic commercial activities and international trade. This military entrepreneurial empire had total assets of over $1 billion, including a $700 million real estate portfolio, steel mills, power plants, and a large portion of China's arms sales trade. Meanwhile, the Department of General Political Tasks opened the Kaili Corporation for business.[68] The navy ran the Songhai Corporation in Shanghai and the Xinghai Corporation in Guangzhou, which included a dozen Hong Kong–based container freighters with a 400,000-ton capacity. Many PLAN conglomerates were controlled by naval "princelings"—children of high-ranking naval officers. The daughter of Admiral Liu Huaqing served as one of Baoli's CEOs.

China's defense minister, General Zhang Aiping, was among the high-ranking officers who opposed the party's decision. He believed that the PLA's participation in business would certainly create interest groups and power-capital establishments that would encourage corruption and power abuse.[69] Nevertheless, most naval officers welcomed the new policy and readied themselves to enter the business world, compete with state-owned enterprises and the private sector, and make a lot of money.

Soon the PLAN owned shipping companies that used hundreds of naval transit vessels for river and oceanic commercial shipping.[70] The fleet commands sought foreign partners from the United States, Taiwan, and Hong Kong to establish profitable joint ventures or construction projects. The PLAN opened and leased twenty-nine naval bases, ports, and facilities for business and commercial purposes.[71] Some naval bases and PLANAF airfields ran department stores, office buildings, hotels, golf clubs, nightclubs, KTVs (karaoke rooms), brothels, and underground casinos. Many squadrons owned supermarkets, restaurants, gas stations, and convenience stores. The East Sea Fleet opened a substantial shopping mall in Shanghai, with hundreds of stores selling imported luxuries, name-brand apparel, electrical appliances, and furniture. A naval base commander leased an antiaircraft artillery regiment, including all AAA cannon, radar system, equipment, vehicles, and facilities, and the base, to a Hong Kong film company for a month-long production. The PLA high command and local governments offered special tax breaks, regulation exemptions, and protective policies to incentivize PLA and PLAN businesses. In fact, most PLAN businesses garnered protection from and connections with local police and security forces. Some foreign investors, especially those from Taiwan and Hong Kong, felt safer conducting business with the navy than with other partners in the military.

But corruption, power abuse, and mismanagements soon swept like a wildfire throughout the navy. Many naval officers accepted bribes, kickbacks, and commissions, just as the other branches had, and used naval facilities, equipment, and warships to make easy profits. Captains and sailors used their warships for smugglings to avoid port inspections and custom searches. Island patrol troops were involved in drug trafficking along the coastline. High-ranking officers sold military secrets to Taiwanese and American intelligence. Some air force bases, equipment warehouses, military hospitals, and defense facilities became available for rent or sale. Some PLAN units resorted to arms sales, human trafficking, and other criminal activities.

Many generals and admirals became millionaires themselves; their children studied in Western countries and Japan, their wives and parents purchased expensive houses, and they bought permanent residency (or "green cards") and citizenship in foreign countries like the United States, Canada, England, France, Australia, and Singapore.[72] Consequently, power-interest groups gradually spread from high-ranking officers to middle-ranking officers, as demonstrated by the high percentage of income not accounted for by traditional means. Senior Colonel Liu Mingfu, a professor at China's NDU, warned the PLA in his book, "The most dangerous enemy the PLA faces today is its own corruption."[73] In his studies on China under Deng Xiaoping, Maurice Meisner argues that the "crown princes and princesses," or children of top military leaders, took advantage of their privileges to benefit themselves. They became "the most prominent symbols of the official profiteering and corruption that overwhelmed the Communist bureaucracy in the late 1980s." Official corruption in the 1990s was so rampant that its scope and scale "shocked even the most hardened of political cynics." For Meisner, corruption was one of the "unintended consequences" of Deng's economic reform. Unfortunately, Deng's own children conducted lucrative businesses, and his policy response to the rampant corruption was "confused, contradictory, and above all, ambiguous."[74] Therefore, rapid economic development coupled with official corruption and an absence of effective legal and social supervising mechanisms, problems that the 1989 Tiananmen demonstration targeted, grew worse and expanded to more industries and governments.

During the 1980s, corruptions, mismanagements, power abuse, and theft of public property were rampant, despite the government's efforts to control them. In the late 1980s, increasing economic stratification, social instability, and political dissatisfaction were highlighted by minority antigovernment revolts and prodemocracy student activities.[75] After former CCP chairman Hu Yaobang died on April 15, 1989, students mourning on their Beijing campus soon became a citywide and then a nationwide prodemocracy demonstration asking for political reforms across the country and protesting corruption and power abuse. Although Deng denounced the movement, hundreds of thousands of students and citizens joined together and continued demonstrating at Tiananmen Square in May.[76] Soon the demonstrations had spread to 116 cities across the country.[77]

On the afternoon on May 19, the Party Center enforced martial law in Beijing. The PLA high command appointed Admiral Liu Huaqing the commander of the PLA Martial Law Forces, including both army and air force. Admiral Liu deployed twenty-two infantry divisions from thirteen armies and ordered the Airborne 15th Army from the air force to move into the capital city under the command of the PLA Martial Law Forces. Many people, including PLA officers, asked questions then and now about why Admiral Liu did not send the PLAN Marine Corps or any naval troops to Tiananmen Square during the suppression. It was said that some naval admirals, including Admiral Li Yaowen, the navy's political commissar, opposed the dispatch of troops to Beijing for use against the student demonstration. During the crisis, infantry troops were sent to guard (or watch) PLAN HQ in Beijing, as the high command had doubts about the navy's loyalty and control.

From May 20, the martial law troop under the command of Liu Huaqing, some 250,000–300,000 strong, began moving toward Beijing. As the Party Center divided, the deployment reflected the CCP elders' uncertainty and anxiety. However, many PLA divisions were stopped in the suburbs by crowds and roadblocks. All martial law troops failed to reach their destinations in the capital as planned.[78] Most generals knew nothing of the movement, and the order came as a surprise.[79] A group of generals, including Zhang Aiping and Ye Fei, signed a letter to Deng Xiaoping that read, "We request that troops not enter the city and that martial law not be carried out in Beijing."[80]

Martial law, however, was ineffective: students remained in Tiananmen Square, and the demonstration on May 23 was the largest since its declaration. By the end of May, the Party Center prepared for a final crackdown. On June 3, the Politburo instructed Admiral Liu Huaqing to put down the "counterrevolutionary riot" by force in Beijing.[81] Admiral Liu established two subcommands, including the City Forward Command and Square Clearing Command, to carry out the Party Center's order. He ordered divisions from the 28th, 38th, and 63rd Armies to move into the capital from the west and divisions from the 15th, 20th, 26th, and 54th Armies from the south. He ordered the Capital First Division and 39th Army to move toward Tiananmen from the east and the 40th and 64th Armies from the north. All infantry soldiers received two hundred rounds of ammunition.[82] Some PLA officers questioned the high command's decision and refused to carry out Liu Huaqing's orders. The 38th Army commander, Xu Qinxian, returned to the hospital to avoid commanding his troops against the demonstrators in Beijing.[83] Although he was arrested immediately, his disobedience shocked his troops and other armies. Rumors soon spread that they would fight against the rebellious 38th Army in Beijing. Xu Feng, commander of the 116th Division, 39th Army, refused to move his troops into the capital by creating communication problems, remaining in an eastern suburb, and delaying his troop movement into the city.

After 9 p.m. that evening, PLA troops forced their way through the streets and opened fire on the protesters about 10 p.m. at West Chang'an Street, about six miles from Tiananmen Square. The protesters and local residents burned public trollies on the street to halt, or at least hinder, the 38th's advance. The troops shot their way through the roadblock and fired on residential buildings along both sides of the street. It was reported that by 10:30 p.m., more than forty people had been killed on West Chang'an

Street.⁸⁴ Around midnight, Yan Hongji, chief of staff of the 38th Army's First Division, led his troops into the city center first. Party propaganda praised his arrival at Tiananmen Square as a "heroic action." Yan himself shot and killed one student while he ordered tanks to ram the protesters at high speed, causing many casualties. Some soldiers refused to fire on unarmed students and civilians. Some dropped their weapons and deserted. Some officers only reluctantly followed their orders and reportedly "disappeared." Some protesters picked up those weapons and returned fire, while their leaders tried convincing them not to but to keep the protest a "peaceful demonstration."⁸⁵

Around 10:30 p.m., the 15th Airborne Army fired on protesters to the south. The protesters tried to burn out the military trucks by throwing flaming objects and other projectiles. During the bloody clash, at least seven hundred civilians were killed, while the 15th Army counted a couple of dozen casualties.⁸⁶ When 70,000–80,000 protesting students remained in the square on the early morning of June 4, the 15th's tanks and armored vehicles forced their way into Tiananmen Square by 1:30 a.m. The troops continued firing on the students. Some protesters returned fire, and a few soldiers were killed during the fight. Both the 15th and 38th Armies boasted the "most kills." By around 5 a.m., PLA troops had ended the protest at Tiananmen Square.

After the Tiananmen Square incident, the PLA conducted investigations of 3,500 officers. About 111 of them were punished because they had "breached discipline in a serious way." Meanwhile, 1,400 soldiers were court-martialed because they "shed their weapons and ran away."⁸⁷ The incident had a negative impact on the PLA, especially the navy. PLAN political commissar Admiral Li Yaowen lost his position and was forced to retire from the navy in April 1990. Nevertheless, Deng Xiaoping continued to insist on his Four Cardinal Principles, including keeping to the socialist road, upholding the people's democratic dictatorship, sticking to the CCP's leadership, and adhering to Marxism-Leninism and Maoist thought. He believed that though the country must keep its door open to the world, stability must be stressed. To guarantee stability, the Communist Party must be in control. However, health problems soon reduced his active political role, as Parkinson's disease, lung ailments, and other problems had made him almost blind and deaf by the mid-1990s. Deng died in Beijing on February 28, 1997.⁸⁸

CHAPTER 6

Sea Power in the Blue Water

The Chinese navy evolved and became one of the world naval powers from 1990 to 2012. Jiang Zemin became China's leader (1990–2002) after Deng's retirement in 1989. Although the year 1991 witnessed the end of the Soviet Union, the Jiang government stayed its course, continuing to promote Deng's modernization policy and agenda through the last decade of the twentieth century. In the 1990s, the PLA expected "reimbursement" from Jiang Zemin after the Tiananmen crisis. From 1990 to 2002, the government doubled its defense budget, with an annual GNP growth rate of 8.6 percent. To further their interests, the high command protected Jiang's new, central leadership based on a coalition of key political institutions. Jiang earned the PLA's political support, and as such his position went unchallenged.

China's rapid increase in overseas trade made the oceans more important to national economic growth. In his early years, Jiang Zemin promoted a pragmatic nationalism to emphasize China's unity, sovereignty, strength, and prosperity, and he gradually shifted the party's ideology from radical communism to moderate nationalism as an ideology to save the state at the end of the Cold War, bringing in one more source of legitimacy for the CCP as the country's ruling party. As Jiang shifted the party's political goals, he faced new challenges such as Tibet, Taiwan, and disputed islands in the ECS and SCS. Jiang Zemin supported Admiral Liu Huaqing's perception of China's sea power, maritime interests, and oceanic sovereignty. Admiral Liu became the CMC's vice chairman in 1990 and a Politburo Standing Committee member in 1992. The PLAN received the lion's share of Jiang's new defense budget as he concurred with Admiral Liu's focus on China's naval development. Jiang Zemin told PLA leaders, "We must prioritize naval construction."[1] The PLA moved away from traditional ground war preparation and began to focus more on new naval warfare.

In the late 2000s, when China had the second largest economy in the world, the country became more dependent on overseas trade. Hu Jintao, Jiang's successor from 2002 to 2012, deliberately maintained successful naval reforms. Yet from its inception, the PLAN's continuously adaptive reforms made its modernization dependent on economic success, and it seemed that the PLAN might forever trail behind Western armed forces. From 2002 to 2012, Hu Jintao nurtured the PLAN's relationship by supporting a growing military professionalism with an emphasis on educational credentials and merit-based system of officer promotion. According to Hu and the new high command, the navy needed a "leap-over" transition from electronic to digital capabilities. By 2012, the Chinese navy expanded from a "coastal fleet" in the 1980s to a "twenty-first-century maritime power" and, as the second largest navy in the world, was surpassed only by the USN.[2]

JIANG'S NAVAL STRATEGY

After the Tiananmen incident, Jiang Zemin continued military reform in favor of the Chinese navy. In 1992, under Jiang's leadership, the National People's Congress (NPC) passed China's First Maritime Law, which codified Liu's conception of "sea as territory," including the country's "sovereignty" over 3 million square kilometers of ocean and seas. From that point, China regarded the oceans and seas as new frontiers. General Chi Haotian, China's defense minister (1993–2003) and the CMC's vice chairman (1995–2003), supported Jiang Zemin's claims of sea power and 3 million square kilometers of "oceanic territory." He believes that "the country's rise and fall depends on its role in the oceans." The Chinese navy should be a blue-water navy, according to General Chi, and "going to the four oceans" is its strategic choice.[3] With the military's support, Jiang Zemin made an important call in November 1996 for the PLA's "two transformations": from an armed force to fight "local war under ordinary conditions" to an army prepared to fight and win "local wars under modern high-tech conditions"; and from an armed force based on quantity to an army based on quality. To carry out Jiang's vision for the future of the PLA, in 1997 the high command made a three-step grand PLA plan for 1998–2040. It became the new guideline for the PLA to prepare "local wars under modern high-tech conditions." The grand plan prioritized the PLAN's modernization under the third-generation command and new efforts in reorganization, institutional reform, and improving sustainability system.

On April 7, 1990, Jiang Zemin attended a PLAN commission ceremony for a new model of Chinese-made submarine. At lunch, Jiang sat with submarine sailors and learned how the new technology worked underwater. The new president stated, "We must recognize the oceans from a strategic point of view, and promote a strong sea perspective of all the Chinese people." On June 23, Jiang visited a SSF training base and told South Sea Fleet commanders, "Since building a strong naval force is a very complicated task, we need to train the best naval officers first." By the late 1990s, about 87 percent of naval officers had a college degree or other higher education certificate. On April 18, 1993, Jiang Zemin visited SSF Hainan Naval Base and met the officers and sailors of an SSF submarine squadron. He told the seamen, "This is the foremost front of China's sea defense."[4] He inscribed this calligraphy at the base: "Prepare for war all the time to defend our southern frontier." Jiang saw the SCS as China's new frontier. On April 29, 1994, Jiang attended the commission ceremony for a new Chinese-made guided-missile destroyer, *112 Harbin*, and toured its missile launchers, weapons system, and new engine technology. Jiang told Captain Wu Hongle at the bridge, "This is China's new modern warship. You are the pioneers of our new naval operations." Jiang asked sailor Yang Chunsheng what was new about the warship. Yang demonstrated to the president four new features, including its antiair missiles, its new engine, antisubmarine helicopters, and a digital warfare system. Jiang was satisfied by the sailor's answer.[5]

A year later, on October 15–19, 1995, Jiang Zemin and Liu Huaqing led all Chinese military leaders to observe a large-scale naval exercise in the Yellow Sea, including nuclear submarines, missile destroyers, missile frigates, fighters, bombers, and helicopters. Jiang told the CMC standing members, "We must prioritize the naval construction and escalate its modernization to safeguard China's sea security and accomplish the great task of national unification."[6] After the naval exercise, Jiang revisited the flagship, the missile destroyer *112 Harbin*, and received Captain Wu's report on the destroyer operations, sailor training, and fire system exercises from the previous year. Thereafter, *112 Harbin* continued its drills, operations, and routine patrols.[7] In February 1997, destroyer *112* led a PLAN fleet as its flagship and visited the United States, Mexico, Peru, and Chile for more than a hundred days, sailing 24,000 nautical miles.[8] From 1989 to 1993, the PLA sent its warships to visit the United States, Thailand, Bangladesh, and India.

In October 1992, Admiral Liu Huaqing was elected as one of seven members on the CCP Politburo's Standing Committee and became one of the country's top national leaders as he helped consolidate Jiang Zemin's control of the PLA. Admiral Liu administrated the PLA's daily operations, managed China's defense budget, oversaw weapons production, conducted military diplomacy, and continued promoting naval development as the CMC vice chairman next to Jiang Zemin. The PLAN purchased new weaponry and imported advanced naval technology from Russia and the West, thereby narrowing the Chinese navy's technological gap with its major Western competitors. Liu purchased two *Sovremenny*-class destroyers (DDG) and four *Kilo*-class diesel electric submarines from Russia. The Russians built the 8,000-ton destroyers in St. Petersburg for the Chinese and sold the first one for $840 million in 1996 and the second one for $1 billion in November 1997. The first Russian destroyer, named *Hangzhou*, arrived at Zhoushan, Zhejiang in February 2000; the second, the *Fuzhou*, arrived in January 2001. From 1993 to 1996, the Chinese warships visited Vladivostok and other Russian seaports.

In the 1990s, the PLAN added more than twenty warships to its force with upgraded electronic countermeasures, radar and sonar, and fire-control systems. According to Liu's plans, three *Song*-class conventionally powered submarines and two nuclear-powered ballistic missile submarines, the Type 094, were constructed.[9] China manufactured Type 052 and Type 054 missile destroyers and Type 053H2G and Type 053H3 missile frigates. The Type 052 destroyers have upgraded antiaircraft, antiship, and electronic combat capabilities. They gained fame as the "Chinese Shield."[10] The Type 052C *Luoyang-II* destroyers were equipped with a phased-array radar for its HQ-9 SAM system. (The HQ-9 is comparable to the United States' Patriot missiles.)

The Type 054A *Jiangkai II* frigates were equipped with the HQ-16 SAM system and had a displacement between 3,600 and 5,500 tons and a speed between 18 and 32 knots. All the new warships and submarines were blue water capable.[11] The navy sent out second-generation destroyers and frigates to visit four countries in the Americas.

In the 1990s, a new domestic, conventionally powered submarine emerged as Type 039, while China designed and developed Type 093 nuclear submarines, Type 094 ballistic missile submarines, and Julang-2 submarine ballistic missile. Many new missiles and electronic warfare systems were manufactured as main battle equipment. Some of the new missiles were used in the 1995–96 Taiwan Strait Crisis by the Jiang administration. Jiang Zemin also supported Liu Huaqing's initiative about China's aircraft carrier. Liu said to his staff that he "could not die with eyes closed without seeing a Chinese carrier."[12] In 2000, China used $20 million to purchase an unfinished Soviet carrier, *Voyage* (about 68 percent completed), from Ukraine for structural studies. Although it took three years and $200 million to tow the *Voyage* (*Varyag*) from Ukraine to Dalian, China, the Chinese navy thus began to make its carrier development a reality. Meanwhile, comprehensive depot vessels displacing 11,000 tons sailed the oceans.

From 1995 to 2001, the PLAN's task groups paid port visits to Indonesia, Australia, the Philippines, South Africa, the United States, Canada, France, Italy, Germany, and Britain. In February–May 1997, Vice Admiral Wang Yongguo, commander of the South Sea Fleet, led the missile destroyers *Zhuhai* (*112*) and *166* and the replenishment oiler *Nancang* (*953*) with 789 sailors and officers to complete a circumnavigation of the Pacific Ocean for ninety-eight days, including port visits to the United States, Mexico, Peru, and Chile. It was the first time the PLAN convoy had crossed the International Date Line (180-degree west longitude) and entered the Western Hemisphere. At the Hawaii and San Diego U.S. Naval Bases, Wang and He Pengfei, deputy commander of the PLAN, visited the U.S. Pacific Command and Naval Pacific Fleet HQ.[13]

The PLANAF continued to purchase Su-30 and Su-32 strike fighters from Russia in the 2000s. The Su-30MK2 has a maximum speed of 1,305 miles per hour, a ceiling altitude of 56,800 feet, and a flying range of 1,900 miles. Meanwhile, the PLAN also introduced its new JH series of fighter-bombers to improve its aerial maritime strike capability. The H-6 twin-engine bombers was a new version of the Russian Tu-16 Badger. The JH-7/FBC-1, nicknamed "Flying Leopard," carries four YJ-82 antiship cruise missiles and air-to-air missiles with a cruising speed of 528 miles per hour. The new planes and their weapon systems brought more firepower over Chinese territorial waters. China also manufactured its SH-5 seaplanes and Z-8 and Z-9 helicopters. From 1997 to 2001, the PLAN expedited its modernization by developing better technology and purchasing more Russian equipment.

In November 1996, Vice Admiral Shi Yunsheng was appointed as the navy's new commander (1996–2003). After joining the PLA in 1956, Shi Yunsheng enrolled in the PLA Air Force Academy in 1958. After his graduation, he became a pilot of the PLANAF in 1962. He served as a squadron commander, wing deputy commander, and regiment deputy commander from 1964 to 1978. Then Shi Yunsheng enrolled in the Naval Command University. He became an air force division commander in 1981 and SSF air force commander in 1983. Ranked rear admiral in 1988, Shi was promoted to PLANAF deputy commander in 1990 and PLAN deputy commander in 1992. He attained the rank of vice admiral in 1994 and admiral in June 2000.

In 1991–98, after significant budget increases and across-the-board pay raises, Jiang Zemin gradually began separating the PLA from commercial activities with the aid of Premier Zhu Rongji and Defense Minister General Zhang Wannian. First, the PLA high command suspended all businesses run by combat units below the divisional level in 1991. Then the CMC banned commercial ventures by combat units below the army level in 1993. PLA companies were reduced from 15,000 to 9,000 by late 1995, and their employees reduced from 860,000 to 780,000. In 1996, the PLA requested that all PLA units terminate their joint-venture ownership and separate from local enterprises. By 1997, 2,937 companies had been transferred from the PLA to the state or local governments with 209,000 employees. Finally, the high command decided that all PLA units, including noncombat units and People's Armed Police (PAP), should end their commercial activities and business involvement in March 1998.[14]

That year, the PLA closed 3,928 companies and businesses and laid off 104,000 employees. Fewer than 2,000 companies remained within the PLA as supportive and welfare enterprises. The high command announced on December 15, 1998 that the PLA and PAP had disconnected from commercial activities. Since the PLA ran many illegal commercial activities and under-the-table businesses, the Party Center launched a nationwide campaign in the second half of 1998 to target PLA-related business crimes, including corruption, smuggling, and illegal transactions.[15]

The highest-ranking officer who faced the death penalty was Vice Admiral Wang Shaoye, deputy commander of the Chinese navy. Wang joined the army after he graduated from college in 1967. He served as a combat technician, engineer, and a staff member in the 38th Army and then was promoted to assistant manager, deputy director, and office chief in the Logistics Department of the Beijing Regional Command. In 1995, Wang Shaoye became the chief of the Construction Engineering Division in the PLA Department of General Logistics. He was appointed as the PLAN deputy commander in 2001. On December 23, 2012, Wang was arrested at the PLAN Command meeting for his corruption and graft, estimated at 160 million yuan RMB, and sentenced to death.[16] In his case, other four major generals and seven senior colonels were also arrested. Facing pressure and punishment, some officers transferred their assets overseas, as most of their income had been obtained illegally. In 2000, the amount of cash sent overseas from China totaled $48 billion, and China became the world's fourth largest country for outflow of capital, after Venezuela, Mexico, and Argentina.[17]

TAIWAN CRISIS AND HAINAN INCIDENT

During his military reform, Jiang Zemin tested the PLA's command and control, combat readiness, and crisis management during the Taiwan Strait missile crisis. Known as the Third Taiwan Strait Crisis, the conflict began in June 1995 when Lee Teng-hui (Li Denghui), ROC president, visited Cornell University in the United States. Jiang Zemin's government tried isolating Taiwan and opposed the U.S. government's permission for Lee Teng-hui's visit. General Chi Haotian, China's defense minister, made a convincing suggestion to Jiang Zemin that it was necessary to use military force to stop further distortion of Sino-American relations.[18] Jiang accepted Chi Haotian's proposal and decided on a show of force that summer. The PLA high command conducted its first round of missile tests from July 21 to 28 in an area thirty-six miles north of Taiwan. At 1 a.m. on July 21, the PLA's Second Artillery Force (SAF, strategic force) launched two short-range ballistic Dongfeng-15 (M-9) surface-to-surface missiles from Jiangxi at about seventy nautical miles from Taiwan's coast. At 12 a.m. and 2 a.m. on July 22, the SAF fired two DF-15 missiles and hit the area within forty miles north of Taiwan. Two more missiles were fired on July 24 and hit the same area.[19] Jiang Zemin employed the military to put pressure on Washington.

Simultaneously, the PLA concentrated large naval and landing forces and launched one wave after another of military exercises, including a joint amphibious landing exercise in the Taiwan Strait.[20] From August 15 to 25, the ESF deployed fifty-nine warships and naval vessels for a large-scale naval attack and amphibious landing exercise. The PLANAF launched 192 sorties and scrambled its fighters and bombers during the naval attack exercise. From October 31 to November 23, the PLA launched another joint amphibious landing campaign on Dongshan Island off the Fujian coast. The navy deployed sixty-three warships, landing craft, and support vessels. The army's 91st Infantry Division conducted landing and beachhead defense. The PLAAF sent fifty fighters, bombers, and other planes to the joint amphibious landing campaign.[21] By late fall, Beijing's military aggression had caused the most serious international crisis since 1958, when Beijing and Taipei had engaged in military conflict over the islands of Jinmen and Mazu.

Before year's end, cross-strait tensions rose drastically. Taiwan's military remained on high alert and declared that it had made all necessary preparations to deal with a possible PLA invasion of the island. In December 1995, the Clinton administration sent its aircraft carrier, the *Nimitz*, to pass through the Taiwan Strait in response to PLA activities. Between January and February 1996, the PLA concentrated 100,000 troops along the coast across the strait from Taiwan and launched another large-scale landing exercise to send a stronger signal to both Taipei and Washington. Through the winter of 1995–96, tensions remained heightened in the strait.[22]

Taiwan prepared for its presidential election in early 1996. It was Taiwan's first general election since 1949. Lee Teng-hui ran on the GMD ticket. To discourage the Taiwanese from voting for Lee, Jiang Zemin conducted a new set of missile tests, accompanied by live fire and naval exercises. Obviously, he used the military to threaten Taiwanese voters. On March 8, 1996, the PLA conducted more missile tests by firing three DF-15 surface-to-surface missiles just twelve miles off Kaohsiung and about twenty-nine nautical miles off Keelung.[23] On the same day, the United States announced the deployment of the *Independence* carrier battle group to international waters near Taiwan. On March 11, the United States deployed the *Nimitz* carrier battle group to the Taiwan area. This was the largest U.S. naval movement in the Asia-Pacific region since the Vietnam War. In response to U.S. naval deployments, China announced more live-fire exercises near Penghu, an ROC-held island group near Taiwan. From March 18 to 25, the PLA deployed three hundred airplanes, guided-missile destroyers, and submarines in the joint exercise at Pingtan Island with 150,000 troops, about seventy nautical miles from the Taiwanese-held islands. The exercise included amphibious landing, paratroopers, and mountain assaults. Meanwhile, several nuclear submarines left their base at Qingdao. Without identifying the Chinese nuclear submarines' locations, the United States instructed the *Nimitz* to stay 350 miles away from the strait.[24]

An imminent PLA invasion, however, did not threaten Taiwan, which stood firm against China's aggressive policy during the missile crisis: its intelligence had obtained information from Major General Liu Liankun of the PLA, deputy director of the Ordnance Division in the Department of General Armaments. Back in 1989, Liu had not favored the PLA's suppression of student movements in Tiananmen Square. As a result, his promotion to lieutenant general was denied in 1990. Soon, one of his subordinates, Colonel Shao Zhengzong, a recruit of the Taiwanese intelligence agents, convinced Liu Liankun to turn. In late 1992, Taiwanese agents, headed by Pang Ta-wei, secretly met Liu, Shao, and other PLA officers in Guangzhou and gave Liu the code name Shaokang 2. Pang Ta-wei incentivized Liu with $20,000 and promised a monthly payment of $3,500, the amount a major general would receive according to the Taiwanese military intelligence pay scale. Liu Liankun accepted the offer. From then on, he provided information on China's major military purchases from Russia, its strategy on retaking some offshore islands, and its plans on the handover of Hong Kong.[25]

Three months before the PLA conducted military exercises and missile attacks threatening Taiwan's first-ever general presidential election, Liu Liankun leaked the entire plan to Taiwanese intelligence. Through Liu, the Taiwanese military found that China would not actually attack if the United States became involved, and its missiles would not fly over Taiwan, nor would they be armed. Therefore, the PLA threats were ineffective. In his speech on March 7, 1996, then–presidential candidate Lee Teng-hui claimed that PLA missiles were not armed and assured the public that he had already prepared several scenarios to deal with the situation. The next day the PLA fired three missiles into Taiwanese waters, but they did not have payloads.[26] The PLA high command immediately realized the presence of a high-ranking spy in their ranks and launched a top-down investigation. In April 1999, PLA counterintelligence arrested Taiwanese spy Ye Bingnan in China. Later that month, after Ye divulged information, Liu Liankun, Shao Zhengzong, and twenty-four PLA officers were arrested. Liu Liankun was executed in August. The PLA learned a hard lesson in the spy war between China and Taiwan through the 1990s. Moreover, Beijing also learned an important lesson from the 1995–96 crisis: that Washington would not watch the PLA attack Taiwan. China has to deal with U.S. intervention in the Taiwan Strait.

The Third Taiwan Strait Crisis was over, and Lee Teng-hui was elected as Taiwan's president on March 23, 1996. China's intimidation was counterproductive and boosted Lee by 5 percent in the polls, earning him a majority of the voters. Beijing continued criticizing Lee as "the general representative of Taiwan's separatist forces, a saboteur of the stability of the Taiwan Straits, a stumbling-block preventing the development of relations between China and the United States, and a troublemaker for the peace and stability of the Asian-Pacific region."[27] Andrew Scobell considers *hawkish* as "the most accurate term to use to describe the words and deeds" of Chinese military during the crisis. Nevertheless, Beijing "achieved most of its goals without resorting to actual warfare: its actions got Taipei and Washington to take China's warnings seriously and resulted in a more chastened and less boisterous Taiwanese

Independence movement."²⁸ Worthing adds, "In the interests of reducing tensions in the Straits, the United States scaled back its arms sales, restricted Taiwanese officials to transit visas, and urged Lee Teng-hui to avoid action that might upset the status quo."²⁹ Robert Ross states that Beijing and Washington tried to protect their strategic positions through the crisis, and both reached their goals with certain strategic benefits.³⁰ The Chinese government still believed in their "compatriots in Taiwan" and maintained the position "in adhering to 'peaceful reunification' and 'one country, two systems.'"

During Lee's term, cross-strait exchange and trade continued to develop rapidly.³¹ From 1988 to 1999, the Taiwanese visited the mainland 16 million times for family reunions, relative visits, sightseeing, or business trips. The total cross-strait trade volume reached $160 billion, and Taiwanese businesses invested $44 billion in China, making it the second largest direct foreign investor in China, surpassed only by Japan. Beijing certainly did not want to slow down the much-needed foreign investment and trade through any aggressive policy or military action.

During his administration, Jiang Zemin had to deal with an unexpected international dispute when a Chinese naval fighter collided with a U.S. spy plane, known as the Hainan Island incident, or 81192 accident, in April 2001. Hainan was and still is the home base for the SSF's submarines. It also had underground facilities capable of supporting nuclear ballistic missile submarines. The Chinese naval fighters were very protective and aggressive over the sea area around the Hainan Island. Since the collision happened over an area in the SCS, both China and the United States disagreed, first, about the overflights by U.S. military aircraft and, second, about the cause of the collision. Third, when the Chinese demanded apologies and the U.S. government refused to give them, China detained twenty-four American crew members in Hainan naval airfield. It was the last international crisis for Jiang Zemin, but the first for President George W. Bush, who had been inaugurated just ten weeks earlier.

Lieutenant Commander Wang Wei was a naval interceptor fighter pilot of the navy's Ninth Air Force Division. He enrolled in a PLA pilot academy in Changchun, Jilin in 1986. After his graduation in 1990, he became a naval pilot and flew more than two thousand sorties. On April 1, 2001, he and his wingman Zhao Yu were patrolling the near waters around Hainan. At 8:36 a.m., they discovered a USN EP-3E Aries II signals intelligence airplane sixty-five to seventy miles southeast of the island. After their report, the PLANAF ordered the two J-8II fighter jets to intercept the American spy plane. Wang Wei flew over the U.S. naval plane and warned, "You have entered our national airspace. Please leave immediately!" Receiving no response, Wang's 81192 (or 81194) fighter tried again and flew closer to the EP-3, just a few meters away.[32] According to Zhao Yu, the U.S. plane made a sudden turn toward Wang's 81192. When Wang's fighter made third pass, they collided in midair. Because the EP-3 was a much larger plane, one of its propellers cut off half of the fighter's tail fin.[33]

The impact of the collision immediately sent the fighter into a nose-down spiral fall. He told Zhao Yu, "I've lost control!" The air control at the Lingshui airfield called Wang and ordered, "81192, please return." Wang, however, could not control his fighter and responded, "This is 81192. I can't return. You carry on, repeat, you carry on!" Zhao yelled into his radio, "Eject! Eject!" Instead Wang tried to bring the fighter out of the spiral dive, but he failed. Then Zhao saw Wang eject from the damaged fighter. Zhao Yu pushed down his fighter to three thousand meters above the sea and looked for Wang's parachute in the water. Without any luck, he reported the location and returned to the base. The PLAN Command ordered the SSF and PLANAF to send warships, search planes, and local islanders to look for the missing pilot. From April 1 to 14, the SSF mobilized more than ten thousand sailors, soldiers, marines, and local fishermen to participate in the search-and-rescue efforts, but they had no success. On April 16, the Chinese navy presumed Wang Wei's death at the age of thirty-three. On April 24, the CMC declared him a national "Naval Air Hero." The SSF established a national martyr's cemetery for Wang Wei.

After the midair collision, the EP-3 could not make it back to base, so it made an emergency landing at the PLAN Lingshui airfield at the Hainan Island. Its crew destroyed intelligence data and sensitive items. Then they were taken to a military facility at Lingshui for interrogations. As soon as the USAF received the information, the U.S. government requested that China release the American crew and plane immediately. The Jiang government demanded three apologies: for destroying the Chinese fighter, for making the Chinese pilot disappear, and for entering China and landing at the Chinese airport without permission.

While both sides maintained their strong positions, negotiations began. After eleven talks, Joseph Prueher, U.S. ambassador to Beijing, delivered the "letter of the two sorries" to Tang Jiaxuan, PRC foreign minister, to defuse the incident. According to the letter, the United States was "very sorry" for the death of Chinese pilot Wang Wei and was "very sorry" the aircraft entered China's airspace and that its landing did not have "verbal clearance." On April 12, the twenty-four EP-3 crew members were sent back. Since the plane was damaged and unable to fly again, the U.S. military disassembled the plane and transported its parts back to the United States. To retaliate, China refused a U.S. warship's entry to Chinese seaport for a scheduled visit. On May 15, the Chinese government also canceled a planned port visit to Hong Kong by the minesweeper USS *Inchon*.

HU AND NAVAL DEVELOPMENT

Hu Jintao became chairman of the CCP at the Sixteenth CCP National Congress after Jiang Zemin retired in November 2012. Hu was elected president of the PRC at the Sixth NPC next March. In September 2004, Jiang left command of the Chinese military, and Hu Jintao became the new civilian commander in chief of the twenty-first-century PLA. Diversity grew within the CMC leadership under Hu Jintao, and competing factions became dynamically interdependent. Several political groups of younger, ambitious, and capable leaders aggressively fought political battles for control of the government and military.[34] Hu tried to maintain a balance in Beijing by emphasizing political and social harmony and nurturing working relations among the different military groups, while also emphasizing the importance of the continuing naval development. He supported military professionalism and the merit-based system of officer promotion. He emphasized that the PLA officers should have college degrees and formal overseas training. By 2005, all naval pilots and naval commanders of warships had a college education.[35]

After taking over the office of commander in chief, Hu Jintao continued to promote Jiang Zemin and Liu Huaqing's conceptions of sea power, oceanic territory, maritime sovereignty, and naval modernization. Hu told the PLA leaders, "China is a big oceanic country. The Chinese navy plays a crucial role in defending our country's sovereignty, security, marine interests, and sea power. It is a glorious mission."[36] In August 2004, Hu chaired a Politburo meeting to mobilize national resources and promote naval modernization. Hu emphasized the escalation of naval transformation and special attention to its combat readiness. In December 2006, Hu met the representatives of the PLAN Tenth Party Committee Conference and told naval leaders to "build a modern, professional, and strong navy to meet China's new demands and development in the new century."[37] During Hu's administration, the navy improved its equipment and weapon systems and received many new warships.

Since 2000, the Chinese navy has commissioned more than thirty new submarines, including sixteen Chinese-manufactured *Song*-class submarines and twelve *Kilo*-class submarines purchased from Russia. Meanwhile, the PLAN designed, manufactured, and completed four *Yuan*-class submarines with an air-independent propulsion system to reduce their vulnerability. The navy received new Type 051C missile destroyers like the *Shijiazhuang*, which has a displacement of seven thousand tons and a navigational speed of over thirty knots, in 2005. The PLAN also received missile frigates like the *Wenzhou*, which has a displacement of four thousand tons, commissioned in September 2005. The PLAN commissioned sixty Type 022 *Houbei* missile-armed catamarans after 2007. These ships are equipped with the sea-skimming YJ-082 supersonic antiship cruise missiles. The Chinese navy is armed with wire-guided, wake-homing torpedoes and shipborne air defense. The PLAN, however, had only limited indigenous technological capabilities in the 1990s. It remained a "learner" rather than an "innovator" in many areas of naval technology in the 2010s.

Hu Jintao appointed Admiral Zhang Dingfa as the new navy commander in 2003 after Shi Yunsheng's retirement. Zhang studied at the Naval Submarine Academy in 1960. After his graduation, Zhang served as a submarine torpedo officer and then a staff member at the Nuclear Submarine Office in the PLAN HQ. From 1973, Zhang Dingfa became a submarine deputy captain and captain. In 1980, he studied at the Naval Command University. In

January 1985, Zhang became an assistant to the chief of staff of the NSF, and then the chief of staff of the Qingdao Naval Base. He enrolled in the graduate curriculum at the NDU in 1988. After 1933, Zhang Dingfa served as the NSF chief of staff, deputy commander, and commander. He became PLAN deputy commander in 2000, president of the PLA Academy of Military Science in 2002, and the navy commander in June 2003. At the April 2004 meeting, Hu Jintao and the Politburo decided on conversion of the *Voyage* (*Varyag*) carrier. On July 27, 2011, the PRC Defense Ministry announced, "China is now remodeling a worn-out aircraft carrier for scientific research, experiment and training." On September 25, 2012, Hu personally launched China's first aircraft carrier, *Liaoning* (CV 16), and gained a new public profile as achieving significant success in the navy's modernization.

From May to September 2002, Vice Admiral Ding Yiping, NSF commander, led the destroyer *Qingdao* and the replenishment oiler *Taicang* with 506 officers and sailors for the PLAN's first circumnavigation of the world, a voyage of 132 days and covering 33,000 nautical miles. During the first voyage around the world, the Chinese convoy visited ten ports in Singapore, Egypt, Turkey, Greece, Ukraine, Portugal, and France. On July 14, the Chinese navy Global Voyage Vessels Formation crossed the Atlantic Ocean for South America. From 2004 to 2011, the PLAN became a Pacific navy and sailed often by Okinawa, Japan. Its large warships also visited the Western Pacific and Indian Ocean.

In the meantime, the Chinese navy participated in joint naval exercises with foreign navies. In October 2003, Chinese warships, seaplanes, and helicopters hosted a joint military exercise with the Pakistani destroyer *Babur* and the comprehensive depot ship *Nasr* in the near waters off Shanghai. On March 12–16, 2004, the Chinese missile destroyer *Harbin* and depot ship *Hongzehu* held a joint exercise in the Yellow Sea with the French navy's antisubmarine destroyer *Latouche-Treville* and frigate *Commandant Birot*. On August 15–24, 2005, the Chinese and Russian navies launched a joint exercise code-named Peace Mission 2005.[38] The first U.S.-Chinese naval exercise took place on September 20, 2006, off the California coast. The Chinese missile destroyer *Qingdao* worked with USS *Shoup* and *Seahawk* helicopters in a joint maritime search-and-rescue exercise. After the U.S.-China joint naval exercise, Rear Admiral Wang Fushan, commander of the Chinese visiting formation, cabled Admiral Gary Roughead, "The commanding skills and professional quality of the US Pacific Fleet impressed us deeply."[39] Then China held the Peace Mission 2007 joint maritime training exercise in the Arabian Sea with seven foreign navies. In September 2007, the British navy held a joint exercise with the PLAN on the Atlantic. British aircraft carrier *Ark Royal* and Chinese missile destroyer *Guangzhou* and comprehensive depot ship *Weishanhu* conducted emergency communication, joint command, and search and rescue. The Chinese navy had several joint naval exercises with the Russian navy in 2005, 2009, and 2012. On April 22–27, 2012, the Chinese navy and Russian navy held a joint exercise on the Yellow Sea. Twenty-three warships, two submarines, thirteen fixed-wing aircraft, nine helicopters, and one special combat unit from each navy participated in the exercise.

After the sudden death of Admiral Zhang Dingfa, Wu Shengli was the navy commander from 2008 to 2017. Admiral Wu grew up in a PLA family. His father, Wu Xian, joined the New Fourth Army during the Anti-Japanese War and became a platoon, company, battalion, and regiment officer from 1938 to 1945. During the civil war, Wu Xian was appointed deputy political commissar of the PLA 35th Army. After his retirement, he prepared his children for the service. All of his sons became PLA members; Wu Shengli joined in 1964. Wu Shengli majored in marine survey after enrolling in the PLA Institute of Surveying and Mapping. After his graduation, Wu worked as navigation officer and deputy captain on four different frigates and destroyers. He served as a frigate and then a destroyer captain for eight years. In July 1994, he was ranked a rear admiral. Captain Wu Shengli was promoted to a fleet captain, naval base chief staff, president of the PLA Dalian Warship Academy, ESF deputy commander, and SSF commander. He became a vice admiral in July 2003. Wu became the PLA deputy chief of the General Staff in April 2004 and the navy's commander in August 2006. He was ranked admiral on June 20, 2007.

Hu Jintao visited the SSF on April 9, 2008. He proclaimed that the Chinese navy was a "strategic, comprehensive, and international force, which plays a pivotal role in defending our oceanic territory, maintaining our sea power, and developing our national maritime interests."[40] Hu told Chinese military leaders at a conference in December 2011 that the navy should "accelerate its transformation and modernization in a sturdy way, and make extended preparations for warfare in order to make greater contributions to safeguard national security."[41] Nan Li emphasizes Hu Jintao's two contributions to China's naval strategy and capability developments. First, Hu requested that the PLA "safeguard China's newly emerging overseas interests, which defines PLAN's far-seas missions." Second, Hu "endorsed the concept of information systems–based system of systems operations, which impacts how PLAN conducts operations."[42] Hu attended the naval parade at Qingdao on April 23, 2009 to celebrate the navy's sixtieth birthday. What was new at this celebration, the largest parade in PLAN history, was that the Chinese navy invited twenty-one foreign warships from fourteen countries to participate, including the U.S., Russian, French, Canadian, Mexican, Indian, and other navies. Before the parade, Hu met foreign naval delegations from twenty-nine countries.[43]

In 2010, China became the largest shipbuilder in the world after its total building tonnage surpassed that of the longtime leader, South Korea. Chinese news agency *Xinhua News* reported, "China built ships with a total deadweight capacity of 65.5 million tons, accounting for 43 percent of the deadweight capacity of ships built in the world."[44] The PLAN was ready to improve its logistical support system for longtime maritime missions by providing better fleet training. China's 2010 *National Defense White Paper* indicated the accelerated construction of "large support vessels."[45] By 2010, the PLAN totaled 300,000 personnel and more than 600 warships, including an aircraft carrier and nuclear submarines. The Chinese navy has an air arm of 430 warplanes and 35,000 personnel and commands China's 12,000-strong marine corps. You Ji examines the PLAN's transformation in the 2000s–10s, when it was "extending its operations from coastal defense to far-seas power projection."[46] Cole believes that the Chinese have "the idea that a great country should have a great Navy." He links Chinese naval efforts to "the nation's economic development" and to "dependence on overseas trade," which have been largely overlooked by other works in the field. He concludes that Chinese maritime strategy attempts to "achieve near-term national security objective and long-term regional maritime dominance."[47]

DISPUTED ISLANDS AND NEAR-SEA PROBLEMS

Hu Jintao continued his nationalistic foreign policy and engaged Japan in the Senkaku Island disputes. The Diaoyu/Senkaku Islands became a testing ground for the Chinese public to judge the military strength, political toughness, and diplomatic skills of the new leadership. In 1995, the China National Offshore Oil Corporation (CNOOC), a state-owned oil and gas company, built the country's first and largest undersea natural gas field, Chunxiao, in the ECS. Although the Chunxiao field is on the Chinese side, it is located only three or four miles west of the median line. Japan feared the Chunxiao field's reserves possibly lay well beyond the Japanese side, and Tokyo opposed any further Chinese exploration of natural gas resources in the same area. Nevertheless, CNOOC continued its explorations and established five more natural gas fields in the area. By 2006, all its gas fields were operational.[48] The resultant increase in China's natural gas reserves was accredited to deepwater drilling and other technological developments. The fields in the ECS are estimated to hold proven reserves of more than 100 billion cubic meters (bcm) of natural gas. China has proven gas reserves of more than 300 bcm within its ECS exclusive economic zone (EEZ). The country has the second largest gas reserves among its Asia-Pacific neighbors. China's 3.1 trillion cubic meters of gas reserves cover 18.45 percent of the region's land area, second only to Australia's 22.16 percent.[49] Tokyo asked Beijing to stop drilling and building gas exploration platforms close to disputed waters. Japan's major concern was that Chinese exploration and production might tap reservoirs that extend into Japan's underwater oil and gas reserves.

As China's oil and gas industries shifted to deepwater exploration, international tensions increased between China and Japan over the sovereignty of areas along the median line in the ECS. In June 2008, Beijing and Tokyo reached an agreement on joint development of hydrocarbon resources in the disputed area. But in the same month, Chinese coast guard vessels accompanied Taiwanese activists approaching Diaoyu Dao/Uotsurishima Island.[50] Contradictory policies profoundly entrenched themselves in Chinese political institutions and policy-making processes. The Japanese, and sometimes the Americans, were confused by the discrepancy between Hu's policy and the PLAN's behavior, but inconsistency in strategic formulations and actual implementation was quite common. From the early 2000s, the disputed islands became the Chinese government's demonstration of strong nationalistic stands against foreign threats that involved territorial integrity, naval strength, political toughness, and diplomatic skills. Any compromise over the islands currently seems exceedingly difficult, if not impossible.

Chinese naval leaders certainly felt an increasing pressure or even a threat from the U.S. naval activities in East Asia. They believed that the United States "has increased its strategic attention to and input in the Asia-Pacific region, further consolidating its military alliances, adjusting its military development, and enhancing its military capabilities."[51] China insists that the United Nations Convention on the Law of the Sea gives coastal states the right to regulate not only economic activities but also foreign military activities in their EEZs. This interpretation has been the root cause of various contentious physical encounters between U.S. and PRC vessels, both military and civilian, in the past. In 2006, a Chinese submarine surfaced near the USS *Kitty Hawk*. In 2007, China denied safe harbor to two small USN minesweepers caught in dangerous weather. Gaye Christoffersen exposes a crisis management system in China's near seas between China, Japan, and the United States and identifies "different configurations for crisis management mechanism," which could escalate tensions in the areas.[52] Since returning the Diaoyu/Senkaku Islands to Japan, the United States has had no legal standing to contest ECS territorial disputes. Nonetheless, the U.S. government recently made it clear that these islands are included within the U.S.-Japanese Mutual Defense Treaty. In other words, the United States can commit its armed forces to defending the disputed areas if Japan requests it.

In 2009, Secretary of State Hillary Clinton told the Japanese foreign minister that the Treaty of Mutual Cooperation and Security between the United States and Japan covers the disputed areas, meaning that the Obama administration could commit U.S. armed forces to Japanese defense of these islands.[53] On March 8, 2009, the USN survey vessel *Impeccable* was confronted by five Chinese navy ships. According to the American accounts, the Chinese ships surrounded and harassed the USS *Impeccable*, which conducted surveillance in an area over which Beijing claimed jurisdiction but other countries consider international waters. The Chinese tried to block the ship and snag its cables with hooks. The Americans used a fire hose to spray water at the Chinese. The chief American intelligence officer called it the "most serious" military incident with China since 2001. On March 12, 2009, when President Barack Obama met with China's foreign minister, Yang Jiechi, he told the Chinese foreign minister that the two countries need to raise "the level and frequency" of military dialogue "in order to avoid future incidents" like the high-seas confrontation.[54]

In November 2012, a U.S. congressional amendment to the National Defense Act included possible defense of the disputed islands in the ECS in the event of armed attacks.[55] In 2013, Secretary of State John Kerry further warned Beijing that although the United States did not take a position on the ultimate sovereignty of the islands, the White House acknowledged they were under Japanese and American government administration and opposed any unilateral actions that sought to undermine Japanese administration.[56] In a May report, the U.S. Department of Defense pointed out, "China began using improperly drawn straight baseline claims around the Senkaku Islands, adding to its network of maritime claims inconsistent with international law."[57] On July 30, the U.S. Senate unanimously passed a resolution condemning China's "use of coercion, threats, or force by naval, maritime security, or fishing vessels and military or civilian aircraft in . . . the East China Sea to assert disputed maritime or territorial claims or alter the status quo."[58] The ECS gained importance as China significantly and urgently focused on building its maritime power, thus the ECS has become one of the major sources of international tension in the Asian-Pacific region in the twenty-first century.

In 2010, China's total energy consumption surpassed that of the United States for the first time ever, making it the world's largest energy consumer. China's economy faces more challenges and pressures than ever, and the export-oriented manufacturing that relied especially on energy resources is no longer sustainable. Therefore, the 12th Five-Year Plan period became crucial in that China entered a period of reforming the energy economy. Then, in 2011, China became the second largest economy in the world, following only the United States. Its energy production and consumption taken together signifies how the national economy operates. China ranked fifth in world oil production in 2011, with more than 4 million barrels a day, about 51 percent of the Asia-Pacific total oil production.⁵⁹ In the meantime, Beijing shifted its strategic priorities from land power to maritime power. China's maritime economic interests, as a net energy importer, are supported by increasing regional and global sea lines of communication.

ANTIPIRACY AND FAR-SEA OPERATIONS

In 2008, Commander Wu Shengli ordered the SSF to prepare the participation in international antipiracy operations off the coast of Somalia to protect Chinese commercial shipping. In June 2008, the UN Security Council passed Resolution No. 1816 to empower member states to "cooperate with the Transitional Federal Government of Somalia (TFG) in the fight against piracy and armed robbery at sea off the coast of Somalia, for which advance notification had been provided by the TFG to the Secretary General."⁶⁰ The security situation for international commercial shipping deteriorated in 2007–8. On April 18, 2007, a Taiwanese ship was hijacked, and one Chinese sailor from Liaoning was killed by Somali pirates. On May 15, two Korean ships (whose crews included ten Chinese sailors) were hijacked. On September 15, 2008, a Hong Kong ship was hijacked; two days later a Chinese ship was captured, and twenty-four Chinese sailors became hostages. In November, three Chinese cargo ships were hijacked. From January to November 2008, China sent 1,265 commercial ships through the Gulf of Aden, about three to five ships every day. Eighty-four Chinese ships, about 20 percent of the total, were attacked, robbed, or hijacked by Somali pirates.⁶¹ At the time, China was the fourth-largest international shipping nation in the world and needed the PLAN's protection.

This was the first time the Chinese navy had sent naval combat force overseas for international humanitarian operations. In November, SSF Command launched three antipiracy exercises involving destroyers, helicopters, naval special forces, and marines. On December 19, China announced it would send its naval fleet to fight against the pirates along the Somali coast. The SSF Command dispatched the missile destroyers Type 052C *Wuhan* and Type 052B *Haikou* (171, flagship) with *Weishanhu* (887), the PLAN's largest supply ship, as the First Group Convoy Formation under the command of

Rear Admiral Du Jingchen, SSF deputy commander. The *Haikou* was the *Luoyang II*-class missile destroyer, manufactured at the Shanghai shipyard, completed in 2003, and commissioned in December 2005. It also participated in the sixth (2010-11) and tenth (2011-12) escort formations. The *Weishanhu* was the *Fuchi*-class supply ship, completed in 2003 at the Shanghai shipyard and commissioned in April 2004. It was 178 meters long and 24.8 meters wide, with a displacement of 20,530 tons, 130 crews, and a speed of 19 knots. It also participated in the second (2009), fifth (2010), sixth (2010), and eleventh (2012) convoy formations. The first formation included 800 sailors and 70 naval special force soldiers.

On December 25, 2008, Rear Admiral Du Jingchen, commander of the First Group Convoy Formation, chaired a captain meeting at SSF Sanya Naval Base and finalized their operation details. The next day, Du Jingchen set sail to the Gulf of Aden as the first PLAN antipirate formation. He instructed the two K-28 Russian-made antisubmarine helicopters to secure the convoy formation. Ten days later, the Chinese fleet arrived at the Gulf of Aden. Although the Chinese shared intelligence with international navies, the fleet engaged the escorts and fought the pirates independently in the gulf. On January 6, 2009, the fleet began its engagement by escorting four Chinese cargo ships through the gulf. On January 29, the Chinese fleet received an emergency call from a Greek merchant ship that was blocked by the pirates' boats. Du Jingchen sent destroyer *Wuhan*, two helicopters, and forty special force troops to rescue the ship. *Wuhan*'s captain fired warning shots, and the helicopters successfully drove the pirates away from the Greek ship before they could board it.

During its four-month operation, Du Jingchen and his fleet responded to all the requests and escorted 212 Chinese and international commercial ships. Du used his helicopters as the "forward eyes" to patrol the areas and report any suspicious pirate activities. Sometimes the helicopters alone could tackle pirates and drive them away. But after pirates got on commercial ships, the Chinese navy faced a kidnapping and hostage situation. Then Du Jingchen sent his warships with naval special force soldiers. During their tour, the Chinese naval special force launched five rescue operations to attack the pirates and release four Chinese and international ships from danger. On March 14, Rear Admiral Du Jingchen was invited to meet Rear Admiral Terence E. McKnight on the USS *Boxer*, which was also part of the escort mission. Nevertheless, Du Jingchen also dealt with his own issues, such as logistical shortages, low morale, communication problems, and lack of knowledge of international law.

Then the PLAN maintained its escort formations in the area by assigning two to three warships on a three-to-four-month basis. To supply the Chinese naval force in the Gulf of Aden, the PLAN proposed to establish a Chinese naval base in Africa to support its antipiracy missions in the region. On April 2, 2009, the Chinese navy sent its Second Group Convoy Formation, including the missile destroyer *Shenzhen* (167) and missile frigate *Huangshan*, to the Somali coast and continued the Chinese escort mission. The *Shenzhen* was an *Luhai*-class, Type 051B missile destroyer, manufactured at the Dalian shipyard in 1995, completed in 1997, and commissioned in February 1999. With a displacement of 6,600 tons and a cruising speed of 31 knots, it had sixteen YJ-12 antiship missiles, two three-tube 324-mm torpedo launchers with Y-7 (copy of U.S. Type MK-46 Mod1) torpedoes, and one eight-tube antiair missile launcher with thirty-two HQ-7 or HQ-16 antiair missiles. The second formation had two Z-9C Chinese-made, improved French AS-565 model helicopters. The new fleet arrived on April 16, and twelve days later Du Jingchen and his fleet left the gulf and returned to the Sanya naval base.

At 8:50 a.m. on May 14, the commander of the Second Group Formation received his helicopter's report on suspicious pirate activity: "One mother ship is towing multiple small boats toward our formation from the left at high speed?" At that moment, the destroyer *Shenzhen* was escorting two commercial ships through the gulf. The commander immediately ordered, "Helicopters, go closer and report. Port Five, both engines four ahead. *Shenzhen*, forward to see. Report to the merchant formation and stay vigilant!" The two helicopters soon reported more details: "One mother ship identified 8.3 nautical miles to starboard. Eighteen small boats sailing toward the formation at high speed." When the pirates locked on a target, they flocked together and rushed toward it. Now the Chinese formation, destroyer *Shenzhen* and two cargo ships, faced a double threat; while the pirate mother ship was hidden in canvas, nearly twenty speedboats were flying at full speed toward the Chinese ships from all directions. There were up to five men in each speedboat. The formation commander ordered the destroyer *Huangshan*, which was anchored nine nautical miles away standby, to come immediately. Meanwhile, the *Shenzhen*'s captain sped up his destroyer ahead of the cargo ships. He ordered the special force soldiers, emergency personnel, and medics to get ready on deck.

About three nautical miles between the *Shenzhen* and pirate speedboats, the helicopters continued to report, "Automatic weapons, rifles, and bazookas on the boats!" The *Shenzhen*'s captain instructed the helicopters to circle low and hover over the speedboats and ordered the sailors and soldiers on deck to "prepare for battle!" The *Shenzhen* had 250 seamen, including 40 officers. It was armed with one double-barrel 100-mm cannon (PJ-33A), four double-barreled 37-mm antiaircraft guns (76A), and two defense cannon (model-1130). Facing the Chinese naval firepower and combat readiness, the pirates seemingly felt intimidated. They stopped their boats about two nautical miles from the destroyer *Shenzhen* and did not attack. After a ten- or fifteen-minute standoff that seemed endless, the pirates turned and sailed off. During the confrontation, without firing a shot or releasing a bomb, the Chinese escort formation successfully drove the enemy away.

Then the ESF Command deployed the Third Group Convoy Formation under the command of Rear Admiral Wang Zhiguo, ESF deputy commander. His formation included two missile frigates, *Zhoushan* (529) and *Xuzhou* (530) and *Qiandaohu* AOE 886, a *Fuchi*-class, 23,000-ton supply ship, on July 16, 2009. The *Zhoushan* was the *Jiangkai II*–class, 054A missile frigate that was commissioned in 2008. It had one 76-mm cannon, two seven-barrel 30-mm (Type 730) defense guns, two four-tube YJ-8 antiship missile launchers, four eight-tube HHQ-16 antiair missile launchers, two Type 81 six-tube 250-mm antisubmarine rocket launchers, two 324-mm three-tube torpedo launchers, and two eighteen-tube multiple-purpose rocket launchers. The missile frigate *Zhoushan* had 190 seamen with a displacement of 4,500 tons and a speed of 27 knots.

At 4 p.m. on August 6, 2009, Rear Admiral Wang Zhiguo received a report that the Chinese cargo ship *Zhenhua* was being chased by pirates in the west of the gulf. Wang ordered the two helicopters to take off and rescue. After a twenty-eight-minute flight, Liu Jinkun, one of the helicopter pilots, discovered that eight pirate boats, three to four nautical miles from the starboard side of the *Zhenhua*, were maneuvering to beset it at high speed. The special force soldiers on his helicopter fired two red warning flares. The speedboats did not respond and continued to approach the *Zhenhua*. Pilot Liu described the situation in his diary: "I could see vaguely eight to nine people on each boat. The boats were all double-motored and sailing at high speed. . . . Our helicopters laid down anchor rods and lowered altitude to terrorize them, half a mile, a quarter mile, 200 yards. . . . The pirates were just before our eyes. We were well within range of the pirates' weapons."[62] Meanwhile, the Chinese soldiers fired explosive bombs in front of the pirate boats and stopped their speedy chase. After a roughly ten-minute confrontation, the leading boat bowed to the mounting pressure and turned to flee. The others followed. To keep them from coming back, Liu and the other pilot continued to hover over the Chinese cargo ship until the pirates disappeared. During its tour, the Third Group Convoy Formation had a joint naval exercise with the Russian navy's escort formation in the area, codenamed Peach Blue Shield, from September 10–18, 2009. Then the Chinese and Russian fleets began their joint escort operation in the gulf. In October, the Chinese formation escorted 174 commercial ships through the Gulf of Aden. On November 20, the Third Group Convoy Formation escorted twenty-six cargo ships in one day.

From December 2008 to February 2011, the PLAN sent ten group formations to the Gulf of Aden and African coast against the pirates, including twenty-five warships and eighteen airplanes and helicopters, totaling 8,400 sailors, marines, and naval special force. They escorted 4,411 Chinese and international commercial ships and rescued fifty-one cargo ships. The special forces troops launched twenty-two rescue operations on thirty-three commercial ships and successfully rescued the Chinese and foreign sailors without any casualty. It was the first time the Chinese navy had conducted joint operations defend national strategic interests at the far sea. It was also the first time the PLAN had engaged in transoceanic military missions for such an extended time period. On November 30, 2011, the spokesman for

China's Defense Ministry announced, "China will continue to dispatch naval convoy formations to the waters of the Gulf of Aden and Somalia for escort work and to further carry out international convoy cooperation."[63] On February 23–24, 2012, the PLAN hosted the first International Symposium on Counter-Piracy and Escort Operations at the PLA Naval Command College in Nanjing. More than five hundred naval officers attended the international symposium, including eighty-four naval representatives from international organizations such as the European Union, NATO, and Baltic and International Maritime Conference. More than twenty foreign navies sent their representatives to the symposium, including the United States, the United Kingdom, France, Germany, and Russia.

In April 2012, Liao Shining, deputy chief of staff of the PLAN, and his warship *Zhenghe* left Lushun for the PLAN's second around-the-world voyage. The *Zhenghe*, a PLAN Type 679 training warship (81), was commissioned in April 1987 with a displacement of 4,500 tons and a speed of 17 knots. It was the first PLAN warship to sail from China to the United States. For the new voyage, Rear Admiral Liao Shining had three hundred officers, naval cadets, and sailors on board. They sailed more than 30,000 nautical miles in five months and visited Vietnam, Malaysia, India, Italy, Spain, Canada, Ecuador, Polynesia, Tonga, Indonesia, and Brunei. During this voyage, the *Zhenghe* docked at Djibouti, Jamaica, and Australia.

CONCLUSION

Xi's New Navy

This historical overview has showed the Chinese navy's operational experience resulting from its strategic changes, institutional reforms, and technological improvement. The PLAN had transformed from a coastal defensive fleet in 1949 to a modern navy by 2009. The analysis explored its continuing reorganization, professionalization, and digitalization, which define the PLAN's characteristics in the twenty-first century. The diachronic discussions have explained the need for reforms and the results of those efforts. The six chapters have told the story of successive generations of Chinese naval officers and sailors, with modernization as the central theme and patterns of their operational behavior. The unique characteristics influence naval reforms and modernization amid political loyalty. The way the Chinese navy carried on long-standing traditions while also making remarkable changes was crucial to building a "rich country with a strong navy."

Upon taking office as commander in chief in 2012, Xi Jinping inherited PLA traditional naval doctrines, and he has drawn on its Cold War strategic concepts but modified China's maritime policy. Chinese leaders today face some familiar international and domestic issues, which prioritized their security concerns, national defense, economic development, and domestic control in the 1950s. Although the international environment has dramatically changed since the end of the Cold War, the PRC apparently replaced the former Soviet Union as the primary challenge to the United States and the post–Cold War world. Of course, China is nothing like it was in 1950, but the CCP's dominant leadership and continuing insecurity, and Xi Jinping's call for the "fighting spirit" against the United States carry on the party's doctrine and Mao Zedong's legacy as one of few Communist survivors as well as a "beneficial participant" in the Cold War.

XI'S MARITIME POLICY

Among the factors influential in China's maritime strategy are national security concerns, international relations, economic resources, and political and social conditions. Chinese military leaders have new security concerns, casting doubt on Western specialists' argument that China feels safer than ever before. Recent interviews show that some PLA officers believe they live in a dangerous world in the twenty-first century, with many uncertainties and potential challenges to China's security.[1] Their concerns are confirmed by Beijing's high command in the *White Paper: China's National Defense*, which made it clear that the country is facing "unprecedented" challenges because "new security threats keep emerging."[2] Their justification and calculation seem reasonable and logical in terms of the ongoing globalization.

Xi Jinping believes in the PLA's active defense and resists the current Asian-Pacific security system under U.S. leadership. As we know, during Mao Zedong's era, the PLA adopted an active defense strategy, challenging the Cold War international system in which two superpowers dominated global affairs. First the PLA fought the American armed forces in Korea in 1950–53, and then it fought the Soviet Union along their borders in 1969–71. Xi Jinping reaffirms Jiang Zemin's post–Cold War doctrine and continues to employ nationalism as an ideology to unite the country and fight for its superpower status, perhaps resulting in one more source of legitimacy for the CCP as the country's ruling party. Xi promoted his global "New Silk Road and Economic Belt" plan to establish a China-centric global system that excludes America. His plan is to connect Africa, Asia, Europe, and Latin America as China repositions itself by creating a new center of gravity in the Asia-Pacific region. On October 24, 2017, the BRI was added to the party's constitution at the CCP 19th National Congress in Beijing. Mao and Xi's strategies on active defense diverge in that the latter had shifted from engaging in land wars in neighboring countries like Korea and Vietnam to preparing for naval warfare in the Taiwan Strait, ECS, and SCS.

The BRI has brought massive trade, finance, transportation, communication, infrastructure, and energy programs, by both sea and land routes, from Chinese coasts to other continents along the ancient Silk Road. As Xi Jinping made his strategic shift, he also developed new, aggressive initiatives in the ECS. In November 2013, Beijing began using the name China's East Sea (Zhongguo Donghai) to define the area and claimed the establishment of an Air Defense Identification Zone (ADIZ), including the disputed Diaoyu/Senkaku Islands.[3] The ADIZ requires all international aircraft to provide their flight information to Chinese authorities before entering the zone. Since then, the PLAAF has regularly patrolled the zones to strengthen the country's effective control over it. Shen Jinke, spokesman for the PRC Defense Ministry, said that the PLAAF's routine patrols intend simply to verify the identities of foreign aircraft and administer official warnings and that it should not impact commercial air traffic. He stated that the PLAAF patrols "are purely defensive and consistent with international norms" and that the PLAAF would also conduct routine air drills in the zone to prepare to deal with any emergency situations.[4]

In 2016, the territorial conflict escalated to military confrontation involving naval vessels, coast guard gunboats, and fighters in the ECS's disputed areas. The ECS has become one of the most worrisome flash points in Asia, an important source of insecurity in the Western Pacific, and possibly a point of contention between the United States and the PLA forces in East Asia. In November, the PLAAF conducted another large-scale air exercise in the ADIZ, involving H-6K heavy bombers, Su-30 fighters, and air tankers. The drill included early warning, reconnaissance, and attacks on air and sea surface targets. The Japanese air force surpassed a previous Cold War annual record by scrambling 1,168 fighter jets in 2017 in response to PLAAF aircraft encroachment into Japanese airspace, and this provoked 851 incidents. Thereafter, China replaced Russia as the major post–Cold War threat to Japanese airspace.

From Mao Zedong to Xi Jinping, Beijing continued its military alliance with Moscow, excluding the two decades of the Sino-Soviet split. Xi Jinping made eight trips to Moscow between 2012 and 2020 with the purpose of strengthening Russia's strategic support to China. By 2014, the two nations had announced a new era of military collaboration as part of an enhanced strategic partnership. In a long-term view, the PLA's investment in Soviet technology and advisory assistance in 1950–60 paid significant dividends during the PLA's modernization in the 1980s–2000s. The partnership between the PRC and the Russian Federation air forces continues to grow through a collaborative engagement launched in the 2010s. This raises serious questions about the future of American security and about whether the United States has anything to fear from Communist China, a potential military superpower. The latest Chinese purchase included Su-35 fighters, accounting for over $1 billion annually from 2012 to 2017.

NEW NAVAL DEVELOPMENT

To avoid or successfully cope with the problems in the ECS, China needs to make considerable progress toward building and fielding a credible naval, air, and even a strategic force, and taking part in the responsibilities that accompany the accumulation of national power in the Western Pacific. The main mission of the PLAN consists of safeguarding maritime rights, protecting coastal lines and sovereignty, and resisting seaborne invasion. Therefore, recent naval training has focused on the naval base defense, maritime transportation protection, antisea lines of communication, antiship operations, maritime blockage, and maritime-land attack. The PLAN held bilateral joint maritime training exercises with the navies of fourteen countries during the past two years, including Russia, the United Kingdom, France, the United States, Pakistan, India, and South Africa. The Chinese navy is the second largest navy in the world, exceeded only by the USN.

The shift in approach to war from a land conflict to naval warfare reflects current security concerns, evolving strategic thoughts, and emphasis on naval combat readiness. In August 2013, Xi Jinping visited the aircraft carrier *Liaoning*, and noted that China should build an even stronger naval force.[5] Later that year, Rear Admiral Jiang Weilie, SSF commander, had an interview after his fleet's sixteen-day exercise in the Western Pacific and through the first chain of islands. The PLAN general said that the purpose of the exercise was to test long-distance operations, antimissile capabilities, and antisubmarine attacks as well as coordination among battleships and fighter jets. They treated the exercise as a real war.[6] In 2015, the PLAAF began patrolling the SCS, including the disputed Paracel and Spratly Islands. Thereafter, confrontations between Chinese and American armed forces in the SCS have aroused serious concerns about security and stability in the

Asia-Pacific region. The USAF continues to fly military aircraft in the ADIZ without informing China, defying China's declaration that the region falls into a Chinese airspace defense zone.

As Xi Jinping carried on active defense strategy and enhanced the party's control of the military, the PLAN continued its military alliance with Russia and promoted the "leap-over" approach for PLA technological improvement. Moreover, Xi repositioned China as the Asia-Pacific regional epicenter, despite experiencing unprecedented demands, facing new challenges, and creating new problems. In April 2013, Beijing announced in its annual *Defense White Paper* that the Chinese navy has the strategic task of meeting the new requirement of China's national interests and security needs.[7] In November 2013, China began construction of its second aircraft carrier. After Wu Shengli retired, Shen Jinlong became the PLAN commander from 2017 to 2021. Admiral Shen made it clear that the PLAN had become more prominent since the turn of the twenty-first century due to a change in China's economic growth, international status, new security concerns, and global strategic priorities. The clearest indication of this new PLAN prominence is that China is developing a blue-water navy. On April 26, 2017, the PLAN launched its new aircraft carrier, *Shandong, Kuznetsov-Mod*, Type 002, at the Dalian shipyard.

To match China's economic superpower status, the Chinese navy acquired more ships, improved its technology, and conducted frequent naval exercises. By 2020, the PLAN had 240,000 naval officers and sailors with an overall battle force of 350 surface ships and submarines; at that same time, the USN had 293 warships. The Chinese navy also had 15,000 marines and 26,000 naval aviation personnel with 690 aircraft. Its tonnage totaled 1.82 million in 2019, making it the second largest navy in the world, surpassed only by the USN. It continued its expansion into the 2020s, commissioning new warships and constructing more naval facilities.

The PLAN has expanded its amphibious assault capabilities by building more landing ships, including amphibious transport docks.[8] Among its most publicized developments is a growing Chinese carrier fleet. The Chinese navy has also expanded its ballistic missile submarine fleet, including Type 094 *Jin*-class SSBNs and long-range *JL-2 SLBM*.[9] In May 2015, the Chinese and

Russian navies conducted the Joint Sea 2015 exercise in the Mediterranean Sea. In August, a larger-scale operation, Joint Sea II, was held in international waters about 250 miles from Japan, involving twenty-two warships and twenty aircraft. Vice Admiral Aleksandr Fedotenkov, the Russian navy's deputy commander in chief, commented on the result of the joint training, which "showed that Russian and Chinese seamen can effectively fulfill tasks in such a difficult region."[10] In the same year, the PLAN conducted three large-scale military exercises in the ECS. The third live-fire exercise on August 24–28 involved more than a hundred naval vessels, dozens of aircraft, and information regarding warfare units. Chinese warships fired various missiles, nearly a hundred of them.[11] Currently, many American and Japanese naval strategists predict that sooner or later there will be a naval clash between their navies or air forces and the PLAN or PLAAF, both of which have become more and more aggressive after acquiring Russian military technology.[12]

HOT SPOTS: A NEW COLD WAR BETWEEN CHINA AND THE UNITED STATES?

Taiwan has emerged as the most dangerous flash point in the growing U.S.-China rivalry. Chinese attacks on Taiwan, to protect Beijing's so-called core interests, are part of China's strategy. The PLA has significantly escalated its military activities directed at Taiwan, including naval and air patrols in the Taiwan Strait, joint exercises to simulate landing campaigns, and antiship missile exercises aimed largely at American intervention against possible PLA attacks on Taiwan. In June 2021, the PLA conducted an amphibious landing exercise in the Taiwan Strait. According to CCTV, "the 72nd Group Army explored the tactics of emergency loading, long-distance transport, beach assaults under complicated sea situations, and the troops' amphibious combat."[13]

The disputed islands in both the ECS and SCS are also possible sources for international discontent and present increasing tension between China and the United States. Hostility toward Japan received nationwide support not only from Chinese senior citizens, who experienced and remember Japanese atrocities in World War II, but also from youth who always suspected Japan's intentions and negative reactions to China's replacing Japan as the dominant economic power in Asia.¹⁴ Nationwide protests occurred in 2012 when the Japanese government purchased three islands from private owners and officially increased its ownership to seven of the eight islands. Seeing the purchase as a way to nationalize the disputed islands, Chinese citizens gathered outside the Japanese embassy in Beijing and held large-scale protests across the country. In 2013, it was reported that the massive Chinese protests seemed "semi-official," since "almost all the voices in China pressing the Okinawa issues are affiliated in some way with the government."¹⁵ The BBC reported in February #2013 that the situation had become "the most serious for Sino-Japanese relations in the post-war period in terms of the risk of military conflict."¹⁶ With popular support, both governments sent more navy and coast guard vessels to the ECS disputed areas.

In 2010–30, the new transformation of the PLA will certainly affect such areas as strategy, doctrine, operational concepts, and combat techniques. For example, an important ongoing change in the PLA doctrine moves away from the traditional defense principle of "never open fire first." It dismisses the timing issue and instead justifies its war efforts as defensive in nature even though Chinese troops may have to open fire first. The new strategy and transformations require the PLA to build up a combat force to win local wars in conditions of informationization. It requires the PLA to prepare itself for defensive operations under the most difficult and complex circumstances. The U.S. Department of Defense pointed out in 2009 that "the pace and scope of China's military transformation have increased in recent years, fueled by acquisition of advanced foreign weapons, continued high rates of investment in its domestic defense and science and technology industries, and far-reaching organizational and doctrinal reforms of the armed forces."¹⁷ The potential for a new cold war between the two countries will loom ever larger if China continues its efforts to create "one world, two systems." History will repeat itself in the 2020s if there is a complete break in diplomatic relations between the two countries or, even more serious, a limited hot war.

NOTES

INTRODUCTION. OPERATION AND TRANSFORMATION

1. President Ma Ying-jeou, meeting with the author and several other members of the Chinese Historians in the United States in his office, Taipei, Taiwan, June 8, 2017. Ma (1950–) was the president of the Republic of China (ROC) from 2008 to 2016.
2. Hans van de Ven, "Introduction," in *Warfare in Chinese History*, ed. van de Ven (Boston: Brill, 2000), 7.
3. 吴杰章少将 [Rear Admiral Wu Jiezhang], 苏小东 [Su Xiaodong], 程志发 [Cheng Zhifa] 主编, 中国近代海军史 [*A History of the Modern Chinese Navy*] (Beijing: PLA Press, 1989), 2. Wu (1931–) served as the director of the Department of Political Tasks at the PLA Naval Aviation Engineering University from 1987 to 1996.
4. 朱增泉中将 [Lieutenant General Zhu Zengquan], 战争史笔记 [*Historical Notes on Chinese Warfare*] (Beijing: People's Literature Press, 2010), 61–62.
5. 吴杰章 [Wu Jiezhang], 苏小东 [Su Xiaodong], 程志发 [Cheng Zhifa], 中国近代海军史 [*A History of the Modern Chinese Navy*], 2–6.
6. 徐焰少将 [Major General Xu Yan], "中国由注重'海防'变为争取'海权'" ["China Shifts Its Focus from 'Coastal Defense' to 'Sea Power'"], in 徐焰讲稿自选集 [*Self-Selected Lecture Essays of Xu Yan*] (Beijing: National Defense University Press, 2014), 204.
7. John Keegan, *A History of Warfare* (New York: Knopf, 1993), 214, 221, 332–33.
8. John King Fairbank, "Introduction: Varieties of the Chinese Military Experience," in *Chinese Ways of Warfare*, ed. Frank Kierman and Fairbank (Cambridge, MA: Harvard University Press, 1974), 6–7.
9. William R. Thompson, "The Military Superiority Thesis and the Ascendancy of Western Eurasia," *Journal of World History* 10, no. 1 (Spring 1999): 1–22.
10. David A. Graff, *The Eurasian Way of War: Military Practice in Seventh-Century China and Byzantium* (London: Routledge, 2016).
11. Peter A. Lorge, *The Reunification of China: Peace through War under the Song Dynasty* (New York: Cambridge University Press, 2015).
12. Jung-Pang Lo, *China as a Sea Power, 1127–1368: A Preliminary Survey of the Maritime Expansion and Naval Exploits of the Chinese People during the Southern Song and Yuan Periods* (Singapore: National University of Singapore Press, 2012).
13. Bruce A. Elleman, *The Making of the Modern Chinese Navy: Special Historical Characteristics* (London: Anthem, 2019), 12.
14. James Waterson, *Defending Heaven: China's Mongol Wars, 1209–1370* (Havertown: Pen & Sword, 2013).
15. 曾公亮、丁度 [Zeng Gongliang and Ding Du], 武经总要 *Wujing zongyao* [*General Outline of Weapons*], in 四库全书 [*Siku quanshu*] (Shanghai: Ancient Classics Press, 2015), 22: 52–55.

16. Description from *Wujing zongyao* [*General Outline of Weapons*] quoted in Ralph D. Sawyer, *Fire and Water: The Art of Incendiary and Aquatic Warfare in China* (Boulder, CO: Westview, 2004), 65.
17. Sawyer, 201.
18. Peter A. Lorge, *The Asian Military Revolution: From Gunpowder to the Bomb* (New York: Cambridge University Press, 2008), 35–36.
19. Peter A. Lorge, *War, Politics, and Society in Early Modern China, 900–1795* (New York: Routledge, 2005), 2, and *Warfare in China to 1600* (Farnham, UK: Ashgate, 2005), 24.
20. Peter Worthing, *A Military History of Modern China: From the Manchu Conquest to Tiananmen Square* (Westport, CT: Praeger, 2007), 14.
21. Paul U. Unschuld, *The Fall and Rise of China: Healing the Trauma of History* (London: Reaktion, 2013).
22. Tonio Andrade, *The Gunpowder Age: China, Military Innovation, and the Rise of the West in World History* (Princeton, NJ: Princeton University Press, 2016).
23. Bruce A. Elleman, *Modern Chinese Warfare, 1795–1989* (London: Routledge, 2001); Mark Felton, *China Station: The British Military in the Middle Kingdom 1839–1997* (Barnsley, UK: Pen & Sword Military, 2013).
24. 刘华清上将 [Admiral Liu Huaqing], 前言 ["Introduction"], in 吴杰章 [Wu Jiezhang], 苏小东 [Su Xiaodong], and 程志发 [Cheng Zhifa], 中国近代海军史 [*A History of the Modern Chinese Navy*], 1.
25. Nicola Di Cosmo, "Introduction," in *Military Culture in Imperial China*, ed. Di Cosmo (Cambridge, MA: Harvard University Press, 2009), 5.
26. Elleman, *The Making of the Modern Chinese Navy*, 73–74.
27. Harold M. Tanner, promotional blurbs for Elleman, *The Making of the Modern Chinese Navy*, back cover.
28. Toshi Yoshihara, *Mao's Army Goes to Sea: The Island Campaigns and the Founding of China's Navy* (Washington, DC: Georgetown University Press, 2022).
29. Yoshihara, iv.
30. Toshi Yoshihara and James R. Holmes, *Red Star over the Pacific: China's Rise and the Challenge to U.S. Maritime Strategy*, 2nd ed. (Annapolis, MD: Naval Institute Press, 2018).
31. James C. Bussert and Bruce A. Elleman, *People's Liberation Army Navy: Combat Systems Technology, 1949–2010* (Annapolis, MD: Naval Institute Press, 2018), 1.
32. Bussert and Elleman, x.
33. Bussert and Elleman, ix.
34. Rear Admiral Michael A. McDevitt, *China as a Twenty-First-Century Naval Power: Theory, Practice, and Implications* (Annapolis, MD: Naval Institute Press, 2020), x.
35. McDevitt, vii.
36. Bernard D. Cole, *The Great Wall at Sea: China's Navy in the Twenty-First Century*, 2nd ed. (Annapolis, MD: Naval Institute Press, 2010), 190.
37. Cole, 42.

38. Among newly declassified Chinese documents in the 2000s, see, for example, 中共中央档案局 [CCP Central Archives], 中共中央文件选集, *1921–1949* [*Selected Documents of the CCP Central Committee, 1921–1949*] (Beijing: CCP Central Party University Press, 1992), vols. 1–18; 中共中央档案局、中央文献研究室、中央组织部 [CCP Central Archives, Central Archival and Manuscript Research Division, and CCP Organization Department, comps.], 中国共产党组织史资料, *1921–1997* [*Archives of the CCP Organization's History, 1921–1997*] (Beijing: CCP Central Committee's Party History Press, 2000), vols. 1–14.
39. For example, 前苏联档案 [Former Soviet Archives], "斯大林与中共代表团会谈记录" ["The Meeting Minutes of Stalin's Negotiations with the CCP Delegation"], June 27, 1949, in 有关刘少奇1949年访苏的俄国档案 [*The Russian Archives of 1949 Liu Shaoqi's Visit in the Soviet Union*]; "斯大林与毛泽东会谈记录" ["The Meeting Minutes of Stalin's Conversation with Mao Zedong"], December 16, 1949, in 有关1950年中苏条约谈判的俄国档案 [*The Russian Archives of the 1950 Treaty Negotiations on the Soviet-Chinese Agreement*].
40. For example, "New Russian Documents on the Korean War," trans. and ed. Kathryn Weathersby, *Cold War International History Project Bulletin* 6–7 (Winter 1995/1996): 30–125.
41. Chinese leaders' papers and manuscripts include 毛泽东 [Mao Zedong], 建国以来毛泽东文稿, *1949–1976* [*Mao Zedong's Manuscripts since the Founding of the State, 1949–1976*] (Beijing: CCP Central Archival and Manuscript Press, 1993), vols. 1–13; 建国以来毛泽东军事文稿 [*Mao Zedong's Military Manuscripts since the Founding of the PRC*] (Beijing: Military Science Press and CCP Central Archival and Manuscript Press, 2010), vols. 1–3; 毛泽东军事文集 [*Collected Military Works of Mao Zedong*] (Beijing: Military Science Press, 1993), vols. 1–6; 毛泽东军事文选 (内部版) [*Selected Military Papers of Mao Zedong: Internal Edition*] (Beijing: PLA Soldiers Press], 1981), vols. 1–2; 毛泽东文选 [*Collected Works of Mao Zedong*] (Beijing: People's Press, 1999), vols. 1–8; 刘少奇 [Liu Shaoqi], 建国以来刘少奇文稿 [*Liu Shaoqi's Manuscripts since the Founding of the State*] (Beijing: CCP Central Archival and Manuscript Press, 2008), vols. 1–7; 周恩来 [Zhou Enlai], 建国以来周恩来文稿 [*Zhou Enlai's Manuscripts since the Founding of the State, 1949–1950*] (Beijing: CCP Central Archival and Manuscript Press, 2008), vols. 1–3; 周恩来军事文选 [*Selected Military Papers of Zhou Enlai*] (Beijing: People's Press, 1997), vols. 1–4.
42. The PRC government documents include 中国外交部办公厅档案资料部 [Archives Department of the General Office, PRC Foreign Ministry], 中国外交档案 [*China's Foreign Affairs Archives*], 北京 [Beijing]; 新华社 [Xinhua News Agency], 新华社文件资料汇编 [*A Collection of Documentary Materials of Xinhua News Agency*] (Beijing: Xinhua News Agency Publishing House, n.d.).
43. 朱德元帅 [Marshal Zhu De], 朱德军事文选 [*Selected Military Writings of Zhu De*] (Beijing: PLA Press, 1986); 彭德怀元帅 [Marshal Peng Dehuai], 彭德怀军

事文选 [*Selected Military Writings of Peng Dehuai*] (Beijing: CCP Central Archival and Manuscript Press, 1988); 刘伯承元帅 [Marshal Liu Bocheng], 刘伯承军事文选 [*Selected Military Writings of Liu Bocheng*] (Beijing: PLA Press, 1992); 聂荣臻元帅 [Marshal Nie Rongzhen], 聂荣臻军事文选 [*Selected Military Writings of Nie Rongzhen*] (Beijing: PLA Press, 1992); 徐向前元帅 [Marshal Xu Xiangqian], 徐向前军事文选 [*Selected Military Writings of Xu Xiangqian*] (Beijing: PLA Press, 1992); 贺龙元帅 [Marshal He Long], 贺龙军事文选 [*Selected Military Writings of He Long*] (Beijing: PLA Press, 1989); 陈毅元帅 [Marshal Chen Yi], 陈毅军事文选 [*Selected Military Papers of Chen Yi*] (Beijing: PLA Press, 1996).

44. 肖劲光大将 [Fleet Admiral Xiao Jinguang], 肖劲光军事文选 [*Selected Military Writings of Xiao Jinguang*] (Beijing: PLA Press, 2003); 刘华清上将 [Admiral Liu Huaqing], 刘华清军事文选 [*Selected Military Writings of Liu Huaqing*] (Beijing: PLA Press, 2008).

45. Part of the research effort resulted in a volume translated and edited by Xiaobing Li, Allan R. Millett, and Bin Yu: *Mao's Generals Remember Korea* (Lawrence: University Press of Kansas, 2001).

CHAPTER 1. LIGHT NAVY FOR COASTAL DEFENSE

1. 张爱萍上将 [General Zhang Aiping], 中国人民解放军 [*The Chinese People's Liberation Army*] (Beijing: Contemporary China Press, 1994), 2:25.
2. Gao Xiaoxing et al., *The PLA Navy* (Beijing: China Intercontinental Press, 2012), 1.
3. 张爱萍 [Zhang Aiping], 中国人民解放军 [*The Chinese People's Liberation Army*], 2:25-26.
4. Marshal Nie Rongzhen, "Beijing's Decision to Intervene," in Li, Millett, and Yu, *Mao's Generals Remember Korea*, 49; Major General Xu Yan, "Chinese Forces and Their Casualties in the Korean War," trans. Xiaobing Li, *Chinese Historians* 6, no. 2 (1991): 52.
5. 徐焰 [Xu Yan], 中国由注重"海防"变为争取"海权" ["China Shifts Its Focus from 'Coastal Defense' to 'Sea Power'"], 206.
6. 中共中央党内指示 [CCP Central Committee's Instruction], 目前形势和党在一九四九年的任务 ["Current Situation and the Party's Tasks in 1949"], drafted by Mao Zedong and passed by the Politburo on January 8, 1949, in 毛泽东军事文集 [*Collected Military Manuscripts of Mao Zedong*] (Beijing: CCP Central Archival and Manuscript Press and Military Science Press, 1993), 5:471-78.
7. 毛泽东 [Mao Zedong], 中国人民站起来了 ["Chinese People Have Stood Up"], in 建国以来毛泽东文稿, 1949-1976 [*Mao Zedong's Manuscripts since the Founding of the State, 1949-1976*] (Beijing: CCP Central Archival and Manuscript Press, 1993), 1:7-8. Hereafter cited as 毛文稿 [*Mao's Manuscripts*].
8. Mao Zedong's words quoted in 肖劲光大将 [Fleet Admiral Xiao Jinguang], 肖劲光回忆录 (续集) [*Memoir of Xiao Jinguang* (Sequel)] (Beijing: PLA Press, 1989), 3-4.

9. 杨国宇少将 [Rear Admiral Yang Guoyu], 当代中国海军 [*Contemporary Chinese Navy*] (Beijing: China's Social Science Press, 1987), 17. Yang served as PLAN deputy commander and chief of staff in 1978-85.
10. 张爱萍 [Zhang Aiping], 中国人民解放军 [*The Chinese People's Liberation Army*], 2:25.
11. 胡彦林上将 [Admiral Hu Yanlin], 威震海疆: 人民海军征战纪实 [*Shocking the Sea: Records of the People's Navy's Battles*] (Beijing: National Defense University Press, 1996), 59. As a fighter pilot in the 1960s, Hu became political commissar of a PLAAF regiment and division in the 1980s. He was appointed director of the Political Tasks Department of the PLANAF in 1990-93 and ranked rear admiral in 1990. Hu was promoted to director of the Political Tasks Department of the PLAN in 1993-2000 and vice admiral in 1995. He became PLAN political commissar in 2003-8 and admiral in 2004.
12. 郑雅茹 [Zheng Yaru], 肖劲光 ["Xiao Jinguaung"], in 中国人民解放军高级将领传 [*Biographies of the PLA's High-Ranking Generals*], 中国人民解放军高级将领传编审委员会编著 [ed. PLA *Biographies of the PLA's High-Ranking Generals* Editorial Committee] (Beijing: PLA Press, 2008), 4:477-78.
13. Fleet Admiral Xiao Jinguang (1903-89) was purged during the Cultural Revolution. For more information on his military career, see 星火燎原编辑部 [*Xinghuo liaoyuan* Composition Department], 中国人民解放军将帅名录 [*PLA Marshals and Generals*] (Beijing: PLA Press, 1992), 1:30-31. Hereafter cited as 将帅名录 [*Marshals and Generals*].
14. 中国人民解放军历史资料丛书编审委员会 [Editorial Board of PLA Historical Archives and Documents Collection Series], ed., 对国民党海军的政治争取工作 ["Political Persuasive Efforts in the GMD Navy"], in 解放战争时期国民党军起义投诚（综合册）[*The Revolts and Realignments of the GMD Forces during the War of Liberation* (combined vol.)] (Beijing: PLA Press, 1996), 375.
15. 胡彦林 [Hu Yanlin], 威震海疆 [*Shocking the Sea*], 78.
16. 杨国宇 [Yang Guoyu], 当代中国海军 [*Contemporary Chinese Navy*], 28-29.
17. 毛泽东、朱德 [Mao Zedong and Zhu De], 嘉勉重庆号起义官兵 ["Congratulation Telegram to the 'Chongqing' Uprising Officers and Sailor"], drafted by Mao, March 24, 1949, in 毛泽东军事文集 [*Collected Military Manuscripts of Mao Zedong*], 5:524-25.
18. 地久、克峰 [Di Jiu and Ke Feng], 潮涨潮落: 国共角逐台湾海峡纪实 [*Ebb and Flow: Records of the CCP-GMD Confrontations in the Taiwan Strait*] (Beijing: China Industrial and Commercial Publishing, 1996), 90.
19. Mao and Zhu's congratulation telegram of May 18, 1949, quoted in 毛泽东年谱, 1893-1949 [*A Chronological Record of Mao Zedong, 1893-1949*], 中共中央文献研究室编 [ed. CCP Central Archival and Manuscript Research Division] (Beijing: CCP Central Archival and Manuscript Press, 1993), 3:502-3.
20. Mao's words quoted in 杨国宇 [Yang Guoyu], 当代中国海军 [*Contemporary Chinese Navy*], 33-34.

21. 宋万贤 [Song Wanxian], 毛泽东与张爱萍上将 ["Mao Zedong and General Zhang Aiping"], in 毛泽东与海军将领 [Mao Zedong and Naval Admirals], 吴殿卿、袁永安、赵小平主编 [ed. Wu Dianqing, Yuan Yong'an, and Zhao Xiaoping] (Beijing: PLA Literature Press, 1999), 95-96.
22. Lin Zun (1905-79) studied at the Naval School in Yantai from 1924 to 1928. Then he enrolled at the Greenwich Royal Navy Academy in Great Britain in 1929, and later he transferred to Portsmouth School for further study of naval aviation. After his graduation, Lin returned in 1934 and served in the GMD navy as deputy captain. He studied submarine technology in Germany from 1937 to 1939. He became captain, naval research officer in the Ministry of Defense, and naval staff in the GMD Chief of Staff Office from 1939 to 1945. He was sent to the United States as naval attaché in the ROC embassy in Washington, DC. Lin became the commander of the GMD navy's Second Fleet in 1946-49. He joined the CCP in 1977. See 星火燎原编辑部 [Xinghuo liaoyuan Composition Department], 将帅名录 [Marshals and Generals], 3:158.
23. 东方鹤 [Dong Fanghe], 张爱萍传 [Biography of Zhang Aiping] (Beijing: People's Press, 2000), 1:559-60.
24. Gao et al., The PLA Navy, 2.
25. 贺茂之 [He Maozhi], 张爱萍 ["Zhang Aiping"], in 中国人民解放军高级将领传编审委员会编著 [ed. PLA Biographies of the High-Ranking Generals Editorial Committee], 中国人民解放军高级将领传 [Biographies of the PLA's High-Ranking Generals], 9:438.
26. Zhang Aiping (1910-2003) became commander of the Zhejiang Military Command and chief of staff of the Third Field Army in 1951-55. He served as deputy director of the National Commission of Defense Science and Technology in 1959-66. He was purged during the Cultural Revolution from 1966 to 1976 and jailed for six years. After his return, Zhang was deputy chief of the PLA General Staff in 1977-80, vice premier in 1980-82, and defense minister in 1982-87. See 星火燎原编辑部 [Xinghuo liaoyuan Composition Department], 将帅名录 [Marshals and Generals], 1:104-5.
27. For example, when the PLA took Beijing in January 1949, 200,000 GMD troops surrendered, and between February and April, 150,000 of them were inducted into the PLA. 军事科学院军事历史研究部 [Military History Research Division, PLA Academy of Military Science (AMS)], 中国人民解放军全国解放战争史 [History of the PLA in the Chinese Liberation War] (Beijing: Military Science Press, 1997), 4:485-86, 488-90; Joseph K. S. Yick, Making Urban Revolution in China: The CCP-GMD Struggle for Beiping-Tianjin, 1945-1949 (Armonk, NY: M. E. Sharpe, 1995), 176-77.
28. 东方鹤 [Dong Fanghe], 张爱萍传 [Biography of Zhang Aiping], 1:572-73.
29. 贺茂之 [He Maozhi], 张爱萍 ["Zhang Aiping"], 9:392.
30. 军事科学院军事历史研究部 [Military History Research Division, PLA-AMS], 中国人民志愿军抗美援朝战史 [War History of the Chinese People's

Volunteer Force to Resist the United States and Aid Korea] (Beijing: Military Science Press, 1990), 236–37; Shu Guang Zhang, *Mao's Military Romanticism: China and the Korean War, 1950–1953* (Lawrence: University Press of Kansas, 1995), 255, 258.

31. When Mao met the former GMD admirals in Beijing, the CCP chairman told them, "Our new [PLA] navy must learn from you. The new and old [revolted GMD] navies must learn from each other." Mao's words are quoted in 杨国宇 [Yang Guoyu], 当代中国海军 [*Contemporary Chinese Navy*], 33–34.
32. Deng Zhaoxiang (1903–98) enrolled in Huangpu (Whampoa) Military Academy in 1914, then studied naval warfare at Wusong Naval School, Yantai Naval Academy, and Nanjing Naval War School from 1919 to 1922. After his graduation, he served as deputy captain. In 1930, Deng went to Britain and studied at the British Greenwich Royal Navy Academy and British Torpedo School. After his return in 1934, he served in the GMD navy as deputy captain, captain, torpedo battalion commander, and staff member of the Second Fleet Command. In May 1948, he became the captain of the *Chongqing*. For more details on Rear Admiral Deng's biography, see 郭金炎 [Guo Jinyan], 大海之子邓兆祥 [*Son of the Sea: Deng Zhaoxiang*] (Beijing: Ocean Wave Publishing, 2004).
33. 杨国宇 [Yang Guoyu], 当代中国海军 [*Contemporary Chinese Navy*], 35–36.
34. 杨国宇 [Yang Guoyu], 当代中国海军 [*Contemporary Chinese Navy*], 34.
35. 肖劲光上将 [Fleet Admiral Xiao Jinguang], 关于组建华南海军机构的问题 ["On the Issues of Establishing Command Headquarters of South China Regional Navy"], in 肖劲光军事文选 [*Selected Military Writings of Xiao Jinguang*] (Beijing: PLA Press, 2003), 234.
36. Gao et al., *The PLA Navy*, 6.
37. 杨国宇 [Yang Guoyu], 当代中国海军 [*Contemporary Chinese Navy*], 16.
38. 韩怀智中将 [Lieutenant General Han Huaizhi], 当代中国军队的军事工作 [*Military Affairs of Contemporary China's Armed Forces*] (Beijing: China's Social Science Press, 1989), 2:65–66.
39. Gao et al., *The PLA Navy*, 110.
40. Bussert and Elleman, *People's Liberation Army Navy*, 2.
41. 毛泽东 [Mao Zedong], 关于兵力部署的意见给林彪的电报 ["My Suggestions on Your Troops Disposition and Battle Array"], October 31, 1949, in 毛文稿 [*Mao's Manuscripts*], 1:107.
42. 中华民国国防部 [Defense Ministry, ROC], 国军后勤史 [*Logistics History of the GMD Armed Forces*] (Taipei: Bureau of Historical and Political Records, Defense Ministry, 1992), 6:199–200.
43. Bruce A. Elleman, *High Seas Buffer: The Taiwan Patrol Force, 1950–1979* (Newport, RI: Naval War College Press, 2012), 5.
44. 中华民国国防部 [Defense Ministry, ROC], 国军后勤史 [*Logistics History of the GMD Armed Forces*], 6:277.

45. 地久、克峰 [Di Jiu and Ke Feng], 潮涨潮落 [*Ebb and Flow*], 90.
46. 胡彦林 [Hu Yanlin], 威震海疆 [*Shocking the Sea*], 33–34.
47. 地久、克峰 [Di Jiu and Ke Feng], 潮涨潮落 [*Ebb and Flow*], 116–18.
48. Chief General Hao Baicun (Hau Pei-stun, ROC army), interview by the author in Taipei, Taiwan, May 1994. Hao served as an ROC army commander on the offshore islands during the PLA attack on Jinmen in 1949. Then he was defense minister of the ROC in the 1980s.
49. Compilation Committee of ROC History, *A History of the Republic of China* (Taipei: Modern China Press, 1981), 2:297. The GMD army officially claimed PLA casualties of about 20,000 men, including 7,200 prisoners. According to the author's interviews both in Taiwan and in China, a figure of 10,000 PLA casualties seems most acceptable.
50. 毛泽东 [Mao Zedong], 关于兵力部署的意见给林彪的电报 ["My Suggestions on Your Troops Disposition and Battle Array"]. In his telegram, Mao advised Lin, "Do not attack the Leizhou Peninsula, much less a chance to attack the Hainan Island." See 毛文稿 [*Mao's Manuscripts*], 1:107.
51. Two CMC telegrams were drafted by Mao to Su Yu. 中央军委 [CMC], 军委关于同意定海作战方案给粟裕等的电报 ["CMC Telegram to Su Yu: Agree the Operation Plan of the Dinghai Campaign"], November 4, 1949; 毛泽东 [Mao Zedong], 关于定海作战部署给粟裕的电报 ["Telegram on the Dinghai Campaign Plan"], November 14. The latter reads, "In view of the military failure on Jinmen, you must check out closely and seriously all problems, such as boat transportation, troop reinforcement, and attack opportunity on the Dinghai Landing. If it is not well prepared, we could rather postpone the attack than feel sorry about it later." In 毛文稿 [*Mao's Manuscripts*], 1:118, 120, 137.
52. 中央军委 [CMC], 军委关于攻击金门岛失利的教训的通报 ["CMC Circular on the Setback and Lessons of the Attack on Jinmen Island"], in 毛文稿 [*Mao's Manuscripts*], 1:101.
53. He Di, "The Last Campaign to Unify China: The CCP's Unrealized Plan to Liberate Taiwan, 1949–1950," in *Chinese Warfighting: The PLA Experience since 1949*, ed. Mark A. Ryan, David M. Finkelstein, and Michael A. McDevitt (Armonk, NY: M. E. Sharpe, 2003), 88.
54. 叶飞上将 [General Ye Fei], 叶飞回忆录 [*Memoirs of Ye Fei*] (Beijing: PLA Press, 1988), 608; staff member of the Tenth Army Group HQ, interview by the author at Hangzhou, Zhejiang, July 6, 2006. Ye was the commander of the Tenth Army Group in 1949–55. See 星火燎原编辑部 [*Xinghuo liaoyuan* Composition Department], 将帅名录 [*Marshals and Generals*], 1:58–59.
55. General Jiang Weiguo (Chiang Wei-kuo, ROC army), interview by the author at Rongzong Hospital, Taipei, Taiwan, May 26, 1994. Jiang Weiguo was the son of Jiang Jieshi (Chiang Kai-shek, ROC president from 1927 to 1975) and the younger brother of Jiang Jingguo (Chiang Ching-kuo, ROC president from 1978 to 1988).

56. Xiaobing Li, *A History of the Modern Chinese Army* (Lexington: University Press of Kentucky, 2007), 223.
57. 前苏联档案 [Former Soviet Archives], 斯大林与中共代表团会谈记录 ["The Meeting Minutes of Stalin's Negotiations with the CCP Delegation"], June 27, 1949, in 有关刘少奇1949年访苏的俄国档案 [*The Russian Archives of 1949 Liu Shaoqi's Visit in the Soviet Union*], 中共党史研究 [*CCP Party History Research*], no. 2 (1998): 15–16.
58. 杨忠义大校 [Commodore Yang Zhongyi], 苏联专家与中国海军航空兵 [*Soviet Experts and Chinese Naval Aviation*] (Beijing: PLA Press, 2013), 10.
59. 杨国宇 [Yang Guoyu], 当代中国海军 [*Contemporary Chinese Navy*], 48–49.
60. 军事科学院军事历史研究部 [Military History Division, PLA-AMS], 中国人民解放军战史 [*War History of the Chinese People's Liberation Army*] (Beijing: Military Science Press, 1987), 3:359.
61. 毛泽东 [Mao Zedong], 渡海作战必须注意的问题 ["Crucial Issues for Cross-Strait Battles"], December 18, 1949, in 毛军事文稿 [*Mao's Military Manuscripts*], 1:104–6.
62. 毛泽东 [Mao Zedong], 关于海南岛作战问题给林彪的电报 ["Telegram to Lin Biao on the Issues of the Battle of Hainan Island"], January 10, 1950, in 毛文稿 [*Mao's Manuscripts*], 1:228–29.
63. 前苏联档案 [Former Soviet Archives], 斯大林与毛泽东会谈记录 ["The Meeting Minutes of Stalin's Conversation with Mao Zedong"], December 16, 1949, in 有关1950年中苏条约谈判的俄国档案 [*The Russian Archives of the 1950 Treaty Negotiations on the Soviet-Chinese Agreement*], in 党史研究 [*Party History Research*], no. 4 (1998): 4.
64. 杨国宇 [Yang Guoyu], 当代中国海军 [*Contemporary Chinese Navy*], 48, 52.
65. Mao's conversation with Pavel Yudin, ambassador of the Soviet Union to China on July 22, 1958, in Mao Zedong, *Mao Zedong on Diplomacy* (Beijing: Foreign Languages Press, 1998), 255.
66. 杨忠义 [Yang Zhongyi], 苏联专家与中国海军航空兵 [*Soviet Experts and Chinese Naval Aviation*], 10–11.
67. 王定烈少将 [Major General Wang Dinglie], 当代中国空军 [*Contemporary Chinese Air Force*] (Beijing: China's Social Science Press, 1989), 78–79. Wang was the chief of staff of the PLAAF in 1975–82.
68. 毛泽东 [Mao Zedong], 关于起义的伞兵第三团加强训练问题给粟裕的电报 ["Telegram to Su Yu on Strengthening the Third Paratroop Regiment Training"], February 4, 1950; 关于同意粟裕调四个师演习海战等问题给刘少奇的电报 ["Telegram to Liu Shaoqi to Agree with Su Yu's Disposing Four Divisions for Landing Campaign Training"] February 10; 关于确定先打定海再打金门的方针的批语 ["Mao's Approval of the Plan to Attack Dinghai First, Jinmen Second"], March 28, in 毛文稿 [*Mao's Manuscripts*], 1:256, 257, 282.
69. 肖劲光大将 [Fleet Admiral Xiao Jinguang], 肖劲光回忆录 [*Memoirs of Xiao Jinguang*] (Beijing: PLA Press, 1988), 2:8, 26.

70. He Di, "The Last Campaign to Unify China," 82–83.
71. 中共中央党史研究室 [Party History Research Division, CCP Central Committee], 中国共产党历史大事记, 1919–1987 [*Major Historical Events of the CCP, 1919–1987*] (Beijing: People's Press, 1989), 191–92.
72. General Ye Fei, interview by the author in Hangzhou, Zhejiang, July 1996. Ye served as the commander of the Tenth Army Group, PLA Third Field Army, in 1949–51.
73. Mao was very dissatisfied with this and later confided, "They [North Koreans] are our next-door neighbor, but they did not consult with us about the outbreak of the war." Mao's quote is in 李海文 [Li Haiwen], 党中央什么时候决定派志愿军出国参战 ["When Did the CCP Central Committee Decide to Send the Volunteers to Fight Abroad?"], 党的文献 [*Party Manuscripts and Archives*], no. 5 (1993): 85.
74. Xiaobing Li, "Truman and Taiwan: A U.S. Policy Change from Face to Faith," in *Northeast Asia and the Legacy of Harry S. Truman: Japan, China, and the Two Koreas*, ed. James I. Matray (Kirksville, MO: Truman State University Press, 2012), 127–28.
75. Hao Bocun, interviews by the author in Taipei, Taiwan, May 23–24, 1994. Hao, as the commander of the front artillery force on Jinmen Island, felt released when he was informed of the U.S. Seventh Fleet's patrol in the Taiwan Strait in June 1950. See also 肖劲光 [Xiao Jinguang], 肖劲光回忆录 [*Memoirs of Xiao Jinguang*], 2:26.
76. 中国人民海军总部 [PLAN General Headquarters], 中国人民解放军海军编年史, 1949–1983 [*The Chronicle of the PLA Navy, 1949–1983*] (Beijing: PLAN Press, 1995), 24; 刘亮 [Liu Liang], 岸防劲旅: 中国人民解放军海军岸防部队 [*Strong Coastal Defense: PLAN Coastal Defense Forces*] (Beijing: Blue Sky, 2014), 4.
77. 毛泽东 [Mao Zedong], 三大运动的伟大胜利 ["The Great Achievements of the Three Glorious Movements"], a speech at the Third Plenary Session of the First National Committee of the Chinese People's Political Consultative Conference, October 23, 1951, in 毛文稿 [*Mao's Manuscripts*], 2:481–86.
78. Yoshihara, *Mao's Army Goes to Sea*, 6.
79. Vice Admiral Liu Daosheng (1915–95) was purged during the Cultural Revolution. For more information, see 星火燎原编辑部 [*Xinghuo liaoyuan* Composition Department], 将帅名录 [*Marshals and Generals*], 1:246–47.
80. 星火燎原编辑部 [*Xinghuo liaoyuan* Composition Department], 将帅名录 [*Marshals and Generals*], 1:358–59.
81. 张爱萍 [Zhang Aiping], 中国人民解放军 [*The Chinese People's Liberation Army*], 2:25–26.
82. 吴殿卿大校 [Commodore Wu Dianqing], 周恩来、朱德指导制定第一个海军三年建设计划 ["Zhou Enlai and Zhu De Give Instructions to Make the

Navy's First Three-Year Development Plan"], 铁军 [*Iron Force*], no. 3 (2013): 21–22. Wu served as deputy chief of the Propaganda Division, PLAN's Political Tasks Department, in the 1990s.

83. 中国人民海军总部 [PLAN General Headquarters], 中国人民解放军海军编年史, 1949–1983 [*The Chronicle of the PLA Navy, 1949–1983*], 43.
84. 肖劲光 [Xiao Jinguang], 肖劲光回忆录 (续集) [*Memoir of Xiao Jinguang* (Sequel)], 2.
85. 吴殿卿大校 [Commodore Wu Dianqing], 组建海军重大决策的历史事实 ["Historical Facts on Important Decisions to Establish the PLA Navy"], 人民海军 [*People's Navy*], no. 9 (October 2002): 4–5.
86. 李东野 [Li Dongye], 忆大连第一海军学校的创建 ["The Founding of the First Naval Academy in Dalian"], in 海军回忆史料 [*The Navy: Memoirs and History Records*] (Classified), 中国人民解放军历史资料丛书海军编审委员会 [ed. Navy Compilation Committee, PLA Historical Documents and Collections Series] (Beijing: Ocean Wave Publishing, 1994), 2:634–37.
87. 夏光 [Xia Guang], 从华东军区海校到海军联校 ["From East China Military Region's Naval School to PLAN Academy"], in 中国人民解放军历史资料丛书海军编审委员会 [Navy Compilation Committee, PLA Historical Documents and Collections Series, ed.] 海军回忆史料 [*The Navy: Memoirs and History Records*] (Classified), 2:631–32.
88. Among the 80,000 Soviet advisers sent to China each year in the 1950s, most were military advisers. See 沈志华 [Shen Zhihua], 毛泽东、斯大林与朝鲜战争 [*Mao Zedong, Stalin, and the Korean War*] (Guangzhou: Guangdong People's Press, 2004), 371–72. Shen found the information in the archives of the Second Division, Defense Intelligence Agency, ROC Defense Ministry, in Taiwan. He believes that the numbers collected by the intelligence agents in the 1950s were incomplete.
89. Kecherjn's quotes are in 沈志华 [Shen Zhihua], 苏联专家在中国 (1948–1960) [*Soviet Experts in China, 1948–1960*] (Beijing: China International Broadcasting Publishing House, 2003), 146.
90. 杨国宇 [Yang Guoyu], 当代中国海军 [*Contemporary Chinese Navy*], 48–49.
91. 杨国宇 [Yang Guoyu], 当代中国海军 [*Contemporary Chinese Navy*], 55.
92. 杨忠义 [Yang Zhongyi], 苏联专家与中国海军航空兵 [*Soviet Experts and Chinese Naval Aviation*], 25, 38.
93. 杨忠义 [Yang Zhongyi], 苏联专家与中国海军航空兵 [*Soviet Experts and Chinese Naval Aviation*], 32–33.
94. 杨忠义 [Yang Zhongyi], 苏联专家与中国海军航空兵 [*Soviet Experts and Chinese Naval Aviation*], 35.
95. 吴殿卿大校 [Commodore Wu Dianqing], 总司令的"海军月" ["The 'Naval Month' of the Commander in Chief"], in 共和国领袖与海军 [*PRC National Leaders and the Navy*], 吴殿卿、袁永安、赵小平主编 [ed. Wu Dianqing, Yuan Yong'an, and Zhao Xiaoping] (Beijing: Ocean Wave Publishing, 2000), 28–32.

96. 杨忠义 [Yang Zhongyi], 苏联专家与中国海军航空兵 [*Soviet Experts and Chinese Naval Aviation*], 180.
97. 南平波 [Nan Pingbo], 潜艇部队初建时期的政治工作 ["The Political Tasks of the Submarine Fleet during Its Formative Years"], in 中国人民解放军历史资料丛书海军编审委会 [Navy Compilation Committee, PLA Historical Documents and Collections Series], 海军回忆史料 [*The Navy: Memoirs and History Records*] (Classified), 2:807.
98. 付继泽、李克明 [Fu Jize and Li Keming], 在苏联三年的潜艇培训 ["Three Years of Submarine Training in the Soviet Union"], 海军回忆史料 [*The Navy: Memoirs and History Records*] (Classified), 1:99–101.
99. 南平波 [Nan Pingbo], 潜艇部队初建时期的政治工作 ["The Political Tasks of the Submarine Fleet during Its Formative Years"], 2:806.
100. Gao et al., *The PLA Navy*, 29.
101. 丁伟 [Ding Wei], 在移动的国土上: 人民海军的创建与发展 ["On the Floating Territory: Creation and Development of the People's Navy"], in 军旗飘飘: 新中国50年军事大事述实 [*PLA Flag Fluttering: The Facts about China's Major Military Events in the Past Fifty Years*], 军事科学院军事历史研究部编 [ed. Military History Division, PLA Academy of Military Science] (Beijing: PLA Press, 1999), 1:97.
102. Bussert and Elleman, *People's Liberation Army Navy*, 6.
103. 储峰 [Chu Feng], 二十世纪50年代中苏军事关系研究 ["Sino-Soviet Military Relations in the 1950s"], 中共中央党校2006年博士论文 (PhD diss., Beijing: CCP Central Party University, 2006), 64.
104. 吴殿卿大校 [Commodore Wu Dianqing], 毛泽东与肖劲光大将 ["Mao Zedong and Fleet Admiral Xiao Jinguang"], in 毛泽东与海军将领 [*Mao Zedong and Naval Admirals*], 吴殿卿、袁永安、赵小平主编 [ed. Wu Dian-qing, Yuan Yong'an, and Zhao Xiaoping] (Beijing: PLA Literature Press, 1999), 25–26.
105. Gao et al., *The PLA Navy*, 16.
106. 杨国宇 [Yang Guoyu], 当代中国海军 [*Contemporary Chinese Navy*], 16.
107. 韩怀智 [Han Huaizhi], 当代中国军队的军事工作 [*Military Affairs of Contemporary China's Armed Forces*], 1:142–43, 144–45.
108. 张爱萍 [Zhang Aiping], 中国人民解放军 [*The Chinese People's Liberation Army*], 1:75–76.
109. 杨国宇 [Yang Guoyu], 当代中国海军 [*Contemporary Chinese Navy*], 156.
110. 胡彦林 [Hu Yanlin], 威震海疆 [*Shocking the Sea*], 91–92.
111. 地久、克峰 [Di Jiu and Ke Feng], 潮涨潮落 [*Ebb and Flow*], 127.
112. 胡彦林 [Hu Yanlin], 威震海疆 [*Shocking the Sea*], 93.
113. 杨国宇 [Yang Guoyu], 当代中国海军 [*Contemporary Chinese Navy*], 161.
114. A decommissioned *Jiefang* is on display today in the square of the Chinese Navy Museum in Qingdao.
115. 韩怀智 [Han Huaizhi], 当代中国军队的军事工作 [*Military Affairs of Contemporary China's Armed Forces*], 1:157.
116. 胡彦林 [Hu Yanlin], 威震海疆 [*Shocking the Sea*], 98.

117. 地久、克峰 [Di Jiu and Ke Feng], 潮涨潮落 [*Ebb and Flow*], 126–27.
118. Yoshihara, *Mao's Army Goes to Sea*, 1.
119. 丁伟 [Ding Wei], 在移动的国土上 ["On the Floating Territory"], 92.
120. 军事科学院军事历史研究部 [Military History Research Division, PLA Academy of Military Science], 中国人民解放军的七十年 [*Seventy Years of the Chinese PLA*] (Beijing: Military Science Press, 1997), 370.
121. 杨国宇 [Yang Guoyu], 当代中国海军 [*Contemporary Chinese Navy*], 181.
122. 张爱萍 [Zhang Aiping], 中国人民解放军 [*The Chinese People's Liberation Army*], 2:55.
123. 胡彦林 [Hu Yanlin], 威震海疆 [*Shocking the Sea*], 101.
124. 胡彦林 [Hu Yanlin], 威震海疆 [*Shocking the Sea*], 104.
125. 杨国宇 [Yang Guoyu], 当代中国海军 [*Contemporary Chinese Navy*], 176–77.
126. General Zhang Aiping had only one infantry army, the 24th Army, available for his amphibious operations along the Zhejiang coast. The number of ECMR troops had been dramatically reduced during the Korean War. The Ninth Army Corps, the main strength of the ECMR, numbering about 150,000 men, including the 20th, 26th, and 27th Armies, left the Zhejiang-Jiangsu region for the Korean War in 1950 and did not return to East China after the war ended in 1953. The 25th Army left Zhejiang for Fujian in 1951. 毛泽东 [Mao Zedong], 给宋时轮、陶勇的电报 ["Telegram to Song Shilun and Tao Yong"] on October 31, 1950, in 毛泽东 [Mao Zedong], 毛泽东军事文选（内部版）[*Selected Military Papers of Mao Zedong: Internal Edition*], 2:667; 徐焰少将 [Major General Xu Yan], 金门之战 [*The Battle of Jinmen*] (Beijing: China's Radio and Television Publishing House, 1992), 171.
127. 地久、克峰 [Di Jiu and Ke Feng], 潮涨潮落 [*Ebb and Flow*], 201–2.
128. 韩怀智 [Han Huaizhi], 当代中国军队的军事工作 [*Military Affairs of Contemporary China's Armed Forces*], 1:333.
129. 军事科学院军事历史研究部 [Military History Research Division, PLA-AMS], 中国人民解放军的七十年 [*Seventy Years of the Chinese PLA*], 371.
130. General Jiang Weiguo (Chiang Wei-kuo, ROC army), interview by the author at Rongzong (Glory General) Hospital in Taipei, Taiwan, May 25–27, 1994.
131. 东方鹤 [Dong Fanghe], 张爱萍传 [*Biography of Zhang Aiping*], 2:655; Xiaobing Li, "New War of Nerves," *Journal of Chinese Political Science* 3, no. 1 (Summer 1997): 70.
132. 徐焰 [Xu Yan], 中国由注重"海防"变为争取"海权" ["China Shifts Its Focus from 'Coastal Defense' to 'Sea Power'"], 206.
133. 肖劲光 [Xiao Jinguang], 肖劲光回忆录（续集）[*Memoir of Xiao Jinguang (Sequel)*], 65.
134. Sherman Xiaogang Lai, "Ensured Loyalty versus Professionalism at Sea: A Historical Review of the PLA Navy, 1949–1982," paper presented at the annual meeting of Chinese Military History Society, Ottawa, Ontario, Canada, April 16, 2016.

CHAPTER 2. "LIMITED NAVAL WARS" IN THE TAIWAN STRAIT

1. 毛泽东 [Mao Zedong], 同意目前不打金门 ["Agree Not to Attack Jinmen Right Now"], in 毛军事文稿 [*Mao's Military Manuscripts*], 2:194. Chen Yi estimated the cost of Jinmen landing campaign about 500 million RMB (about $200 million at that time). Mao told Chen in the telegram, "[We] don't have that much, at least in 1954 [we] should not use such a huge amount of money."
2. 毛泽东 [Mao Zedong], 建设一支强大的海军 ["Build a Strong Naval Force"], Mao's speech at the CCP Enlarged Politburo meeting on December 4, 1953, in 毛军事文稿 [*Mao's Military Manuscripts*], 2:192.
3. Lai, "Ensured Loyalty versus Professionalism at Sea," 15.
4. 周恩来 [Zhou Enlai], 关于美蒋"共同防御条约"的声明 ["Statement against the US-Jiang Mutual Defense Treaty"], in 周恩来军事活动记事 [*Chronicle of Zhou Enlai's Military Affairs*], 《周恩来军事活动记事》编写组编著 [Compilation Team of *Chronicle of Zhou Enlai's Military Affairs*] (Beijing: CCP Central Archival and Manuscript Press, 2000), 2:351.
5. For "probe action" interpretations, see Tang Tsou, *The Embroilment over Quemoy: Mao, Chiang, and Dulles* (Salt Lake City: University of Utah Press, 1959); Robert W. Barnett, *Quemoy: The Use and Consequence of Nuclear Deterrence* (Cambridge, MA: Harvard University Press, 1960).
6. 徐焰 [Xu Yan], 中国由注重"海防"变为争取"海权" ["China Shifts Its Focus from 'Coastal Defense' to 'Sea Power'"], 207.
7. Ming-Yen Tsai, *From Adversaries to Partners: Chinese and Russian Military Cooperation after the Cold War* (Westport, CT: Praeger, 2003), 25–27.
8. The words of China's defense minister and vice premier, Marshal Peng Dehuai, are quoted in 张爱萍 [Zhang Aiping], 中国人民解放军 [*The Chinese People's Liberation Army*], 2:33.
9. Bussert and Elleman, *People's Liberation Army Navy*, 18.
10. 徐焰 [Xu Yan], 中国由注重"海防"变为争取"海权" ["China Shifts Its Focus from 'Coastal Defense' to 'Sea Power'"], 205–6.
11. Xiaobing Li, "PLA Attacks and Amphibious Operations during the Taiwan Strait Crises of 1954–55 and 1958," in *Chinese Warfighting: The PLA Experience since 1949*, ed. Mark A. Ryan, David M. Finkelstein, and Michael A. McDevitt (New York: M. E. Sharpe, 2003), 143–72.
12. 胡彦林 [Hu Yanlin], 威震海疆 [*Shocking the Sea*], 78–79. Vice Admiral Fang Qiang became the deputy commander of the PLAN in 1979–82.
13. 沈志华 [Shen Zhihua], 苏联专家在中国 [*Soviet Experts in China*], 139.
14. 沈志华 [Shen Zhihua], 苏联专家在中国 [*Soviet Experts in China*], 139–40.
15. 储峰 [Chu Feng], 二十世纪50年代中苏军事关系研究 ["Sino-Soviet Military Relations in the 1950s"], 70–71.
16. 中国人民解放军海军政治部 [PLAN Department of Political Tasks], 中国人民解放军海军编年史, 1949–1983 [*Chronicle of the PLAN, 1949–1983*] (Beijing: PLA Press, 1985), 135.

17. Bussert and Elleman, *People's Liberation Army Navy*, 64.
18. 侯向之 [Hou Xiangzhi], 《二四协定》的签定 ["The Conclusion of February 4 Agreement"], in 中国人民解放军历史资料丛书: 海军回忆史料 [*PLA Historical Sources Series: The Navy's Memoirs and Records*] (Classified), 海军编审委员会 [ed. Navy Editorial Committee] (Beijing: Ocean Wave Publishing, 1994], 2:1047.
19. 储峰 [Chu Feng], 二十世纪50年代中苏军事关系研究 ["Sino-Soviet Military Relations in the 1950s"], 71.
20. 中国人民解放军海军政治部 [PLAN Department of Political Tasks], 中国人民解放军海军编年史, 1949-1983 [*Chronicle of the PLAN, 1949-1983*], 135.
21. Cole, *The Great Wall at Sea*, 8.
22. 张爱萍 [Zhang Aiping], 中国人民解放军 [*The Chinese People's Liberation Army*], 2:33.
23. Chen Jian, *Mao's China and the Cold War* (Chapel Hill: University of North Carolina Press, 2001), 62.
24. Bussert and Elleman, *People's Liberation Army Navy*, 6.
25. 任秀生大校 [Commodore Ren Xiusheng], 华东军区海军舰船修造工作的回顾 ["Recollection of ECMR Navy's Shipbuilding and Rebuilt"], in 中国人民解放军历史资料丛书: 海军回忆史料 [*PLA Historical Source Collection Series: The Navy: Memoirs and History Records*] (Classified), 海军编审委员会 [ed. Navy Editorial Committee] (Beijing: Ocean Wave Publishing, 1994], 2:1002.
26. 任秀生 [Ren Xiusheng], 华东军区海军舰船修造工作的回顾 ["Recollection of ECMR Navy's Shipbuilding and Rebuilt"], 88-89.
27. 储峰 [Chu Feng], 二十世纪50年代中苏军事关系研究 ["Sino-Soviet Military Relations in the 1950s"], 72.
28. 储峰 [Chu Feng], 71-72.
29. 杨国宇 [Yang Guoyu], 当代中国海军 [*Contemporary Chinese Navy*], 83. Yang served as deputy commander and chief of staff of the PLAN from 1978 to 1985.
30. 沈志华 [Shen Zhihua], 苏联专家在中国 [*Soviet Experts in China*], 407.
31. 刘伯承元帅 [Marshal Liu Bocheng], 对作战情报系第二届毕业班的讲话 ["Speech to the Second Graduating Class of the Department of Operation and Intelligence"], in 刘伯承军事文选 [*Selected Military Papers of Liu Bocheng*] (Beijing: PLA Press, 1992), 518.
32. For more details on Vice Admiral Fang Qiang, see 星火燎原编辑部 [*Xinghuo liaoyuan* Composition Department], 将帅名录 [*PLA Marshals and Generals*], 1:184-85.
33. For more details on Rear Admiral Zhang Xuesi (1916-70), see 星火燎原编辑部 [*Xinghuo liaoyuan* Composition Department], 将帅名录 [*PLA Marshals and Generals*], 3:73-74.
34. For more information on Admiral Liu Huaqing (1916-2011), see 刘华清上将 [Admiral Liu Huaqing], 刘华清回忆录 [*Memoir of Liu Huaqing*] (Beijing: PLA Press, 2004).

35. 张爱萍 [Zhang Aiping], 中国人民解放军 [*The Chinese People's Liberation Army*], 1:540.
36. Major Guo Haiyun, interviews by the author in Chengde, Hebei Province, July 2006. Guo served as the chief of staff of the Second Battalion, 611th Regiment, 64th AAA Division in 1967–69. See also 军事科学院军事历史研究部 [Military History Research Division, PLA-AMS], 中国人民解放军的七十年 [*Seventy Years of the Chinese PLA*], 455, 461.
37. 毛泽东 [Mao Zedong], 海空军强大起来了就能够收复台湾 ["Strong Naval and Air Forces Can Take Over Taiwan"], in 毛军事文稿 [*Mao's Military Manuscripts*], 2:227–28.
38. CMC document, "The CMC Decision on Strengthening the Struggle against the Jiang's Gang in the Southeastern Coastal Areas, January 1954," quoted in 韩怀智 [Han Huaizhi], 当代中国军队的军事工作 [*Military Affairs of Contemporary China's Armed Forces*], 1:256.
39. Lieutenant General Xu Changyou, interview by the author in Shanghai, April 2000. Xu served as General Zhang Aiping's aide and then deputy secretary general of the CMC. He was vice political commissar of the East Sea Fleet at the time of the interview.
40. 东方鹤 [Dong Fanghe], 张爱萍传 [*Biography of Zhang Aiping*], 2:663–64; Xiaobing Li, "PLA Attacks and Amphibious Operations during the Taiwan Straits Crises of 1954–55 and 1958," 146.
41. Nie Fengzhi was made a lieutenant general in 1955. He served as air force commander of Fuzhou Military Region in 1958 and deputy commander of Fuzhou Military Region from 1960 to 1962. Nie became air force commander and deputy commander of Nanjing Military Region from 1962 to 1966. He was jailed from 1966 to 1975 during the Cultural Revolution. From 1975 to 1977, he returned as deputy commander of Nanjing Military Region and became its commander in 1977–82. For more details on Lieutenant General Nie Fengzhi (1914–92), see 星火燎原编辑部 [*Xinghuo liaoyuan* Composition Department], 将帅名录 [*Marshals and Generals*], 1:406–7.
42. The First Marine Division was disbanded in 1957 and reorganized as the Shanghai Security Force. The PLAN did not have a marine corps until 1980. See 杨国宇 [Yang Guoyu], 当代中国海军 [*Contemporary Chinese Navy*], 56–57.
43. Zhongtian Han, "The PRC's Naval-Air Campaign in the East China Sea, 1954–1955," paper presented at the Chinese Military History Society annual meeting (via Zoom), May 10, 2020.
44. Ma Guansan (1913–91) was ranked rear admiral in 1961. For more details on Ma, see 星火燎原编辑部 [*Xinghuo liaoyuan* Composition Department], 将帅名录 [*PLA Marshals and Generals*], 2:26.
45. 卢辉少校 [Major Lu Hui], 三军战一江 [*Joint Operation against Yijiangshan*] (Beijing: China United Literature, 2014), 54–55.
46. 胡彦林 [Hu Yanlin], 威震海疆 [*Shocking the Sea*], 192.

47. 杨国宇 [Yang Guoyu], 当代中国海军 [*Contemporary Chinese Navy*], 196.
48. 聂凤智中将 [Lieutenant General Nie Fengzhi], 海陆空军联合作战解放一江山岛 ["Join Force with the Army and Navy to Liberate the Yijiangshan Island"], in 中国人民解放军历史资料丛书: 空军回忆史料 [*PLA Historical Source Collection Series: The Air Force: Memoirs and History Records*] (Classified), 空军编审委员会 [ed. Air Force Editorial Committee] (Beijing: PLA Press, 1999), 1:231–32.
49. General Jiang Weiguo (Chiang Wei-kuo, ROC army), interview by the author at Rongzong Hospital in Taipei, Taiwan, May 25–27, 1994. General Jiang, when asked during the interview about his father's secret visit to the Dachens, pointed out that his father recognized the strategic importance of these islands after the Korean War. Jiang Jieshi (Chiang Kai-shek) made his trip to these offshore islands without informing any ROC officials or American representatives in Taiwan other than his naval commanders.
50. General Jiang Weiguo, interview by the author at Rongzong Hospital in Taipei, Taiwan, May 25–27, 1994.
51. 台湾外交部长叶公超 [ROC Foreign Minister Ye Gongchao], "至顾维钧大使电报" [Telegram to Ambassador Gu Weijun], "台澎外岛防御问题, 大陈情况摘要" ["Defense Issues on the Offshore Islands beyond Taiwan and Penghu: The Key Points of the Dachen Situation"], 1954年5月17日, (43) 电字第209号 [Tele No. 209], 台湾档案管理局 [Taiwan Archival Administration], 外交部档案 [*Foreign Ministry Archives*], 档号 [File No.]: 0042/426.2/1.
52. 地久、克峰 [Di Jiu and Ke Feng], 潮涨潮落 [*Ebb and Flow*], 205–6.
53. Part of the reason Jiang Jieshi ordered continuous counterattacks was the presence of two U.S. intelligence agents (CIA) on the Dongji Islands when the PLA landed. They hid in caves and escaped from the island the next evening. For more details, see 雷华建、王冀城 [Lei Huajian and Wang Jicheng], 新中国海战内幕 [*Inside Story of New China's Naval Warfare*] (Beijing: China International Translations and Publishing House, 1993), 71–72.
54. 地久、克峰 [Di Jiu and Ke Feng], 潮涨潮落 [*Ebb and Flow*], 206.
55. Mao's instruction quoted in 卢辉 [Lu Hui], 三军战一江 [*Joint Operation against Yijiangshan*], 57.
56. 毛泽东 [Mao Zedong], 不要先向挑衅的美舰开炮 ["Do Not Open Fire First on the Aggressive American Warships"], Mao's instruction in his reply to Su Yu's report on June 2, 1954, in 毛军事文稿 [*Mao's Military Manuscripts*], 2:212.
57. 毛泽东 [Mao Zedong], 给周恩来的电报 [Telegram to Zhou Enlai], July 23, 1954, in 毛泽东外交文选 [*Selected Diplomatic Papers of Mao Zedong*] (Beijing: CCP Central Archival and Manuscript Press, 1994), 159–61.
58. The CCP Politburo's decision was later rewritten as "Proposal for a Collective Peace in Asia, September 1954," against U.S. secretary of state John Foster Dulles's proposal for the Southeast Asian Treaty Organization. The CCP

proposal was included in *Important Documents concerning the Question of Taiwan* (Beijing: Foreign Languages Press, 1955), 145–46.

59. CMC order quoted in 叶飞 [Ye Fei], 叶飞回忆录 [*Memoirs of Ye Fei*], 642–43.
60. 许峰源 [Hsu Feng-Yuan], 迁台初期台湾对沿海岛屿的防御策略调整 (1950–1955) ["Adjustment of Taiwan's Outer Islands Defense Strategy (1950–1955)"], 档案半年刊 [*Archives Semiannual*] 21, no. 1 (June 2022): 37.
61. 毛泽东 [Mao Zedong], 对再次炮击金门计划的批语 ["Instruction on the Next Bombardment of Jinmen's Plan"], September 14, 1954, in 毛军事文稿 [*Mao's Military Manuscripts*], 2:234.
62. 东方鹤 [Dong Fanghe], 张爱萍传 [*Biography of Zhang Aiping*], 2:664–65; Li, "PLA Attacks and Amphibious Operations during the Taiwan Straits Crises of 1954–55 and 1958," 148.
63. 马冠三少将 [Rear Admiral Ma Guansan], 鏖战东海忆当年 ["Remember the Combat Years in the East China Sea"], in 三军挥戈战东海 [*Combined Forces Wield Spears and Fight in the East China Sea*], 聂凤智等 [ed. Nie Fengzhi et al.] (Beijing: PLA Press, 1985), 29. Ma was ZFC deputy commander in charge of the naval force.
64. 胡彦林 [Hu Yanlin], 威震海疆 [*Shocking the Sea*], 219.
65. 陆其明 [Lu Qiming], 奇袭太平号: 人民海军鱼雷快艇首次海战纪实 ["Ambush Taiping: The Story of the First Battle of the PLAN Torpedo Boats"], in 三军挥戈战东海 [*Combined Forces Wield Spears and Fight in the East China Sea*], 聂凤智等 [ed. Nie Fengzhi et al.] (Beijing: PLA Press, 1985), 197–98.
66. 马冠三 [Ma Guansan], 鏖战东海忆当年 ["Remember the Combat Years in the East China Sea"], 29.
67. 周官英大校 (台湾海军) [Commodore Zhou Guan-ying (ROC navy)], 忆往事, 话太平: 记太平军舰遇伏始末 ["Remember the History: A Complete Story of How *Taiping* Was Ambushed"], 海军学刊 [*Journal of the Navy*] 44, no. 1 (February 2010): 112.
68. 陆其明 [Lu Qiming], 奇袭太平号 ["Ambush *Taiping*"], 201–2.
69. 东方鹤 [Dong Fanghe], 张爱萍传 [*Biography of Zhang Aiping*], 2:674–75; 韩怀智 [Han Huaizhi], 当代中国军队的军事工作 [*Military Affairs of Contemporary China's Armed Forces*], 1:216–17; Li, "PLA Attacks and Amphibious Operations during the Taiwan Straits Crises of 1954–55 and 1958," 152.
70. 许峰源 [Hsu Feng-Yuan], 迁台初期台湾对沿海岛屿的防御策略调整 (1950–1955) ["Adjustment of Taiwan's Outer Islands Defense Strategy (1950–1955)"], 39.
71. Mao's instructions quoted in 何迪 [He Di], 台海危机和中国对金门、马祖政策的形成 ["Taiwan Strait Crisis and China's Policy-Making toward Jinmen and Mazu"], 美国研究 [*American Studies*] 3, no. 1 (Fall 1988): 40.
72. 胡士弘 [Hu Shihong], 横槊东海 ["Couching the Lance in the East China Sea"], in 三军挥戈战东海 [*Army, Navy, and Air Force Fight in the East China Sea*], 聂凤智等 [ed. Nie Fengzhi et al.] (Beijing: PLA Press, 1986), 50. Hu

was the chief of radio operation of the 180th Regiment in the Yijiangshan landing campaign.
73. 马冠三 [Ma Guansan], 鏖战东海忆当年 ["Remember the Combat Years in the East China Sea"], 29.
74. 聂凤智中将 [Lieutenant General Nie Fengzhi], 云击鹰翔震海空 ["Soaring Eagles Strike and Shake the Sea and Sky"], in 三军挥戈战东海 [Army, Navy, and Air Force Fight in the East China Sea], 聂凤智等 [ed. Nie Fengzhi et al.] (Beijing: PLA Press, 1986), 16. Nie was ZFC deputy commander in the Yijiangshan landing campaign.
75. 胡彦林 [Hu Yanlin], 威震海疆 [Shocking the Sea], 222.
76. 韩怀智 [Han Huaizhi], 当代中国军队的军事工作 [Military Affairs of Contemporary China's Armed Forces], 1:215–16.
77. Vice Admiral Tao Yong (1912–67) died by suicide in 1967. For more details on Tao Yong, see 星火燎原 编辑部 [Xinghuo liaoyuan Composition Department], 将帅名录 [PLA Marshals and Generals], 1:432–33.
78. 崔向华大校、陈大鹏 [Commodore Cui Xianghua and Chen Dapeng], 陶勇将军传 [Biography of Vice Admiral Tao Yong] (Beijing: PLA Press, 1989), 406.
79. 杨忠义 [Yang Zhongyi], 苏联专家与中国海军航空兵 [Soviet Experts and Chinese Naval Aviation], 214–15.
80. 卢辉 [Lu Hui], 三军战一江 [Joint Operation against Yijiangshan], 126.
81. 杨忠义 [Yang Zhongyi], 苏联专家与中国海军航空兵 [Soviet Experts and Chinese Naval Aviation], 220.
82. 韩怀智 [Han Huaizhi], 当代中国军队的军事工作 [Military Affairs of Contemporary China's Armed Forces], 1:220–21.
83. 地久、克峰 [Di Jiu and Ke Feng], 潮涨潮落 [Ebb and Flow], 210–12.
84. 卢辉 [Lu Hui], 三军战一江 [Joint Operation against Yijiangshan], 206.
85. In February 1955, the U.S. Seventh Fleet deployed aircraft carriers, cruisers, and up to forty destroyers, to cover the evacuation of the Dachens. See *New York Times*, January 25 and February 7, 1955.
86. 韩怀智 [Han Huaizhi], 当代中国军队的军事工作 [Military Affairs of Contemporary China's Armed Forces], 1:222–23.
87. U.S. State Department, "Memorandum of Discussion at the 232nd Meeting of the National Security Council, January 20, 1955," *FRUS, 1955–1957* (Washington, DC: U.S. Government Printing Office, 1986), 2:70–71.
88. Gordon H. Chang, "To the Nuclear Brink: Eisenhower, Dulles, and the Quemoy-Matsu Crisis," *International Security* 12 (Spring 1988): 106.
89. Eisenhower, "The President News Conference, March 16, 1955," *FRUS, 1955–1957*, 2:332–33.
90. Xinhua News Agency, *China's Foreign Relations: A Chronology of Events, 1949–1988* (Beijing: Foreign Languages Press, 1989), 525.
91. Among the recent books published in China on PLA amphibious operations are 罗选优 [Luo Xuanyou], 中越台海战争征战纪实 [*Battle Records of the*

Sino-Vietnam and Taiwan Strait Wars] (Urumqi: Xinjiang People's Press, 2004); 沈卫平 [Shen Weiping], 8.23炮击金门 [*The August 23 Bombardment of Jinmen*] (Beijing: Huayi Publishing, 1999); 李健 [Li Jian], 台海两岸战事回顾 [*History of the Military Conflicts over the Taiwan Strait*] (Beijing: China Literature Publishing, 1996); 地久、克峰 [Di Jiu and Ke Feng], 潮涨潮落 [*Ebb and Flow*]; 徐焰 [Xu Yan], 金门之战 [*The Battle of Jinmen*].

92. Mao's words quoted in 沈卫平 [Shen Weiping], 8.23炮击金门 [*The August 23 Bombardment of Jinmen*] (Beijing: Huayi Publishing, 1999), 1:52, 54.
93. Mao's speech at the CMC meeting on July 18, 1958, in 毛军事文集 [*Mao's Military Papers*], 6:442–43.
94. Hao Bocun, interview by the author in Taipei, Taiwan, May 1994. Hau served as the garrison commander on Jinmen from 1957 to 1960. Then, in the 1970s and 1980s, Hau became the chief staff of the GMD army and the defense minister of the ROC. He retired from the military and served as the ROC premier in 1990–93.
95. 沈卫平 [Shen Weiping], 8.23炮击金门 [*The August 23 Bombardment of Jinmen*], 2:723.
96. 徐焰 [Xu Yan], 金门之战 [*The Battle of Jinmen*], 205–6; Xiaobing Li, "New War of Nerves," *Journal of Chinese Political Studies* 3, no. 1 (Summer 1997): 59.
97. 韩怀智 [Han Huaizhi], 当代中国军队的军事工作 [*Military Affairs of Contemporary China's Armed Forces*], 2:387.
98. Former FFC HQ's staff officer (PLA colonel ret.), interview by the author in Hangzhou, Zhejiang, April 2000.
99. 叶飞 [Ye Fei], 叶飞回忆录 [*Memoirs of Ye Fei*], 653–54; Xiaobing Li, "PLA Attacks and Amphibious Operations during the Taiwan Strait Crises of 1954–55 and 1958," 159.
100. General Jiang Weiguo, interviews by the author in Taipei, Taiwan, May 25–27, 1994.
101. 沈卫平 [Shen Weiping], 8.23炮击金门 [*The August 23 Bombardment of Jinmen*], 1:50, 62.
102. 毛泽东 [Mao Zedong], 关于把握打金门时机给彭德怀、黄克诚的信 ["Letter to Peng Dehuai and Huang Kecheng about Timing the Attack of Jinmen, August 18, 1958"], in 毛文稿 [*Mao's Manuscripts since 1949*], 7:326–27.
103. 叶飞 [Ye Fei], 叶飞回忆录 [*Memoirs of Ye Fei*], 651–52.
104. Vladislav M. Zubok, "The Mao-Khrushchev Conversation, July 31–August 3, 1958, and October 2, 1959," in "New Evidence on the Cold War in Asia," *Cold War International History Project Bulletin* 12–13 (Fall/Winter 2001): 244–46.
105. Beidaihe is a beach area located at the border of Hebei and Liaoning Provinces where Chinese leaders regularly take vacations and hold meetings during summer.

Notes to Pages 75–77   **219**

106. 毛泽东 [Mao Zedong], 关于停止在深圳方面的演习准备打金门的批语 ["Instruction on Stopping Military Exercise at Shenzhen and Preparing the Attack on Jinmen"], in 毛文稿 [*Mao's Manuscripts since 1949*], 7:348.
107. 沈卫平 [Shen Weiping], 8.23炮击金门 [*The August 23 Bombardment of Jinmen*], 1:188.
108. Ye had deployed a large bombardment force, including artillery units from the 20th, 28th, and 31st Armies; Third Artillery Division; and the naval coastal artillery units, which all participated. 叶飞 [Ye Fei], 叶飞回忆录 [*Memoirs of Ye Fei*], 655–56.
109. 徐焰 [Xu Yan], 金门之战 [*The Battle of Jinmen*], 224–28.
110. The PLA high command's telegram quoted in 沈卫平 [Shen Weiping], 8.23炮击金门 [*The August 23 Bombardment of Jinmen*], 1:220.
111. The Jinmen GMD garrison had received the intelligence information before the PLA bombardment. President Jiang Jieshi inspected the GMD troops on Jinmen on August 20, 1958, three days before the PLA bombardment. Generals Jiang Weiguo and Hao Bocun, interviews by the author in Taipei, Taiwan, May 1994. See also 国防部史政编译局 [History Compilation and Translation Bureau, ROC Defense Ministry], 8-23 炮战胜利30周年纪念文集 [*Recollection for the 30th Anniversary of the Victorious August 23 Artillery Battle*] (Taipei, Taiwan: Defense Department Printing, 1989), 1, 55.
112. 徐焰 [Xu Yan], 金门之战 [*The Battle of Jinmen*], 228–30; 沈卫平 [Shen Weiping], 8.23炮击金门 [*The August 23 Bombardment of Jinmen*], 1:229–30; Xiaobing Li, Chen Jian, and David L. Wilson, trans. and eds., "Mao Zedong's Handling of the Taiwan Strait Crisis of 1958: Chinese Recollections and Documents," *Cold War International History Project Bulletin* 6–7 (1996): 208–9.
113. Hao Bocun, interview by the author in Taipei, Taiwan, May 1994.
114. 国防部史政编译局 [History Compilation and Translation Bureau, ROC Defense Ministry], 8-23 炮战胜利30周年纪念文集 [*Recollection for the 30th Anniversary of the Victorious August 23 Artillery Battle*], 25–26, 181.
115. Hao Bocun, interview by the author in Taipei, Taiwan, May 1994.
116. FFC HQ's staff officer, interview by the author in Hangzhou, Zhejiang, April 2000.
117. 毛泽东 [Mao Zedong], 在军委关于对台湾和沿海蒋占岛屿军事斗争的指示搞上的批语 ["Instruction on the CMC Orders for the Military Operations against the Jiang-Occupied Offshore Islands in the Taiwan Strait, September 3, 1958"], in 毛文稿 *Mao's Manuscripts since 1949*, 7:376–77; 徐焰 [Xu Yan], 金门之战 [*The Battle of Jinmen*], 250–51; 沈卫平 [Shen Weiping], 8.23炮击金门 [*The August 23 Bombardment of Jinmen*], 1:359–60.
118. Vice Admiral Roland N. Smoot (USN), "As I Recalled: The U.S. Taiwan Defense Command," U.S. Naval Institute *Proceedings* 110, no. 9, 979 (September 1984): 56–59.
119. 叶飞 [Ye Fei], 叶飞回忆录 [*Memoirs of Ye Fei*], 659–61.

120. 沈卫平 [Shen Weiping], 8.23炮击金门 [*The August 23 Bombardment of Jinmen*], 1:398–400.
121. 徐焰 [Xu Yan], 金门之战 [*The Battle of Jinmen*], 250–51.
122. 沈卫平 [Shen Weiping], 8.23炮击金门 [*The August 23 Bombardment of Jinmen*], 2:500.
123. Elleman, *High Seas Buffer*, 103; Smoot, "As I Recalled," 56–59.
124. Li, "PLA Attacks and Amphibious Operations during the Taiwan Strait Crises of 1954–55 and 1958," 163.
125. Hao Bocun, interview by the author in Taipei, Taiwan, May 1994.
126. 韩怀智 [Han Huaizhi], 当代中国军队的军事工作 [*Military Affairs of Contemporary China's Armed Forces*], 1:395, 405.
127. Elleman, *High Seas Buffer*, 103; Joseph E. Bouchard, *Command in Crisis: Four Case Studies* (New York: Columbia University Press, 1991), 74.
128. 章长蓉少将 [Rear Admiral Zhang Changrong, ROC navy, ret.], 回顾八二三台海战役之海军作战 ["Recollection of the Naval Battles in the 8-23 Battle of the Taiwan Strait"], 海军学术 [*Naval Studies*] 52, no. 5 (2018): 13–14.
129. 王定烈 [Wang Dinglie], 当代中国空军 [*Contemporary Chinese Air Force*], 334–36.
130. 林虎中将 [Lieutenant General Lin Hu (PLAAF)], 保卫祖国领空的战斗 [*Air Battles to Defend Motherland's Airspace*] (Beijing: PLA Press, 2002), 57–58.
131. 张爱萍 [Zhang Aiping], 中国人民解放军 [*The Chinese People's Liberation Army*], 1:193–94.
132. 王定烈 [Wang Dinglie], 当代中国空军 [*Contemporary Chinese Air Force*], 342–43.
133. 王海上将 [General Wang Hai (PLAAF)], 我的战斗生涯 [*My Military Career*] (Beijing: CCP Central Archival and Manuscript Press, 2000), 190. Wang was the commander of the PLAAF from 1985 to 1992.
134. 王定烈 [Wang Dinglie], 当代中国空军 [*Contemporary Chinese Air Force*], 338–43; 徐焰 [Xu Yan], 金门之战 [*The Battle of Jinmen*], 212–14; 沈卫平 [Shen Weiping], 8.23炮击金门 [*The August 23 Bombardment of Jinmen*], 1:128–45.
135. Major General Peng Deqing (1911–99) served as vice minister of China's Transportation Ministry in 1965–81 and minister of transportation in 1981–83. For more details, see 星火燎原编辑部 [*Xinghuo liaoyuan* Composition Department], 将帅名录 [*Marshals and Generals*], 3:525.
136. Admiral Peng Deqing's notes quoted in 沈卫平 [Shen Weiping], 8.23炮击金门 [*The August 23 Bombardment of Jinmen*], 1:290.
137. 胡彦林 [Hu Yanlin], 威震海疆 [*Shocking the Sea*], 263–64.
138. Zhang Yimin's interview (1993) quoted in 沈卫平 [Shen Weiping], 8.23炮击金门 [*The August 23 Bombardment of Jinmen*], 1:308.
139. 台湾国防部军务局 [Department of Military Affairs, ROC Defense Ministry], 八二三台海战役 [*The 8-23 Battle of the Taiwan Strait*] (Taipei: Department of Military Affairs, ROC Defense Ministry, 1998), 113.

140. Li Maoqin's interview (1993) quoted in 沈卫平 [Shen Weiping], 8.23炮击金门 [*The August 23 Bombardment of Jinmen*], 1:330–35. Li was the chief engineer on *PT-175* during the 1958 battle.
141. Su Yu's instruction quoted in 胡彦林 [Hu Yanlin], 威震海疆 [*Shocking the Sea*], 271.
142. Zhang Yimin's interview (1993) quoted in 沈卫平 [Shen Weiping], 8.23炮击金门 [*The August 23 Bombardment of Jinmen*], 1:349–50.
143. 地久、克峰 [Di Jiu and Ke Feng], 潮涨潮落 [*Ebb and Flow*], 233.
144. 章长蓉 [Zhang Changrong], 回顾八二三台海战役之海军作战 ["Recollection of the Naval Battles in the 8-23 Battle of the Taiwan Strait"], 12.
145. 俊涛 [Jun Tao], 炮击金门 ["Bombardment of Jinmen"], 中华传奇 [*The Legacy of China*], no. 179 (November 2004): 72.
146. 毛泽东 [Mao Zedong], 关于暂停炮击和发表《告台湾同胞书》给彭德怀、黄克诚的信 ["Letter to Peng Dehuai and Huang Kecheng about Suspending the Bombardment and Releasing the 'Message to Compatriots in Taiwan,' October 5-6, 1958"], in 毛文稿 *Mao's Manuscripts since 1949*, 7:437.
147. 沈卫平 [Shen Weiping], 8.23炮击金门 [*The August 23 Bombardment of Jinmen*], 2:842; 国防部史政编译局 [History Compilation and Translation Bureau, ROC Defense Ministry], 8-23 炮战胜利30周年纪念文集 [*Recollection for the 30th Anniversary of the Victorious August 23 Artillery Battle*], 30, 34.
148. 徐焰 [Xu Yan], 金门之战 [*The Battle of Jinmen*], 268–69.
149. 毛泽东 [Mao Zedong], 在第十五次最高国务会议上谈国际形势 ["Speech on International Situation at the Fifteenth Conference of the Supreme State Council, September 8, 1958"], in 毛泽东外交文选 [*Selected Diplomatic Papers of Mao Zedong*], 348–52.
150. Wu Lengxi, "Inside Story of the Decision Making during the Shelling of Jinmen," in "Mao Zedong's Handling of the Taiwan Straits Crisis of 1958: Chinese Recollections and Documents," trans. and ed. Xiaobing Li, Chen Jian, and David L. Wilson, *Cold War International History Project Bulletin* 6-7 (1995/1996): 215.

CHAPTER 3. NAVAL STRATEGY AND COMBAT EXPERIENCE
1. Chen Jian and Xiaobing Li, "China and the End of the Cold War," in *The Cold War: From Détente to the Soviet Collapse*, ed. Malcolm Muir Jr. (Lexington: Virginia Military Institute Press, 2006), 121–22.
2. For example, Premier Zhou said on April 29, 1968 that the Soviet Union (like America) was apparently circulating and containing China. Zhou's words quoted in 李丹慧 [Li Danhui], 中苏在援越抗美问题上的矛盾与冲突 (1965–1972) ["Conflicts between China and the Soviet Union in Their Efforts to Aid Vietnam and Resist America"], in 冷战与中国 [*The Cold War and China*], 章百家、牛军主编 [ed. Zhang Baijia and Niu Jun] (Beijing: Global Knowledge], 2002), 373n1.

3. Former Soviet major (Red Army, ret.) and KGB agents, interviews by the author in 2004 and 2009. See also Major T., "Russian Missile Officers in Vietnam," and Russian Agent (KGB), "Russian Spies in Hanoi," in *Voices from the Vietnam War: Stories from American, Asian, and Russian Veterans*, ed. Xiaobing Li (Lexington: University Press of Kentucky, 2010), 65–72, 93–100.
4. 杨奎松 [Yang Kuisong], 美苏冷战的起源对中国革命的影响 ["Origins of the U.S.-Soviet Cold War and Its Impact on China's Revolution"], in 冷战与中国 [*The Cold War and China*], 章百家、牛军主编 [ed. Zhang Baijia and Niu Jun] (Beijing: Global Knowledge Publishing, 2002), 51–88.
5. Mao's words quoted in 赵小平 [Zhao Xiaoping], 毛泽东与吴瑞林中将 ["Mao Zedong and Lieutenant General Wu Ruilin"], in 毛泽东与海军将领 [*Mao Zedong and His Admirals and Generals*] (Beijing: PLA Literature Press, 1999), 206.
6. Tsai, From *Adversaries to Partners*, 25–27.
7. 储峰 [Chu Feng], 二十世纪50年代中苏军事关系研究 ["Sino-Soviet Military Relations in the 1950s"], 88–89.
8. 肖劲光 [Xiao Jinguang], 肖劲光回忆录（续集）[*Memoir of Xiao Jinguang (Sequel)*], 172–73.
9. 中国人民解放军历史资料丛书编审委员会 [The Editorial Board of Collected Historical Documents of the PLA], 海军历史资料 [*Historical Documents of the Navy*] (Beijing: PLA Press, 2006), 147–55.
10. 沈志华 [Shen Zhihua], 苏联专家在中国 [*Soviet Experts in China*], 407.
11. Kecherjin's quotes are in 沈志华 [Shen Zhihua], 苏联专家在中国 [*Soviet Experts in China*], 146–47.
12. Mao, "Talk to Yudin, Ambassador of the Soviet Union to China," on July 22, 1958, in *Mao Zedong on Diplomacy*, 254.
13. 罗时叙 [Luo Shixu], 由蜜月到反目：苏联专家在中国 [*From Honeymoon to Betrayal–Soviet Experts in China*] (Beijing: Shijie zhishi chubanshe [World Knowledge Publishing], 1999), 55–57.
14. 王焰 [Wang Yan], 彭德怀传 [*Biography of Peng Dehuai*] (Beijing: Contemporary China Press, 1993), 542–43.
15. 《彭德怀传》编写组 [Peng Dehuai Biography Compilation Team], 一个真正的人：彭德怀 [*A Real Man: Peng Dehuai*] (Beijing: People's Press, 1994), 225.
16. 沈志华 [Shen Zhihua], 苏联专家在中国 [*Soviet Experts in China*], 358–59.
17. 肖劲光 [Xiao Jinguang], 肖劲光回忆录 [*Memoirs of Xiao Jinguang*], 2:175–82.
18. 聂荣臻元帅 [Marshal Nie Rongzhen], 聂荣臻回忆录 [*Memoir of Nie Rongzhen*] (Beijing: PLA Press, 1984), 2:553.
19. 沈志华 [Shen Zhihua], 苏联专家在中国 [*Soviet Experts in China*], 146.
20. 胡彦林 [Hu Yanlin], 威震海疆 [*Shocking the Sea*], 77.
21. 沈志华 [Shen Zhihua], 苏联专家在中国 [*Soviet Experts in China*], 267.
22. Mao's conversation with Yudin in 沈志华 [Shen Zhihua], 苏联专家在中国 [*Soviet Experts in China*], 251.

23. 沈志华 [Shen Zhihua], 苏联专家在中国 [*Soviet Experts in China*], 299.
24. Zubok, "The Mao-Khrushchev Conversation, July 31–August 3, 1958, and October 2, 1959," 244–46.
25. "Document No. 1: The First Conversation of N. S. Khrushchev with Mao Zedong, Hall of Huaizhentang, Beijing, July 31, 1958; The Mao-Khrushchev Conversation, July 31–August 3, 1958 and October 2, 1959," in "New Evidence on the Cold War in Asia," trans. and intro. Vladislav M. Zubok, *Cold War International History Project Bulletin* 12–13 (2001): 252.
26. "Document No. 1: The First Conversation of N. S. Khrushchev with Mao Zedong, Hall of Huaizhentang, Beijing, July 31, 1958," 253.
27. 徐明德 [Xu Mingde], 第一座超长波电台的建设 ["The Construction of the First Long-Wave Radio Station"], in 海军: 回忆史料 [*The Navy: Memoirs and History Records*], 中国人民解放军历史资料丛书海军编审委员会 [ed. PLA Navy History Editorial Committee] (Classified Documents) (Beijing: Ocean Wave Publishing, 1994), 2:920–22.
28. "Document No. 1: Mao's Talk to Yudin," 254–55.
29. "Document No. 1: The First Conversation of N. S. Khrushchev with Mao Zedong, Hall of Huaizhentang, Beijing, July 31, 1958," 256–57.
30. "Document No. 1: The First Conversation of N. S. Khrushchev with Mao Zedong," 258–59.
31. "Document No. 1: The First Conversation of N. S. Khrushchev with Mao Zedong," 260.
32. 《周恩来军事活动记事》编写组 [Compilation Team of *Chronicle of Zhou Enlai's Military Affairs*], 周恩来军事活动记事 [*Chronicle of Zhou Enlai's Military Affairs*], 2:456.
33. 沈志华 [Shen Zhihua], 苏联专家在中国 [*Soviet Experts in China*], 307.
34. Xiaobing Li, *A History of the Modern Chinese Army*, 188–89.
35. 沈志华 [Shen Zhihua], 苏联专家在中国 [*Soviet Experts in China*], 358–59.
36. Lorenz M. Lüthi, "Sino-Soviet Split," in *China at War*, ed. Xiaobing Li (Santa Barbara, CA: ABC-CLIO, 2012), 406–9.
37. Mark A. Ryan, David M. Finkelstein, and Michael A. McDevitt, "Patterns of PLA Warfighting," introduction to *Chinese Warfighting: The PLA Experience since 1949*, ed. Ryan, Finkelstein, and McDevitt (Armonk, NY: M. E. Sharpe, 2003), 15.
38. Mao's quotes are from 王焰 [Wang Yan], 彭德怀传 [*Biography of Peng Dehuai*], 624–26.
39. Ellis Joffe, *The Chinese Army after Mao* (Cambridge, MA: Harvard University Press, 1987), 16.
40. Fang Zhu, *Gun Barrel Politics: Party-Army Relations in Mao's China* (Boulder, CO: Westview, 1998), 103.
41. After his fall, in 1965, Peng had a chance to prove his innocence and loyalty by serving as the deputy director of the "remote regional reconstruction" in Sichuan, but he did not survive the Cultural Revolution of 1966–76. He

was arrested again in 1966 and sent back to Beijing where he was criticized, denounced, and tortured through the rest of the 1960s and early 1970s. Peng died in jail on November 29, 1974. After Mao's death in 1976, the Central Committee announced Peng's rehabilitation in 1978, and his funeral was held in Beijing later that year.

42. 姚莲瑞 [Yao Lianrui], 彭大将军的沉冤 ["The Injustice of Marshal Peng"], in 军旗飘飘: 新中国50年军事大事述实 [*PLA Flag Fluttering: The Facts about China's Major Military Events in the Past Fifty Years*], 军事科学院军事历史研究部 [ed. Military History Division, PLA Academy of Military Science] (Beijing: PLA Press, 1999), 1:293.

43. For more details on the radical political movements in the 1950s, such as the Three Antis movement, Five Antis movement, and Anti-Rightist movement, see Xiaobing Li, *Civil Liberties in China* (Santa Barbara, CA: ABC-CLIO, 2010), 5-6.

44. 李作鹏中将 [Lieutenant General Li Zuopeng], 关于海军工作情况的汇报材料 ["Investigation Report on the Current Situations of the Navy"], in 李作鹏回忆录 [*Memoir of Li Zuopeng*] (Hong Kong: Beixing Publishing, 2011), 509-10.

45. 李作鹏 [Li Zuopeng], 关于海军工作情况的汇报材料 ["Investigation Report on the Current Situations of the Navy"], 510.

46. Lieutenant General Li Zuopeng (1914-2009) was purged as a member of Lin Biao's clique after Lin was killed in a plane crash in 1971. Li was arrested in late September 1971, dismissed from all his military positions in 1972, and expelled from the CCP in August 1973. He was sentenced to seventeen years in prison by the PRC Supreme Court on January 25, 1981 because of his involvement in Lin's plot against Mao Zedong and the Party Center as one of the leading members. For more information on his military and political career, see 星火燎原 编辑部 [Xinghuo liaoyuan Composition Department], 将帅名录 [*Marshals and Generals*], 1:274-75.

47. 郑雅茹 [Zheng Yaru], 肖劲光 ["Xiao Jinguaung"], 4:529.

48. 李作鹏 [Li Zuopeng], 李作鹏回忆录 [*Memoir of Li Zuopeng*], 516.

49. Lai, "Ensured Loyalty versus Professionalism at Sea," 23.

50. 崔向华、陈大鹏 [Cui Xianghua and Chen Dapeng], 陶勇将军传 [*Biography of Vice Admiral Tao Yong*], 447.

51. Deng Xiaoping, "A Historic Meeting of the PLA," in *Selected Works of Deng Xiaoping* (Beijing: Foreign Languages Press, 1994), 1:179.

52. Lieutenant Wang Xiangcai (PLAAF, ret.), interviews by the author in Harbin, Heilongjiang, August 2003.

53. Deng, "A Historic Meeting of the PLA," 1:180.

54. Deng, "A Historic Meeting of the PLA," 1:181.

55. 徐焰少将 [Major General Xu Yan], 中国空军的艰难起步和辉煌前景 ["A Tough Start and the Bright Future of the Chinese Air Force"], in 徐焰讲稿

自选集 [*Self-Selected Lectures of Xu Yan*] (Beijing: National Defense University Press, 2014), 284.
56. 杨忠义 [Yang Zhongyi], 苏联专家与中国海军航空兵 [*Soviet Experts and Chinese Naval Aviation*], 180-81.
57. The air force bases in east coast cities like Shanghai, Hangzhou, and Ningbo were also used by Zhang's jets in the air campaigns.
58. 王定烈 [Wang Dinglie], 当代中国空军 [*Contemporary Chinese Air Force*], 324.
59. 林虎 [Lin Hu], 保卫祖国领空的战斗 [*Air Battles to Defend Motherland's Airspace*], 49. Lin served as the commander of the PLAAF 18th Division in 1956 and as deputy commander of the PLAAF in 1985 and was appointed an air force lieutenant general in 1988.
60. 王定烈 [Wang Dinglie], 当代中国空军 [*Contemporary Chinese Air Force*], 345; 国防部史政编译局 [History Compilation and Translation Bureau, ROC Defense Ministry], 8-23 炮战胜利30周年纪念文集 [*Recollection for the 30th Anniversary of the Victorious August 23 Artillery Battle*], 33-34.
61. Li, *A History of the Modern Chinese Army*, 188-89.
62. Bussert and Elleman, *People's Liberation Army Navy*, 84.
63. 卢小萍 [Lu Xiaoping], 中国人民解放军空军 [*The Air Force of the Chinese People's Liberation Army*] (Beijing: China Continental Media, 2012), 67-68.
64. 中共中央文献研究室 [CCP Central Archival and Manuscript Research Division], 周恩来年谱, 1949-1976 [*A Chronological Record of Zhou Enlai, 1949-1976*] (Beijing: CCP Central Archival and Manuscript Press, 1997), 2:648.
65. 杨国宇 [Yang Guoyu], 当代中国海军 [*Contemporary Chinese Navy*], 353-54. Rear Admiral Yang served as the deputy commander and chief of staff of the PLAN in 1978-85.
66. 胡彦林 [Hu Yanlin], 威震海疆 [*Shocking the Sea*], 318-19. Hu became PLAN's political commissar in 2003-8 and admiral in 2004.
67. 林虎 [Lin Hu], 保卫祖国领空的战斗 [*Air Battles to Defend Motherland's Airspace*], 243-44.
68. 王成志 [Wang Chengzhi], 空中卫士 ["The Airspace Defenders"] 军旗飘飘: 新中国50年军事大事述实, 1949-1999 [*PLA Flag Fluttering: Facts of China's Major Military Events in Fifty Years, 1949-1999*], 军事科学院军事历史研究部 [Military History Research Division, PLA-AMS] (Beijing: PLA Press, 1999), 1:424.
69. 卢小萍 [Lu Xiaoping], 中国人民解放军空军 [*The Air Force of the Chinese People's Liberation Army*], 111.
70. 胡彦林 [Hu Yanlin], 威震海疆 [*Shocking the Sea*], 303.
71. 张力等 [Zhang Li et al.], 徐学海先生访问记录 ["Interview of Vice Admiral Xu Xuehai"], in 海军人物访问记录 [*Interview Records of Naval Admirals*], 张力、曾金兰编 [ed. Zhang Li and Zeng Jinlan] (Taipei: Institute of Modern China, Academia Sinica, 2002), 2:87-88.

72. 段与衡将军访问记录 ["Interview Records of Major General Duan Yuheng"], in 尘封的作战计划: 国光计划—口述历史 [*Oral History: Historical Operational Plan–Guoguang Jihua*], 彭大年编 [ed. Peng Danian] (Taipei: Department of Military Affairs, ROC Defense Ministry, 2005), 198.
73. 王蜀宁上校 [Captain Wang Shuning (ROC navy)], 八六海战评析 ["Analysis of the August 6 Naval Battle"], 海军学术 [*Naval Studies*] 42, no. 6 (December 2008): 38.
74. Wu Ruilin (1915–95) was involved in the Lin Biao incident in 1969–71 and purged from all his naval positions in September 1972. For more details on Lieutenant General Wu, see 星火燎原编辑部 [*Xinghuo liaoyuan* Composition Department], 将帅名录 [*Marshals and Generals*], 1:296–97.
75. 吴瑞林中将 [Lieutenant General Wu Ruilin], 吴瑞林回忆录 [*Memoirs of Wu Ruilin*] (Beijing: China Archival Publishing, 1995), 3:117–19.
76. 何森 [He Sen], 海上较量: 解放军海军取得八六海战与崇武海战胜利 [*Battles at Sea: PLA Navy's Victories of the Battles of the August Sixth and Chongwu*] (Jilin: Jilin Publishing, 2011), 32–33.
77. 军事科学院军事历史研究部 [Military History Division, PLA-AMS], 中国人民解放军的七十年 [*Seventy Years of the PLA*], 533.
78. Kong Zhaonian (1925–2019) became commander of the Shantou Marine Security District in 1969, deputy commander of the Guangzhou Naval Base in 1970, deputy commander of the Chinese navy in 1973–79, and deputy commander of the ESF in 1983–89.
79. 胡彦林 [Hu Yanlin], 威震海疆 [*Shocking the Sea*], 320–22.
80. 王成志 [Wang Zhicheng], 潮涨潮落: 打击海上窜扰之敌 ["Ebb and Flow: Defeat the Enemy Force at Sea"], in 军旗飘飘: 新中国50年军事大事述实 [*PLA Flag Fluttering: The Facts about China's Major Military Events in the Past Fifty Years*], 军事科学院军事历史研究部编 [ed. Military History Division, PLA Academy of Military Science] (Beijing: PLA Press, 1999), 2:437.
81. Zhou's instruction cited in 何森 [He Sen], 海上较量 [*Battles at Sea*], 29.
82. 杨国宇 [Yang Guoyu], 当代中国海军 [*Contemporary Chinese Navy*], 383.
83. 高晓星等 [Gao Xiaoxing et al.], 中国人民解放军海军 [*The PLA Navy*] (Beijing: China Intercontinental Press, 2012), 42–44.
84. 韩怀智 [Han Huaizhi], 当代中国军队的军事工作 [*Military Affairs of Contemporary China's Armed Forces*], 1:351.
85. 何森 [He Sen], 海上较量 [*Battles at Sea*], 34.
86. 军事科学院军事历史研究部 [Military History Division, PLA Academy of Military Science], 中国人民解放军的七十年 [*Seventy Years of the PLA*], 533.
87. 胡彦林 [Hu Yanlin], 威震海疆 [*Shocking the Sea*], 333–34.
88. Wu Ruilin's order to "keep fighting" quoted in 高晓星等 [Gao Xiaoxing et al.], 中国人民解放军海军 [*The PLA Navy*], 43.
89. 杨国宇 [Yang Guoyu], 当代中国海军 [*Contemporary Chinese Navy*], 386.

90. 毛泽东 [Mao Zedong], 对击沉国民党"剑门"、"章江"两舰战斗经验总结报告的批语 ["Instructions on the Battle Report on Combat Experience in Sinking Two GMD Warships of *Jianmen* and *Zhangjiang*"], August 15, 1965, in 毛军事文稿 [*Mao's Military Manuscripts*], 3:325.
91. 周恩来 [Zhou Enlai], 在接见海军作战有功人员时的指示 ["Instructions at the Meeting with Naval Combat Meritorious Personnel"], in 周恩来军事文选 [*Selected Military Papers of Zhou Enlai*], 4:530.
92. 高晓星等 [Gao Xiaoxing et al.], 中国人民解放军海军 [The PLA Navy], 40.
93. 刘广凯上将 [Admiral Liu Guangkai (ROC navy)], 刘广凯将军报国忆往 [*Admiral Liu Guangkai's Recollection of Defending the Country*] (Taipei: Institute of Modern China, Academia Sinica, 1994), 268-69.
94. 刘广凯 [Liu Guangkai], 刘广凯将军报国忆往 [*Admiral Liu Guangkai's Recollection of Defending the Country*], 270.
95. 邢祖援将军访问记录 ["Interview Records of Major General Xing Zuyuan"], in 尘封的作战计划: 国光计划–口述历史 [*Oral History: Historical Operational Plan–Guoguang Jihua*], 彭大年编 [ed. Peng Danian] (Taipei: Department of Military Affairs, ROC Defense Ministry, 2005), 61-62.
96. 王蜀宁 [Wang Shuning], 八六海战评析 ["Analysis of the August 6 Naval Battle"], 39-40.
97. Zhou's instructions cited in the endnotes of 周恩来 [Zhou Enlai], 在接见海军作战有功人员时的指示 ["Instructions at the Meeting with Naval Combat Meritorious Personnel"], in 周军事文选 [*Zhou's Military Papers*], 4:531.
98. 韩怀智 [Han Huaizhi], 当代中国军队的军事工作 [*Military Affairs of Contemporary China's Armed Forces*], 1:352.
99. 杨国宇 [Yang Guoyu], 当代中国海军 [*Contemporary Chinese Navy*], 387.
100. 胡彦林 [Hu Yanlin], 威震海疆 [*Shocking the Sea*], 345.
101. 王成志 [Wang Zhicheng], 潮涨潮落 [*Ebb and Flow*], 2:443.
102. Elleman, *High Sea Buffer*, 115.
103. 《周恩来军事活动纪事》编写组 [Chronicle of Zhou Enlai's Military Affairs Editorial Group], 周恩来军事活动纪事 [*Chronicle of Zhou Enlai's Military Affairs*], 2:622.
104. Gao et al., *The PLA Navy*, 40.
105. 钟坚 [Zhong Jian], 导读: 英雄不回头 ["Introduction: The Hero No Return"], in 看不见的屏障: 决定台湾命运的第七舰队 [*Invisible Shell: The Seventh Fleet and Taiwan's Fate*], 吴润睿译 [trans. Wu Runrui] (Xinbei, Taiwan: Eight Banner Culture, 2017), 21.

CHAPTER 4. THE VIETNAM WAR AND SOUTH CHINA SEA
1. The quote of the "May 16 Circular" is from Zhu, *Gun Barrel Politics*, 116.
2. Zhu, *Gun Barrel Politics*, 181.
3. There have been several speculations about the crash of Lin Biao's plane, including a Chinese missile attack, running out of fuel, or simply an accident.

See 高文谦 [Gao Wenqian], 晚年周恩来 [*Zhou Enlai's Later Years*] (Hong Kong: Mingjing Publishing, 2003), 350-55; 黄耀、严敬棠 [Huang Yao and Yan Jingtang], 林彪一生 [*The Life of Lin Biao*] (Beijing: PLA Literature Press, 2004), 490-507; 叶永烈 [Ye Yonglie], 高层较量 [*Power Struggle at the Top*] (Urumqi: Xinjiang People's Press, 2004), 369-76.

4. Mao's new political campaign to "Criticize Lin and Confucius" (批林批孔) purged most of Lin's generals and eliminated his military programs in 1972-73. By September 1973, 75 percent of the PLA officers had gone through the "reeducation" program. For details, see 军事科学院军事历史研究部 [Military History Division, PLA Academy of Military Science], 中国人民解放军的七十年 [*Seventy Years of the Chinese PLA*] (Beijing: Military Science Press, 1997), 566-68.

5. For more details on Admiral Su Zhenhua (1912-79), see 星火燎原编辑部 [*Xinghuo liaoyuan* Composition Department], 中国人民解放军将帅名录 [*PLA Marshals and Generals*] (Beijing: PLA Press, 1992), 1:72-73. 解放军将帅名录.

6. Among the recent publications in China on the Vietnam War of 1965-73 are 郭谨良 [Guo Jinliang], 亲历越战 [*The Vietnam War in My Eyes*] (Beijing: PLA Literature Press, 2005); 军事科学院军事历史研究部 [Military History Division, PLA Academy of Military Science], 美国侵越战争史 [*War History of U.S. Invasion of Vietnam*] (Beijing: Military Science Press, 2004); 罗选优 [Luo Xuanyou], 中越台海战争 [*The Sino-Vietnam and Taiwan Strait Wars*] (Beijing: Jinghua Publishing, 2007); 陈湃 [Chen Pai], 越战亲历记 [*My Personal Experience in the Vietnam War*] (Zhengzhou: Henan People's Press, 1997); 王贤根大校 [Colonel Wang Xiangen], 援越抗美实录 [*Historical Records of Aiding Vietnam and Resisting the United States*] (Beijing: International Culture Publishing, 1990). Wang served in the HQ of the PLA Engineering Corps during the Vietnam War.

7. Pierre Asselin, *Hanoi's Road to the Vietnam War, 1954-1965* (Berkeley: University of California Press, 2013), 59.

8. Mao decided that China must support the "magnificent armed struggles" in South Vietnam and Laos unconditionally during a party conference of the CCP Central Committee at Beidaihe in August 1962. 杨奎松 [Yang Kuisong], 毛泽东与印度支那战争 ["Mao Zedong and the Indochina Wars"], 中国与印度支那战争 [*China and the Indochina Wars*], 李丹慧主编 [ed. Li Danhui] (Hong Kong: Heaven and Earth Books, 2000), 72-73.

9. 张世鸿、张炎平、吴迪 [Zhang Shihong, Zhang Yanping, and Wu Di], 胡志明小道上的701天 [*701 Days on the Ho Chi Minh Trail*], 328, 338.

10. 韩念龙 [Han Nianlong], 当代中国外交 [*Foreign Affairs of Contemporary China*] (Beijing: China's Social Science Press, 1990), 159.

11. 王贤根大校 [Senior Colonel Wang Xiangen], 援越抗美实录 [*Historical Records of Aiding Vietnam and Resisting the United States*], 47. Wang served as a staff member at the PLA Engineering Corps HQ.

12. 李珉 [Li Min], 想起那个年代 ["Remember Those Years"], in 血洒越南—60年代援越抗美战地采访纪实 [*Blood Shed in Vietnam: Reports and Records from the Battleground of Assisting Vietnam and Resisting the United States. in the 1960s*], 尚力科、邢志远主编 [eds. Shang Like and Xing Zhiyuan] (Beijing: China Human Resources Publishing, 1993), 229-30.
13. 紫丁 [Ziding], 李强传 [*Biography of Li Qiang*], 259.
14. 王贤根 [Wang Xiangen], 中国秘密大发兵 [*China's Secret Dispatch of a Large Force*], 129-30.
15. 杨国宇 [Yang Guoyu], 当代中国海军 [*Contemporary Chinese Navy*] (Beijing: China's Social Science Press, 1987), 412-13. Yang served as the deputy commander and chief of staff of the PLAN in 1978-85.
16. 紫丁 [Ziding], 李强传 [*Biography of Li Qiang*], 259-60.
17. General Creighton Abrams is quoted in Michael Kelley, *Where We Were in Vietnam: A Comprehensive Guide to the Firebases, Military Installations, and Naval Vessels of the Vietnam War* (Central Point, OR: Hellgate Press, 2002), F-33.
18. 紫丁 [Ziding], 李强传 [*Biography of Li Qiang*], 278.
19. Chen, *Mao's China and the Cold War*, 228, table 1.
20. Gary R. Hess, *Vietnam: Explaining America's Lost War* (Malden, MA: Blackwell, 2009), 86.
21. Xiaobing Li, *The Dragon in the Jungle: The Chinese Army in the Vietnam War* (New York: Oxford University Press, 2020), chap. 2.
22. 曲爱国 [Qu Aiguo], 中国支援部队在越南战场的军事行动 ["Operations of the Chinese Supporting Forces in the Vietnam War"], 50.
23. 胡彦林上将 [Admiral Hu Yanlin], 威震海疆: 人民海军征战纪实 [*Shocking the Sea: Records of the People's Navy's Battles*] (Beijing: National Defense University Press, 1996), 318-19. Hu became the navy's political commissar in 2003-8 and admiral in 2004.
24. 杨国宇 [Yang Guoyu], 当代中国海军 [*Contemporary Chinese Navy*], 415.
25. Spencer C. Tucker, *Vietnam* (Lexington: University Press of Kentucky, 1999), 120.
26. Major General Xu Changyou, interviews by the author in Shanghai, April 25-27, 2000. Xu served as the deputy secretary general of the CMC in 1995-99 and deputy political commissar of the ESF Air Force of the PLAN in 2000-2004. See also Marshal Xu Xiangqian, "The Purchase of Arms from Moscow," in *Mao's Generals Remember Korea*, trans. and ed. Xiaobing Li, Allan R. Millett, and Bin Yu (Lawrence: University Press of Kansas, 2001), 144-46. Marshal Xu served as chief of the PLA General Staff and vice chairman of the CMC during the Korean War. Then he became the PRC vice premier from 1965 to 1980 and defense minister in 1978-81. He planned China's invasion of Vietnam in 1979.
27. Xu Changyou, interviews by the author in Shanghai, April 25-27, 2000; see also 李可、郝生章 [Li Ke and Hao Shengzhang], 文化大革命中的人民解放军 [*The PLA in the Cultural Revolution*], chaps. 2-8.

28. Colonel Jerry Noel Hoblit (USAF, ret.), interviews by the author in Edmond, Oklahoma, April 2005. Born in 1936, Jerry Hoblit graduated from U.S. Military Academy, West Point, in 1958. He then chose a commission in the USAF. He was initially trained to fly the F-100 Super Sabre before switching to the F-105 and being sent to fly and fight in Vietnam. Captain Hoblit was a USAF F-105F pilot of 357th Tactical Fighter Squadron, 355th Tactical Fighter Wing, Tuy Hoa Air Base, Vietnam, in 1966–67. He received three Silver Stars, three Distinguished Flying Crosses, the Legion of Merit, and the Air Force Cross before he retired from the air force as a colonel in 1982.
29. 胡彦林 [Hu Yanlin], 威震海疆 [*Shocking the Sea*], 361.
30. Colonel Yan Guitang, interview by the author in Xi'an, Shaanxi, July 29–30, 2006. Yan served as a staff member at the PLA DGS.
31. 李宝祥 [Li Baoxiang], 援越扫雷的技术保障工作 ["Technology Improvement: Help Vietnam to Clean the Mines"] in 援越抗美 [*Aid Vietnam and Resist America*], 曲爱国、鲍明荣、肖祖跃编 [eds. Qu, Bao, and Xiao], 301–2. Li was the senior engineer of the PLA Naval Research Institute in 1965–73.
32. For more details on Operation Linebacker I, see Tucker, *Vietnam*, 170–71.
33. 来光祖 [Lai Guangzu], 周总理运筹援越扫雷 ["Premier Zhou Organizes the Mine-Sweeping in Vietnam"], 299.
34. 萧石忠 [Xiao Shizhong], 扑灭印度支那战火的一次重要军事行动 ["An Important Military Operation to Put Out War Flames in Indochina"], 2:461.
35. 郭保兰 [Guo Baolan], 援越扫雷 ["Help Vietnam to Clean the Mines"], in 中国人民解放军历史资料丛书: 海军回忆史料 [*PLA Historical Sources Series: The Navy's Memoirs and Records*] (Classified), 海军编审委员会 [ed. Navy Editorial Committee] (Beijing: Ocean Wave Publishing, 1994), 2:1168.
36. 张寿瀛 [Zhang Shouying], 赴越扫雷的回顾 ["Memoir of Mine-Sweeping Experience in Vietnam"], 306–7.
37. 杨国宇 [Yang Guoyu], 当代中国海军 [*Contemporary Chinese Navy*], 423–24.
38. 萧石忠 [Xiao Shizhong], 扑灭印度支那战火的一次重要军事行动 ["An Important Military Operation to Put Out War Flames in Indochina"], 2:461.
39. 张寿瀛 [Zhang Shouying], 赴越扫雷的回顾 ["Memoir of Mine-Sweeping Experience in Vietnam"], 306.
40. 郭保兰 [Guo Baolan], 援越扫雷 ["Help Vietnam to Clean the Mines"], 2:1171.
41. 胡彦林 [Hu Yanlin], 威震海疆 [*Shocking the Sea*], 368–69.
42. 田铭、夏三保、陈康明 [Tian Ming, Xia Sanbao, and Chen Kangming], 越南人民的功臣 ["A Hero for the Vietnamese People"], in 援越抗美–中国支援部队在越南 [*Aid Vietnam and Resist the United States: Recollections of China's Supporting Forces in Vietnam*], 曲爱国少将、鲍明荣、肖祖跃编 [ed. Major General Qu Aiguo, Bao Mingrong, and Xiao Zuyue] (Beijing: Military Science Press, 1995), 313. Tian Ming was captain of the PLAN 312-05 minesweeper in 1972–73.

43. 崔向华大校、陈大鹏 [Commodore Cui Xianghua and Chen Dapeng], 陶勇将军传 [*Biography of Vice Admiral Tao Yong*] (Beijing: PLA Press, 1989), 447.
44. 崔向华、陈大鹏 [Cui Xianghua and Chen Dapeng], 陶勇将军传 [*Biography of Vice Admiral Tao Yong*], 448.
45. 崔向华大校 [Commodore Cui Xianghua], 毛泽东与陶勇中将 ["Mao Zedong and Vice Admiral Tao Yong], in 毛泽东与海军将领 [*Mao Zedong and His Admirals*] (Beijing: PLA Literature Publishing, 1999), 243.
46. Ye Qun's words quoted in 李可、郝生章 [Li Ke and Hao Shengzhang], 文化大革命中的人民解放军 [*The PLA in the Cultural Revolution*], 89.
47. 刘永路 [Liu Yonglu], 毛泽东与张学思少将 ["Mao Zedong and Rear Admiral Zhang Xuesi"], in 毛泽东与海军将领 [*Mao Zedong and His Admirals*] (Beijing: PLA Literature, 1999), 315.
48. Mao's words quoted in 杨肇林大校 [Commodore Yang Zhaolin], 毛泽东与苏振华上将 ["Mao Zedong and Admiral Su Zhenhua"], in 毛泽东与海军将领 [*Mao Zedong and His Admirals*] (Beijing: PLA Literature Publishing, 1999), 82.
49. For the last phase of the Cultural Revolution, see Gao Meng and Yan Jiaqi, *Wenhua dageming shi nian shi* [*Ten Years of the Cultural Revolution*], chaps. 6–7; 李可、郝生章 [Li Ke and Hao Shengzhang], 文化大革命中的人民解放军 [*The PLA in the Cultural Revolution*]; Meisner, *Mao's China*, chap. 20.
50. 星火燎原编辑部 [*Xinghuo liaoyuan* Composition Department], 将帅名录 [*Marshals and Generals*], 1:72–73.
51. Admiral Su's words quoted in 杨国宇 [Yang Guoyu], 当代中国海军 [*Contemporary Chinese Navy*], 395.
52. 胡彦林 [Hu Yanlin], 威震海疆 [*Shocking the Sea*], 387–88.
53. Li, "Xisha Islands Defensive Campaign (1974)," 503.
54. 丁伟 [Ding Wei], 保卫领海主权的军事行动–西沙群岛自卫反击战实录 ["Military Operations to Defend China's Sovereignty–Historical Records of the Self-Defense Battle of the Xisha Islands"], in 军旗飘飘: 新中国50年军事大事述实 [*PLA Flag Fluttering: The Facts about China's Major Military Events in the Past Fifty Years*], 军事科学院军事历史研究部编 [ed. Military History Division, PLA Academy of Military Science] (Beijing: PLA Press, 1999), 2:581.
55. Gao et al., *The PLA Navy*, 63.
56. 杨国宇 [Yang Guoyu], 当代中国海军 [*Contemporary Chinese Navy*], 396.
57. 丁伟 [Ding Wei], 保卫领海主权的军事行动 ["Military Operations to Defend the Water Sovereignty"], 2:583.
58. 胡彦林 [Hu Yanlin], 威震海疆 [*Shocking the Sea*], 393.
59. 赵小平 [Zhao Xiaoping], 坐镇总参谋部，决胜南中国海 ["Command in the DGS and Victory in the South China Sea"], 187–88.
60. Li Ruyi was the charge-man on *274*. His memoir was quoted in Gao et al., *The PLA Navy*, 66.

61. 杨国宇 [Yang Guoyu], 当代中国海军 [*Contemporary Chinese Navy*], 397.
62. 丁伟 [Ding Wei], 保卫领海主权的军事行动 ["Military Operations to Defend the Water Sovereignty"], 2:586-87.
63. 胡彦林 [Hu Yanlin], 威震海疆 [*Shocking the Sea*], 395.
64. 杨国宇 [Yang Guoyu], 当代中国海军 [*Contemporary Chinese Navy*], 398.
65. Gao et al., *The PLA Navy*, 81.
66. James C. Bussert and Bruce A. Elleman, *People's Liberation Army Navy: Combat Systems Technology, 1949-2010* (Annapolis, MD: Naval Institute Press, 2018), 19.
67. 李琼 [Li Qiong], 海上长城: 中国人民解放军海军60年 [*The Great Wall at Sea: 60 Years of the PLA Navy*] (Jilin: Jilin Publishing, 2011), 53.
68. Bussert and Elleman, *People's Liberation Army Navy*, 66.
69. Mao's words quoted in Gao et al., *The PLA Navy*, 121.
70. Bernard D. Cole, *The Great Wall at Sea: China's Navy in the Twenty-First Century*, 2nd ed. (Annapolis, MD: Naval Institute Press, 2010), 12.
71. 陈右铭 [Chen Youming], 第一代核潜艇的诞生 ["The Birth of the First Nuclear Submarine"], in 中国人民解放军历史资料丛书：海军回忆史料 [*PLA Historical Sources Series: The Navy's Memoirs and Records*] (Classified), 海军编审委员会 [ed. Navy Editorial Committee] (Beijing: Ocean Wave Publishing, 1994), 2:1080-81.
72. 陈右铭 [Chen Youming], 第一代核潜艇的诞生 ["The Birth of the First Nuclear Submarine"], 2:1100.
73. Gao et al., *The PLA Navy*, 86-87.

CHAPTER 5. REFORM AND NEW STRATEGY

1. 刘华清 [Liu Huaqing], 刘华清回忆录 [*Memoir of Liu Huaqing*], 358.
2. 刘华清 [Liu Huaqing], 350.
3. For the details of arresting the Gang of Four, see Deng Rong, *Deng Xiaoping and the Cultural Revolution—A Daughter Recalls the Critical Years*, trans. Sidney Shapiro (Beijing: Foreign Languages Press, 2002), chap. 55, "Thoroughly Smash the Gang of Four," 436-43.
4. For more information on Admiral Su Zhenhua (1912-79), see 星火燎原编辑部 [*Xinghuo liaoyuan* Composition Department], 将帅名录 [*PLA Marshals and Generals*], 1:72.
5. Deng became the second generation of the CCP political and military leadership. See Cheng Li, *China's Leaders: The New Generation* (Lanham, MD: Rowman & Littlefield, 2001), 7-9.
6. Among the recent publications in English on the Sino-American rapprochement are William Burr, ed., *The Kissinger Transcripts: The Top-Secret Talks with Beijing and Moscow* (New York: New Press, 1999); Jim Mann, *About Face: A History of America's Curious Relationship with China, from Nixon to Clinton* (New York: Knopf, 1999); Rosemary Foot, *The Practice of Power: US Relations with China*

since 1949 (Oxford: Oxford University Press, 1997); Robert Ross, *Negotiating Co-operation: The United States and China, 1969–1989* (Stanford, CA: Stanford University Press, 1995).
7. Warren I. Cohen, *America's Response to China: A History of Sino-American Relations*, 5th ed. (New York: Columbia University Press, 2010), 206.
8. Cohen, 207.
9. Tian Fuzi, *Zhongyeu zhanzheng jishilu* (Factual Records of the Sino-Vietnam War), 92, 328.
10. Gerald Segal, "Foreign Policy," in Goodman and Segal, *China in the Nineties*, 173.
11. Henry J. Kenny's interviews with Vietnamese colonels and a general; quote from his article, "Vietnamese Perceptions of the 1979 War with China," in *Chinese Warfighting: The PLA Experience since 1949*, ed. Mark A. Ryan, David M. Finkelstein, and Michael A. McDevitt (New York: M. E. Sharpe, 2003), 232.
12. Kenny, "Vietnamese Perceptions of the 1979 War with China," 232.
13. As General Xiong Guangkai, deputy chief of the General Staff, states, "Promoting RMA (Revolution of Military Affairs) with Chinese characteristics purports that we need to study and draw on the experience as well as lessons of RMA in other countries and of each hi-tech local war. Yet we cannot copy the entire mode of RMA of other countries." Xiong, "On Revolution in Military Affairs," a conference presentation at the "Chinese Scientists' Forum on Humanities" on April 16, 2003, in Xiong, *International Strategy and Revolution in Military Affairs* (Beijing: Tsinghua University Press, 2003), 183.
14. Deng, "Streamline the Army and Raise Its Combat Effectiveness," a speech at an enlarged meeting of CMC Standing Committee on March 12, 1980, *Selected Works of Deng Xiaoping*, 2:284–87.
15. Deng, "Speech at an Enlarged Meeting of the CMC, June 4, 1985," *Selected Works of Deng Xiaoping*, 3:131.
16. Deng, "Speech at an Enlarged Meeting of the CMC, June 4, 1985," 133.
17. Dean Chen, "Sea Power and the Chinese State: China's Maritime Ambitions," Heritage Foundation, July 11, 2011, www.heritage.org/asia/report/sea-power-and-the-chinese-state-maritime-ambitions.
18. 杨国宇 [Yang Guoyu], 当代中国海军 [*Contemporary Chinese Navy*], 437–38. Yang served as the deputy commander and chief of staff of the PLAN in 1978–85.
19. 吴瑞虎 [Wu Ruihu], 三代驱逐舰启程中南海—党和国家领导人关心驱逐舰部队建设记事 ["Three Generations of Destroyers Started from Zhongnanhai: History Shows How CCP and PRC Leaders Cared about Construction of the Destroyer Fleet"], in 共和国领袖与海军 [*National Leaders and China's Navy*], 吴殿卿、袁永安、赵小平主编 [ed. Wu Dianqing, Yuan Yong'an, and Zhao Xiaoping] (Beijing: Ocean Wave Publishing, 2000), 289.

20. 中国人民解放军历史资料丛书编审委员会 [The Editorial Board of Collected Historical Documents of the PLA], 海军历史资料 [*Historical Documents of the Navy*], 169.
21. Lai, "Ensured Loyalty versus Professionalism at Sea," 41.
22. For more details on General Ye Fei (1914-99), see 星火燎原编辑部 [*Xinghuo liaoyuan* Composition Department], 将帅名录 [*PLA Marshals and Generals*], 1:58-59.
23. 叶飞 [Ye Fei], 叶飞回忆录 [*Memoir of Ye Fei*], 811-14.
24. 吴殿卿 [Wu Dianqing], 叶飞 ["Ye Fei"], in 中国人民解放军高级将领传 [*Biographies of the Leading Generals of the Chinese People's Liberation Army*], 《中国人民解放军高级将领传》编审委员会编著 [ed. *Biographies of the PLA's High-Ranking Generals* Editorial Committee] (Beijing: PLA Press, 2007), 107-8.
25. Deng's words quoted in 吴殿卿 [Wu Dianqing], 叶飞 ["Ye Fei"], 170.
26. 叶飞 [Ye Fei], 叶飞回忆录 [*Memoir of Ye Fei*], 829-31.
27. Deng Xiaoping says, "We should try to solve this problem while we are still around, because it will be hard for others to do so after we've left the scene." Deng's speech at an enlarged meeting of the standing committee of the PLAN Party Committee on July 29, 1979, in *Selected Works of Deng Xiaoping*, 2nd ed., 2:198.
28. 杨国宇 [Yang Guoyu], 当代中国海军 [*Contemporary Chinese Navy*], 500-501.
29. Deng, "The Organizational Line Guarantees the Implementation of the Ideological and Political Lines," a speech to attendees at an enlarged meeting of the standing committee of the PLAN Party Committee on July 29, 1979, in *Selected Works of Deng Xiaoping*, 2:198.
30. 叶飞 [Ye Fei], 叶飞回忆录 [*Memoir of Ye Fei*], 832.
31. 吴殿卿 [Wu Dianqing], 乘长风破万里浪 ["Ride a Long Wind and Thousands of Miles of Waves"], in 共和国领袖与海军 [*National Leaders and China's Navy*], 吴殿卿、袁永安、赵小平主编 [ed. Wu Dianqing, Yuan Yong'an, and Zhao Xiaoping] (Beijing: Ocean Wave Publishing, 2000), 229-30.
32. 吴殿卿 [Wu Dianqing], 乘长风破万里浪 ["Ride a Long Wind and Thousands of Miles of Waves"], 232.
33. Deng's words quoted in 杨国宇 [Yang Guoyu], 当代中国海军 [*Contemporary Chinese Navy*], 437-38.
34. 杨国宇 [Yang Guoyu], 当代中国海军 [*Contemporary Chinese Navy*], 481-82.
35. Gao et al., *The PLA Navy*, 86.
36. 杨国宇少将 [Rear Admiral Yang Guoyu], 天涯迎飞舟 ["Receiving the Rocket on the Other Side of the World"], in 中国海军走向深蓝, 1980-2010 [*The Chinese Navy Goes to Blue Water, 1980-2010*], 左津玲主编 [ed. Zuo Jinling] (Beijing: PLA Press, 2014), 16.
37. 杨国宇 [Yang Guoyu], 当代中国海军 [*Contemporary Chinese Navy*], 642.

38. 胡彦林 [Hu Yanlin], 威震海疆 [*Shocking the Sea*], 475-76. Hu became the navy's political commissar in 2003-8 and admiral in 2004.
39. 杨国宇 [Yang Guoyu], 天涯迎飞舟 ["Receiving the Rocket on the Other Side of the World"], 23.
40. 张爱萍 [Zhang Aiping], 中国人民解放军 [*The Chinese People's Liberation Army*], 2:31.
41. 叶飞 [Ye Fei], 叶飞回忆录 [*Memoir of Ye Fei*], 852-53.
42. 陈右铭 [Chen Youming], 第一代核潜艇的诞生 ["The Birth of the First Nuclear Submarine"], in 中国人民解放军历史资料丛书: 海军回忆史料 [*PLA Historical Sources Series: The Navy's Memoirs and Records*] (Classified), 海军编审委员会 [ed. Navy Editorial Committee] (Beijing: Ocean Wave Publishing, 1994], 2:1100.
43. Richard A. Bitzinger, Michael Raska, Collin Koh Swee Lean, and Kelvin Wong Ka Weng, "Locating China's Place in the Global Defense Economy," in *Forging China's Military Might: A New Framework for Assessing Innovation*, ed. Tai Ming Cheung (Baltimore: Johns Hopkins University Press, 2014), 180.
44. For more information on Admiral Li Yaowen (1918-2018), see 星火燎原编辑部 [*Xinghuo liaoyuan* Composition Department], 将帅名录 [*Marshals and Generals*], 2:494.
45. 刘华清 [Liu Huaqing], 刘华清回忆录 [*Memoir of Liu Huaqing*], 342-44.
46. 刘华清 [Liu Huaqing], 刘华清回忆录 [*Memoir of Liu Huaqing*], 271-76.
47. David Shambaugh, *Modernizing China's Military: Progress, Problems, and Prospects* (Berkeley: University of California Press, 2002), 68.
48. Shambaugh, *Modernizing China's Military*, 67.
49. 杨国宇 [Yang Guoyu], 当代中国海军 [*Contemporary Chinese Navy*], 712.
50. 聂奎聚中将 [Vice Admiral Nie Kuiju], 扬帆起航向大洋 ["Set Sail to the Oceans"], in 中国海军走向深蓝, 1980-2010 [*The Chinese Navy Goes to Blue Water, 1980-2010*], 左津玲主编 [ed. Zuo Jinling] (Beijing: PLA Press, 2014), 74. Nie Kuiju (1926-92) was the deputy commander of the PLAN from 1982 to 1988 and commander of the East China Sea Fleet from 1985 to 1989.
51. 胡彦林 [Admiral Hu Yanlin], 威震海疆 [*Shocking the Sea*], 501.
52. 赵国臣中将 [Vice Admiral Zhao Guochen], 难忘首次南极考察 ["Unforgettable the First Expedition to the South Pole"], in 中国海军走向深蓝, 1980-2010 [*The Chinese Navy Goes to Blue Water, 1980-2010*], 左津玲主编 [ed. Zuo Jinling] (Beijing: PLA Press, 2014), 57. Zhao Guochen (1935-94) was the commander of the Lushun Naval Base from 1985 to 1990 and chief of staff of the PLAN from 1990 to 1994.
53. 胡彦林 [Hu Yanlin], 威震海疆 [*Shocking the Sea*], 550-51.
54. Sarah Raine and Christian Miere, *Regional Disorder: The South China Sea Disputes* (London: Routledge, 2013), 17-19, 42-43.
55. Ministry of National Defense, ROC, "MND Admits Strategic Value of Spratly Airstrip," *Taipei Times*, January 6, 2006.

56. Among Ma Ying-jeou's books are *Diaoyutai lieyu zhuquan zhengyi: Huigu yu zhanwang* [*Disputed Sovereignty of Diaoyu Islands: The Past and Future*] (Taipei: ROC Government Printing, 1996) and *Cong xin haiyangfa lun Diaoyutai lieyu yu Donghai huajie wenti* [*New Oceanic Regulations: Issues of the Diaoyu Islands and Border of the East China Sea*] (Taipei: Zhengzhong Books, 1986).
57. 张驭涛 [Zhang Yutao], 新中国军事大事纪要 [*Chronicle of Major Military Events of China*] (Beijing: Military Science Press, 1998), 485.
58. 胡彦林 [Hu Yanlin], 威震海疆 [*Shocking the Sea*], 562.
59. 张驭涛 [Zhang Yutao], 新中国军事大事纪要 [*Chronicle of Major Military Events of China*], 491.
60. 胡彦林 [Hu Yanlin], 威震海疆 [*Shocking the Sea*], 554-59.
61. 胡彦林 [Hu Yanlin], 威震海疆 [*Shocking the Sea*], 559-61.
62. 张驭涛 [Zhang Yutao], 新中国军事大事纪要 [*Chronicle of Major Military Events of China*], 492.
63. 胡彦林 [Hu Yanlin], 威震海疆 [*Shocking the Sea*], 571.
64. General Xiong Guangkai, "The International Strategic Situation at the Dawn of the New Century." Xiong was interviewed by the staff writer of *Study Times*. An article based on the interview was published by the journal on December 30, 2000, 10-13.
65. 军事科学院军事历史研究部 [Military History Division, PLA-AMS], 中国人民解放军的七十年 [*Seventy Years of the Chinese PLA*], 662.
66. Senior Colonel Yang Shaojun, interview by the author at the PLA Academy of Logistics in Beijing, July 1994.
67. 张驭涛 [Zhang Yutao], 新中国军事大事纪要 [*Chronicle of Major Military Events of China*], 427.
68. China National Industrial and Commercial Administration Bureau, *Gongsi dengji guanli wenjian huibian* [*Collected Documents of Company Registration and Administration*] (Beijing: China Society Press, 1990), 268.
69. 张胜 [Zhang Sheng], 从战争中走来 [*Coming from the War*] (Beijing: Three Alliances Publishing, 2013), 641-42; 东方鹤 [Dong Fanghe], 张爱萍传 [*Biography of Zhang Aiping*], 2:1095-96.
70. 军事科学院军事历史研究部 [Military History Research Division, PLA-AMS], 中国人民解放军的八十年 [*Eighty Years of the Chinese PLA*] (Beijing: Military Science Press, 2007), 520.
71. 军事科学院军事历史研究部 [Military History Division, PLA-AMS], 中国人民解放军的七十年 [*Seventy Years of the Chinese PLA*], 665.
72. R. Keith Schoppa argues, "For many in China, the actions cost the army a huge amount of respect." Schoppa, *Revolution and Its Past: Identities and Change in Modern Chinese History*, 3rd ed. (New York: Prentice Hall, 2011), 422.
73. 刘明福 [Liu Mingfu], 为什么解放军能赢 [*Why the PLA Is Able to Win*] (Beijing: PAP Press, 2012), 9-11.

74. Maurice Meisner, *Mao's China and After: A History of the People's Republic* (New York: Free Press, 1999), 475–76; Maurice Meisner, *The Deng Xiaoping Era: An Inquiry into the Fate of Chinese Socialism, 1978–1994* (New York: Hill & Wang, 1996), 304–21.
75. Xiaobing Li, "Introduction: Social-Economic Transition and Cultural Reconstruction in China," in *Social Transition in China*, ed. Jie Zhang and Xiaobing Li (Lanham, MD: University Press of America, 1998), 1–18.
76. Deng's views were reflected in an April 26, 1989 editorial in the *Renmin ribao (People's Daily)*. See Zhang Liang, ed., *The Tiananmen Papers: The Chinese Leadership's Decision to Use Force against Their Own People—in Their Own Words* (New York: Public Affairs, 2001), 71–75.
77. Zhang, *The Tiananmen Papers*, 121–22.
78. Martial Law Troop Command, "Martial Law Situation Report, no. 3, May 19," in Zhang, *The Tiananmen Papers*, 227.
79. Zhang, *The Tiananmen Papers*, 265.
80. Zhang Liang's book listed eight generals, while the others had different numbers. For example, seven generals were mentioned in an essay collection edited by Suzanne Ogden, Kathleen Hartford, Lawrence Sullivan, and David Zweig, *China's Search for Democracy: The Student and the Mass Movement of 1989* (Armonk, NY: M. E. Sharpe, 1992), 292.
81. Party Central Office Secretariat, "Minutes of the Politburo Standing Committee Meeting, June 3, 1989," in Zhang, *The Tiananmen Papers*, 368–70.
82. Louisa Lim, *The People's Republic of Amnesia* (New York: Oxford University Press, 2014). 17.
83. Harlan Jencks, "Civil-Military Relations in China: Tiananmen and After," *Problems of Communism* 40 (May–June 1991): 22.
84. Wu Renhua, *Martial Law Troops in the June Fourth Incident* (Los Angeles: Truth Publishing, 2009), 131–33, 145–47.
85. Shi Wusui, "The June 4th Remembered by Both Sides of the Gun," Secret China, June 1, 2020, http://www.secretchina.com/news/2020/06/01/935091.html. First Lieutenant Li Xiaoming retired from the PLA in 1993 and became an electrical engineer in Shenyang. He went to Australia in 2000 and enrolled in Double Es MS Program at Royal Melbourne Institute of Technology.
86. The official statistics listed 264 deaths, including 23 college students and 20 PLA soldiers and officers. The Beijing Red Cross estimated 2,600 deaths, and China Radio International reported in Beijing on June 4 that "several thousand people, mostly innocent citizens" had been killed by "heavily armed soldiers." Zhang, *The Tiananmen Papers*, 385, 389.
87. Extracts from military security report are included in a CMC document, dated December 29, 1989.
88. Xiaobing Li, "Reforming the People's Army: Military Modernization in China," *Journal of Southwest Conference on Asian Studies* 5 (2005): 17.

CHAPTER 6. SEA POWER IN THE BLUE WATER

1. 陈万军、袁华智、司彦文 [Chen Wanjun, Yuan Huazhi, and Si Yanwen], 春风鼓浪好杨帆–江泽民主席关心人民海军现代化建设记事 ["Ride the Spring Wind and Waves: Historical Records of President Jiang Zemin's Efforts in the Modernization of the People's Navy"], in 共和国领袖与海军 [*Chinese Leaders and the Navy*], 吴殿卿、袁永安、赵小平 [ed. Wu Dianqing, Yuan Yong'an, and Zhao Xiaoping] (Beijing: Ocean Wave Publishing, 2000), 300.
2. Cole, *The Great Wall at Sea*, x.
3. 迟浩田上将 [General Chi Haotian], 前言 ["Introduction"], in 中国海军走向深蓝, 1980-2010 [*The Chinese Navy Goes to Blue Water, 1980-2010*], 左津玲主编 [ed. Zuo Jinling] (Beijing: PLA Press, 2014), vii.
4. 陈万军、袁华智、司彦文 [Chen Wanjun, Yuan Huazhi, and Si Yanwen], 春风鼓浪好杨帆 ["Ride the Spring Wind and Waves"], 301.
5. 吴瑞虎 [Wu Ruihu], 三代驱逐舰启程中南海 ["Three Generations of Destroyers Started from Zhongnanhai"], 291–92.
6. 新华社 [New China News], 人民海军70年: 党中央关心人民海军建设发展纪实 ["70 Years of the People's Navy: The Historical Facts of the Party Center's Support to Construction and Development of the People's Navy"], 新华社新媒体 [*New China's News Media*], April 22, 2019, www.baijiahao.baidu.com/s?id=16315103827060121248&wfr.
7. 陈万军、袁华智、司彦文 [Chen Wanjun, Yuan Huazhi, and Si Yanwen], 春风鼓浪好杨帆 ["Ride the Spring Wind and Waves"], 302–4.
8. 王永国中将 [Vice Admiral Wang Yongguo], 横跨太平洋首次出访美洲四国 ["Across the Pacific: The First Voyage to Four Countries in Americas"], in 中国海军走向深蓝, 1980-2010 [*The Chinese Navy Goes to Blue Water, 1980-2010*], 左津玲主编 [ed. Zuo Jinling] (Beijing: PLA Press, 2014), 185. Wang, ranked rear admiral in 1988 and vice admiral in 1996, was the commander of the South China Sea Fleet and deputy commander of the PLA Guangzhou Military Region from 1994 to 2002.
9. 刘华清 [Liu Huaqing], 刘华清回忆录 [*Memoir of Liu Huaqing*], 477.
10. Gao et al., *The PLA Navy*, 107.
11. 李琼 [Li Qiong], 海上长城: 中国人民解放军海军60年 [*The Great Wall at Sea: 60 Years of the PLA Navy*] (Jilin: Jilin Publishing, 2011), 55.
12. Liu's words quoted in You Ji, *China's Military Transformation: Politics and War Preparation* (Cambridge, UK: Polity, 2016), 194.
13. 王永国 [Wang Yongguo], 横跨太平洋首次出访美洲四国 ["Across the Pacific: The First Voyage to Four Countries in Americas"], 191.
14. 张万年上将 [General Zhang Wannian], 张万年自传 [*Autobiography of Zhang Wannian*] (Beijing: PLA Press, 2011), 2:361–65. Zhang Wannian (1928–2015) was CMC vice chairman in 1995–2003 and in charge of terminating PLA commercial activities.

15. 张万年 [Zhang Wannian], 张万年自传 [*Autobiography of Zhang Wannian*], 2:382–83.
16. 张万年 [Zhang Wannian], 张万年自传 [*Autobiography of Zhang Wannian*], 2:396–97.
17. Orville Schell and John Delury, *Wealth and Power: China's Long March to the Twenty-First Century* (New York: Random House, 2013), 64–65.
18. For more discussions on General Chi Haotian's hard-line position, see John F. Copper, "The Origins of Conflict across the Taiwan Strait: The Problem of Differences in Perceptions," in *Across the Taiwan Strait: Mainland China, Taiwan, and the 1995–1996 Crisis*, ed. Suisheng Zhao (London: Routledge, 1999), 43; You Ji, "Changing Leadership Consensus: The Domestic Context of War Game," in Zhao, *Across the Taiwan Strait*, 91–93.
19. 张驭涛 [Zhang Yutao], 新中国军事大事纪要 [*Chronicle of Major Military Events of China*], 608.
20. For a detailed overview of the 1995–96 Taiwan Strait Crisis, see Qimao Chen, "The Taiwan Strait Crisis: Causes, Scenarios, and Solutions," in *Across the Taiwan Strait: Mainland China, Taiwan, and the 1995–1996 Crisis*, ed. Suisheng Zhao (London: Routledge, 1999), 127–62.
21. 张驭涛 [Zhang Yutao], 新中国军事大事纪要 [*Chronicle of Major Military Events of China*], 610.
22. William Perry and Ashton Carter, *Preventive Defense: A New Security for America* (Washington, DC: Brookings Institute, 1999), 92–93.
23. Patric Tyler, *A Great Wall: Six Presidents and China* (New York: Public Affairs, 1999), 33, 195.
24. William Perry, the U.S. secretary of defense, made a public statement on March 11, 1996 about the large U.S. naval maneuver near the Taiwan Strait. For Perry's statement, see *American Forces Press Service*, March 11; the Department of Defense, *News Briefings*, March 12, 14, and 16, 1996.
25. 胡润民 [Hu Runmin], 台湾军情局的疯狂岁月 ["The Crazy Era of Taiwan's Military Intelligence Bureau"], 环球人物 [*Global People*], no. 5 (2011): 21–24.
26. 张万年 [Zhang Wannian], 张万年自传 [*Autobiography of Zhang Wannian*], 2:433–35. Zhang was CMC vice chairman and the commander of the 1996 PLA joint exercise along the eastern coast.
27. Taiwan Affairs Office and the Information Office, PRC State Council, "The One-China Principle and the Taiwan Issue, February 2000," in *White Papers of the Chinese Government, 2000–2001*, comp. Information Office, PRC State Council (Beijing: Foreign Languages Press, 2003), 29.
28. Andrew Scobell, *China's Use of Military Force: Beyond the Great Wall and the Long March* (Cambridge: Cambridge University Press, 2003), 189.
29. Worthing, *A Military History of Modern China*, 197.
30. Worthing, 122.

31. Worthing, 31.
32. Some Chinese sources say it was 81194. For example, see 新华社 [Xinhua News Agency], 我国著名的航空史学家陈应明为海空卫士王伟亲属制作"铁血战机"模型 ["China's Well-Known Aviation Historian Chen Yingming Makes a 'Hero Martyr's Fighter' Model for Wang Wei's Family"], April 18, 2001. See also 周日新 [Zhou Rixin], 中国航空图志 [*Pictographic Records of Chinese Aviation*] (Beijing: Beijing Aerospace University Press, 2008).
33. The U.S. government stated that the Chinese fighter bumped the wing of the larger, slower, and less maneuverable EP-3. The Chinese government used Zhao's account that the American plane "veered at a wide angle toward the Chinese," in the process ramming the J-8II.
34. Xiansheng Tian, "When Chongqing Challenges Beijing: The Bo Xilai Case," in *Evolution of Power: China's Struggle, Survival, and Success*, ed. Xiaobing Li and Xiansheng Tian (Lanham, MD: Lexington Books, 2014), 323.
35. Author interview with the officer at Langfang, Hebei, July 28, 2002. The provincial commander sent out a survey form to all of the officers of its regiments in 2003. The survey provides a mixed report on the only-child officers. Some are liberal and democratic, emphasize individual competition and equal opportunity, and dislike political control. For more details, see Xiaobing Li, "The Impact of Social Changes on the PLA: A Chinese Military Perspective," in *Civil-Military Relations in Today's China: Swimming in a New Sea*, ed. David M. Finkelstein and Kristen Gunness (Armonk, NY: M. E. Sharpe, 2007), 26–47.
36. Hu Jintao's words quoted in 迟浩田 [Chi Haotian], 前言 ["Introduction"], in 中国海军走向深蓝, 1980–2010 [*The Chinese Navy Goes to Blue Water, 1980–2010*], viii.
37. 新华社 [New China News], 胡锦涛会见海军代表 ["Hu Jintao Meets Naval Representatives"], 中国新闻网 [*China News*], December 28, 2006. www.chinanews.com.cn/gn/news/2006/12-28.
38. 李琼 [Li Qiong], 海上长城: 中国人民解放军海军60年 [*The Great Wall at Sea: 60 Years of the PLA Navy*], 15.
39. Rear Admiral Wang Fushan's telegram quoted in Gao et al., *The PLA Navy*, 195.
40. Hu's words quoted in 李琼 [Li Qiong], 海上长城: 中国人民解放军海军60年 [*The Great Wall at Sea: 60 Years of the PLA Navy*], 73.
41. "Hu Jintao Tells China Navy: Prepare for Warfare," BBC News, December 7, 2011, www.bbc.com/news/world-asia-china-16063607.
42. Nan Li, "China's Evolving Naval Strategy and Capabilities in the Hu Jintao Era," in *Assessing the People's Liberation Army in the Hu Jintao Era*, ed. Roy Kamphausen, David Lai, and Travis Tanner (Carlisle, PA: U.S. Army War College, 2014), 257.
43. 新华社 [New China News], 胡锦涛出席庆祝人民海军成立60周年海上阅兵活动 ["Hu Jintao Attends the Naval Parade to Celebrate the People's Navy's 60th Birthday"], 中国台湾网 [*China's Taiwan News*], April 23, 2009, www.taiwan.cn/xwzx/jrbd/200904/t20090424_876110.htm.

44. Wang Guangqun, "China Rises to Top in Ranks of Ship Makers," Xinhua News Agency, May 9, 2011, http://news.xinhuanet.com/english2010/china/2011-05/09/c_13865547.htm.
45. Information Office of the State Council, *China's National Defense in 2010* (Beijing: State Council Information Office, 2011), http://www.gov.cn/english/official/2011-03/31/content_1835499.htm.
46. You Ji, *China's Military Transformation*, 181.
47. Cole, *The Great Wall at Sea*, xix, 187, 190.
48. Xiaobing Li and Michael Molina, eds., *Oil: A Cultural and Geographic Encyclopedia of Black Gold* (Santa Barbara, CA: ABC-CLIO, 2014), 1:42–43.
49. Li and Molina, 2:464, 467.
50. Hsiu-Chuan Shih and Flora Wang, "Officials Drop Plan to Visit Diaoyutais," *Taipei Times*, June 18, 2008.
51. Information Office, PRC State Council, *White Papers of China's National Defense* (Beijing: Foreign Languages Press, 2008), 8.
52. Christoffersen, "Crises as Impetus for Institutionalization," 74.
53. Hillary Clinton, "Secretary Clinton Joint Press Availability with Japanese Foreign Minister Seiji Maehara," October 27, 2010, www.state.gov/secretary/rm/2010/10/150110.htm.
54. P. Baker, "Obama Calls for Military Dialogue with China," *New York Times*, March 12, 2009.
55. U.S. Senate, *National Defense Authorization Act for Fiscal Year 2013*, H.R. 4310: Sec. 1251 (Washington, DC: U.S. Government Printing Office, 2013).
56. K. Mori, "Kerry Spells Out Policy on Senkaku Islands," UPI, April 15, 2013, www.upi.com/Top_News/World-News/2013/04/15.
57. Office of the U.S. Secretary of Defense, *Military and Security Developments Involving the People's Republic of China*, 2013, 12, http://www.defenselink.mil/pubs/pdfs/China_Military_Report_13.pdf.
58. U.S. Senate, *National Defense Authorization Act for Fiscal Year 2013*, H.R. 4310: Sec. 1251.
59. Xiaobing Li, "Sino-Japanese Maritime Conflicts and Security Concerns in the East China Sea," in *Maritime Security in the Indian Ocean and Western Pacific: Heritage and Contemporary Challenges*, ed. Howard M. Hensel and Amit Gupta (London: Routledge, 2018), 249.
60. UN Resolution No. 1816 quoted in Gao et al., *The PLA Navy*, 138.
61. 新华社 [Xinhua News Agency], 中国海军出击亚丁湾 ["The Chinese Navy Dispatched to the Gulf of Aden"], 参考消息 [*Reference News*], December 27, 2008, 1–2.
62. Helicopter pilot Liu Jinkun's diary quoted in Gao et al., *The PLA Navy*, 143.
63. Chinese Defense Ministry's spokesman's announcement quoted in Gao et al., *The PLA Navy*, 148.

CONCLUSION. XI'S NEW NAVY

1. Among the interviews with the PLA officers by the author are Major Sun Lizhou, Second Department of the PLA General Staff, Beijing; the deputy commander, Jilin Provincial Command, Changchun, Jilin; and Major General Guan Zhichao (retired), at the PLA Political Academy, Nanjing.
2. Information Office, the PRC State Council, "The Security Situation," in *White Papers of China's National Defense in 2008*, http://English.people.com.cn/90001/90776/90785/6578688.html.
3. You Ji, *China's Military Transformation*, 10, 72, 77–78.
4. *PLA Daily*, "China's Establishment of the Air Defense Identification Zone (ADIZ) in the East China Sea, January 22, 2014," http://eng.chinamil.com.cn/view/2014-01.
5. C. Huang and T. Ng, "Xi Jinping Sends Signal to Neighbors with High-Profile Tour of Liaoning Aircraft Carrier," *South Chinese Morning Post*, August 31, 2013, 1–3.
6. General Jiang Weilie, interview by a reporter on April 9, 2013, PRC Defense Ministry, www.mod.gov.cn.
7. Information Office, the PRC State Council, *The Diversified Employment of China's Armed Forces (China's Defense White Paper)*, April 2013, http://www.chinadaily.com.cn/language_tips/news/2013-04/17/content_16414985.htm.
8. U.S. Defense Intelligence Agency, *China Military Power: Modernizing a Force to Fight and Win* (Washington, DC: U.S. Government Printing Office, 2019), 70.
9. Dean Cheng, "Assessing Threats to US Vital Interests: China," Heritage Foundation, 2021, www.heritage.org/2021-index-us-military-strength/assessing-threats-us-vital-interests/china.
10. Vice Admiral Fedotenkov's praise is quoted in Franz-Stefan Gady, "Russian and China Kick Off Naval Exercise in Sea of Japan," *The Diplomat*, August 24, 2015, http://thediplomat.com/2015/08/Russian-and-china-kick-off-naval-exercise-in-sea-of-japan.
11. M. Rajagopalan, "China Conducts Air, Sea Drills in East China Sea," *Reuters*, August 27, 2015, http://www.reuters.com/articles/us-china-defense-idUSKCN0QW1EX20150827.
12. Xiaobing Li, paper presented at the conference "Large-Scale Amphibious Warfare in Chinese Military Strategy," organized by China Maritime Studies Institute, U.S. Naval War College, May 4–6, 2021.
13. Kevin Catapano, "China Conducts Assault Landing Drills as Invasion Attempt Looks Inevitable," *Western Journal*, June 10, 2021, http://westernjournal.com/china-conducts-assault-landing-drills-invasion-attempt-looks-inevitable/.
14. Robert G. Sutter, *Foreign Relations of the PRC: The Legacies and Constraints of China's International Politics since 1949*, 2nd ed. (Lanham, MD: Rowman & Littlefield, 2018), 217.

15. J. Perlez, "Sentiment Builds in China to Press Claim for Okinawa," *New York Times*, June 13, 2013, http://www.nytimes.com/2013/06/14/world/asia.html.
16. BBC, "Viewpoints: How Serious Are China-Japan Tensions?" *BBC Chinese (UK)*, February 8, 2013, http://news.bbc.co.uk/chinese/trad/hi/newsid_7450000.stm.
17. Office of the U.S. Secretary of Defense, *Annual Report to Congress: Military Power of the People's Republic of China*, 2009, http://www.defenselink.mil/pubs/pdfs/China_Military_Report_09.pdf.

SELECTED BIBLIOGRAPHY

CHINESE-LANGUAGE SOURCES [中文资料]

ARCHIVES, MANUSCRIPTS, AND MILITARY PAPERS [档案文稿及军事文件]

陈毅 [Chen Yi]. 陈毅军事文选 [*Selected Military Writings of Chen Yi*]. Beijing: PLA Press, 1996.

贺龙 [He Long]. 贺龙军事文选 [*Selected Military Writings of He Long*]. Beijing: PLA Press, 1989.

刘伯承 [Liu Bocheng]. 刘伯承军事文选 [*Selected Military Writings of Liu Bocheng*]. Beijing: PLA Press, 1992.

刘华清 [Liu Huaqing]. 刘华清军事文选 [*Selected Military Writings of Liu Huaqing*]. Beijing: PLA Press, 2008.

刘少奇 [Liu Shaoqi]. 建国以来刘少奇文稿 [*Liu Shaoqi's Manuscripts since the Founding of the State*]. 7 vols. Beijing: CCP Central Archival and Manuscript Press, 2008. Cited as 刘文稿 [*Liu's Manuscripts*].

毛泽东 [Mao Zedong]. 建国以来毛泽东军事文稿 [*Mao Zedong's Military Manuscripts since the Founding of the PRC*]. 3 vols. Beijing: Military Science Press and CCP Central Archival and Manuscript Press, 2010. Cited as 毛军事文稿 [*Mao's Military Manuscripts*].

———. 建国以来毛泽东文稿, 1949–76 [*Mao Zedong's Manuscripts since the Founding of the State, 1949–1976*]. 13 vols. Beijing: CCP Central Archival and Manuscript Press, 1993. Cited as 毛文稿 [*Mao's Manuscripts*].

———. 毛泽东军事文集 [*Collected Military Works of Mao Zedong*]. 6 vols. Beijing: CCP Central Archival and Manuscript Press and Military Science Press, 1993.

———. 毛泽东军事文选（内部版）[*Selected Military Papers of Mao Zedong: Internal Edition*]. 2 vols. Beijing: PLA Soldiers Press, 1981.

———. 毛泽东外交文选 [*Selected Diplomatic Papers of Mao Zedong*]. Beijing: CCP Central Archival and Manuscript Press, 1994.

———. 毛泽东文选 [*Collected Works of Mao Zedong*]. 8 vols. Beijing: People's Press, 1999.

———. 毛泽东选集 [*Selected Works of Mao Zedong*]. 5 vols. Beijing: People's Press, 1979.

聂荣臻 [Nie Rongzhen]. 聂荣臻军事文选 [*Selected Military Writings of Nie Rongzhen*]. Beijing: PLA Press, 1992.

彭德怀 [Peng Dehuai]. 彭德怀军事文选 [*Selected Military Writings of Peng Dehuai*]. Beijing: CCP Central Archival and Manuscript Press, 1988.

前苏联档案 [Former Soviet Archives]. 斯大林与毛泽东会谈记录 ["The Meeting Minutes of Stalin's Conversation with Mao Zedong"], December 16, 1949, in 有关1950年中苏条约谈判的俄国档案 [*The Russian Archives of the 1950*

Treaty Negotiations on the Soviet-Chinese Agreement], in 中共党史研究 [*CCP Party History Research*], no. 4 (1998): 1–13.

———. 斯大林与中共代表团会谈记录 ["The Meeting Minutes of Stalin's Negotiations with the CCP Delegation"], June 27, 1949, in 有关刘少奇1949年访苏的俄国档案 [*The Russian Archives of 1949 Liu Shaoqi's Visit in the Soviet Union*]. 中共党史研究 [*CCP Party History Research*], no. 2 (1998): 12–25.

台湾档案管理局 [Taiwan Archival Administration]. 外交部档案 [*Foreign Ministry Archives*], 台北 [Taipei].

肖劲光 [Xiao Jinguang]. 肖劲光军事文选 [*Selected Military Writings of Xiao Jinguang*]. Beijing: PLA Press, 2003.

新华社 [Xinhua News Agency]. 新华社文件资料汇编 [*A Collection of Documentary Materials of Xinhua News Agency*]. Beijing: Xinhua News Agency Publishing House, n.d.

徐向前 [Xu Xiangqian]. 徐向前军事文选 [*Selected Military Writings of Xu Xiangqian*]. Beijing: PLA Press, 1992.

中共中央档案局 [CCP Central Archives]. 中共中央文件选集, 1921–49 [*Selected Documents of the CCP Central Committee, 1921–1949*]. 18 vols. Beijing: CCP Central Party University Press], 1992.

中共中央档案局、中央文献研究室、中央组织部 [CCP Central Archives, Central Archival and Manuscript Research Division, and CCP Organization Department, comps.]. 中国共产党组织史资料, 1921–97 [*Documents of the CCP Organization's History, 1921–1997*]. 14 vols. Beijing: CCP Central Committee's Party History Press, 2000.

中国外交部办公厅档案资料部 [Archives Department of the General Office, PRC Foreign Ministry]. 中国外交档案 [*China's Foreign Affairs Archives*], 北京 [Beijing].

中国人民海军旅顺基地 [Lushun Naval Command, PLA Navy]. 林彪、李作鹏反党乱军罪行文件汇编 ["Document Collection on Lin Biao and Li Zuopeng's Criminal Activities of Attacking the Party and Betraying the PLA, October 1971"]. In 批林批李资料 [*Political Files against the Lin-Li Group (1971–1972)*]. 旅顺海军基地档案室] *Lushun Naval Base Archives*, Lushun, Liaoning.

周恩来 [Zhou Enlai]. 建国以来周恩来文稿 [*Zhou Enlai's Manuscripts since the Founding of the State, 1949–1950*]. 3 vols. Beijing: CCP Central Archival and Manuscript Press, 2008.

周恩来 [Zhou Enlai]. 周恩来军事文选 [*Selected Military Papers of Zhou Enlai*]. 4 vols. Beijing: People's Press, 1997.

朱德 [Zhu De]. 朱德军事文选 [*Selected Military Writings of Zhu De*]. Beijing: PLA Press, 1986.

OFFICIAL CHRONICLES, RECOLLECTIONS, AND MEMOIRS
[官方记事及回忆录]

柴成文 [Chai Chengwen]. 板门店谈判纪事 [*The True Stories of the Panmunjom Negotiations*]. Beijing: Current Affairs Press, 2000.

陈湃 [Chen Pai]. 越战亲历记 [*My Personal Experience in the Vietnam War*]. Zhengzhou: Henan People's Press, 1997.

陈右铭 [Chen Youming]. 第一代核潜艇的诞生 ["The Birth of the First Nuclear Submarine"]. In 中国人民解放军历史资料丛书: 海军回忆史料 [*PLA Historical Sources Series: The Navy's Memoirs and Records*] (Classified), 海军编审委员会 [ed. Navy Editorial Committee]. Beijing: Ocean Wave Publishing, 1994.

段与衡将军访问记录 ["Interview Records of Major General Duan Yuheng"]. In 尘封的作战计划——国光计划——口述历史 [*Oral History: Historical Operational Plan–Guoguang Jihua*], 彭大年编 [ed. Peng Danian]. Taipei: Department of Military Affairs, ROC Defense Ministry, 2005.

葛楚民编 [Ge Chumin, ed.]. 老战士轶事 [*Personal Stories of the Veterans*]. Beijing: China Outreaching and Translation Publishing, 2000.

国防部军务局 [Department of Military Affairs, ROC Defense Ministry]. 八二三台海战役 [*The 8-23 Battle of the Taiwan Strait*]. Taipei: Department of Military Affairs, ROC Defense Ministry, 1998.

国防部史政编译局 [History Compilation and Translation Bureau, ROC Defense Ministry]. 8-23 炮战胜利30周年纪念文集 [*Recollection for the 30th Anniversary of the Victorious August 23 Artillery Battle*]. Taipei, Taiwan: Defense Department Printing, 1989.

洪学智 [Hong Xuezhi]. 洪学智回忆录 [*Memoirs of Hong Xuezhi*]. Beijing: PLA Press, 2007.

侯向之 [Hou Xiangzhi]. 《二四协定》的签定 ["The Conclusion of February 4 Agreement"]. In 中国人民解放军历史资料丛书: 海军回忆史料 [*PLA Historical Sources Series: The Navy's Memoirs and Records*] (Classified), 海军编审委员会编 [ed. Navy Editorial Committee], 2:1046-56. Beijing: Ocean Wave Publishing, 1994.

胡润民 [Hu Runmin]. 台湾军情局的疯狂岁月 ["The Crazy Era of Taiwan's Military Intelligence Bureau"], 环球人物 [*Global People*], no. 5 (2011).

胡士弘 [Hu Shihong]. 横槊东海 ["Couching the Lance in the East China Sea"]. In 三军挥戈战东海 [*Army, Navy, and Air Force Fight in the East China Sea*], 聂凤智等 [edited by Nie Fengzhi et al.], 38-58. Beijing: PLA Press, 1986.

李宝祥 [Li Baoxiang]. 援越扫雷的技术保障工作 ["Technology Improvement: Help Vietnam to Clean the Mines"]. In 援越抗美 [*Aid Vietnam and Resist America*], 曲爱国、鲍明荣、肖祖跃编 [eds. Qu, Bao, and Xiao]: 301-5.

李东野 [Li Dongye]. 忆大连第一海军学校的创建 ["The Founding of the First Naval Academy in Dalian"]. In 海军回忆史料 [*The Navy: Memoirs and History Records*] (Classified), 2:634-53.

李珉 [Li Min]. 想起那个年代 ["Remember Those Years"]. In 血洒越南–60年代援越抗美战地采访纪实 [*Blood Shed in Vietnam: Reports and Records from the Battleground of Assisting Vietnam and Resisting the U.S. in the 1960s*], 尚力科、邢志远主编 [eds. Shang Like and Xing Zhiyuan]: 228-45.

李作鹏 [Li Zuopeng]. 李作鹏回忆录 [*Memoir of Li Zuopeng*]. Hong Kong: Beixing Publishing House, 2011.

林虎 [Lin Hu]. 保卫祖国领空的战斗 [*Air Battles to Defend Motherland's Airspace*]. Beijing: PLA Press, 2002.

刘广凯 [Liu Guangkai]. 刘广凯将军报国忆往 [*Admiral Liu Guangkai's Recollection of Defending the Country*]. Taipei: Institute of Modern China, Academia Sinica, 1994.

刘华清 [Liu Huaqing]. 刘华清回忆录 [*Memoir of Liu Huaqing*]. Beijing: PLA Press, 2004.

马冠三 [Ma Guansan]. 鏖战东海忆当年 ["Remember the Combat Years in the East China Sea"]. In 三军挥戈战东海 [*Combined Forces Wield Spears and Fight in the East China Sea*], 聂凤智等 [edited by Nie Fengzhi et al.], 26-33. Beijing: PLA Press, 1985.

南平波 [Nan Pingbo]. 潜艇部队初建时期的政治工作 ["The Political Tasks of the Submarine Fleet during Its Formative Years"]. In 海军回忆史料 [*The Navy: Memoirs and History Records*] (Classified), 2:806-14.

聂凤智 [Nie Fengzhi]. 海陆空军联合作战解放一江山岛 ["Join Force with the Army and Navy to Liberate the Yijiangshan Island"]. In 中国人民解放军历史资料丛书: 空军回忆史料 [*PLA Historical Source Collection Series: The Air Force: Memoirs and History Records*] (Classified), 空军编审委员会 [edited by Air Force Editorial Committee], 1:231-48. Beijing: PLA Press, 1999.

———. 云击鹰翔震海空 ["Soaring Eagles Strike and Shake the Sea and Sky"]. In 三军挥戈战东海 [*Army, Navy, and Air Force Fight in the East China Sea*], 聂凤智等 [edited by Nie Fengzhi et al.], 11-25. Beijing: PLA Press, 1986.

聂奎聚 [Nie Kuiju]. 扬帆起航向大洋 ["Set Sail to the Oceans"]. In 中国海军走向深蓝, 1980-2010 [*The Chinese Navy Goes to Blue Water, 1980-2010*], 左津玲主编 [edited by Zuo Jinling]. Beijing: PLA Press, 2014.

聂荣臻 [Nie Rongzhen]. 聂荣臻回忆录 [*Memoir of Nie Rongzhen*]. 2 vols. Beijing: PLA Press, 1984.

任秀生 [Ren Xiusheng]. 华东军区海军舰船修造工作的回顾 ["Recollection of ECMR Navy's Shipbuilding and Rebuilt"]. In 海军回忆史料 [*The Navy: Memoirs and History Records*] (Classified), 2:997-1009.

尚力科、邢志远主编 [Shang Like and Xing Zhiyuan, eds.]. 血洒越南—60年代援越抗美战地采访纪实 [*Blood Shed in Vietnam: Reports and Records from the Battleground of Assisting Vietnam and Resisting the U.S. in the 1960s*]. Beijing: Human Resources Publishing House, 1993.

王海 [Wang Hai]. 我的战斗生涯 [*My Military Career*]. Beijing: CCP Central Archival and Manuscript Press, 2000.

王永国 [Wang Yongguo]. 横跨太平洋首次出访美洲四国 ["Across the Pacific: The First Voyage to Four Countries in Americas"]. In 中国海军走向深蓝, 1980-2010 [*The Chinese Navy Goes to Blue Water, 1980-2010*], 左津玲主编 [ed. Zuo Jinling], 184-201. Beijing: PLA Press, 2014.

吴瑞林 [Wu Ruilin]. 吴瑞林回忆录 [*Memoirs of Wu Ruilin*]. Beijing: China Archival Publishing, 1995.

夏光 [Xia Guang]. 从华东军区海校到海军联校 ["From East China Military Region's Naval School to PLAN Academy"]. In 中国人民解放军历史资料丛书海军编审委会 [PLA Historical Documents and Collections Series: Navy Compilation Committee], 海军回忆史料 [*The Navy: Memoirs and History Records*] (Classified), 2:621-33.

———. 肖劲光回忆录 [*Memoirs of Xiao Jinguang*]. Beijing: PLA Press, 1988.

肖劲光 [Xiao Jinguang]. 肖劲光回忆录 (续集) [*Memoir of Xiao Jinguang* (Sequel)]. Beijing: PLA Press, 1989.

邢祖援将军访问记录 ["Interview Records of Major General Xing Zuyuan"]. In 尘封的作战计划—国光计划—口述历史 [*Oral History: Historical Operational Plan–Guoguang Jihua*], 彭大年编 [edited by Peng Danian]. Taipei: Department of Military Affairs, ROC Defense Ministry, 2005.

徐明德 [Xu Mingde]. 第一座超长波电台的建设 ["The Construction of the First Long-Wave Radio Station"]. In 海军: 回忆史料 [*The Navy: Memoirs and History Records*], 中国人民解放军历史资料丛书海军编审委员会 [edited by PLA Navy History Editorial Committee] (Classified Documents). Beijing: Ocean Wave Publishing, 1994.

杨国宇 [Yang Guoyu]. 天涯迎飞舟 ["Receiving the Rocket on the Other Side of the World"]. In 中国海军走向深蓝, 1980-2010 [*The Chinese Navy Goes to Blue Water, 1980-2010*], 左津玲主编 [edited by Zuo Jinling]. Beijing: PLA Press, 2014.

叶飞 [Ye Fei]. 叶飞回忆录 [*Memoirs of Ye Fei*]. Beijing: PLA Press, 1988.

章长蓉 [Zhang Changrong]. 回顾八二三台海战役之海军作战 ["Recollection of the Naval Battles in the 8-23 Battle of the Taiwan Strait"]. 海军学术 [*Naval Studies*] 52, no. 5 (2018): 6-15.

张力等 [Zhang Li et al.]. 徐学海先生访问记录 ["Interview of Vice Admiral Xu Xuehai"]. In 海军人物访问记录 [*Interview Records of Naval Admirals*], 张力、曾金兰编 [edited by Zhang Li and Zeng Jinlan]. Taipei: Institute of Modern China, Academia Sinica, 2002.

张世鸿、张炎平、吴迪 [Zhang Shihong, Zhang Yanping, and Wu Di]. 胡志明小道上的701天 [*701 Days on the Ho Chi Minh Trail*]. Beijing: PLA Literature Press, 2007.

张万年 [Zhang Wannian]. 张万年自传 [*Autobiography of Zhang Wannian*]. Beijing: PLA Press, 2011.

张驭涛 [Zhang Yutao]. 新中国军事大事纪要 [*Chronicle of Major Military Events of China*]. Beijing: Military Science Press, 1998.

赵国臣 [Zhao Guochen]. 难忘首次南极考察 ["Unforgettable the First Expedition to the South Pole"]. In 中国海军走向深蓝, 1980-2010 [*The Chinese Navy Goes to Blue Water, 1980-2010*], 左津玲主编 [edited by Zuo Jinling]. Beijing: PLA Press, 2014.

中共中央党史研究室 [Party History Research Division, CCP Central Committee]. 中国共产党历史大事记, 1919-87 [*Major Historical Events of the CCP, 1919-1987*]. Beijing: People's Press, 1989.

中共中央文献研究室 [CCP Central Archival and Manuscript Research Division]. 毛泽东年谱, 1893-1949 [*A Chronological Record of Mao Zedong, 1893-1949*]. 3 vols. Beijing: CCP Central Archival and Manuscript Press, 1993.

中共中央文献研究室 [CCP Central Archival and Manuscript Research Division]. 毛泽东传, 1893-1949 [*Biography of Mao Zedong, 1893-1949*]. 2 vols. Beijing: CCP Central Archival and Manuscript Press, 1996.

中共中央文献研究室 [CCP Central Archival and Manuscript Research Division]. 周恩来年谱, 1949-76 [*A Chronological Record of Zhou Enlai, 1949-1976*]. Beijing: CCP Central Archival and Manuscript Press, 1997.

中共中央文献研究室 [CCP Central Archival and Manuscript Research Division]. 朱德年谱, 1886-1976 [*A Chronological Record of Zhu De, 1886-1976*]. Beijing: People's Press, 1986.

中国军事顾问团编辑组 [Chinese Military Advisory Group Compilation Team]. 中国军事顾问团援越抗法实录: 当事人的回忆 [*The Records of the Chinese Military Advisory Group in the War to Aid Vietnam and Resist France: Personal Accounts of the Veterans*]. Beijing: CCP Party History Press, 2002.

中国人民解放军海军政治部 [PLAN Department of Political Tasks]. 中国人民解放军海军编年史, 1949-83 [*Chronicle of the PLA Navy, 1949-1983*]. Beijing: PLA Press, 1985.

中国人民解放军历史资料丛书编审委员会 [The Editorial Board of Collected Historical Documents of the PLA]. 海军历史资料 [*Historical Documents of the Navy*]. Beijing: PLA Press, 2006.

中国人民解放军历史资料丛书编审委员会 [PLA Historical Documents and Collections Series Compilation Committee]. 解放战争时期国民党军起义投诚 (综合册) [*The Revolts and Realignments of the GMD Forces during the War of Liberation* (combined vol.)]. Beijing: PLA Press, 1996.

中国人民解放军历史资料丛书海军编审委会 [Navy Compilation Committee, PLA Historical Documents and Collections Series]. 海军回忆史料 [*The Navy: Memoirs and History Records*] (Classified). Beijing: Ocean Wave Publishing, 1994.

中华民国国防部 [Defense Ministry, ROC]. 国军后勤史 [*Logistics History of the GMD Armed Forces*]. 8 vols. Taipei, Taiwan: Bureau of Historical and Political Records, Defense Ministry, 1992.

《周恩来军事活动记事》编写组编著 [Compilation Team of *Chronicle of Zhou Enlai's Military Affairs*]. 周恩来军事活动记事 [*Chronicle of Zhou Enlai's Military Affairs*]. Beijing: CCP Central Archival and Manuscript Press, 2000.

周官英 [Zhou Guan-ying]. 忆往事, 话太平: 记太平军舰遇伏始末 ["Remember the History: A Complete Story of How *Taiping* Was Ambushed"]. 海军学刊 [*Journal of the Navy*] 44, no. 1 (February 2010): 106-14.

左津玲主编 [Zuo Jinling, ed.]. 中国海军走向深蓝, 1980-2010 [*The Chinese Navy Goes to Blue Water, 1980-2010*]. Beijing: PLA Press, 2014.

BOOKS, ARTICLES, AND OTHER MATERIALS [书刊资料]

陈万军、袁华智、司彦文 [Chen Wanjun, Yuan Huazhi, and Si Yanwen]. 春风鼓浪好杨帆——江泽民主席关心人民海军现代化建设记事 ["Ride the Spring Wind and Waves: Historical Records of President Jiang Zemin's Efforts in the Modernization of the People's Navy"]. In 共和国领袖与海军 [*Chinese Leaders and the Navy*], 吴殿卿、袁永安、赵小平编 [edited by Wu Dianqing, Yuan Yong'an, and Zhao Xiaoping], 299–306. Beijing: Ocean Wave Publishing, 2000.

迟浩田 [Chi Haotian]. 前言 ["Introduction"]. In 中国海军走向深蓝, 1980–2010 [*The Chinese Navy Goes to Blue Water, 1980–2010*], 左津玲主编 [edited by Zuo Jinling], vii–viii. Beijing: PLA Press, 2014.

储峰 [Chu Feng]. 二十世纪50年代中苏军事关系研究 ["Sino-Soviet Military Relations in the 1950s"], 中共中央党校2006年博士论文 [PhD diss., Beijing: CCP Central Party University, 2006].

崔向华、陈大鹏 [Cui Xianghua and Chen Dapeng]. 陶勇将军传 [*Biography of Vice Admiral Tao Yong*]. Beijing: PLA Press, 1989.

地久、克峰 [Di Jiu and Ke Feng]. 潮涨潮落: 国共角逐台湾海峡纪实 [*Ebb and Flow: Records of the CCP-GMD Confrontations in the Taiwan Strait*]. Beijing: China Industrial and Commercial Publishing, 1996.

丁伟 [Ding Wei]. 在移动的国土上: 人民海军的创建与发展 ["On the Floating Territory: Creation and Development of the People's Navy"]. In 军事科学院军事历史研究部 [Military History Division, PLA-AMS], 军旗飘飘: 新中国50年军事大事述实 [*PLA Flag Fluttering: The Facts about China's Major Military Events in the Past 50 Years*], 1:90–105. Beijing: PLA Press, 1999.

东方鹤 [Dong Fanghe]. 张爱萍传 [*Biography of Zhang Aiping*]. Beijing: People's Press, 2000.

高文谦 [Gao Wenqian]. 晚年周恩来 [*Zhou Enlai's Later Years*]. Hong Kong: Mingjing Publishing, 2003.

高晓星等 [Gao Xiaoxing et al.]. 中国人民解放军海军 [*The PLA Navy*]. Beijing: China Intercontinental Press, 2012.

郭晋良 [Guo Jinliang]. 亲历越战 [*My Experience in the Vietnam War*]. Beijing: PLA Literature Publishing, 2005.

郭金炎 [Guo Jinyan]. 大海之子邓兆祥 [*Son of the Sea: Deng Zhaoxiang*]. Beijing: Ocean Wave Publishing, 2004.

韩怀智 [Han Huaizhi]. 当代中国军队的军事工作 [*Military Affairs of Contemporary China's Armed Forces*]. Beijing: China's Social Science Press, 1989.

韩念龙 [Han Nianlong]. 当代中国外交 [*Foreign Affairs of Contemporary China*]. Beijing: China's Social Science Press, 1988.

何迪 [He Di]. 台海危机和中国对金门、马祖政策的形成 ["Taiwan Strait Crisis and China's Policy-Making toward Jinmen and Mazu"]. 美国研究 [*American Studies*] 3, no. 1 (Fall 1988): 19–45.

何森 [He Sen]. 海上较量：解放军海军取得八六海战与崇武海战胜利 [*Battles at Seas: PLA Navy's Victories of the Battles of the August Sixth and Chongwu*]. Jilin: Jilin Publishing, 2011.

贺茂之 [He Maozhi]. 张爱萍 ["Zhang Aiping"]. In 中国人民解放军高级将领传编审委员会编著 [edited by PLA *Biographies of the High-Ranking Generals* Editorial Committee], 中国人民解放军高级将领传 [*Biographies of the PLA's High-Ranking Generals*], 9:417-52.

胡海波、于洪军 [Hu Haibo and Yu Hongjun]. 跟着毛泽东打天下 [*Follow Mao Zedong to Seize All under the Heaven*]. Changsha: Hunan People's Press, 2009.

胡彦林 [Hu Yanlin]. 威震海疆：人民海军征战纪实 [*Shocking the Sea: Records of the People's Navy's Battles*]. Beijing: National Defense University Press, 1996.

黄耀、严敬棠 [Huang Yao and Yan Jingtang]. 林彪一生 [*The Life of Lin Biao*]. Beijing: PLA Literature Press, 2004.

军事科学院军事历史研究部 [Military History Research Division, PLA-AMS]. 军旗飘飘：新中国50年军事大事述实 [*PLA Flag Fluttering: The Facts about China's Major Military Events in the Past 50 Years*]. Beijing: PLA Press, 1999.

———. 中国人民解放军全国解放战争史 [*History of the PLA in the Chinese Liberation War*]. Beijing: Military Science Press, 1997.

———. 中国人民解放军的八十年 [*Eighty Years of the Chinese PLA*]. Beijing: Military Science Press, 2007.

———. 中国人民解放军的七十年 [*Seventy Years of the Chinese PLA*]. Beijing: Military Science Press, 1997.

———. 中国人民解放军战史 [*War History of the Chinese People's Liberation Army*]. Beijing: Military Science Press, 1987.

———. 中国人民志愿军抗美援朝战史 [*War History of the Chinese People's Volunteer Force to Resist the United States and Aid Korea*]. Beijing: Military Science Press, 1990.

俊涛 [Jun Tao]. 炮击金门 ["Bombardment of Jinmen"]. 中华传奇 [*The Legacy of China*], no. 179 (November 2004): 64-80.

李丹慧 [Li Danhui]. 中苏在援越抗美问题上的矛盾与冲突 (1965-72) ["Conflicts between China and the Soviet Union in Their Efforts to Aid Vietnam and Resist America"]. In 冷战与中国 [*The Cold War and China*], 章百家、牛军主编 [edited by Zhang Baijia and Niu Jun], 372-414. Beijing: Global Knowledge Publishing, 2002.

李海文 [Li Haiwen]. 党中央什么时候决定派志愿军出国参战 ["When Did the CCP Central Committee Decide to Send the Volunteers to Fight Abroad?"]. 党的文献 [*Party Manuscripts and Archives*], no. 5 (1993): 72-95.

李健 [Li Jian]. 台海两岸战事回顾 [*History of the Military Conflicts over the Taiwan Strait*]. Beijing: China Literature Publishing, 1996.

李琼 [Li Qiong]. 海上长城：中国人民解放军海军60年 [*The Great Wall at Sea: 60 Years of the PLA Navy*]. Jilin: Jilin Publishing, 2011.

Selected Bibliography

雷华建、王冀城 [Lei Huajian and Wang Jicheng]. 新中国海战内幕 [*Inside Story of New China's Naval Warfare*]. Beijing: China International Translations and Publishing, 1993.

刘华清 [Liu Huaqing]. 前言 ["Introduction"]. In 中国近代海军史 [*A History of the Modern Chinese Navy*], 吴杰章、苏小东、程志发主编 [edited by Wu Jiezhang, Su Xiaodong, and Cheng Zhifa], 1–5.

刘亮 [Liu Liang]. 岸防劲旅: 中国人民解放军海军岸防部队 [*Strong Coastal Defense: PLAN Coastal Defense Forces*]. Beijing: Blue Sky Publishing, 2014.

刘明福 [Liu Mingfu]. 为什么解放军能赢 [*Why the PLA Can Win*]. Beijing: PAP Press, 2012.

卢辉 [Lu Hui]. 三军战一江 [*Joint Operation against Yijiangshan*]. Beijing: China United Literature Publishing, 2014.

陆其明 [Lu Qiming]. 奇袭太平号: 人民海军鱼雷快艇首次海战纪实 ["Ambush Taiping: The Story of the First Battle of the PLAN Torpedo Boats"]. In 三军挥戈战东海 [*Combined Forces Wield Spears and Fight in the East China Sea*], 聂凤智等 [edited by Nie Fengzhi et al.], 194–202. Beijing: PLA Press, 1985.

卢小萍 [Lu Xiaoping]. 中国人民解放军空军 [*The Air Force of the Chinese People's Liberation Army*]. Beijing: China Continental Media Publishing, 2012.

罗时叙 [Luo Shixu]. 由蜜月到反目: 苏联专家在中国 [*From Honeymoon to Betrayal–Soviet Experts in China*]. Beijing: Global Knowledge Publishing, 1999.

罗选优 [Luo Xuanyou]. 中越台海战争征战纪实 [*Battle Records of the Sino-Vietnam and Taiwan Strait Wars*]. Urumqi: Xinjiang People's Press, 2004.

《彭德怀传》编写组 [Peng Dehuai Biography Compilation Team]. 彭德怀传 [*Biography of Peng Dehuai*]. Beijing: Contemporary China Press, 2006.

《彭德怀传》编写组 [Peng Dehuai Biography Compilation Team]. 一个真正的人: 彭德怀 [*A Real Man: Peng Dehuai*]. Beijing: People's Press, 1994.

沈卫平 [Shen Weiping]. 8.23炮击金门 [*The August 23 Bombardment of Jinmen*]. Beijing: Huayi Publishing, 1999.

沈志华 [Shen Zhihua]. 毛泽东、斯大林与朝鲜战争 [*Mao Zedong, Stalin, and the Korean War*]. Guangzhou: Guangdong People's Press, 2004.

———. 苏联专家在中国 (1948-60) [*Soviet Experts in China, 1948–1960*]. Beijing: China International Broadcasting Publishing, 2003.

宋万贤 [Song Wanxian]. 毛泽东与张爱萍上将 ["Mao Zedong and General Zhang Aiping"]. In 吴殿卿、袁永安、赵小平主编 [*Mao Zedong and Naval Admirals*], 毛泽东与海军将领 [edited by Wu Dianqing, Yuan Yong'an, and Zhao Xiaoping], 85–98.

王定烈 [Wang Dinglie]. 当代中国空军 [*Contemporary Chinese Air Force*]. Beijing: China's Social Science Press, 1989.

王蜀宁 [Wang Shuning]. 八六海战评析 ["Analysis of the August 6 Naval Battle"]. 海军学术 [*Naval Studies*], 42, no. 6 (December 2008): 38.

王贤根 [Wang Xiangen]. 中国秘密大发兵：援越抗美实录 [*China's Secret Dispatch of a Large Force: True Story of Aiding Vietnam and Resisting the U.S.*]. Ji'nan: Ji'nan Publishing House, 1992.

———. 援越抗美实录 [*True Stories of Aiding Vietnam and Resisting America*]. Beijing: Global Cultural Publishing, 1990.

王焰 [Wang Yan]. 彭德怀传 [*Biography of Peng Dehuai*]. Beijing: Contemporary China Press, 1993.

王成志 [Wang Zhicheng]. 潮涨潮落: 打击海上窜扰之敌 ["Ebb and Flow: Defeat the Enemy Force at Sea"]. In 军旗飘飘: 新中国50年军事大事述实 [*PLA Flag Fluttering: The Facts about China's Major Military Events in the Past Fifty Years*], 军事科学院军事历史研究部编 [edited by Military History Division, PLA Academy of Military Science]. Beijing: PLA Press, 1999.

吴殿卿 [Wu Dianqing]. 乘长风破万里浪 ["Ride a Long Wind and Thousands of Miles of Waves"]. In 共和国领袖与海军 [*National Leaders and China's Navy*], 吴殿卿、袁永安、赵小平主编 [edited by Wu Dianqing, Yuan Yong'an, and Zhao Xiaoping]. Beijing: Ocean Wave Publishing, 2000.

———. 蓝色档案: 新中国海军大事纪实 [*Blue Archives: The Major Events of the Chinese Navy*]. Taiyuan: Shanxi Publishing, 2015.

———. 毛泽东与肖劲光大将 ["Mao Zedong and Fleet Admiral Xiao Jinguang"]. In 吴殿卿、袁永安、赵小平主编 [*Mao Zedong and Naval Admirals*], 毛泽东与海军将领 [edited by Wu Dianqing, Yuan Yong'an, and Zhao Xiaoping, 1–35.

———. 叶飞 ["Ye Fei"]. In 中国人民解放军高级将领传 [*Biographies of the Leading Generals of the Chinese People's Liberation Army*], 《中国人民解放军高级将领传》编审委员会编著 [edited by Biographies of the PLA's High-Ranking Generals Editorial Committee]. Beijing: PLA Press, 2007.

———. 周恩来、朱德指导制定第一个海军三年建设计划 ["Zhou Enlai and Zhu De Give Instructions to Make the Navy's First Three-Year Development Plan"]. 铁军 [*Iron Force*], no. 3 (2013): 18–29.

———. 总司令的"海军月" ["The 'Naval Month' of the Commander in Chief"]. In 共和国领袖与海军 [*PRC National Leaders and the Navy*], 吴殿卿、袁永安、赵小平主编 [edited by Wu Dianqing, Yuan Yong'an, and Zhao Xiaoping], 27–33.

———. 组建海军重大决策的历史事实 ["Historical Facts on Important Decisions to Establish the PLA Navy"]. 人民海军 [*People's Navy*], no. 9 (October 2002): 1–13.

吴殿卿、袁永安、赵小平主编 [Wu Dianqing, Yuan Yong'an, and Zhao Xiaoping, eds.]. 共和国领袖与海军 [*PRC National Leaders and the Navy*]. Beijing: Ocean Wave Publishing, 2000.

———. 毛泽东与海军将领 [*Mao Zedong and Naval Admirals*]. Beijing: PLA Literature Press, 1999.

吴杰章 [Wu Jiezhang]、苏小东 [Su Xiaodong]、and 程志发 [Cheng Zhifa]. 中国近代海军史 [*A History of the Modern Chinese Navy*]. Beijing: PLA Press, 1989.

吴瑞虎 [Wu Ruihu]. 三代驱逐舰启程中南海——党和国家领导人关心驱逐舰部队建设记事 ["Three Generations of Destroyers Started from Zhongnanhai: History Shows How CCP and PRC Leaders Cared about Construction of the Destroyer Fleet"]. In 共和国领袖与海军 [*National Leaders and China's Navy*], 吴殿卿、袁永安、赵小平主编 [edited by Wu Dianqing, Yuan Yong'an, and Zhao Xiaoping], 285-92. Beijing: Ocean Wave Publishing, 2000.

吴润睿译 [Wu Runrui, trans.]. 看不见的屏障：决定台湾命运的第七舰队 [*Invisible Shell: The Seventh Fleet and Taiwan's Fate*]. Xinbei, Taiwan: Eight Banner Culture Publishing, 2017.

新华社 [New China News]. 胡锦涛会见海军代表 ["Hu Jintao Meets Naval Representatives"]. 中国新闻网 [*China News*], December 28, 2006. www.chinanews.com.cn/gn/news/2006/12-28.

新华社 [Xinhua News Agency]. 胡锦涛出席庆祝人民海军成立60周年海上阅兵活动 ["Hu Jintao Attends the Naval Parade to Celebrate the People's Navy's 60th Birthday"]. 中国台湾网 [*China's Taiwan News*], April 23, 2009. www.taiwan.cn/xwzx/jrbd/200904/t20090424_876110.htm.

———. 人民海军70年：党中央关心人民海军建设发展纪实 ["70 Years of the People's Navy: The Historical Facts of the Party Center's Support to Construction and Development of the People's Navy"]. 新华社新媒体 [*New China's News Media*], April 22, 2019. www.baijiahao.baidu.com/s?id=16315103827060121248&wfr.

———. 我国著名的航空史学家陈应明为海空卫士王伟亲属制作"铁血战机"模型 ["China's Well-Known Aviation Historian Chen Yingming Makes a 'Hero Martyr's Fighter' Model for Wang Wei's Family"]. 新华社新媒体 [*New China's News Media*], April 18, 2001.

———. 中国海军出击亚丁湾 ["The Chinese Navy Dispatched to the Gulf of Aden"], 参考消息 [*Reference News*], December 27, 2008.

星火燎原编辑部 [*Xinghuo liaoyuan* Composition Department]. 中国人民解放军将帅名录 [*PLA Marshals and Generals*]. Beijing: PLA Press, 1992. Cited as 将帅名录 [*Marshals and Generals*].

许峰源 [Xu Feng-Yuan]. 迁台初期台湾对沿海岛屿的防御策略调整 (1950-55) ["Adjustment of Taiwan's Outer Islands Defense Strategy (1950-1955)"]. 档案半年刊 [*Archives Semiannual*] 21, no. 1 (June 2022): 28-43.

徐焰 [Xu Yan]. 金门之战 [*The Battle of Jinmen*]. Beijing: China's Radio and Television Publishing, 1992.

———. 军事家毛泽东 [*Mao Zedong as a Military Leader*]. Beijing: CCP Central Archival and Manuscript Press, 1995.

———. 徐焰讲稿自选集 [*Self-Selected Lectures of Xu Yan*]. Beijing: National Defense University Press, 2014.

———. 中国空军的艰难起步和辉煌前景 ["A Tough Start and the Bright Future of the Chinese Air Force"]. In 徐焰讲稿自选集 [*Self-Selected Lectures of Xu Yan*], 281-91.

———. 中国由注重"海防"变为争取"海权" ["China Shifts Its Focus from 'Coastal Defense' to 'Sea Power'"]. In 徐焰讲稿自选集 [Self-Selected Lectures of Xu Yan], 203-11.

杨国宇 [Yang Guoyu]. 当代中国海军 [Contemporary Chinese Navy]. Beijing: China's Social Science Press, 1987.

杨奎松 [Yang Kuisong]. 毛泽东与印度支那战争 ["Mao Zedong and the Indochina Wars"]. In 中国与印度支那战争 [China and the Indochina Wars], 李丹慧主编 [ed. Li Danhui], 12-28. Hong Kong: Heaven and Earth Books, 2000.

———. 美苏冷战的起源对中国革命的影响 ["Origins of the U.S.-Soviet Cold War and Its Impact on China's Revolution"]. In 冷战与中国 [The Cold War and China], 章百家、牛军主编 [edited by Zhang Baijia and Niu Jun], 51-88. Beijing: Global Knowledge Publishing, 2002.

杨忠义 [Yang Zhongyi]. 苏联专家与中国海军航空兵 [Soviet Experts and Chinese Naval Aviation]. Beijing: PLA Press, 2013.

姚莲瑞 [Yao Lianrui]. 彭大将军的沉冤 ["The Injustice of Marshal Peng"]. In 军旗飘飘: 新中国50年军事大事述实 [PLA Flag Fluttering: The Facts about China's Major Military Events in the Past Fifty Years], 军事科学院军事历史研究部 [edited by Military History Division, PLA Academy of Military Science]. Beijing: PLA Press, 1999.

叶永烈 [Ye Yonglie]. 高层较量 [Power Struggle at the Top]. Urumqi: Xinjiang People's Press, 2004.

张爱萍 [Zhang Aiping]. 中国人民解放军 [The Chinese People's Liberation Army]. Beijing: Contemporary China Press, 1994.

章百家、牛军主编 [Zhang Baijia and Niu Jun, eds.]. 冷战与中国 [The Cold War and China]. Beijing: Global Knowledge Publishing, 2002.

赵小平 [Zhao Xiaoping]. 毛泽东与吴瑞林中将 ["Mao Zedong and Lieutenant General Wu Ruilin"]. In 毛泽东与海军将领 [Mao Zedong and His Admirals and Generals]. Beijing: PLA Literature Press, 1999.

郑雅茹 [Zheng Yaru]. 肖劲光 ["Xiao Jinguaung"]. In 中国人民解放军高级将领传 [Biographies of the PLA's High-Ranking Generals], 中国人民解放军高级将领传编审委员会编著 [edited by PLA Biographies of the High-Ranking Generals Editorial Committee], 4:465-81.

中国人民革命军事博物馆 [China National Revolutionary Military Museum]. 中国战争发展史 [The Historical Development of Chinese Warfare]. Beijing: People's Press, 2002.

中国人民海军总部 [PLAN General Headquarters]. 中国人民解放军海军编年史, 1949-83 [The Chronicle of the PLA Navy, 1949-1983]. Beijing: PLAN Press, 1995.

中国人民解放军高级将领传编审委员会编著 [PLA Biographies of the High-Ranking Generals Editorial Committee, ed]. 中国人民解放军高级将领传 [Biographies of the PLA's High-Ranking Generals]. Beijing: PLA Press, 2008.

钟坚 [Zhong Jian]. 导读: 英雄不回头 ["Introduction: The Hero No Return"]. In 看不见的屏障: 决定台湾命运的第七舰队 [*Invisible Shell: The Seventh Fleet and Taiwan's Fate*], 吴润睿译 [translated by Wu Runrui]. Xinbei, Taiwan: Eight Banner Culture Publishing, 2017.

周日新 [Zhou Rixin]. 中国航空图志 [*Pictographic Records of Chinese Aviation*]. Beijing: Beijing Aerospace University Press, 2008.

朱增泉 [Zhu Zengquan]. 战争史笔记 [*Historical Notes on Chinese Warfare*]. Beijing: People's Literature Press, 2010.

紫丁 [Ziding]. 李强传 [*Biography of Li Qiang*]. Beijing: People's Press, 2004.

ENGLISH-LANGUAGE SOURCES

DOCUMENTS, MEMOIRS, AND PAPERS

Bui, Tin. *Following Ho Chi Minh: The Memoirs of a North Vietnamese Colonel*. London: Hurst, 1995.

CCP Central Committee. *Selected Documents of the Fifteenth CCP National Congress*. Beijing: New Star Publishing, 1997.

Clinton, Hillary. "Secretary Clinton Joint Press Availability with Japanese Foreign Minister Seiji Maehara." October 27, 2010. www.state.gov/secretary/rm/2010/10/150110.htm.

Deng Rong. *Deng Xiaoping and the Cultural Revolution—a Daughter Recalls the Critical Years*. Translated by Sidney Shapiro. Beijing: Foreign Languages Press, 2002.

Deng Xiaoping. *Selected Works of Deng Xiaoping*. 3 vols. Beijing: Foreign Languages Press, 1994.

"Document No. 1: The First Conversation of N. S. Khrushchev with Mao Zedong, Hall of Huaizhentang, Beijing, July 31, 1958; The Mao-Khrushchev Conversation, July 31–August 3, 1958 and October 2, 1959." In "New Evidence on the Cold War in Asia," translated and with an introduction by Vladislav M. Zubok, *Cold War International History Project Bulletin* 12–13 (Fall/Winter 2001): 242–47.

Important Documents concerning the Question of Taiwan. Beijing: Foreign Languages Press, 1955.

Information Office, the PRC State Council. *China's National Defense in 2010*. Beijing: State Council Information Office, 2011. http://www.gov.cn/english/official/2011-03/31/content_1835499.htm.

Information Office, the PRC State Council. *The Diversified Employment of China's Armed Forces* (*China's Defense White Paper*), April 2013. http://www.chinadaily.com.cn/language_tips/news/2013-04/17/content_16414985.htm.

Information Office, the PRC State Council. "The Security Situation." In *White Papers of China's National Defense in 2008*. http://English.people.com.cn/90001/90776/90785/6578688.html.

Jiang Weilie, interview by a reporter on April 9, 2013. PRC Defense Ministry, www.mod.gov.cn.

Li, Xiaobing, Chen Jian, and David L. Wilson, trans. and eds. "Mao Zedong's Handling of the Taiwan Strait Crisis of 1958: Chinese Recollections and Documents." *Cold War International History Project Bulletin* 6–7 (Winter 1995/1996): 208–19.

Major T. "Russian Missile Officers in Vietnam." In *Voices from the Vietnam War: Stories from American, Asian, and Russian Veterans*, edited by Xiaobing Li, 65–72. Lexington: University Press of Kentucky, 2010.

Mao Zedong. *Mao Zedong on Diplomacy*. Beijing: Foreign Languages Press, 1998.

Mao Zedong. *Selected Works of Mao Tse-tung*. 4 vols. Beijing: Foreign Languages Press, 1977.

"New Russian Documents on the Korean War." Translated and edited by Kathryn Weathersby. *Cold War International History Project Bulletin* 6–7 (Winter 1995/1996): 30–125.

Nie Rongzhen. "Beijing's Decision to Intervene." In *Mao's Generals Remember Korea*, translated and edited by Xiaobing Li, Allan R. Millett, and Bin Yu, 38–60. Lawrence: University Press of Kansas, 2001.

Perry, William (Secretary of U.S. Defense Department). Public statement on March 11, 1996, *American Forces Press Service*, March 11; the Department of Defense, *News Briefings*, March 12, 14, and 16, 1996.

Research Department of Party Literature, CCP Central Committee, ed. *Major Documents of the People's Republic of China–Selected Important Documents since the Third Plenary Session of the Eleventh CCP Central Committee*. Beijing: Foreign Languages Press, 1991.

Ridgway, Matthew B. *The Korean War*. Garden City, NY: Doubleday, 1967.

Smoot, Roland N. "As I Recalled: The U.S. Taiwan Defense Command." U.S. Naval Institute *Proceedings* 110, no. 9, 979 (September 1984): 46–63.

Taiwan Affairs Office and the Information Office, PRC State Council. "The One-China Principle and the Taiwan Issue, February 2000." In *White Papers of the Chinese Government, 2000–2001*, comp. Information Office, PRC State Council. Beijing: Foreign Languages Press, 2003.

U.S. Defense Intelligence Agency. *China Military Power: Modernizing a Force to Fight and Win*. Washington, DC: U.S. Government Printing Office, 2019.

U.S. Department of State. *Foreign Relations of the United States: China, Korea, Vietnam, and Indochina, 1945–1972*. 8 vols. Washington, DC: U.S. Government Printing Office, 1982–97. Cited as FRUS.

U.S. Secretary of Defense. *Annual Report to Congress: Military Power of the People's Republic of China, 2008*. http://www.defenselink.mil/pubs/pdfs/China_Military_Report_08.pdf.

U.S. Secretary of Defense. *Annual Report to Congress: Military Power of the People's Republic of China, 2009*. http://www.defenselink.mil/pubs/pdfs/China_Military_Report_09.pdf.

U.S. Secretary of Defense. *Military and Security Developments Involving the People's Republic of China, 2013*, 12. http://www.defenselink.mil/pubs/pdfs/China_Military_Report_13.pdf.

U.S. Senate. *National Defense Authorization Act for Fiscal Year 2013, H.R. 4310: Sec. 1251.* Washington, DC: U.S. Government Printing Office, 2013.

Weathersby, Kathryn, trans. and ed. "New Russian Documents on the Korean War." *Cold War International History Project Bulletin* 6–7 (Winter 1995/1996): 30–93.

Wu Lengxi. "Inside Story of the Decision Making during the Shelling of Jinmen." In "Mao Zedong's Handling of the Taiwan Straits Crisis of 1958: Chinese Recollections and Documents," translated and edited by Li, Chen, and Wilson, *Cold War International History Project Bulletin* 6–7 (Winter 1995/1996): 208–19.

Xinhua News Agency. *China's Foreign Relations: A Chronology of Events, 1949–1988.* Beijing: Foreign Languages Press, 1989.

Xu Xiangqian. "The Purchase of Arms from Moscow." In Li, Millett, and Yu, *Mao's Generals Remember Korea*, 139–46.

Zhang, Shuguang, and Jian Chen, eds. *Chinese Communist Foreign Policy and the Cold War in Asia: New Documentary Evidence, 1944–1950.* Chicago: Imprint Publications, 1996.

Zubok, Vladislav M. "The Mao-Khrushchev Conversation, July 31–August 3, 1958, and October 2, 1959." In "New Evidence on the Cold War in Asia," *Cold War International History Project Bulletin* 12–13 (Fall/Winter 2001): 239–64.

BOOKS, ARTICLES, AND OTHER MATERIALS

Allen, Kenneth W., Dean B. Cheng, David M. Finkelstein, and Maryanne Kevlehan. "Institutional Reforms of the Chinese People's Liberation Army: Overview and Challenges." *Project Asia*, CRM D0005777.A1. Alexandria, VA: CNA Corporation, May 2002.

Ambrose, Stephen E., and Douglas G. Brinkley. *Rise to Globalism: American Foreign Policy since 1938.* New York: Penguin, 1997.

Andrade, Tonio. *The Gunpowder Age: China, Military Innovation, and the Rise of the West in World History.* Princeton, NJ: Princeton University Press, 2016.

Baker, P. "Obama Calls for Military Dialogue with China." *New York Times*, March 12, 2009.

Barnett, Robert W. *Quemoy: The Use and Consequence of Nuclear Deterrence.* Cambridge, MA: Harvard University Press, 1960.

BBC. "Questions and Answers: China-Japan Islands Row." *BBC News (UK)*, September 11, 2012. http://www.bbc.co.uk/news/world-asia-pacific-11341139.

———. "Viewpoints: How Serious Are China-Japan Tensions?" *BBC Chinese (UK)*, February 8, 2013. http://news.bbc.co.uk/chinese/trad/hi/newsid_7450000.stm.

Bernstein, Thomas P., and Hua-yu Li. *What China Learns from the Soviet Union, 1949–Present.* Lanham, MD: Lexington Books, 2010.

Bin Yu. "What China Learned from Its 'Forgotten War' in Korea." In Li, Millett, and Yu, *Mao's Generals Remember Korea*, 9–29.

Bitzinger, Richard A., Michael Raska, Collin Koh Swee Lean, and Kelvin Wong Ka Weng. "Locating China's Place in the Global Defense Economy." In *Forging China's Military Might: A New Framework for Assessing Innovation*, edited by Tai Ming Cheung. Baltimore: Johns Hopkins University Press, 2014.

Black, Jeremy. *Rethinking Military History*. London: Routledge, 2004.

Blasko, Dennis J. *The Chinese Army Today: Tradition and Transformation for the 21st Century*. 2nd ed. New York: Routledge, 2012.

Bouchard, Joseph E. *Command in Crisis: Four Case Studies*. New York: Columbia University Press, 1991.

Buerk, R. "Japan to Free Chinese Boat Captain." *BBC Chinese (UK)*, September 24, 2010. http://news.bbc.co.uk/chinese/trad/hi/newsid_7450000.stm.

Burkitt, Laurie, Andrew Scobell, and Larry M. Wortzel, eds. *The Lessons of History: The Chinese People's Liberation Army at 75*. Carlisle, PA: Army War College Strategic Studies Institute, 2003.

Burr, William, ed. *The Kissinger Transcripts: The Top-Secret Talks with Beijing and Moscow*. New York: New Press, 1999.

Bussert, James C., and Bruce A. Elleman. *People's Liberation Army Navy: Combat Systems Technology, 1949–2010*. Annapolis, MD: Naval Institute Press, 2018.

Catapano, Kevin. "China Conducts Assault Landing Drills as Invasion Attempt Looks Inevitable." *Western Journal*, June 10, 2021. http://westernjournal.com/china-conducts-assault-landing-drills-invasion-attempt-looks-inevitable/.

Chang, Gordon H. *Friends and Enemies: The United States, China, and the Soviet Union*. Stanford, CA: Stanford University Press, 1990.

———. "To the Nuclear Brink: Eisenhower, Dulles, and the Quemoy-Matsu Crisis." *International Security* 12 (Spring 1988): 82–116.

Chen, Dean. "Sea Power and the Chinese State: China's Maritime Ambitions." Heritage Foundation, July 11, 2011. www.heritage.org/asia/report/sea-power-and-the-chinese-state-maritime-ambitions.

Chen Jian. *Mao's China and the Cold War*. Chapel Hill: University of North Carolina Press, 2001.

Chen Jian and Xiaobing Li. "China and the End of the Cold War." In *The Cold War: From Détente to the Soviet Collapse*, edited by Malcolm Muir Jr., 120–31. Lexington: Virginia Military Institute Press, 2006.

Chen, Qimao. "The Taiwan Strait Crisis: Causes, Scenarios, and Solutions." In *Across the Taiwan Strait: Mainland China, Taiwan, and the 1995–1996 Crisis*, edited by Suisheng Zhao, 127–62. London: Routledge, 1999.

Cheng, Dean. "Assessing Threats to US Vital Interests: China." www.heritage.org/2021-index-us-military-strength/assessing-threats-us-vital-interests/china.

Cheng, Sijin. "Conscription: From the Masses." In *Civil-Military Relations in Today's China: Swimming in a New Sea*, edited by David M. Finkelstein and Kristen Gunness, 235–54. Armonk, NY: M. E. Sharpe, 2006.

Cheung, Tai Ming, ed. *Forging China's Military Might: A New Framework for Assessing Innovation*. Baltimore: Johns Hopkins University Press, 2014.
Christensen, Thomas J. *Useful Adversaries: Grand Strategy, Domestic Mobilization, and Sino-American Conflict, 1947–1958*. Princeton, NJ: Princeton University Press, 1996.
Christoffersen, Gaye. "Crises as Impetus for Institutionalization: Maritime Crisis Management Mechanisms in China's Near Seas." In *China's Strategic Priorities*, edited by Jonathan H. Ping and Brett McCormick, 62–79. London: Routledge, 2016.
Cohen, Warren I. *America's Response to China: A History of Sino-American Relations*. 6th ed. New York: Columbia University Press, 2019.
Cole, Bernard D. *The Great Wall at Sea: China's Navy in the Twenty-First Century*. 2nd ed. Annapolis, MD: Naval Institute Press, 2010.
Compilation Committee of ROC History. *A History of the Republic of China*. Taipei, Taiwan: Modern China Press, 1981.
Copper, John F. "The Origins of Conflict across the Taiwan Strait: The Problem of Differences in Perceptions." In *Across the Taiwan Strait: Mainland China, Taiwan, and the 1995–1996 Crisis*, edited by Suisheng Zhao, 41–76. London: Routledge, 1999.
Cowley, Robert, ed. *The Cold War: A Military History*. New York: Random House, 2005.
Di Cosmo, Nicola, ed. *Military Culture in Imperial China*. Cambridge, MA: Harvard University Press, 2009.
Dreyer, Edward L. "Continuity and Change." In *A Military History of China*, extended ed., edited by Robin Higham and David Graff, 19–38. Lexington: University Press of Kentucky, 2012.
Ebon, Martin. *Lin Piao: The Life and Writings of China's New Ruler*. New York: Stein and Day, 1970.
Elleman, Bruce A. *High Seas Buffer: The Taiwan Patrol Force, 1950–1979*. Newport, RI: Naval War College Press, 2012.
———. *The Making of the Modern Chinese Navy: Special Historical Characteristics*. London: Anthem, 2019.
———. *Modern Chinese Warfare, 1795–1989*. London: Routledge, 2001.
Engstrom, Jeffrey. *Systems Confrontation and System Destruction Warfare: How the Chinese People's Liberation Army Seeks to Wage Modern Warfare*. Santa Monica, CA: RAND Corporation, 2018.
Fairbank, John K., Rosemary Foot, and Frank A. Kierman Jr., eds. *Chinese Ways in Warfare*. Cambridge, MA: Harvard University Press, 1974.
Fairbank, John K., Edwin O. Reischauer, and Albert M. Craig. *East Asia: Transition and Transformation*. Rev. ed. Boston: Houghton Mifflin, 1989.
Fang, Qiang, and Xiaobing Li, eds. *Corruption and Anticorruption in Modern China*. Lanham, MD: Lexington Books, 2019.

Felton, Mark. *China Station: The British Military in the Middle Kingdom 1839–1997*. Barnsley, UK: Pen & Sword Military, 2013.
Finkelstein, David M. "Three Key Issues Affecting Security in the Asia-Pacific Region." In *Asia-Pacific Security: New Issues and New Ideas*, edited by China Association for Military Science, 110–16. Beijing: Military Science Publishing, 2014.
———. *Washington's Taiwan Dilemma, 1949–1950: From Abandonment to Salvation*. Fairfax, VA: George Mason University Press, 1993.
Finkelstein, David M., and Kristen Gunness, eds. *Civil-Military Relations in Today's China: Swimming in a New Sea*. Armonk, NY: M. E. Sharpe, 2007.
Foot, Rosemary. *The Practice of Power: US Relations with China since 1949*. Oxford: Oxford University Press, 1997.
Fravel, M. Taylor. *Active Defense: China's Military Strategy since 1949*. Princeton, NJ: Princeton University Press, 2019.
———. *Strong Borders, Secure Nation: Cooperation and Conflict in China's Territorial Disputes*. Princeton, NJ: Princeton University Press, 2008.
Gady, Franz-Stefan. "Russian and China Kick Off Naval Exercise in Sea of Japan." *The Diplomat*, August 24, 2015. http://thediplomat.com/2015/08/Russian-and-china-kick-off-naval-exercise-in-sea-of-japan.
Gao Xiaoxing et al. *The PLA Navy*. Beijing: China Intercontinental Press, 2012.
Godwin, Paul H. B., and Alice L. Miller. "China's Forbearance Has Limits: Chinese Threat and Retaliation Signaling and Its Implications for a Sino-American Military Confrontation." In *China Strategic Perspectives* No. 6. Washington, DC: National Defense University Institute for National Strategic Studies, 2013.
Goldman, Merle, and Roderick MacFarquhar, eds. *The Paradox of China's Post-Mao Reforms*. Cambridge, MA: Harvard University Press, 1999.
Graff, David A. *The Eurasian Way of War: Military Practice in Seventh-Century China and Byzantium*. London: Routledge, 2016.
Graff, David A., and Robin Higham, eds. *A Military History of China*. Extended ed. Lexington: University Press of Kentucky, 2012.
Granados, Ulises. "The US Factor in China's Dispute with Japan over the Diaoyu/Senkaku Islands: Balancing Washington's 'Rebalancing' in East Asian Waters." In *China's Strategic Priorities*, edited by Jonathan H. Ping and Brett McCormick, 80–96. London: Routledge, 2016.
Han, Zhongtian. "The PRC's Naval-Air Campaign in the East China Sea, 1954–1955." Paper presented at the Chinese Military History Society annual meeting (via Zoom), May 10, 2020.
He Di. "The Last Campaign to Unify China: The CCP's Unrealized Plan to Liberate Taiwan, 1949–1950." In *Chinese Warfighting: The PLA Experience since 1949*, edited by Mark A. Ryan, David M. Finkelstein, and Michael A. McDevitt, 73–90. Armonk, NY: M. E. Sharpe, 2003.
Hensel, Howard M., and Amit Gupta, eds. *Maritime Security in the Indian Ocean and Western Pacific: Heritage and Contemporary Challenges*. London: Routledge, 2018.

Huang, Cary, and Teddy Ng. "Xi Jinping Sends Signal to Neighbors with High-Profile Tour of Liaoning Aircraft Carrier." *South Chinese Morning Post*, August 31, 2013.

Huei, Pang Yang. *Strait Rituals: China, Taiwan, and the United States in the Taiwan Strait Crises, 1954–1958*. Hong Kong: Hong Kong University Press, 2019.

"Hu Jintao Tells China Navy: Prepare for Warfare." *BBC News*, December 7, 2011. www.bbc.com/news/world-asia-china-16063607.

Hyer, Eric, Zhang Qingmin, and Jordan Hamzawi. "Analyzing China's Foreign Policy: Domestic Politics, Public Opinion, and Leaders." In *China's Strategic Priorities*, edited by Jonathan H. Ping and Brett McCormick, 43–61. London: Routledge, 2016.

Jencks, Harlan. "Civil-Military Relations in China: Tiananmen and After." *Problems of Communism* 40 (May–June 1991): 12–27.

Jennings, R. "Taiwan Protests as Japan Holds Fishing Boat Captain." *BBC Chinese (UK)*, June 13, 2008. http://news.bbc.co.uk/chinese/trad/hi/newsid_7450000/newsid_7452300/7452336.stm.

Joffe, Ellis. *The Chinese Army after Mao*. Cambridge, MA: Harvard University Press, 1987.

———. *Party and Army: Professionalism and Political Control in the Chinese Officer Corps, 1948–1964*. Cambridge, MA: Harvard University Press, 1967.

Johnston, Alastair I. "Prospects for Chinese Nuclear Force Modernization: Limited Deterrence versus Multilateral Arms Control." In *China's Military in Transition*, edited by David Shambaugh and Richard H. Yang. New York: Oxford University Press, 1997.

Kamphausen, Roy, David Lai, and Travis Tanner, eds. *Assessing the People's Liberation Army in the Hu Jintao Era*. Carlisle, PA: U.S. Army War College, 2014.

Kau, Michael Y. M., ed. *The Lin Biao Affair: Power Politics and Military Coup*. White Plains, NY: International Arts and Science Press, 1975.

Keegan, John. *A History of Warfare*. New York: Knopf, 1993.

Kenny, Henry J. "Vietnamese Perceptions of the 1979 War with China." In *Chinese Warfighting: The PLA Experience since 1949*, edited by Mark A. Ryan, David M. Finkelstein, and Michael A. McDevitt, 217–40. Armonk, NY: M. E. Sharpe, 2003.

Khoo, Nicholas. *Collateral Damage: Sino-Soviet Rivalry and the Termination of the Sino-Vietnamese Alliance*. New York: Columbia University Press, 2011.

Kierman, Frank, and John King Fairbank, eds. *Chinese Ways of Warfare*. Cambridge, MA: Harvard University Press, 1974.

Lai, Benjamin. *The Chinese People's Liberation Army since 1949*. Oxford: Osprey, 2012.

Lai, Sherman Xiaogang. "Ensured Loyalty versus Professionalism at Sea: A Historical Review of the PLA Navy, 1949–1982." Paper presented at the annual meeting of Chinese Military History Society (CMHS), Ottawa, Ontario, Canada, April 16, 2016.

Lewis, John, and Xue Litai. *China Builds the Bomb*. Stanford, CA: Stanford University Press, 1991.
Li, Cheng. *China's Leaders: The New Generation*. Lanham, MD: Rowman & Littlefield, 2001.
Li Danhui and Yafeng Xia. *Mao and the Sino-Soviet Split, 1959–1973: A New History*. Lanham, MD: Lexington Books, 2018.
Li, Nan. "China's Evolving Naval Strategy and Capabilities in the Hu Jintao Era." In *Assessing the People's Liberation Army in the Hu Jintao Era*, edited by Roy Kamphausen, David Lai, and Travis Tanner. Carlisle, PA: U.S. Army War College, 2014.
———, ed. *Chinese Civil-Military Relations: The Transformation of the People's Liberation Army*. New York: Routledge, 2006.
Li, Xiaobing. *Attack at Chosin: The Chinese Second Offensive in Korea*. Norman: University of Oklahoma Press, 2020.
———. *Building Ho's Army: Chinese Military Assistance to North Vietnam*. Lexington: University Press of Kentucky, 2019.
———. *China's Battle for Korea: The 1951 Spring Offensive Campaign*. Bloomington: Indiana University Press, 2014.
———. "China's Intervention and the CPVF Experience in the Korean War." In *The Korean War at Fifty: International Perspectives*, edited by Mark F. Wilkinson, 130–49. Lexington: Virginia Military Institute Press, 2004.
———. *Civil Liberties in China*. Santa Barbara, CA: ABC-CLIO, 2010.
———. *The Cold War in East Asia*. London: Routledge, 2018.
———. *The Dragon in the Jungle: The Chinese Army in the Vietnam War*. New York: Oxford University Press, 2020.
———. *A History of the Modern Chinese Army*. Lexington: University Press of Kentucky, 2007.
———. "The Impact of Social Changes on the PLA: A Chinese Military Perspective." In *Civil-Military Relations in Today's China: Swimming in a New Sea*, edited by David M. Finkelstein and Kristen Gunness, 26–47. Armonk, NY: M. E. Sharpe, 2007.
———. "Large-Scale Amphibious Warfare in Chinese Military Strategy." Paper presented at the naval symposium organized by China Maritime Studies Institute, U.S. Naval War College, May 4–6, 2021.
———. *Modern China: Understanding Modern Nations*. Santa Barbara, CA: ABC-CLIO, 2016.
———. "New War of Nerves." *Journal of Chinese Political Science* 3, no. 1 (Summer 1997): 56–73.
———. "PLA Attacks and Amphibious Operations during the Taiwan Strait Crises of 1954–55 and 1958." In *Chinese Warfighting: The PLA Experience since 1949*, edited by Mark A. Ryan, David M. Finkelstein, and Michael A. McDevitt, 143–72. New York: M. E. Sharpe, 2003.

———. "Reforming the People's Army: Military Modernization in China." *Journal of Southwest Conference on Asian Studies* 5 (2005): 1–19.
———. "Sino-Japanese Maritime Conflicts and Security Concerns in the East China Sea." In *Maritime Security in the Indian Ocean and Western Pacific: Heritage and Contemporary Challenges*, edited by Howard M. Hensel and Amit Gupta, 243–60. London: Routledge, 2018.
———. "Truman and Taiwan: A U.S. Policy Change from Face to Faith." In *Northeast Asia and the Legacy of Harry S. Truman: Japan, China, and the Two Koreas*, edited by James I. Matray, 119–44. Kirksville, MO: Truman State University Press, 2012.
———. *Voices from the Vietnam War: Stories from American, Asian, and Russian Veterans*. Lexington: University Press of Kentucky, 2010.
Li, Xiaobing, and Qiang Fang, eds. *Sino-American Relations: A New Cold War*. Leiden: Amsterdam University Press, 2022.
Li, Xiaobing, Allan R. Millett, and Bin Yu, trans. and eds. *Mao's Generals Remember Korea*. Lawrence: University Press of Kansas, 2001.
Li, Xiaobing, and Michael Molina, eds. *Oil: A Cultural and Geographic Encyclopedia of Black Gold*. Santa Barbara, CA: ABC-CLIO, 2014.
Li, Xiaobing, and Patrick Fuliang Shan, eds. *Ethnic China: Identity, Assimilation, and Resistance*. Lanham, MD: Lexington Books, 2015.
Li, Yue, and Chen Liu. "Runaway Chinese Officials and International Chase." In *Corruption and Anticorruption in Modern China*, edited by Qiang Fang and Xiaobing Li, 187–204. Lanham, MD: Lexington Books, 2019.
Li, Zhisui. *The Private Life of Chairman Mao: The Memoirs of Mao's Personal Physician*. New York: Random House, 1994.
Lim, Louisa. *The People's Republic of Amnesia*. New York: Oxford University Press, 2014.
Lo, Jung-Pang. *China as a Sea Power, 1127–1368: A Preliminary Survey of the Maritime Expansion and Naval Exploits of the Chinese People during the Southern Song and Yuan Periods*. Singapore: National University of Singapore Press, 2012.
Lorge, Peter A. *The Asian Military Revolution: From Gunpowder to the Bomb*. New York: Cambridge University Press, 2008.
———. *The Reunification of China: Peace through War under the Song Dynasty*. New York: Cambridge University Press, 2015.
———. *War, Politics, and Society in Early Modern China, 900–1795*. New York: Routledge, 2005.
———. *Warfare in China to 1600*. Farnham, UK: Ashgate, 2005.
Lüthi, Lorenz M. *The Sino-Soviet Split: Cold War in the Communist World*. Princeton, NJ: Princeton University Press, 2008.
———. "Sino-Soviet Split." In *China at War*, edited by Xiaobing Li. Santa Barbara, CA: ABC-CLIO, 2012.
Lu Xiaoping. *The PLA Air Force*. Beijing: China Intercontinental Press, 2012.
Macaes, Bruno. *Belt and Road: A Chinese World Order*. London: Hurst, 2019.

Mann, Jim. *About Face: A History of America's Curious Relationship with China, from Nixon to Clinton*. New York: Knopf, 1999.
Mattis, Peter. *Analyzing the Chinese Military: A Review Essay and Resource Guide on the People's Liberation Army*. Kindle ed., 2015.
McDevitt, Michael A. *China as a Twenty-First-Century Naval Power: Theory, Practice, and Implications*. Annapolis, MD: Naval Institute Press, 2020.
Meisner, Maurice. *The Deng Xiaoping Era: An Inquiry into the Fate of Chinese Socialism, 1978–1994*. New York: Hill & Wang, 1996.
———. *Mao's China and After: A History of the People's Republic*. New York: Free Press, 1999.
Mori, K. "Kerry Spells Out Policy on Senkaku Islands." *UPI*, April 15, 2013. www.upi.com/Top_News/World-News/2013/04/15.
Muir, Malcolm, Jr., and Mark F. Wilkinson, eds. *The Most Dangerous Years: The Cold War, 1953–1975*. Lexington: Virginia Military Institute, 2005.
O'Dowd, Edward C. *Chinese Military Strategy in the Third Indochina War: The Last Maoist War*. London: Routledge, 2007.
Ogden, Suzanne, Kathleen Hartford, Lawrence Sullivan, and David Zweig. *China's Search for Democracy: The Student and the Mass Movement of 1989*. Armonk, NY: M. E. Sharpe, 1992.
Perlez, J. "Sentiment Builds in China to Press Claim for Okinawa." *New York Times*, June 13, 2013. http://www.nytimes.com/2013/06/14/world/asia.html.
Perry, William, and Ashton Carter. *Preventive Defense: A New Security for America*. Washington, DC: Brookings Institute, 1999.
Peters, Richard, and Xiaobing Li. *Voices of the Korean War: Personal Stories of American, Korean, and Chinese Soldiers*. Lexington: University Press of Kentucky, 2004.
PLA Academy of Military Science (AMS). "The Unforgotten Korean War: Chinese Perspective and Appraisals." 3 vols. Unpublished manuscript written by PLA officer-historians and sponsored by the Office of Net Assessment, Office of the U.S. Secretary of Defense, 2006.
PLA Daily. "China's Establishment of the Air Defense Identification Zone (ADIZ) in the East China Sea, January 22, 2014." http://eng.chinamil.com.cn/view/2014-01.
Raine, Sarah, and Christian Miere. *Regional Disorder: The South China Sea Disputes*. London: Routledge, 2013.
Rajagopalan, M. "China Conducts Air, Sea Drills in East China Sea." *Reuters*, August 27, 2015. http://www.retuers.com/articles/us-china-defense-idUSKCN0QW1EX20150827.
Roberts, Priscilla, ed. *Behind the Bamboo Curtain: China, Vietnam, and the World beyond Asia*. Stanford, CA: Stanford University Press, 2006.
Robinson, Thomas. "The Sino-Soviet Border Conflicts of 1969: New Evidence Three Decades Later." In *Chinese Warfighting: The PLA Experience since 1949*, edited by Mark A. Ryan, David M. Finkelstein, and Michael A. McDevitt, 198–216. Armonk, NY: M. E. Sharpe, 2003.

Ross, Robert. *Negotiating Co-operation: The United States and China, 1969–1989*. Stanford, CA: Stanford University Press, 1995.
Ryan, Mark A., David M. Finkelstein, and Michael A. McDevitt, eds. *Chinese Warfighting: The PLA Experience since 1949*. Armonk, NY: M. E. Sharpe, 2003.
Saunders, Phillip C., Arthur S. Ding, Andrew Scobell, Andrew N. D. Yang, and Joel Wuthnow, eds. *Chairman Xi Remakes the PLA: Assessing Chinese Military Reforms*. Washington, DC: National Defense University Press, 2019.
Sawyer, Ralph D. *Fire and Water: The Art of Incendiary and Aquatic Warfare in China*. Boulder, CO: Westview, 2004.
———. *The Seven Military Classics of Ancient China*. New York: Basic Books, 2007.
Schell, Orville, and John Delury. *Wealth and Power: China's Long March to the Twenty-First Century*. New York: Random House, 2013.
Schoppa, R. Keith. *Revolution and Its Past: Identities and Change in Modern Chinese History*. 3rd ed. New York: Prentice Hall, 2011.
Scobell, Andrew. *China's Use of Military Force: Beyond the Great Wall and the Long March*. Cambridge: Cambridge University Press, 2003.
Shambaugh, David. *Modernizing China's Military: Progress, Problems, and Prospects*. Berkeley: University of California Press, 2002.
Shambaugh, David, and Richard H. Yang, eds. *China's Military in Transition*. New York: Oxford University Press, 1997.
Sheng, Michael M. *Battling Western Imperialism: Mao, Stalin, and the United States*. Princeton, NJ: Princeton University Press, 1997.
Shen Zhihua and Danhui Li. *After Leaning to One Side: China and Its Allies in the Cold War*. Stanford, CA: Stanford University Press, 2011.
Shen Zhihua and Yafeng Xia. *Mao and the Sino-Soviet Partnership, 1945–1959: A New History*. Lanham, MD: Lexington Books, 2017.
Shih, Hsiu-Chuan, and Flora Wang. "Officials Drop Plan to Visit Diaoyutais." *Taipei Times*, June 18, 2008.
Sunzi. *The Art of War*. In *The Seven Military Classics of Ancient China*, translated and edited by Ralph D. Sawyer. New York: Basic Books, 2007.
Sutter, Robert G. *Foreign Relations of the PRC: The Legacies and Constraints of China's International Politics since 1949*. 2nd ed. Lanham, MD: Rowman & Littlefield, 2018.
Swope, Kenneth, ed. *Warfare in China since 1600*. New York: Routledge, 2005.
Szonyi, Michael. *Cold War Island: Quemoy on the Front Line*. New York: Cambridge University Press, 2008.
Thompson, William R. "The Military Superiority Thesis and the Ascendancy of Western Eurasia." *Journal of World History* 10, no. 1 (Spring 1999): 1–22.
Tian, Xiansheng. "When Chongqing Challenges Beijing: The Bo Xilai Case." In *Evolution of Power: China's Struggle, Survival, and Success*, edited by Xiaobing Li and Xiansheng Tian, 323–50. Lanham, MD: Lexington Books, 2014.
Tsai, Ming-Yen. *From Adversaries to Partners: Chinese and Russian Military Cooperation after the Cold War*. Westport, CT: Praeger, 2003.

Tsou, Tang. *The Embroilment over Quemoy: Mao, Chiang, and Dulles.* Salt Lake City: University of Utah Press, 1959.

Tucker, Nancy Bernkopf. *Strait Talk: United States–Taiwan Relations and the Crisis with China.* Cambridge, MA: Harvard University Press, 2009.

Tyler, Patric. *A Great Wall: Six Presidents and China.* New York: Public Affairs, 1999.

Unschuld, Paul U. *The Fall and Rise of China: Healing the Trauma of History.* London: Reaktion, 2013.

van de Ven, Hans, ed. *Warfare in Chinese History.* Boston: Brill, 2000.

———. "War in the Making of Modern China." In *Modern Asian Studies* 30, no. 4 (October 1996): 737–56.

Wang Guangqun. "China Rises to Top in Ranks of Ship Makers." Xinhua News Agency, May 9, 2011. http://news.xinhuanet.com/english2010/china/2011-05/09/c_13865547.htm.

Wang, Yuan-Kang. *Harmony and War: Confucian Culture and Chinese Power Politics.* New York: Columbia University Press, 2010.

Westad, Odd Arne, ed. *Brothers in Arms: The Rise and Fall of the Sino-Soviet Alliance, 1945–1963.* Washington, DC, and Stanford, CA: Woodrow Wilson Center Press and Stanford University Press, 1998.

Whiting, Allen S. *The Chinese Calculus of Deterrence: India and Indochina.* Ann Arbor: University of Michigan Press, 1975.

Wilson, Jeanne L. *Strategic Partners: Russian-Chinese Relations in the Post-Soviet Era.* Armonk, NY: M. E. Sharpe, 2004.

Worthing, Peter. *A Military History of Modern China: From the Manchu Conquest to Tiananmen Square.* Westport, CT: Praeger, 2007.

Wortzel, Larry M. "China's Foreign Conflicts since 1949." In *A Military History of China*, extended ed., edited by David Graff and Robin Higham, 267–84. Lexington: University Press of Kentucky, 2012.

———. *The Dragon Extends Its Reach: Chinese Military Power Goes Global.* Herndon, VA: Potomac Books, 2013.

Xinhua News Agency. *China's Foreign Relations: A Chronology of Events, 1949–1988.* Beijing: Foreign Languages Press, 1989.

Xiong Guangkai. *International Strategy and Revolution in Military Affairs.* Beijing: Tsinghua University Press, 2003.

———. "On Revolution in Military Affairs." Conference presentation at the "Chinese Scientists' Forum on Humanities," Beijing, April 16, 2003.

Xu Yan. "Chinese Forces and Their Casualties in the Korean War." Translated by Xiaobing Li. *Chinese Historians* 6, no. 2 (1991): 45–64.

Yates, Stephen J. "Why Taiwan's Security Needs to Be Enhanced" (October 25, 1999); "China's Taiwan White Paper Power Play" (February 29, 2000); "Taiwan: A Celebration of Democracy" (March 17, 2000); and "Better US Treatment of Taiwan" (September 11, 2000). Heritage Foundation, www.heritage.org/search?contains=taiwan.

Yick, Joseph K. S. *Making Urban Revolution in China: The CCP-GMD Struggle for Beiping-Tianjin, 1945–1949*. Armonk, NY: M. E. Sharpe, 1995.

Yoshihara, Toshi. *Mao's Army Goes to Sea: The Island Campaigns and the Founding of China's Navy*. Washington, DC: Georgetown University Press, 2022.

Yoshihara, Toshi, and James R. Holmes. *Red Star over the Pacific: China's Rise and the Challenge to U.S. Maritime Strategy*. 2nd ed. Annapolis, MD: Naval Institute Press, 2018.

You, Ji. "Changing Leadership Consensus: The Domestic Context of War Game." In *Across the Taiwan Strait: Mainland China, Taiwan, and the 1995–1996 Crisis*, edited by Suisheng Zhao, 77–98. London: Routledge, 1999.

———. *China's Military Transformation: Politics and War Preparation*. Cambridge: Polity, 2016.

Yu, Bin. "What China Learned from Its 'Foreign War' in Korea." In Li, Millett, and Yu, *Mao's Generals Remember Korea*, 9–29.

Zhai, Qiang. "Beijing and the Vietnam Conflict, 1964–1965: New Chinese Evidence." *Cold War International History Project Bulletin* 6–7 (Winter 1995/1996): 233–50.

———. *China and the Vietnam War, 1950–1975*. Chapel Hill: University of North Carolina Press, 2000.

———. "Reassessing China's Role in the Vietnam War: Some Mysteries Explored." In *China and the United States: A New Cold War History*, edited by Xiaobing Li and Hongshan Li, 97–118. New York: University Press of America, 1998.

Zhang, Jie, and Xiaobing Li, eds. *Social Transition in China*. Lanham, MD: University Press of America, 1998.

Zhang, Shu Guang. "Beijing's Aid to Hanoi and the United States–China Confrontations, 1964–1968." In *Behind the Bamboo Curtain: China, Vietnam, and the World beyond Asia*, edited by Priscilla Roberts, 259–88. Stanford, CA: Stanford University Press, 2006.

———. *Deterrence and Strategic Culture: Chinese American Confrontations, 1949–1958*. Ithaca, NY: Cornell University Press, 1992.

———. *Mao's Military Romanticism: China and the Korean War, 1950–1953*. Lawrence: University Press of Kansas, 1995.

Zhang, Xiaoming. "Air Combat for the People's Republic: The People's Liberation Army Air Force in Action, 1949–1969." In *Chinese Warfighting: The PLA Experience since 1949*, edited by Mark A. Ryan, David M. Finkelstein, and Michael A. McDevitt, 270–300. New York: M. E. Sharpe, 2003.

———. *Deng Xiaoping's Long War: The Military Conflict between China and Vietnam, 1979–1991*. Chapel Hill: University of North Carolina Press, 2015.

———. "High-Altitude Duel: The CIA's U-2 Spy Plane Overflights and China's Air Defense Force, 1961–1968." *Journal of Military History* 86, no. 1 (January 2022): 132–59.

---. *Red Wings over the Yalu: China, the Soviet Union, and the Air War in Korea.* College Station: Texas A&M University Press, 2002.
Zhao, Suisheng, ed. *Across the Taiwan Strait: Mainland China, Taiwan, and the 1995–1996 Crisis.* London: Routledge, 1999.
Zhu, Fang. *Gun Barrel Politics: Party-Army Relations in Mao's China.* Boulder, CO: Westview Press, 1998.
Zubok, Vladislav M. "The Mao-Khrushchev Conversation, July 31–August 3, 1958 and October 2, 1959." In "New Evidence on the Cold War in Asia," *Cold War International History Project Bulletin* 12–13 (Fall/Winter 2001): 239–64.

INDEX

2-4 Agreement, 55-56, 87
6-4 Agreement, 52-53, 54-55
6-4 Tiananmen Incident, 13, 162, 164, 174; demonstrations, 163; firing on students, 165; martial law, 163
8-6 Naval Battle, 107
8-23 Artillery Battle, 76-78, 80

Abrams, Creighton, 122
Aden, Gulf of, 186, 187-88, 189, 190
ADIZ (air defense identification zone), 194, 195
Africa, 6, 188, 190; coast, 13, 186-87, 193
air battles, 62-63, 79-80, 100, 101-102, 105
aircraft, Chinese, 16, 84; bombers, 33; C-75 bombers, 93, 102, 168, 173; coastal transits, 37; exercises, 173; fighters, 33, 80, 168, 173; H-5, 100; H-6, 148, 171, 194; J-5, 80, 99, 104; J-6, 100, 103, 104; J-7, 100; J-8, 106, 177; JH-7, 155, 171; La-9, 32; MiG-9, 32; MiG-15, 32, 71, 85, 96-97, 100, 101; MiG-15bis, 63; MiG-17, 79-80, 99, 101-4; MiG-19, 100, 105; naval planes, 54; Russian-made, 37, 56, 99, 170; SH-5, 171; Su-30, 170, 194; Su-32, 170; Su-35, 195; torpedo bombers, 37, 56, 80; training, 56; Tu-2, 32, 70; WP-5, 100; Yer-10, 32; Yun-5, 99
aircraft, Taiwanese, F-47 bomber, 61, 63, 101; F-84, 79-80, 86, 100; F-84G, 79; F-86, 80, 101-2; P-51, 62; P2V, 102-3; PT-5, 99; PT-6, 100; RB-57A, 102; RB-57D, 102; RF-84, 79-80; RF-101A, 102, 103-4
aircraft, U.S., 125; A-6, 125, 127; A-7, 127; AQM-34A, 105; EP-3, 177-78; F-105s, 124-26; P-3C, 150; spy planes, 100, 102-6, 176-78; U-2, 102; UAV, 105-6
aircraft carrier, 74, 140, 154, 170, 173-4
Aleutian Island, 153
amphibious landing, 12, 15, 29-30, 31, 37, 43, 44, 53, 150, 196; exercises, 173-74; joint operation, 67-70, 71-72; planning, 58, 60, 61-62; training, 31, 60
Andong Naval Academy, 23
Anshan (DD 101), 52,
Antarctica, 153; expeditions of, 155
anti-aircraft artillery (AAA), 32, 33, 56, 89, 161; 37-mm guns, 39, 123; 57-mm guns, 123; 75-mm cannons, 123; 100-mm cannons, 123; casualties of, 125; friendly fire, 80; in Vietnam, 122-24; regiments, 57-58; technology, 125
Anti-Japanese War. See Resistant War against Japan.
Argentina, 172
Art of War, The, 2
artillery, 73-75, 76-78, 84; 102-mm howitzers, 74; 122-mm howitzers, 74; 152-mm howitzers, 74; 155-mm cannons, 74; battles of, 76-78; losses of, 77, 84
ARVN (Army of Vietnam, South), 126, 134, 150
Australia, 1, 26, 162, 170, 191

Baiyanshan Island, 68-69
Bangladesh, 169
Beidaihe, 75
Beijing, 9, 12, 29, 32, 72, 73, 82, 85, 175, 178, 184-85, 194; Military Region of, 172

Belov, Georgiy, 32
Belt and Road Initiative (BRI), 10, 193
Bohai Shipyard, 138
Britain, 20, 26, 162, 170; *Ark Royal*, 181; *Aurora*, 20; *Bendigo*, 26; *Bowmanville*, 26; Greenwich Royal Naval College, 23; navy of, 19, 20, 181, 191, 195
Brunei, 191
Bush, George W., 176
Byzantine Empire, 4

Caishi, Battle of, 5
Cambodia, 122
Canada, 162, 170, 182, 191
Cao Cao, 3
CCYL (Chinese Communist Youth League), 24
Central Military Commission (CMC), 18, 21, 52, 57, 58, 67-68, 94, 141, 155, 178; order of, 65, 84, 158, 171-72; planning meetings of, 72-73
Changchun, 176; *Changchun* (DD 102), 52, 88
Changsha, 26
Chen Genfa, 10
Chen Shui-bian, 157
Chen Weiwen, 157, 158-59
Chen Yi, 11, 21, 35, 50
Chengdu, 80, 94
Chenjia, Battle of, 5
Chenshan Island, 47
Chi Haotian, 159, 167, 172-73
Chibi (Red Cliff), Battle of, 3
Chile, 169, 170
China, People's Republic of (PRC), 9, 43, 142, 157, 184, 192; defense minister of, 22, 52, 94, 150, 161, 167, 171, 172; GNP, 160, 166; Maritime Law, 167; relations with Taiwan, 175-76; supply to Vietnam, 122

China, Republic of (ROC), 1, 157; government, 11, 20
China National Offshore Oil Corporation (CNOOC), 183
Chinese Civil War, 12, 15, 26, 30, 36, 60, 152, 181
Chinese Communist Party (CCP), 9, 26, 192; Seventh National Congress, 33; Eighth National Congress, 117; Ninth National Congress, 118; 19th national Congress, 193; 1959 Lushan Conference, 86, 93-94; membership, 23; Party Center, 12, 17, 30, 31, 141, 160-61, 163, 172; purge by, 23; party system, 24
Chinese People's Revolution Military Museum, 67
Chinese People's Volunteer Force (CPVF), 59, 108, 152
Chongqing, 20, 23, 27, 30
Chosin Reservoir, Battle of, 80, 152
Clinton, Bill, 173
Clinton, Hillary, 184
coastal artillery, 37, 39, 152; 100-mm cannons, 74; 105-mm howitzers, 74; 122-mm guns, 74; 130-mm cannons, 38, 56, 78, 81; 152-mm howitzers, 74; 180-mm guns, 56; 1958 Taiwan Strait Crisis and, 73, 74, 76-78, 84; bombardment by, 70, 76
Cold War, 2, 11, 67, 84, 85, 166, 192, 193
Commission of Science, Technology, and Industry for National Defense (CSTIND), 144, 151-52, 153
commercial fishing, 47, 59, 61, 86
cruiser, 64, 74, 80
Cui Yudong, 108
Cultural Revolution, 24, 117-18, 125, 131, 137-38, 142, 145-46, 147, 153

Da Nang, 106, 126
Dachen Islands, 48, 58–72; attack at, 65; defense of, 70; garrison of, 62; withdrawal from, 72
Dalian, 37, 56, 170; shipyard of, 55, 188,
Dalian Naval College, 24, 57
Dalian Naval Shipbuilding College, 147, 181
Deng Hua, 31
Deng Xiaoping, 10, 12, 160, 164, 166; Cultural Revolution and, 117, 128, 142, 163; death of, 165; navy and, 112, 134, 140, 144, 145, 146–8, 153; reform by, 141, 143–44, 160
Deng Zhaoxiang, 20; career of, 23
Dengbu Island, landing of, 15, 28
destroyers, 37, 64, 74, 116, 132–34, 136, 140, 145, 151–52, 168, 179; 25-mm guns, 136; 130-mm cannons, 136; exercises, 173–74, 180; guided-missile, 130, 136, 144, 147–48, 155, 179; Luda-class, 136; Luoyang-class, 169, 187; operations of, 149, 158–59; Russian-made, 52; Sovremenny-class, 169; training by Russians, 53–54, 88–89
Diaoyu Island, 183-4. See also Senkaku Island.
Ding Yiping, 180
Dingling Island, 89
disputed islands, 166, 184; in ECS, 183-4; in SCS, 12, 119, 131
Djibouti, 191
Dongji Island, 58, 65; counterattacks, 63; landing of, 59–62, 65
Dongshan Island, 107, 109, 112, 173; Battle of, 48–49
Dongting, 81
Du Jingchen, 187–88
Dulles, John Foster, 64, 72
Dun Xingyun, 40

East Asia, 51, 85, 153, 184
East China Military Region (ECMR), 15, 22, 58; air force of, 59–60; intelligence of, 66
East China Naval Academy, 24, 25; Soviet advisors at, 25
East China Sea (ECS), 10, 29, 47, 58-60, 68, 72, 74–76, 166, 183–85, 193, 194
East Chongwu, Battle of, 107, 114–16
East Sea Fleet (ESF), 49, 51, 80–81, 84, 94–96, 106-7, 109, 114–15, 146, 151, 160, 181; AAA troops of, 123, 125; exercises, 173
ECMR Navy, 18, 21, 22, 24, 42, 50, 58, 59–60, 80; anti-blockade, 46–47; establishment of, 15, 21; in the 1954-55 Taiwan Strait Crisis, 61–62; ships of, 25
Ecuador, 191
EEZ (exclusive economic zone), 183-84
Egypt, 180
Eisenhower, Dwight, 49; administration of, 77; nuclear threat of, 72
escort ships, 66, 131
ex-ROC naval personnel, 16, 19, 23; distrust, 24; purged of, 24; realignment, 24; recruitment of, 22, 58; controlling ships, 18; as instructors, 24

Fang Qiang, 46, 53; career of, 57
Fang Zhengping, 112
first island chain, 153
First Naval Academy, 30
First Naval Aviation Academy, 39
fishermen, 61
France, 162, 170, 180, 181; navy of, 180, 191, 195
frigates, 57, 60, 61, 62, 64, 80, 81, 131, 133, 135–36, 140, 151-2, 168, 179; 18th Brigade, 94; 20-mm guns,

274 Index

83; 37-mm guns, 135; 40-mm guns, 83; 76-mm cannons, 83; 100-mm cannons, 135; Jiangkai II, 170; operations, 157, 158–59, 188; ship-to-ship missiles, 130, 135, 188
Fujian, 73, 74, 75, 79–81
Fujian Front Command, 73, 76–77, 78, 79, 81, 84, 115, 145; planning meetings of, 74
Fushun (DD 104), 52
Fuzhou, 79–80; *Fuzhou*, 169
Fuzhou Military Region, 114, 115

Gang of Four, 131, 141, 142
Gao Island, 66
Gao Shaoying, 104
Gao Xizeng, 149
Geneva Conference, 67
Geng Biao, 150
Germany, 170, 191
GMD (Guomindang), 15, 43, 78
Gorshkov, Sergei, 6, 140
Great Leap Forward Movement, 51, 85, 93–94
Greece, 180
Gu Weijun, 62
Guan Zhichao, 11
Guangdong, 73, 79
Guangzhou, 24, 43, 44, 45, 108–9, 161, 174; *Guangzhou*, 26, 61, 145; Military Region of, 49, 108; Riverine Defense Command of, 18, 24, 43, 44–46, 49, 59; shipyard, 55
guerrilla warfare, 42
Guishan, 45
Gulf of Aden, 13
gunboats, 47, 48, 49, 57, 60, 62, 64, 82, 83; brigade of, 80–81
Guo Baolan, 127

Haikou, 105; *Haikou*, 186, 187
Haimen, 108, 109

Hainan Island, 105, 106, 108, 121, 122, 126, 131, 156, 168, 176–8; defense of, 27, 31, 43–44; landing of, 15, 30–31, 33, 43–44
Haiphong, 127
Han dynasty, 2, 3
Hangzhou, 32; *Hangzhou*, 169
Hanoi, 121, 123, 126, 142–43
Hao Bocun, 77
Harbin, 168–69, 180
He Long, 11; navy and, 113, 114
helicopters, 152, 155, 168, 188; HQ-7 missile, 188; HQ-16 missiles, 188; Seahawk, 180; Z-8, 171; Z-9, 171, 188
Hengyang, 94–5
Hoblit, Jerry N., 125–26
Ho Chi Minh, 119
Ho Chi Minh Trail, 119–20
Ho Chi Minh Trail at Sea, 122
Hong Kong, 26, 44, 161, 162, 175, 178, 186
Hong Xuezhi, 43, 44, 46
Hou Zhenlu, 11
Hu Jiaheng, 107, 109–10, 111–12, 114
Hu Jintao, 13, 167, 178, 183; navy and, 178–79, 180, 181–82
Hu Yanlin, 61, 131, 155, 157
Hu Yaobang, 163
Hu Zongnan, 48
Hua Guofeng, 141–42
Hua Keyi, 83
Huang Chaotian, 59, 60; in the 1954–55 Taiwan Strait Crisis, 67–69, 71
Huang Kecheng, 94
Huang'an, 19–20, 26
Huanghe, 26
Huangshan, 188
Hue, 126
Hui'an, 26
Huludao, 41, 138

India, 1, 6, 80, 169, 182, 191, 195
Indian Ocean, 154, 180
Indonesia, 170, 191
Indo-Pacific region, 1, 10
Italy, 170, 191

Jamaica, 191
Japan, 1, 56, 153, 162, 176, 183, 184–85, 194, 197; 19th Artillery Regiment, 74; navy, 19, 26; pirates of, 4
Ji Xingwen, 76
Ji'an, 26
Jian Ming, 39
Jiang Jieshi, 17, 22, 27, 43, 48, 62, 72, 86, 107; Jinmen defense and, 73, 75–78, 84; navy and, 113
Jiang Qing, 117, 131, 141
Jiang Weiguo, 30, 62
Jiang Weilie, 195
Jiang Zemin, 13, 141, 151, 166, 178, 193; 1995–96 Taiwan Strait Crisis and, 170, 172–75; two transformations, 167; Hainan Island Incident and, 176-8; military reform, 167, 171, 172; navy and, 168, 170
Jiangnan Shipyard, 136
Jianmen, 107–9, 110, 111, 114
Jiefang, 45
Jiaoxian, 40
Jilin (DD 101), 52
Jin dynasty, 5,
Ji'nan Military Region, 49, 152
Jingangshan Radar Station, 109, 111–12
Jinmen Island, 48, 64, 109; 1958 Taiwan Strait Crisis and, 72–76, 77–79; blockade of, 72–74, 76, 84; bombardment of, 64-5, 73–76, 102, 146; defense of, 27, 30, 73, 76; landing of: 15, 28–9, 31, 74; Liaoluo Bay, 76; supply of, 73, 76–77, 79, 82–83
Joint Institute of Nuclear Submarine, 137
joint operation, 58–60, 61, 81; joint exercises, 173–74, 180–81, 195, 196–97

Kaifeng, 61
Kalasovski, Mikhail, 38, 39
Kang Zhiqiang, 84
Kerry, John, 185
KGB, 57,
Khrushchev, Nikita, 55, 75, 85, 87, 89, 90–92
KMT, *See* GMD.
Kong Zhaonian, 108–12; career of, 109
Korea, 10, 51, 64, 152, 186, 193
Korea, North (DPRK), 33, 142; North Korean People's Army, 59
Korea, South (ROK), 1, 182
Korean War, 12, 16, 33, 37, 42, 46, 48, 100, 108, 193; Armistice of, 50, 72; veterans, 59, 70, 80, 86; weapons from, 123
Kublai Khan, 3
Kunming, 94–95
Kuznestsov Naval Academy, 57

Lai Sanyang, 145
landing ships, 62, 71, 81–82, 152, 173; 20-mm guns, 82; 40-mm guns, 82
Langjishan Island, 48
Lee Teng-hui, 172–73, 175–76
Li Chuqun, 159
Li Fuxiang, 133
Li Huaizhang, 44
Li Keru, 40,
Li Yaowen, 159, 163; career of, 152–53, 165
Li Zhuan, 107, 110–11

Li Zuopeng, 86, 98–99, 112; career of, 97–98, 130; Cultural Revolution and, 118, 128–29
Liancheng, 79
Lianyunguang, 20
Liaoning, 180
Liao Zhengguo, 129
Liaoluo Bay, 78
Lighting, Operation, 77
Lin Biao, 11, 29, 30, 75; Cultural Revolution and, 117, 128–29; death of, 130; defense minister, 97, 99; fall of, 118; rise of, 86, 94
Lin Hu, 79, 100
Lin Weixian, 71
Lin Wenhu, 45
Lin Zun, 20–1
Lingfu, 23
Lingjiang, 69
Liu Bocheng, 11, 56
Liu Chengsi, 96–8
Liu Daosheng, 39, 42, 104, 105, 149–50; career of, 35–36, 57
Liu Guangkai, 113
Liu Huaqing, 6–7, 11, 140–41, 161, 168; as PLAN commander, 141, 151–54; blue-water navy, 140, 152, 153–54; career of, 57, 141, 151–52; Deng Xiaoping and, 151; Hu Jintao and, 178–79; Jiang Zemin and, 151, 166–67, 169; plans of, 153–54, 155; Tiananmen Incident and, 163–66; visions of, 154, 170
Liu Jinkun, 190
Liu Liankun, 174–75
Liu Shaoqi, 10, 30; Cultural Revolution and, 117, 128; navy and, 112; Vietnam and, 120,
Liu Weihuan, 109
Liu Zigeng, 148,
local war, 2, 51, 58, 85, 143, 168
Long March, 138, 154

Luo Ruiqing, 103, 106; navy and, 116; Vietnam and, 119–20
Luo Shunchu, 35, 37, 42; career of, 36, 57
Luoyang, 26
Luqiao, 97, 104
Lushun Naval Base, 55, 56, 151, 156
LVT, 78–79, 84

Ma Guansan, 59, 61; career of, 60; in the 1954–55 Taiwan Strait Crisis, 65–71
Ma Ying-jeou, 1, 157
Mahan, Alfred T, 6, 140
Mai Xiande, 111, 113
Malaysia, 157, 191
Manchu: 7,
Mao Zedong: 8, 10, 20, 27, 93–94, 104, 142, 192, 193; 1954–55 Taiwan Strait Crisis and, 67–68; 1958 Taiwan Strait Crisis and, 72–77, 84; assassination of, 118; critique against Lin, 118, Cultural Revolution and, 117; death of, 129, 131, 141; the Korean War and, 12, 35; landing and, 29, 30–32, 33; navy and, 16, 18, 21, 35, 40, 42, 63, 105, 112, 130–31, 137, 153; Taiwan and, 35; Russian relations and, 32, 33, 37, 85–86, 87, 90–91, 102; strategy of, 50, 52; U.S. armed forces and, 64; Vietnam and, 119–20, 127, 134
Mao Yuanxin, 141
Maritime interests, 141, 144, 153, 166
maritime sovereignty, 144, 166
marine survey ships, 149
Mazu Island, 48, 81
McKnight, Terence E., 188
Meijian, 82
Meisong, 81
Mexico, 169, 170, 172, 182
Middle East, 72

mine layers, 152
minesweepers, 61, 132-34, 136, 151-52; manufacturing of, 138; model-311, 126, 127; model-312, 126, 127
minesweeping, 47-48, 127-28
Ming dynasty, 3
Ministry of Foreign Affairs, 152, 178
missiles, 56, 87, 135-36, 151-52, 168; ballistic, 136, 148, 154, 155, 170, 176; boats, 136, 152; CSS-N-3, 154; Dongfeng-15, 173, 174; guided, 130; Hongqi-8, 151; Hongying-5, 151; HQ-9; HQ-16, 170; Julang-1, 149; Julang-2, 170; Qianwei-1, 151; SAMs, 125, 169-70; Shrike, 125-6; Sidewinder, 101-102; SY-2, 154; tests, 173-75; Vympel K-13, 102; YJ-82, 171, 179
Mongols, 5
Moscow, 12, 52, 56, 73, 89, 91

Nancang, 170
Nanchang, 103; *Nanchang*, 25
Nancongshan Island, 47
Nanjing, 20, 21, 24, 32
Nanjing Military Region, 49
Nanjing Institute for Foreign Languages, 56-57
Nanjing Naval Academy, 21, 36, 37, 38
Nanjishan Island, 72
National People's Congress (NPC), 167, 178
Naval Aeronautical Engineering Institute, 147
Naval Amphibious Warfare Institute, 147
Naval Aviation College, 147
naval battles, 49, 61, 65-66, 69, 109-11, 115-16, 131-34; ships sunk, 48, 68, 69, 81, 82, 111, 116, 134
Naval Command University, 43, 138, 147, 171, 179, 191

naval exercises, 168
Naval Officer Academy, 147
Naval University of Engineering, 147
Naval Submarine Academy, 147
Naval War College, 10
Ngo Dinh Diem, 119
Nie Fangzhi, 59-60, 61-62; career of, 59; 1954-55 Taiwan Strait Crisis and, 67-70; 1958 Taiwan Strait Crisis and, 73, 75, 79
Nie Jukui, 149
Nie Rongzhen, 11, 33, 103, 137-38
Ningbo, 40, 89
Nixon, Richard, 126-27
NLF (Viet Cong), 119-20, 121-22
Normandy, 69
North Sea Fleet (NSF), 23, 49, 51, 103, 147, 151; AAA troops of, 123; HQ, 56, 156, 180
North Vietnamese Army (NVA), 121; Air Defense-Air Force Command, 123; navy of, 121, 128
Northeast China Military Region, 21
nuclear submarine, 89-90, 130, 136, 137, 148-49, 152, 155, 168; exercises, 173-74; Han-class, 138, 154; technology of, 144, 151, 170; Xia-class, 154
nuclear weapons, 136; deterrence of, 2, 136-7

Obama, Barack, 184, 185
oceanic-going development, 141
oceanic rescue vessels, 149
oceanic territory, 167
Okinawa, 69, 180
Opium War, 6

Pacific Ocean, 138-39, 148, 149, 150, 153, 154, 170, 174, 180, 185; Western, 194, 195
Pakistan, 180, 195

Palm Island, 133
Pang Ta-wei, 174–75
Paracel Islands, 119, 131, 147, 148–49, 155, 195; Battle of, 119, 132–35, 150, 156, 157
patrol (PC) boats, 61, 86, 109–12, 131; 25-mm guns, 108, 110; 37-mm guns, 108, 110; 41st Brigade, 108; 75-mm cannons, 108; manufacturing of, 114; operations, 115
Pearl River, 43, 44
Peng Dehuai, 11, 52, 73, 87, 89, 91; 1958 Taiwan Strait Crisis and, 74–76, 80; fall of, 85–86, 93–94
Peng Deqing, 73, 75, 80–83
Penghu, 174
People's Armed Police (PAP), 171–72
people's war, 89, 143
Peru, 169, 170
Philippines, 153, 157, 170
Pingtan Island, 79–80
pirates, 186–90, 191
PLA (People's Liberation Army), 1, 58, 85–86, 89, 138; Academy of Military Science (AMS), 21, 156, 180; active defense, 2, 10; area denial, 153; assistance to North Vietnam, 121, 142; budget, 141, 144, 160, 166, 171; commercialization, 161–63, 171–72; corruption, 162–3, 172; Department of General Armaments, 174; Department of General Logistics, 172; Department of General Political Tasks, 161; Department of General Staff, 22, 58, 75, 97, 104, 114, 119–20, 131, 161; exercises, 175; high command, 17, 33, 94, 95, 117, 149, 173; intelligence, 175; Martial Law Force, 163–66; modernization, 87, 153; purges of, 94, 118; reform, 12, 88, 140, 143–44, 153; supply to Vietnam, 121

PLA Air Force (PLAAF), 16, 50, 51, 56, 86, 99, 121, 194; First Division, 62; Second Division, 62, 63; Fourth Division, 79–80; Fourth Regiment, 62; Sixth Regiment, 62; Ninth Division, 80; 20th Bomber Regiment, 68; 31st AAA Division, 123; 61st AAA Division, 123; Air Force Academy, 96, 171; bombers, 173; air raids, 71–72; deployments of, 73, 79, 95; exercises, 173–4; fighters, 173; pilots, 33, 86, 100; USAF and, 58
PLA Army, 9, 16, 43, 50, 51, 121; Second Division: 46; Second Field Army: 38, 41; Third Field Army: 15, 21, 25, 28–29, 33, 59, 146; Fourth Field Army, 29, 30, 33, 38, 43, 46, 97; Seventh Army Group, 33; Eighth Army Group, 33; Eighth Route Army, 19, 36, 60, 132; Ninth Army Group, 33, 70, 80; 10th Army Group, 28, 41, 74, 145; 11th Army Group, 38; 12th Army Group, 18, 19, 35–36; 13th Army Group, 33, 46; 15th Army, 163, 164, 165; 15th Army Group, 30–31, 43–44, 97; 19th Army Group, 33; 20th Army, 59, 63, 164; 21st Army, 28; 22nd Army, 80; 23rd Army, 70, 80; 26th Army, 164; 27th Army, 59, 80; 28th Army, 28, 29, 164; 31st Army, 156; 35th Army, 25, 181; 38th Army, 164, 165, 172; 39th Army, 164; 40th Army, 31, 32, 36, 43–44, 164; 43rd Army: 31, 32, 43–44; 44th Army: 46; 54th Army, 164; 60th Division, 62, 63, 71; 61st Division: 28; 63rd Army, 164; 91st Division, 173; 115th Division, 97; 116th Division, 164; 129th Division, 151; 173rd Division: 46; 178th Regiment, 71;

180th Regiment, 62, 71; Capital First Division, 164; New Fourth Army, 19, 80, 181; landing troops of, 133-34, 173-74
PLA Combat Engineering Corps, 121
PLA Marine Corps, 150-51, 163, 196
PLA Navy (PLAN), 1, 35, 44, 58, 61, 89, 121, 134-35, 163, 195, 196; annual budget, 13, 52; antipiracy operations, 13, 186-89, 189-90; auxiliary vessels, 149, 152; aviation: 36, 39-40; Aviation Engineering University, 3; birth of, 15, 21; bombers, 68, 152; budget, 160, 166; commanders of, 15, 18, 39-40; close combat: 45; combat tactics, 42-3; commercialization, 161-3; doctrine of, 15; exercises, 173-74, 180-1 history, 7, 12, 88; HQ, 42, 53, 108, 114, 118, 129, 131, 150, 163, 177, 179; light navy policy, 15-16, 36-37, 42, 51, 52-53; modernization, 144, 153; operations, 148-50, 192; purges of, 118; Russian technology, 87-88, 119; shipping to Vietnam, 121; strategy, 37, 86, 153; tactics, 65-67; training, 57; technology, 154, 155, 167, 192; warships of, 169-70, 196; world-class navy, 8-9
PLA Strategic Force, 173-74; exercises, 175
PLAN Air Force (PLANAF), 57, 58, 99, 101, 121, 161, 171, 177, 196; First Division, 40; Second Division, 100, 101; Fourth Division, 101, 103, 104, 105; Sixth Division, 96, 97; Ninth Division, 176; 16th Division, 101-102; 18th Division, 79; air battles, 61, 100; air raids, 70; bombers, 57, 101, 173; defectors of, 96-98; exercises, 173-74; fighters, 40, 57, 60, 68, 152, 155, 173, 176-77; in the 1954-55 Taiwan Strait Crisis, 60-61, 68-70; in the 1958 Taiwan Strait Crisis, 81, 84; pilots of, 68, 79-80, 96, 100, 102-3, 171, 176; patrol of, 148, 176-77; recon planes, 152; torpedo bomber division, 40; training, 101
PLAN Marine Corps, 59-60; First Division, 60
Politburo, 17, 50, 117, 180; meetings of, 64, 127, 179; Standing Committee of, 57, 75, 141, 166
Polynesia, 191
Portugal, 180
princelings, 161
prisoner of war (POW), 10
Prueher, Joseph, 178

Qiandaohu, 189
Qiao Xingyi, 124-25
Qing dynasty, 3; army, 6; navy, 7
Qingdao, 20, 24, 26, 38-40, 52, 53-54, 104, 144, 174; *Qingdao*, 180
Qingdao Naval Base (QNB), 18, 23, 38, 39-41, 51, 147, 154, 180
Quadrilateral Security Dialogue, 1

Rao Shousheng, 147
Red Army, 18, 21, 35, 59, 70, 80, 97, 108, 145, 151
Red Guards, 117-18, 128-29
Resistant War against Japan, 19, 21, 60
ROC Air Force: 27, 32, 87, 97, 111-12; Black Bat Squadron, 102-3; engagements, 62-63, 100-2; fighters, 79; raids, 18, 27-28, 32, 60, 63, 101; patrol, 43
ROC Army, 48; Ninth Division, 76; 18th Army, 29; 19th Army, 29; 25th Regiment (ROC), 76; 27th Regiment, 76

ROC Navy, 27, 28, 32, 46, 64, 106, 116; First Fleet, 19; Second Fleet, 20, 24, 25, 27–28, 107; Third Fleet, 45–46; anti-GMD rebellions, 19; attacks, 43; blockade, 44; *Changzhi*, 25; convoy, 82; defections of, 19, 20–21; destroyer, 61; frigates, 26, 61; in the 1954–55 Taiwan Strait Crisis, 66–68; in the 1958 Taiwan Strait Crisis, 81–82, 84; patrol boats, 61; training, 20; warships, 26, 46, 48–49, 63, 69–70, 76, 108; *Zhonghai*, 81–82; *Zhongquan*, 68
Rolling Thunder, Operation, 112–23
Roughhead, Gary, 181
Rong Wen, 5
Ruijin, 26, 61; sunk of, 63, 65
Russia, 56, 169, 175; navy of, 180, 181, 190, 191, 197

Sakhalin Islands, 153
San Diego, 170
Sanmen Bay, 60, 101
Sanmen Island, 46
Sanya, 105, 187
sea power, 141, 153, 166, 167
searchlight, 77
Second Industrial Ministry, 137, 144
second island chain, 148, 153
Senkaku Island, 184, 194. *See also* Diaoyudao.
Shanghai, 21, 25, 26, 32, 40, 80, 95, 106, 115, 116, 129, 141, 155, 161, 180, 187; harbor of, 47–48, 150
Shantou, 79, 108, 109
Shantoushan Island, 47
Shao Jianming, 48
Shao Zhengzong, 174–75
Shen Jinlong, 196
Shenyang, 32; *Shenyang*, 20, 26
Shenzhen, 188–9; 37-mm AAA guns, 189; 100-mm cannons, 189
Shi Yunsheng, 179; career of, 171
Shi Zhenshan, 103
Shijiazhuang, 179
shipbuilding, 41–2, 119, 135–36, 139, 144, 182, 186; development, 152, 179; Russian assistance, 54–55, 87
shipping, 47, 86
Shu Jicheng, 105, 106
Sicily, 69
Sihanouk harbor, 122
Singapore, 162, 180
Sino-American Ambassador Talks, 72, 75
Sino-Soviet Friendship and Mutual Assistance Treaty, 32
Sino-Soviet joint naval exercises, 53, 57
Sino-Soviet split, 55, 85, 87, 90–91, 92–93, 106, 125, 136, 137, 194
Sino-US relations, normalization, 84, 142
Sino-Vietnam Border War, 142–3, 156, 157
Sixth Industrial (Shipbuilding) Ministry, 137, 144, 151
Smoot, Roland, 77
Somali, 186–89
Song dynasty, 3; navy, 4–5; Southern, 5
South Africa, 170, 195
South-Central Military Region Navy (SCMRN), 42, 45–46, 51, 58
South China Sea (SCS): 1, 2, 10, 29, 119, 131–5, 148, 150, 155, 156, 166, 176, 193, 195, 197
South Sea Fleet (SSF), 49, 51, 58, 80–81, 109, 112, 145, 148–49, 176, 177; AAA troops of, 123; HQ, 53, 108, 110, 171, 181; operations, 148, 156, 157, 158–59, 170, 186; training, 150–51, 168; warships, 177
Southeast Asia, 6, 119
Soviet Air Force, 56, 61; divisions in China, 32, 33

Soviet Naval Advisory Group, 32, 38
Soviet Navy, 40, 56, 69; Naval Academy, 36; Leningrad Military and Political Academy, 18, 35; Leningrad Naval Academy, 94; technology, 41; Voroshilov Naval Command Academy, 57
Soviet Union, 26, 30, 32, 41, 56, 192; advisors: 17, 25, 30, 37–39, 52–53, 56, 61–62, 69–70, 87–89, 90, 92–93; aid, 16, 32, 35, 37, 52, 87; archives, 10; collapse, 13, 166; joint fleet, 90–91; model, 52, 99; naval assistance, 27, 30, 37, 87; Red Army, 38, 39, 56, 69, 89; technology: 16, 37, 52, 86, 101, 135–36; training in, 37, 88, 151
Spain, 191
speed boats, 81–82; 37-mm guns, 83
Spratly Island, 148, 156–57, 195; Battle of, 151, 158–59
Spring and Autumn, 3
Stalin, Joseph, 30, 37, 39, 50, 87
State Council, 155, 158
Su Yu, 29, 31, 33, 64, 82
Su Zhenhua, 11, 99, 130–1, 134, 140, 141–42, 145; Cultural Revolution and, 118, 131
submarine, 16, 36, 138–9, 168, 176, 196; 22nd Squadron, 94; Kilo-class, 169, 179; manufacturing, 56, 136, 151, 170, 179; Ming-class, 136; *Romeo*-class, 136; Russian-made, 37, 40, 54, 94; sinking of, 94–96; Song-class, 169, 179; training, 40, 96, 179; Yuan-class, 179
Submarine Academy, 156, 179
submarine hunters, 80–81, 82, 107, 136, 151; 20-mm guns, 83, 107, 110; 40-mm guns, 107, 110; 73rd Squadron, 109; 76-mm cannons, 83, 107, 110; in battles, 132–35

Sui dynasty, 4
Sun Quan, 3
support ships, 56
Sunzi (Sun-tzu), 2

Taihangshan, 26
Taihe, 45
Taipei, 27, 67, 104, 173, 175
Taiping, 65–66; sunk of, 67, 68
Taiping Island, 157
Taisheng, 81–82
Taiwan, 35, 43, 77, 153, 161, 162, 166, 174, 186; defense, 27; government of, 72; intelligence, 174–75; landing on, 1, 33, 197; liberation of, 64; psychological warfare of, 97–98
Taiwan Strait, 10, 15, 16, 27, 49, 64, 100, 193, 197; 1954–55 Crisis, 12, 51, 58, 65–69, 146; 1958 Crisis, 12, 51, 72–79, 81–84, 101–2, 146; 1995–96 Crisis, 170, 172–75; U.S. and, 34, 73; warships, 26, 46, 48
Taiwan-U.S. Mutual Defense Treaty, 51
Tang dynasty, 3, 4, 7
Tang Jiahua, 150
Tang Jiaxuan, 178
Tang Tingrang, 66
Tanzhushan Island, 47
Tao Hanzhang, 110
Tao Yong, 70, 84, 95–96; death of, 118, 129
Thailand, 126, 169
third island chain, 153
Three Kingdoms, 3
Tibet, 33, 166
Tie Jianhai, 66–67
Tonga, 191
Tonkin, Gulf of, 106, 120, 121, 148, 156
torpedo (PT) boats, 16, 36, 41, 80, 86, 108, 152; First Squadron,

68–69, 82; 11th Brigade, 108; 31st Squadron, 65–67, 82; brigade of, 80–81; collision, 83; fleet of, 52; manufacturing of, 42, 136; operations, 60, 65–69, 81–82, 109, 110–11, 115; Russian-made, 54, 65; squadrons of, 62; training, 23, 41, 81
Toumen Island, 62
tributary system, 6
Truman, Harry, 34
Tuojiang, 83
Turkey, 180

Ukraine, 170, 180
UN Force, 16, 125
U.S. (United States), 20, 26, 74, 161, 169, 170, 175, 184, 192, 194; government of, 72, 142, 172, 177–78, 184–85, 198; Hainan Island Incident and, 176–78; Taiwan policy, 33, 72
USAF (U.S. Air Force), 68, 102, 196; Fourth Air Force, 102; information on, 121, 126, 177–78; planes of, 68, 104–5, 106
U.S. armed forces, 35, 58; Taiwan Patrol Force, 77
U.S. Congress, 185; 1955 Formosa Resolution of, 72
U.S.-Japanese Mutual Defense Treaty, 184
USN (U.S. Navy), 51, 64, 119, 167, 177, 191; Seventh Fleet, 34, 49, 64, 68, 74, 116; assistant operations, 72, 78–79; *Boxer*, 188; escorts by, 77–78; *Independence*, 174; information on, 121, 126; joint exercise with PLAN, 180–81, 195; *Kitty Hawk*, 184; mine-laying, 127; naval technology, 119, 126; *Nimitz*, 173, 174; Pacific Fleet, 170; *Decker*,

65; *Helena*, 77–78; *Impeccable*, 184; *Inchon*, 178; *Leonard F. Mason*, 116; *O'Brien*, 116; *Shoup*, 180; warships of, 77, 121, 126, 178

Van Tian Dung, 121
Venezuela, 172
Vietnam, 64, 157, 191, 193
Vietnam, North (DRV), 119, 120, 127
Vietnam, South, 119–20, 121, 131
Vietnam War, 12, 119, 126, 131, 174
Vladivostok, 21, 169
VNN (Vietnam Navy), 12, 119, 121, 131, 157; in battle, 132–35, 158–59; *Ly Thuong Kiet* (HQ 16), 133–35; *Nhat Tao* (HQ 10), 132–5; *Tran Binh Trong* (HQ 5), 133–35; *Tran Khanh Du* (HQ 4), 132–34, warships of, 132, 158
Vo Nguyen Giap, 121
Voyage, 170, 180

Wang Bingnan, 75
Wang Faquan, 96
Wang Fushan, 181
Wang Hongkun, 42
Wang Honglin, 104
Wang Hongxi, 104
Wang Jin, 108
Wang Shangrong, 76, 78
Wang Wanli, 103
Wang Wei, 176–77
Wang Xiangyi, 105
Wang Xuedong, 11
Wang Yongguo, 170
Wang Yunshan, 107, 111–12
Wang Zhen, 150
Wang Zhiguo, 189–90
Wang Zizhong, 102
Wanshan, landing of, 44–46
Warring States, 2
Washington, 62, 67, 142, 173, 175

water mines, MK-42, 126, 127; MK-50, 126; MK-52, 126, 127, 128
Way of War (WOW), Chinese, 4, 17; Western, 4
Wei Hengwu, 115–16
Wei Mingsen, 132–35
Weishanhu, 186, 187
Weiyuan, 83
Wenzhou, 179
West, 44, 169
World War I, 19
World War II, 3, 19, 20, 26, 61, 65, 69, 80, 97, 125, 145, 151, 152, 197; Allied Forces, 19, 26
Wu Buyun, 156
Wu Changwu, 104
Wu Dianqing, 37
Wu Hongle, 168–69
Wu Jiezhang, 3
Wu Ruilin, 108–11, 112
Wu Shengli, 181, 186, 196
Wu Xian, 181
Wuchang, 26
Wuhan, 28, 136; *Wuhan*, 186, 187
Wuhu, 42
Wuqiu Island, 114
Wusongkou, 80, 149

Xi Jinping, 8, 10, 13, 192–96
Xia Guang, 38
Xiamen, 28, 29, 74, 75, 81
Xi'an, 26
Xiao Dewan, 134
Xiao Hua, 39
Xiao Jinguang, 11, 15, 16, 31, 33, 35, 80; 1958 Taiwan Strait Crisis and, 81, 83–84; career of, 18–19, 86, 145; issues, 49, 95, 118, 141; Mao and, 18, 42, 104; Russians and, 37–38, 87–89; Zhou and, 34, 89
Xie Xiangpeng, 104
Xingguo, 61, 63, 65

Xiongdi Island, 109–10
Xisha Island. *See* Paracel Island.
Xu Changyou: 11
Xu Feng, 164
Xu Fengming, 82
Xu Qinxiao, 164
Xu Xiangqian, 11
Xu Yan, 3, 49
Xu Zhiming, 138–9
Xu Zuyuan, 113
Xuzhou, 32; *Xuzhou*, 189

Yan'an, 26, 61
Yang Chengwu, 121
Yang Guoyu, 44, 149
Yang Jiechi, 185
Yang Li, 39
Yang Shangkun, 159
Yang Zhiliang, 159
Yangzi River, 21, 26, 27, 28, 47–48, 160
Yantai, 20, 147
Ye Fei, 11, 140, 150–1, 153, 164; 1954–55 Taiwan Strait Crisis and, 64; 1958 Taiwan Strait Crisis and, 73–78; as PLAN political commissar, 145–48, 150; career of, 145
Ye Jianying, 11, 130, 134, 141, 150
Ye Qun, 129
Yellow River, 26
Yellow Sea, 180
Yi Yaocai, 38
Yijiangshan, 53; casualties of, 71; defense of, 70; garrison of, 67, 68–9, 71; landing of, 67–71
Yongchang, 114, 115–16
Yongle Island, 131, 132
Yongtai, 114, 115–16
Yu Dawei, 75, 76
Yulin Naval Base, 132, 149, 156, 157
Yuan dynasty, 3, 5, 6
Yudin, Pavel, 32, 88, 90–91

Zahalov, Vasilievich, 38
Zeng Kelin, 40
Zhang Aiping, 22, 24, 25, 31, 35, 150, 161, 164; career, 21–22; in the 1954–55 Taiwan Strait Crisis, 58–60; 61–63, 65–71, 73–78
Zhang Dingfa, 179–80, 181
Zhang Jie, 76
Zhang Lianzhong, 140; as PLAN commander, 156–58; career of, 156
Zhang Minglong, 94–95
Zhang Shouying, 109, 112, 127–28
Zhang Wannian, 171
Zhang Xiuchun, 99
Zhang Xueliang, 23–24
Zhang Xuesi, 23, 57, 83–84, 106–7, 110; death of, 118, 129
Zhang Xusan, 88, 149
Zhang Yimin, 69–70, 81–83, 115–16; "three rules" of, 81
Zhang Yuanpei, 131–34
Zhangjiang, 107–12, 114
Zhanjiang, 145
Zhao De'an, 79
Zhao Huichun, 39, 40
Zhao Jiarang, 76

Zhao Yiping, 38
Zhao Yu, 177
Zhejiang Command, 58
Zhejiang Front Command, 59, 61–62; in the 1954–55 Taiwan Strait Crisis, 67–70
Zheng Benji, 82
Zheng He, 6; *Zhenghe*, 191
Zhenhua, 189–90
Zhou Enlai, 10, 34–35, 51, 103, 104, 105, 109, 152; 1954–55 Taiwan Strait Crisis and, 72; navy and, 112–13, 114–15, 116; nuclear submarine and, 90, 137; Russian relations and, 88, 91–93; Vietnam and, 127
Zhou Guanying, 66–67
Zhou Kelin, 104
Zhou Renjie, 115
Zhou Wenjie, 53
Zhoushan, 27, 94, 160, 169; landing of: 15, 33; *Zhoushan*, 189
Zhoutian Radar Station, 109
Zhu De, 10, 11, 20; navy and, 21, 39–40, 105
Zhu Rongji, 171
Zhuhai, 170

ABOUT THE AUTHOR

Xiaobing Li is a professor of history and the Don Betz Endowed Chair in International Studies at the University of Central Oklahoma. He holds a PhD from Carnegie Mellon University and is the author of *The Dragon in the Jungle: The Chinese Army in the Vietnam War*, *Attack at Chosin: The Chinese Second Offensive in Korea*, *Building Ho's Army: Chinese Military Assistance to North Vietnam*, *The History of Taiwan*, and *The Cold War in East Asia*. He is also the executive editor of the *Chinese Historical Review*. He served in the PLA in China and lives in Edmond, Oklahoma.

The Naval Institute Press is the book-publishing arm of the U.S. Naval Institute, a private, nonprofit, membership society for sea service professionals and others who share an interest in naval and maritime affairs. Established in 1873 at the U.S. Naval Academy in Annapolis, Maryland, where its offices remain today, the Naval Institute has members worldwide.

Members of the Naval Institute support the education programs of the society and receive the influential monthly magazine *Proceedings* or the colorful bimonthly magazine *Naval History* and discounts on fine nautical prints and on ship and aircraft photos. They also have access to the transcripts of the Institute's Oral History Program and get discounted admission to any of the Institute-sponsored seminars offered around the country.

The Naval Institute's book-publishing program, begun in 1898 with basic guides to naval practices, has broadened its scope to include books of more general interest. Now the Naval Institute Press publishes about seventy titles each year, ranging from how-to books on boating and navigation to battle histories, biographies, ship and aircraft guides, and novels. Institute members receive significant discounts on the Press' more than eight hundred books in print.

Full-time students are eligible for special half-price membership rates. Life memberships are also available.

For more information about Naval Institute Press books that are currently available, visit www.usni.org/press/books. To learn about joining the U.S. Naval Institute, please write to:

Member Services
U.S. Naval Institute
291 Wood Road
Annapolis, MD 21402-5034
Telephone: (800) 233-8764
Fax: (410) 571-1703
Web address: www.usni.org